CW01284422

BIBLICAL COMMENTARY AND TRANSLATION IN LATER MEDIEVAL ENGLAND

Drawing extensively on unpublished manuscript sources, this study uncovers the culture of experimentation that surrounded biblical exegesis in fourteenth-century England. In an area ripe for revision, Andrew Kraebel challenges the accepted theory (inherited from Reformation writers) that medieval English Bible translations represent a proto-Protestant rejection of scholastic modes of interpretation. Instead, he argues that early translators were themselves part of a larger scholastic interpretive tradition, and that they tried to make that tradition available to a broader audience. Translation was thus one among many ways that English exegetes experimented with the possibilities of commentary. With a wide scope, the book focuses on works by writers from the heretic John Wyclif to the hermit Richard Rolle, alongside a host of lesser-known authors, including Henry Cossey and Nicholas Trevet, and many anonymous texts. The study provides new insight into the ingenuity of medieval interpreters willing to develop new literary-critical methods and embrace intellectual risks.

ANDREW KRAEBEL is Assistant Professor of English at Trinity University in San Antonio, Texas. His essays on medieval literature and commentary have appeared in *Speculum*, *JMEMS*, and *Traditio*, among other journals, as well as in such volumes as *Interpreting Scripture in Judaism, Christianity, and Islam: Overlapping Inquiries* (Cambridge, 2016), and *The Cambridge Handbook of Literary Authorship* (Cambridge, 2019). He is the editor of the *Sermons of William of Newburgh* (2010), and, with Ardis Butterfield and Ian Johnson, he is editing a collection of essays on *Literary Theory and Criticism in the Later Middle Ages* (Cambridge).

CAMBRIDGE STUDIES IN MEDIEVAL LITERATURE

Founding Editor
Alastair Minnis, *Yale University*

General Editor
Daniel Wakelin, *University of Oxford*

Editorial Board
Anthony Bale, *Birkbeck, University of London*
Zygmunt G. Barański, *University of Cambridge*
Christopher C. Baswell, *Barnard College and Columbia University*
Mary Carruthers, *New York University*
Rita Copeland, *University of Pennsylvania*
Roberta Frank, *Yale University*
Alastair Minnis, *Yale University*
Jocelyn Wogan-Browne, *Fordham University*

This series of critical books seeks to cover the whole area of literature written in the major medieval languages – the main European vernaculars, and medieval Latin and Greek – during the period *c.*1100–1500. Its chief aim is to publish and stimulate fresh scholarship and criticism on medieval literature, special emphasis being placed on understanding major works of poetry, prose, and drama in relation to the contemporary culture and learning which fostered them.

Recent titles in the series
Sara Harris *The Linguistic Past in Twelfth-Century Britain*
Erik Kwakkel and Rodney Thomson (eds.) *The European Book in the Twelfth Century*
Irina Dumitrescu *The Experience of Education in Anglo-Saxon Literature*
Jonas Wellendorf *Gods and Humans in Medieval Scandinavia: Retying the Bonds*
Thomas A. Prendergast and Jessica Rosenfeld (eds.) *Chaucer and the Subversion of Form*
Katie L. Walter *Middle English Mouths*
Lawrence Warner *Chaucer's Scribes*
Glenn D. Burger and Holly A. Crocker (eds.) *Medieval Affect, Feeling, and Emotion*
Robert J. Meyer-Lee *Literary Value and Social Identity in the Canterbury Tales*
Andrew Kraebel *Biblical Commentary and Translation in Later Medieval England*

A complete list of titles in the series can be found at the end of the volume.

BIBLICAL COMMENTARY AND TRANSLATION IN LATER MEDIEVAL ENGLAND

Experiments in Interpretation

ANDREW KRAEBEL

Trinity University

CAMBRIDGE
UNIVERSITY PRESS

CAMBRIDGE
UNIVERSITY PRESS

University Printing House, Cambridge CB2 8BS, United Kingdom

One Liberty Plaza, 20th Floor, New York, NY 10006, USA

477 Williamstown Road, Port Melbourne, VIC 3207, Australia

314–321, 3rd Floor, Plot 3, Splendor Forum, Jasola District Centre, New Delhi – 110025, India

79 Anson Road, #06–04/06, Singapore 079906

Cambridge University Press is part of the University of Cambridge.

It furthers the University's mission by disseminating knowledge in the pursuit of education, learning, and research at the highest international levels of excellence.

www.cambridge.org
Information on this title: www.cambridge.org/9781108486644
DOI: 10.1017/9781108761437

© Andrew Kraebel 2020

This publication is in copyright. Subject to statutory exception and to the provisions of relevant collective licensing agreements, no reproduction of any part may take place without the written permission of Cambridge University Press.

First published 2020

Printed in the United Kingdom by TJ International Ltd, Padstow Cornwall

A catalogue record for this publication is available from the British Library.

Library of Congress Cataloging-in-Publication Data
NAMES: Kraebel, A. B. (Andrew Brock), 1983– author.
TITLE: Biblical commentary and translation in later medieval England : experiments in interpretation / Andrew Kraebel.
DESCRIPTION: New York : Cambridge University Press, 2020. | Series: Cambridge studies in medieval literature | Includes bibliographical references and index.
IDENTIFIERS: LCCN 2019037735 (print) | LCCN 2019037736 (ebook) | ISBN 9781108486644 (hardback) | ISBN 9781108708128 (paperback) | ISBN 9781108761437 (epub)
SUBJECTS: LCSH: Bible–Commentaries–History and criticism. | Bible–Criticism, interpretation, etc.–England–History–Middle Ages, 600-1500. | Bible–Translating–England–History–To 1500. | Bible. English–Versions–History–To 1500.
CLASSIFICATION: LCC BS491.3 .K73 2020 (print) | LCC BS491.3 (ebook) | DDC 220.60942/09023–dc23
LC record available at https://lccn.loc.gov/2019037735
LC ebook record available at https://lccn.loc.gov/2019037736

ISBN 978-1-108-48664-4 Hardback

Cambridge University Press has no responsibility for the persistence or accuracy of URLs for external or third-party internet websites referred to in this publication and does not guarantee that any content on such websites is, or will remain, accurate or appropriate.

For Allie

Contents

List of Figures	*page* viii
Acknowledgments	x
List of Abbreviations and Conventions	xiii

Introduction		1
1	Interpretive Theories and Traditions	21
2	Eclectic Hermeneutics: Biblical Commentary in Wyclif's Oxford	54
3	Richard Rolle's Scholarly Devotion	91
4	Moral Experiments: Middle English Matthew Commentaries	133
Epilogue: John Bale's Dilemma		176

Appendices

A	Subject Matter Symbols in Wyclif's Postils	188
B	The Texts and Revisions of Rolle's *Latin Psalter*	192
C	The Durham Matthew Prologue	203

Notes	218
Bibliography	273
Index of Manuscripts	296
General Index	299

Figures

1. HEHL MS HM 148, f. 27^r (detail).   *page* 14
2. CUL MS Add. 3470, p. 150 (detail). Reproduced by kind permission of the Syndics of Cambridge University Library.   22
3. Cambridge, Christ's College MS 11, f. 21^v. Reproduced by kind permission of the Master and Fellows of Christ's College.   47
4. Oxford, St. John's College MS 171, f. 241^r (detail). Reproduced by permission of the President and Fellows of St. John's College, Oxford.   61
5. BodL MS Bodley 716, f. 2^r (detail). Reproduced with permission of the Bodleian Libraries, the University of Oxford.   71
6. BL MS Add. 37049, f. 52^v. © The British Library Board.   92
7. BodL MS Bodley 953, f. 2^v. Reproduced with permission of the Bodleian Libraries, the University of Oxford.   108
8. Aberdeen Univ. Lib. MS 243, f. 3^r (detail). © The University of Aberdeen.   109
9. BodL MS Rawl. A. 389, f. 13^r. Reproduced with permission of the Bodleian Libraries, the University of Oxford.   119
10. BL MS Cotton Faustina B. vi (part 2), f. 8^v. © The British Library Board.   130
11. BL MS Stowe 39, f. 16^v. © The British Library Board.   131
12. BL MS Egerton 842, f. 14^v. © The British Library Board.   138
13. BL MS Egerton 842, f. 200^r (detail). © The British Library Board.   144
14. BodL MS Bodley 143, f. 137^r. Reproduced with permission of the Bodleian Libraries, the University of Oxford.   148
15. CUL MS Kk.2.9, f. 73^v (detail). Reproduced by permission of the Syndics of Cambridge University Library.   151

16 Cambridge, Trinity College MS B.1.38, f. 110^r. Reproduced by permission of the Master and Fellows of Trinity College, Cambridge. 152
17 John Bale, *The Image of Both Churches* (London: John Day, 1550), sig. N1^v–N2^r. Reproduced from the copy at the Beinecke Library, Yale University. 179

Acknowledgments

This book took quite a while to write, and its completion was made possible by many individuals and institutions. Crucial to this project was the generosity of various libraries and their staffs, who gave me access to manuscripts and early printed books in their collections and consistently provided generous assistance: in Oxford, the Bodleian and the libraries of St. John's College (Petra Hofmann, Stewart Tiley, and Ruth Ogden) and Magdalen College (Christine Ferdinand and Daryl Green); in Cambridge, the University Library and the libraries of Christ's College (Amelie Roper, Samantha Hughes, and John Wagstaff) and Trinity College (Nicolas Bell); in London, the British Library and Lambeth Palace Library; the Sir Duncan Rice Library at the University of Aberdeen (Kim Downie); Durham Cathedral Library (Janet Gunning); Hereford Cathedral Library (Rosemary Firman); the library of the Shrewsbury School (Robin Brooke-Smith); and the Beinecke Library at Yale, where I am especially grateful for the generosity of Ray Clemens and Kathryn James. A fellowship from the Mrs. Giles Whiting Foundation provided a year of funding to support the dissertation in which some of these chapters began, and the Graduate School and Beinecke Library at Yale provided more funding at various points, including a John Enders Fellowship and an A. Bartlett Giamatti Fellowship. At Trinity in San Antonio, a startup grant and appointment as Mr. and Mrs. Patrick Swearingen Faculty Fellow helped to support further research and writing, and additional funds from Trinity's Associate Vice President for Academic Affairs, first Mark Brodl and now David Ribble, have helped to defray costs associated with securing reproductions of images and permission to publish them.

I am very lucky in my friends and colleagues, who have answered specific questions and discussed and debated some of the broader issues broached in this book, and some of whom have read and offered helpful feedback on individual chapters. Leah Schwebel and Steve Rozenski have to start the list, and Ralph Hanna and Nicholas Watson similarly set themselves apart with their generosity and encouragement. For help with a range of issues, my thanks to Andrew Albin, Alexander Andrée, Frederic Clark, Mordechai Cohen, Andrew Cole, Rita Copeland, William Courtenay, Gilbert Dahan, Tony Edwards, Brian FitzGerald, Kantik Ghosh, Vincent Gillespie, Cédric Giraud, Jill Havens, Anne Hudson, Mary Kate Hurley, Ian Johnson, Kathleen Kennedy, Michael Kuczynski, David Lawton, Ian Levy, Constant Mews, Barbara Newman, Denis Renevey, Arthur Russell, Michael Sargent, Elizabeth Scala, Richard Sharpe, Michael Van Dussen, Nancy Bradley Warren, Katherine Zieman, and Barbara Zimbalist. Though their deaths came at different points in this project, Mary Dove and Jeremy Catto both offered valuable advice, and even some unpublished materials, for which I remain grateful. At Trinity, I have enjoyed the support and guidance of my colleagues in the Department of English, and Victoria Aarons, Willis Salomon, and Claudia Stokes in particular have been sensitive readers of individual chapters and reliable sources of sound advice and encouragement. Two Trinity undergraduates were especially helpful, Olivia Mulder in preparing the symbols used in Appendix A, and Katie Funderburg in gathering together – meticulously and patiently – an abundance of information about manuscripts of Rolle's Latin. Daniel Wakelin is a wonderful series editor, and his comments, as well as the reports by the two anonymous readers, did much to pull the book into its final form. Emily Hockley and her staff have my thanks for seeing it through publication with such care.

This project began when I was in graduate school at Yale, where I benefited from an exceptionally talented cohort of fellow students. Laura Saetveit Miles, Sarah Novacich, Tessie Prakas, Aaron Pratt, Madeleine Saraceni, Samantha Seal, Joe Stadolnik, Trevor Verot, and Eric Weiskott have all made this book better. I'm very grateful, too, to the faculty who taught me how to do this kind of work, in particular Roberta Frank, Ardis Butterfield, Margot Fassler, Denys Turner, David Scott Kastan, David Quint, Marcia Colish, Barbara Shailor, Chris Kraus, James John, Mary Rouse and Richard Rouse, Walter Goffart, and Traugott Lawler. Even more time and care were given by my dissertation committee, Jessica Brantley, Ian Cornelius, and Alastair Minnis, and their intellectual generosity and guidance have been crucial to this project. To Alastair in particular, and to Florence, I owe more than I can express, and I am deeply grateful for their friendship and constant support. So much of what follows has been shaped by ongoing conversations with Alastair, and by his often bracing and always generous feedback. I hope what I offer here comes close to the standard he's set for me. Maybe Smalley would've liked it, too.

It is also hard to express how much I owe my family, and how grateful I am for their love and support. My brothers, Rob and Alex, have always kept things fun, and my parents, Janet and Rick, together with my late grandparents, made sure I grew up with a love of learning, literature, and history, and with models of all the humane values. They have contributed in deep and meaningful ways to this book and to how I think about all of these things.

My wife, Allie Kieffer, has read almost all of this book in at least a few different forms. She's taught me a lot, especially about how ideas work in history and the best ways to write about them, and this would have been a much more boring book without her. It's dedicated to her, therefore, with love and gratitude.

Abbreviations and Conventions

BAV	Vatican City, Biblioteca Apostolica Vaticana
BL	London, British Library
BM	Bibliothèque municipale
BnF	Paris, Bibliothèque nationale de France
BodL	Oxford, Bodleian Library
BRUC	A. B. Emden, *Biographical Register of the University of Cambridge to 1500*
BRUO	A. B. Emden, *Biographical Register of the University of Oxford to A.D. 1500*
CBMLC	Corpus of British Medieval Library Catalogues
CCCM	Corpus Christianorum, Continuatio Mediaevalis
CCSL	Corpus Christianorum, Series Latina
CSEL	Corpus Scriptorum Ecclesiasticorum Latinorum
CUL	Cambridge, University Library
DMLBS	*Dictionary of Medieval Latin from British Sources* (logeion.uchicago.edu)
EAEB	*Earliest Advocates of the English Bible*, ed. Mary Dove
EETS	Early English Text Society
es	Extra Series
os	Original Series
HEHL	San Marino, Henry E. Huntington Library
JMEMS	*Journal of Medieval and Early Modern Studies*
MÆ	*Medium Ævum*
MED	*Middle English Dictionary* (quod.lib.umich.edu/m/med)
MGT	Troyes, Médiathèque du Grand Troyes
MMBL	N. R. Ker et al., *Medieval Manuscripts in British Libraries*
ÖNB	Vienna, Österreichische Nationalbibliothek
PG	*Patrologia Graeca*
PL	*Patrologia Latina*

PNK	Prague, Národní knihovna
Stegmüller	Friedrich Stegmüller, *Repertorium Biblicum Medii Aevi* (cited by entry number)

The range of sources on which this study draws has required a somewhat unusual set of conventions for the presentation of texts, though I have tried to keep things as simple as possible. Apart from consistently rendering Latin *j* as *i*, I have preserved the orthography of all quotations as they appear in the cited manuscripts and printed editions, but I have standardized capitalization and punctuation, sometimes repunctuating earlier editions to reflect my understanding of the text. Abbreviations are generally expanded, though some conventional abbreviations (&, w^t, y^r) are retained in the early modern material quoted in the Epilogue. Corrections to quotations from manuscripts and early printed sources, sometimes drawn from other witnesses to the text and sometimes simply required by the sense of the passage, are given in square brackets; only more elaborate corrections receive comment in the notes. Square brackets in my translations either note ambiguities in the text or function as short explanatory glosses. Translations are my own, though I note earlier renderings that I have consulted in the case of particularly dense texts. For the sake of space, Latin quotations in the notes have not been translated, and I have generally only supplied them when the quoted material is unpublished.

Introduction

Dominus habitans in me est *illuminacio mea* contra tenebras ignorancie, vt iam discernam inter bonum et malum, *et salus mea* contra infirmitatem spiritualem, vt iam firmus resistam peccato. *Quem t[i]mebo?* Preter ipsum nullum. Vtique *Dominus protector vite mee*, id est defensor a malis contra impetus et insidias. *A quo trepidabo*, positus in prouectu virtutum? Audiant hos versus qui solitarios esse non audent, cum iste qui habet Deum illuminatorem et protectorem a nullo trepidat. Non enim timidi sunt homines nisi propter vite reprehensibilis conscienciam. Sciatis ergo vos timidi quod a societate multorum potestis propter peccata vestra a demonibus rapi ad infernum, et in solitudine Deo protegente securi eritis. Deponite itaque malam vitam vestram que in nullo loco effugiet manum Dei vltricem.[1]

The Lord dwelling within me is *my light* against the shadows of ignorance, allowing me to distinguish between the good and the wicked, *and my health* against spiritual illness, allowing me firmly to withstand sin. *Whom shall I fear?* None but him. *The Lord is the protector of my life*, i.e., my defender against the assaults and snares of the wicked. *Of whom shall I*, set in the progression of virtues, *be afraid?* Let those who do not dare to be solitaries hear these verses, for such a one who has God as his light and protector is afraid of no one. For men are only fearful from a sense of guilt for their reprehensible life. Know then, ye fearful, that from the fellowship of many people demons can snatch you to hell because of your sins, while in solitude, with God as your protector, you will be secure. Lay aside, then, your wicked life, which will not offer any refuge from the vengeful hand of God.

This forceful, perhaps overbearing call to flee from the world occurs in a commentary on the Psalms by the Yorkshire hermit Richard Rolle (d. 1349), one of the most influential religious writers of later medieval England. Though elsewhere in this work, out of a concern that he might "appear to exalt [his] own state," Rolle says he will avoid glossing a particular verse as having to do with religious solitaries, he does not hesitate to present himself *qua* hermit as the ideal speaker of Ps. 26.1.[2] With the Lord as his light and his spiritual health (or salvation), the solitary is confident of his fate at the end of time, while those still living "in the fellowship of many people," apparently both secular and religious, may be snatched to hell at any moment. Though coming at the end of his reading of this verse, this identification makes Rolle's initial string of glosses seem, in retrospect, to be not general statements of spiritual self-assurance so much as specific claims about the exegete's authority, and, taken this way, they do indeed reflect views found elsewhere in his writings.[3] The notion of God as a light "dwelling within" him, for example, seems to echo claims of divine inspiration for his exegesis, while his ability to distinguish between the good and the wicked may reflect his belief that he will be among the elect who assist in judging souls, and his need for protection against "assaults and snares" recalls his repeated attacks on those who question his solitary lifestyle and, especially, the frequent relocation of his hermitage.[4] Here, then, Rolle draws on the Psalmist's text (*hos versus*) to articulate a bold account of the authority of both his vocation and his writing.

While his warning to those too afraid to be solitaries is his own contribution to the interpretation of this verse, however, the hermit has adapted the opening series of glosses from his major source, the mid-twelfth-century *Magna glosatura* of Peter Lombard (d. 1160), a basic reference work of scholastic Psalter exegesis.[5] Throughout his commentary, Rolle draws on the Lombard's interpretive offerings, sometimes supplementing them with new glosses of his own and sometimes, as here, presenting them in ways that alter his source's meaning. (In the *Glosatura*, this psalm is interpreted in the voice of any faithful Christian, who can draw confidence from his or her participation in the Church's sacraments.)[6] In one sense, Rolle's approach is typical of scholastic commentators, who regularly engage with a range of sources, sometimes affirming long-standing interpretations, sometimes arguing over whether a gloss presents the literal or spiritual meaning of a verse, and sometimes drawing on newly available material or the insights of new interpretive theories to devise original readings of the biblical text. Yet Rolle also departs from these norms in subtle but significant ways, especially insofar as his disagreements with the Lombard are based not on his engagement with new scholastic theories or newly available sources – which, considering his short career as a student at Oxford, were probably unknown to him – but rather on his ecstatic experiences, especially his distinctive accounts of physical heat and heavenly song, and the authority he derived from them.[7] Rolle's exegesis, in other words, brings together standard glosses that would form the basis of almost any scholastic Psalter commentary with more idiosyncratic ones focused on his distinctive devotional program. Yet it is not simply the case that Rolle uses commentary to authorize his way of life. Though this kind of enhanced authority may be an effect of his exegetical writing and may occasionally – as in Ps. 26.1 – be the focus of his glosses, it would be more accurate to say that, in this work as a whole, he has attempted to contribute to the longer tradition of biblical commentary by bringing his spiritual insights to bear on the interpretation of Scripture, and he thereby expands the scope of scholastic commentary to include more overtly mystical materials. Rolle turns commentary into a form of writing that is at once scholastic and devotional.[8]

This book charts the complex and dynamic field of scholastic biblical commentary in fourteenth-century England, arguing that this form of writing attracted exegetes – authors of commentaries – because of its potential to serve as a site of intellectual and interpretive creativity and experimentation. Biblical commentary afforded writers an opportunity to try out new ways of reading, to explore the implications of new interpretive theories or the relevance of newly discovered sources, to think in different languages, and to develop ideas about a seemingly endless range of issues, reflecting the broad heterogeneity of the biblical text. Almost inevitably, commentators were attracted to this form as an oblique way of accruing authority to their writing, with their original material presented as the meaning of the supremely authoritative text of Holy Writ. Yet their glosses are often tentative, put forward as one or more of many different ways of interpreting an inexhaustibly rich source, and this pragmatic provisionality was reinforced by the attitude with which exegetes by and large approached earlier efforts at interpretation.[9] That is, at the same time as they turned to commentary as a vehicle for exploring new ideas, scholastic exegetes persistently engaged with a vast inherited tradition of interpretation, complexly contradictory patristic and earlier medieval glosses, through which they sifted, sometimes seeking to reconcile conflicting authorities, and in relation to which they positioned their own contributions. Indeed, discerning the intellectual contours of this received body of glosses was itself a significant undertaking, prompting a wide range of creative solutions, new scholarly tools, and different forms of scholastic writing.[10] In sum, then, the commentators whose work forms the core of this book were thoughtfully poised between the new and the old, at once committed to the authoritative traditions of reading gathered in sources like the *Magna glosatura* and eager to find ways to make their own distinctive contributions to the ongoing project of biblical interpretation.

Within this larger field of scholastic commentary, the work of exegetes in England in the fourteenth century is at once more specific and distinctive. At the same time as it saw the production of new commentaries aimed at readers within the universities, English exegesis across the fourteenth century is characterized by an increasing interest in commentary's potential as a demotic literary form, an expansion of the work of scholastic exegesis that is captured perfectly (and influentially) in Rolle's glosses. To put it another way, beginning in the 1310s and 1320s, more and more writers sought to adapt the conventional sources and interpretive strategies of scholastic commentary to meet the needs of readers with at most a limited university education.[11] Initially, this work was done in the same language as most scholastic exegesis, Latin, but especially in the second half of the century, commentators began to turn to Middle English to supply sometimes startlingly complex interpretive material for a wide range of non-specialist readers, including vowed religious women, monastic lay brothers, and a laity with increasingly ambitious devotional aspirations. As so many attempts to define and extend the possibilities of biblical commentary as a literary form with a potentially broad appeal, these efforts at vernacular exegesis represent some of the most significant and consequential experiments in scholastic interpretation in fourteenth-century England, and they provide a crucial context for the creation of the Wycliffite Bible versions, the first complete translations of Scripture into English, which need to be understood not just in relation to scholastic commentary, but as expressions of its development into the vernacular.

At least in part, then, this study seeks to develop the narrative of late medieval university exegesis begun in the scholarship of Beryl Smalley, whose treatment of the fourteenth century was more narrowly focused than her work on earlier scholasticism.[12] But it argues that a fuller account of scriptural commentary in this period must look beyond the universities and include a range of texts that have not typically been addressed in studies like Smalley's, works – like Rolle's – composed for a broader audience and informed by priorities that are now less commonly associated with scholastic exegesis. To overlook these texts, or to treat them as somehow less than deserving of the title of scholastic commentary, almost inevitably results in an impoverished view of English (including Anglo-Latin) exegesis in this period, and it risks falling into easy binarisms, of intellectual and affective, Latin and vernacular, elite and demotic. As we will see, commentary was capacious enough to cut across – without necessarily collapsing – all of these distinctions.

Beyond opening new texts to critical inquiry, then, this understanding of its capaciousness and creativity challenges assumptions about scholastic commentary that have been too common in recent literary and historical scholarship. Indeed, commentary has been seen as a tool wielded by the Latin-educated clergy in an attempt to limit allowable understandings of Scripture, and commentaries are thus often taken as more likely to constrain interpretive inquiry than to encourage it. According to this view, "glossing is a gesture of appropriation," one which "undertakes to speak the text, to assert authority over it, ... to limit or close it to the possibility of heterodox or unlimited significance. ... Glossing seeks to find one answer, impose one interpretation on the meaning" of the biblical text.[13] Likewise, the later medieval Bible has been described as "protected by its Latin glosses" and thereby "meshed in an intertextuality" that guarded against the possibility of dissenting interpretations.[14] Yet, though some examples could surely be found to support them, these caricaturing views are unfortunately misleading with regard to the larger phenomenon of medieval biblical commentary. To be sure, exegetes do often express an anxiety that Holy Writ could be misinterpreted, leading to theological error or heresy – though it is frequently the exegete himself (including Rolle in his work on the Psalms) who fears that *he* will misinterpret Scripture in a way that leads to further confusion and fosters misunderstanding.[15] At the same time as commentators sought to avoid what they considered misreadings, however, their notion of proper interpretation rarely limited the biblical text to a single meaning. Indeed, "it is typical of the commentator to see the text as a 'rich' entity, a practically inexhaustible store of meanings."[16] An exegete "does not close down the meaning of a text but opens it up to further examination," and "the task of commentary is to multiply problems, not to solve them."[17] This interpretive richness is often paired with a complex play of different voices. More than just seeking "to speak the text," the commentator can move from quoting his author to ventriloquizing him with a paraphrasal gloss, and he may then go on to offer further glosses in his own critical voice, as we have seen Rolle doing in his treatment of Ps. 26. The issue of voicing becomes all the more complex with the introduction of interpretations drawn from earlier authorities – "the ghosts that float through the [commentary's] pages" – such that the text becomes something of an echo chamber, with "many different voices offer[ing] a polyphony of interpretations."[18]

Admittedly, these positive valuations have all been taken from discussions of the tradition of commentary on classical Greek and Latin poetry, in some cases describing commentary as it is ideally carried out by classicists today. But the following chapters argue for the perhaps startling degree to which these descriptions can also account for medieval exegesis of biblical literature.[19] Scholastic exegetes worked with a more or less established body of authoritative sources, which could not simply be jettisoned but rather demanded their critical engagement almost as much as the biblical text itself. As we will see, at least one commentator was willing to reclassify all earlier commentaries on a specific biblical book as spiritual, identifying his gloss as the book's first literal treatment – but this is an extreme case, and most exegetes sought to position themselves as extending earlier exegetical undertakings, opening the biblical text to new interpretive possibilities without foreclosing others.[20] Commentary thus presents a very specific instance of what Patricia Clare Ingham has recently described more generally as "the ambivalent status of newness" in the later Middle Ages, with writers "not regularly cast[ing] innovation as utterly distinct from the old."[21] And the same basic interpretive moves that scholastic exegetes found in their authoritative sources – the careful consideration of how to break the text into lemmata, for example, and paraphrasal glosses introduced with the phrase *quasi diceret* or *ac si dicat* (as though he said) – allowed them to explore afresh the many different things a single text could be made to say.[22]

Of course, it is one thing to recover an understanding of commentary as a robust and experimental kind of literature, and quite another to see Middle English biblical translations as part of that larger field of scholastic exegesis. The translations produced in the second half of the fourteenth century, and especially the Wycliffite versions, have typically been thought to reject scholastic interpretive priorities. In contrast to earlier English translations, which were "hedged about with interpretive commentary," we are told that the translators responsible for the Wycliffite versions "wanted [Scripture's] meaning to radiate forth in as unimpeded a way as possible," and they consequently "hated . . . interpretive glossing."[23] The notion of "a Bible liberated from a corrupt academia and its associated intellectual practices" has been identified as "central to the thought of Wyclif and his later followers," who instead favored "the notion of an unglossed, indeed *deglossed* biblical text."[24] Again, these translations supposedly gave "English readers naked Scripture, not only independent of its Latin source . . . but freed from the influence of the schools."[25] As we will see below, this perceived division between scholastic exegesis and Wycliffite biblicism is at best misleading, and it potentially obscures the important ways in which Wycliffite translation was itself a scholastic project. To be sure, there is some basis in Wycliffite writings for the idea that inspired readers can, in theory, interpret Scripture without the aid of glosses, but it hardly follows that Wyclif and his disciples were doggedly hostile to scholastic exegesis in a way that sets them apart from their contemporaries. For one thing, Wyclif was himself the author of an extensive series of scholastic commentaries on the entirety of Scripture, writings which, as we will see, he continued to revise throughout his career. Moreover, many manuscripts of the translations produced by his followers include marginal glosses drawing on some of the same sources as his commentaries, and the vernacular Wycliffite commentary known as the *Glossed Gospels* is one of the major monuments of Middle English scholasticism.[26] Just as importantly, the Wycliffite translations can themselves be considered a kind of commentary, a series of attempts to interpret the meaning of the Vulgate by rendering its text in a new language, sometimes reflecting the insights on offer in standard scholastic (Latin) glosses.[27] Certainly, not all later readers would have recognized these translations as originating from a tradition of scholastic commentary, and copies lacking marginal glosses could have been especially prone to novel interpretive approaches and sensibilities – but the monolingual presentation of these manuscripts may now just as easily obscure their continuing contribution to the enterprise of scholastic interpretation.[28]

The implications of understanding translation as a mode of commentary will be explored at length in the following chapters. But rather than taking up this issue as it relates to the different versions of the Wycliffite Bible, which have received considerable attention in recent scholarship,[29] the argument of this book will focus instead on English works that include translations of individual biblical books *and* extensive interpretive prose, glosses compiled from Latin sources or devised by the English exegete himself. These works, in other words, are substantial biblical commentaries written in English. Further, most of the vernacular examples discussed below adhere to a common form, with a short quotation of the Latin text (typically a single verse) followed by a close translation and a more or less extensive selection of commentary, these different registers typically being distinguished with some combination of underlining, the use of rubrication or paraph marks, or a hierarchy of scripts (more on this below). To give equal weight to their two vernacular elements, namely, the English renderings of biblical material and the English glosses that follow, I propose to refer to these texts as "commentary-translations."[30] Though cumbersome, this description is useful for insisting that these works participate in a larger project of scholastic exegesis, while also emphasizing that, by translating Scripture into a new language, they develop that tradition in novel ways – ones which initially would have been unfamiliar even to their authors, however well versed they may have been in traditions of Latin exegesis. These writings represent, as we will see, a sustained experiment in English prose, and if, as David Lawton has said, the "intellectual tradition" of modern literary criticism "stemmed above all from biblical commentary," then these commentary-translations could be considered the beginning of that tradition in English.[31]

Though they represent the expansion of scholastic interpretive discourses into a new language, however, it would be wrong to see these commentary-translations simply as an instance of academic work diffusing outward from the university to reach a broader or more demotic audience. This is not a straightforward case of "the business of Latin hermeneutics being continued in the vernacular."[32] In this regard, the more capacious and expansive notion of scholastic commentary advocated here is especially important, since one of the earliest (and certainly the most influential) English commentary-translations of biblical literature was *not* written by a master active in Oxford or Cambridge, but rather by Rolle, the Hermit of Hampole, who we have already seen was seeking to put scholastic commentary to differing devotional uses in Latin as well. In his second commentary on the Psalms – written in the vernacular and now called the *English Psalter* – and in early works written in imitation of it, biblical commentary-translation was crafted outside the universities as a means of providing some of the interpretive tools of scholastic commentary to enrich, specifically, *devotional* reading in the vernacular. In the second half of the century, the work of producing new commentary-translations would be taken up by Oxford theologians with considerably more training (and considerably more extensive resources on which to draw), but the texts made by these writers still reflected the devotional priorities established in earlier works, with the example of the *English Psalter* continuing to exercise considerable influence. And, as we will see, early in the fifteenth century, Rolle's vernacular text was even regarded as an authoritative source of scholastic interpretation by an Oxford master writing a commentary in Latin.[33] By treating these texts as important models of vernacular scholasticism, later academic writers seem to have acknowledged that the task of expanding commentary into the vernacular, of experimenting with the kind of work commentaries could do, had already been undertaken by writers outside the schools.

The appeal of these commentary-translations is similarly far from straightforward.[34] To be sure, much of the impetus must have come from the commentators' sense of pastoral obligation, an impulse to provide suitable writings that would benefit vowed female religious and poorly educated members of the clergy, as well as more ambitious laywomen and men.³⁵ Just as importantly, the production of these texts seems likely to have met a demand from their would-be readers – but, again, the importance of Rolle's *English Psalter* as an early example of this kind of literature means that this demand was more complex than might otherwise be expected. On the one hand, as Claire Waters has argued, already in the thirteenth century vernacular religious texts were "focused on the disciplining of the laity, in the sense of making them *discipuli*," students who "engaged cooperatively in the project of their own education," and it could be the case that English learners, already imagining themselves as gaining some mediated access to the scholastic classroom, wanted their study to include the interpretation of Holy Writ as well.³⁶ In this regard, commentary seems to have functioned as a kind of "prestige discourse" to which readers sought access, a desirability which challenges the recent claim that the growth of vernacular religious literature was concomitant with a loss of status of "the ways of knowing fostered by the university."³⁷ On the other hand, the early association of vernacular exegesis with Rolle's authoritative and charismatic *persona* may itself have contributed to the appeal of this kind of writing. At least some readers may have sought out commentary-translations because they were the sort of thing that Rolle wrote, suggested by the misattribution to the hermit of the *Pety Job* (a poeticization of the commentary-translation form focused on selections from Job) or Richard Maidstone's *Penitential Psalms* (another poeticization of the form, discussed in Chapter 3).³⁸ Lacking in all of these explanations, however, is a sense of the contestative relationship between Latin and the vernacular that has often characterized discussions of translation and late medieval English literature, the notion that "the new hermeneutical performance" of these vernacular glosses displaces "antecedent commentaries" and has, more profoundly, the potential to "displace Latin as the linguistic system within which exegesis is practiced."³⁹ Certainly, intellectual resources being limited, the expansion of commentary into a new language means that some writers who would otherwise have glossed Scripture in Latin produced English texts instead, but the composition of these vernacular commentaries was carried out alongside the continuing (and more copious) production of new Latin glosses. This is not to say, then, that English biblical exegesis operated in some kind of humble fealty to the master discourse of Latin, but rather that vernacular commentators persistently position their writings as part of a larger biblical-interpretive field, one which was at once multilingual and predominantly Latin.⁴⁰

As the foregoing discussion should suggest, the university remained critical for the development of biblical exegesis, even when its faculty was responding to trends originating outside its walls. More specifically, the chapters that follow reveal Oxford to have been a significant center of exegetical activity across the fourteenth century, though more intensely in some periods than others. This is not to dispute the claim, initially made by Smalley and supported by William Courtenay, that fourteenth-century Oxford saw the production of fewer biblical commentaries than had been the case in earlier centuries (and especially in comparison to Paris).[41] Almost all of the commentaries discussed here were known to Smalley and Courtenay, and even when we extend our view to include scholastic exegesis composed outside the university, in English and in Latin, the numbers will still come in below those of the two previous centuries. By considering the interpretive experiments on offer in these commentaries, then, this book does not seek to argue that exegesis was any more ubiquitous or popular a form of writing in fourteenth-century Oxford than these earlier studies would suggest. However, at the same time as Courtenay sees schoolmen turning increasingly to the possibilities for professional advancement on offer in the study of canon law, and at the same time as Kantik Ghosh sees theologians turning increasingly to the intellectual tools of speculative philosophy to adjudicate questions of hermeneutics and interpretive authority, it remains the case that some particularly influential writers favored biblical commentary as a mode in which to explore and experiment with their ideas.[42] Such exegetes built on a substantial body of work, and their efforts, though fewer than in past decades, nevertheless represent a major category of scholastic literature, one with an ever larger appeal for readers beyond the university. The purpose of this book, then, is to recover the intellectual contours and complicated interpretive commitments of these unstudied texts, and thereby to gain a fuller sense of why commentary continued to attract writers and readers even in the face of such professional and institutional change.

By advocating for a more capacious view of scholastic exegesis in fourteenth-century England, one that includes texts in Latin and English, this book has implications beyond an understanding of the commentaries that are its focus. Put simply, it indicates the broader relevance of biblical exegesis for medieval vernacular culture, especially – though by no means limited to – vernacular religious culture. Of course, tracing all of these implications lies beyond the scope of this study, but before presenting a more detailed outline of my argument, it will nevertheless be useful to consider some examples illustrating the sort of implications I have in mind, and, relatedly, to address one further methodological issue.

* * *

Introduction

Among other things, the understanding of fourteenth-century biblical exegesis advanced here can support a reassessment of the kind of reading described and encouraged in some of the most familiar texts of Middle English devotion, and it can help us revisit and reinterpret various crucial moments in these texts. Consider, for example, Chapter 58 of the *Book of Margery Kempe*, in which Kempe finds a priest who is willing to "red to hir many a good boke of hy contemplacyon and other bokys, as the Bybyl wyth doctowrys therupon, Seynt Brydys boke, Hyltons boke, Boneventur, *Stimulus Amoris*, *Incendium Amoris*, and swech other."[43] Not only is it impossible to determine which exegetical text is being described with the phrase "the Bybyl wyth doctowrys therupon," it is also very difficult to be sure of the language in which this work would have been written. One editor has suggested that this is a reference to the Wycliffite Bible, perhaps a copy with the kind of extensive marginalia mentioned above.[44] Yet this identification assumes a kind of monolingualism not justified by the fuller passage, which includes at least one other title that Kempe's priest would necessarily have read in Latin, translating and interpreting for her as he went.[45] If the phrase does describe a glossed biblical book, one in which interpretive material appears in the form of discrete notes arranged around the text of Scripture, then this work could be in either Latin or English, and, if Latin, it could just as easily describe a volume of the *Glossa ordinaria* as an informally annotated book, perhaps a small pandect with interpretations added by the reader.[46] Then again, it is not entirely clear that this phrase must describe only a single volume, and it could be that Kempe's priest read to her from the Bible (in Latin or English) and also from the writings of the Fathers compiled in a commentary *upon* a specific biblical book. (The prepositions *super* and *in* are both commonly used for this purpose.) In this case, it would simply be impossible to know which commentary or commentaries (again, in Latin or English) the *Book*'s author has in mind.

Similar uncertainty appears in another early fifteenth-century devotional work, Nicholas Love's *Mirror of the Blessed Life of Jesus Christ*. In a passage not found in his Ps.-Bonaventuran source, Love claims that he does not need to discuss the topic of temptation at greater length, since authoritative material on that subject can readily be found elsewhere:

> In þe whiche processe bene many gude notabilittes touchyng temptacion of man in þis world, of þe whiche Seynt Gregoury and oþere doctours speken in þe exposition of þis gospell, *Ductus est Iesus in desertum*, &c., and specialy Crisostome in *Inperfecto*, þe whech for þei bene sufficiantly writen, not onely in Latyne but also in English, we passen ouere at þis tyme.[47]

As one of the great orthodox authors of the Arundelian Church, Love has been seen as a staunch opponent of vernacular Scripture, and it has been argued that his *Mirror* was meant to serve as "an official alternative" to the Wycliffite Bible.[48] It may be unsurprising, then, that the *Mirror*'s editor has seen this passage as gesturing toward other works of orthodox devotional prose, such as the *Chastising of God's Children*, which includes a citation of the *Opus Imperfectum* (though not on this specific lemma or topic).[49] While this would be a strangely unhelpful (and inaccurate) citation of the *Chastising*, however, the quotation of a biblical lemma (in this case Matth. 4.1) *is* a standard way to cite commentaries, and it is easy enough to find these specific glosses in any number of exegetical works on Matthew's Gospel, where the biblical passage would be underlined and (as the start of a chapter) marked with a prominent initial. Further, as Love says, this is true not just for "Latyne" commentaries – including the *Glossa* or the *Catena Aurea* of Thomas Aquinas – but also for English ones, Wycliffite and non-Wycliffite alike.[50] To be sure, there is nothing here to indicate that Love is specifically sending his reader to the Wycliffite *Glossed Gospels*, but this passage could be evidence of his familiarity with those texts, and perhaps too his belief that they are as reliable a way to find patristic "notabilittes" as Latin commentaries. Familiar with the generally compilatory quality of scholastic glosses and with at least some recent efforts at vernacular exegesis, Love seems to be acknowledging that his readers will potentially have access to a range of different commentaries, in Latin and the vernacular, in which this material could be found.[51]

Though both emphasize the potential relevance of scholastic exegesis to vernacular devotion, these two examples differ in the kind of exegetical reading they expect or describe. Perhaps more familiar, Love is sending the *Mirror*'s readers to commentaries on Matthew with the expectation *not* that they will study the entire interpretive text, or even a whole chapter of it, but rather that they will seek out a limited number of glosses on a specific verse. He treats commentaries as a kind of reference work, with almost encyclopedic offerings that can be consulted in a selective and piecemeal manner. The scene of reading described in Kempe's *Book*, in contrast, where exegetical material (in whatever form) is put alongside different works of "hy contemplacyon," suggests a more sustained engagement with longer passages of commentary, read (along with the other "bokys") over the course of "vii yer er viii yer."[52] Rather than focusing on a discrete gloss, Kempe (aided by her priest) seems to be reading the exegetical text as a kind of devotional work not so much to be consulted as to be pored over at length – though this writing, unlike the others, is explicitly aimed at recovering the meanings of the more authoritative text of Scripture.

These different ways of approaching exegesis correspond to contrasting reading practices now generally described as either monastic or scholastic. The older of the two practices, "monastic *lectio* was a spiritual exercise which involved steady reading to oneself, interspersed by prayer, and pausing for rumination on the text." In contrast, the growth of the cathedral schools in the twelfth century and, thereafter, the development of universities encouraged reading as "a process of study which involved ... consultation for reference purposes."[53] Scholastic commentaries written in Latin are, naturally enough, typically seen as supporting this latter approach, while at least some of the Middle English works discussed in Chapters 3 and 4 have been described as encouraging a form of quasi-monastic rumination.[54] While the differences between these two ways of reading are certainly real, however, it does not at all follow that a text necessarily reflects only one or the other of them, nor should we be too quick to map these practices neatly onto differences in language. As we will see below, some authors of commentary-translations appear to have anticipated a more prolonged ("monastic") approach to their writings while, at the same time, including features that allow for the kind of quick reference favored in "scholastic" reading, and others present short glosses apparently designed to support the "more fragmented, piecemeal reading style" associated with scholasticism, even as their prologues call for sustained devotional engagement.[55] Almost all of these texts, in other words, seem to anticipate more than one way of reading.

Both kinds of readerly engagement are supported by the formal and stylistic details of these commentaries, and, in particular, by the ways they were handled by their scribes. As suggested above, though certainly with some variation, the persistent signaling of biblical lemmata with underlining or a hierarchy of scripts, and (in the case of commentary-translations) the use of paraphs, underlining, or rubrication to distinguish close translations of Scripture from the commentator's interpretations, worked to parse the different textual registers and the different voices presented in exegetical prose. These visual signals facilitated, on the one hand, a piecemeal approach to the text, making it relatively easy to locate the commentator's treatment of a specific chapter, verse, or even an individual word of Holy Writ in what were almost always formidably lengthy works. On the other hand, and perhaps counterintuitively, the same markings that divided the text into discrete segments could also enable its reading as continuous prose, working as visual cues to indicate the voicing of different words and

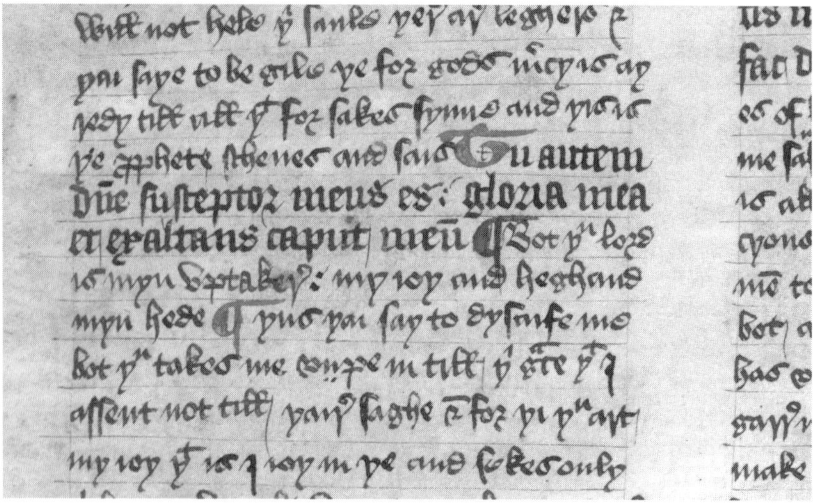

Figure 1   HEHL MS HM 148, f. 27ʳ (detail).

phrases and thus how these parts should be fitted into the larger whole. Such continuous reading seems to be anticipated in some commentaries, even when their arrangement on the page enables the consultation of specific isolated passages. Toward the end of his treatment of Ps. 3.2 in the *English Psalter*, for example, Rolle asserts that "Gods mercy is ay redy till all þat forsakes synne," which (he claims) is what "þe Prophete sheues and sais" in the following verse, provided in Latin immediately after this gloss.[56] In HEHL MS HM 148, as in most other early copies of the *Psalter*, the more prominent script used for the Latin would make it easy enough to locate (and isolate) this verse and Rolle's interpretation of it (see Fig. 1). At the same time, despite this shift in language and (as Anne Hudson says) the "visual differentiation of biblical text from commentary," by ending his gloss with a speech cue for the next verse ("sheues and sais: *Tu autem* ... ") Rolle suggests that any break here is just a matter of indexical convenience, that the interpretive argument of his commentary continues from one verse to the next.[57] Further division is suggested by the paraph marks which the scribe of HM 148 has added immediately before and after the close translation that follows the Latin, but, again, these can help rather than hinder continuous reading. They might, for example, allow a reader with limited Latin to skip immediately from the speech cue at the end of the gloss to the close translation of the next verse – or even to the paraphrase with which the interpretation of Ps. 3.3 begins. (This last possibility is somewhat complicated by the gesture back to the previous verse at the start of the paraphrase, with "þai say" echoing the *multi dicunt* of Ps. 3.2.) Alternatively, if one does read the English gloss followed immediately by the Latin of the next verse, then the paraphs may usefully serve to bracket the close translation, flagging it as a repetition of the material that has just been read in another language. While these details of the commentary-translation's presentation (found also in English works on Matthew, discussed in Chapter 4) would evidently help a reader seeking the kind of quick consultation recommended by Love, they could also have been of use to Kempe's priest, as he sought to work carefully (and devotionally) through the text, its translation, and the "doctowrys therupon."

In part because of the unusual demands of exegetical prose – the need to keep the biblical text distinct and readily locatable while also allowing its integration into the surrounding interpretive material – commentaries have featured prominently in the foundational studies of the organization and presentation of manuscripts in the later Middle Ages, and work on exegesis has tended to be especially attentive to the arrangement of these texts in manuscript.[58] The work of scribes figures prominently in this book as well, in part because (lacking editions of these commentaries) manuscripts provide the only means of accessing their offerings, and in part because of the importance (as in the case of the *English Psalter*) of these visual cues for interpreting the commentary itself. Beyond considering the *mise-en-page* of these texts, however, and the readerly engagement enabled by these modes of presentation, this study raises the thorny issue of how the authors of commentaries could have contributed not just to the content of their texts but also to how those texts were presented. Certainly, I do not disagree with the general notion that medieval authors "seldom determine, and never long control, the physical appearance of their texts," and it is always necessary to keep in mind the influence of established conventions for presenting the different registers of exegesis, familiar to scribes and commentators alike.[59] Nevertheless, the exegetes discussed below were themselves inevitably thoughtful users of manuscripts, and I argue that they could often help to *shape* the appearance of their works, not so much by fussily overseeing their earliest scribes as by creating complex texts that worked within and extended established norms and compelled (or at least encouraged) particular scribal handlings. In some cases, we will see scribes struggling to coordinate a commentary's prose with marginal additions in a way that suggests some engagement – whether on the part of these scribes or those who produced their exemplars – with messily revised authorial working copies.⁶⁰ In others, details of copying or the construction of volumes indicate that scribes were assembling their texts from materially discrete sources, drawing (in the case of some portions of the *Glossed Gospels*, for example) on a marked-up copy of a gospel translation, on another volume with a catena of vernacular glosses, and on yet another bibliographical unit supplying the prologues.⁶¹ These conclusions, of course, are largely based on the probabilistic reconstruction of details of lost manuscripts, the exemplars of the surviving commentaries, and they are some of the more speculative arguments offered in this book. But, taken as a whole, they indicate what may have been an unusually high level of authorial influence on (and, in some cases, concern for) the scribal treatment of texts, one which seems most likely to stem from the relative complexity, and the experimental quality, of the texts themselves.

This book begins with two chapters focused on Latin commentaries produced by Oxford theologians of the fourteenth century, with almost all of these texts now receiving sustained scholarly attention for the first time. Exploring commentaries on the Psalter from the early decades of the century, works by Thomas Waleys OP, Nicholas Trevet OP, and Henry Cossey OFM, Chapter 1 argues for the continuing importance of commentary traditions specific to individual biblical books, even as scholastic theorists (including Bonaventure and Aquinas) attempted to articulate interpretive principles applicable across the entirety of Scripture. While earlier studies have tended to treat these generalizing theories as representing the hermeneutic commitments of medieval exegetes, I contend that such theories complexly arise from, and only imperfectly align with, the diverse range of interpretive approaches established in successive commentaries on particular biblical books (or groups of books), with the result that a phrase like "medieval biblical hermeneutics" can only ever be used as a rough shorthand for the great variety of interpretive theories found in these works. The Psalter provides a particularly clarifying case study in this regard, insofar as it was the object of more exegetical attention than perhaps any other biblical book, with a commentary tradition that established a clear set of interpretive priorities specific to its prophetic content and poetic form – and insofar as the resulting book-specific hermeneutic was particularly difficult to reconcile with Thomistic theory. The works of Waleys, Trevet, and Cossey illustrate these discrepancies, but, more importantly, their texts also reveal that at least some exegetes were aware of the competing claims of generalizing scholastic theories and earlier book-specific commitments, and sought to balance them in their new commentaries.

Such balancing continues in Chapter 2, which takes up commentaries written in the 1370s, focusing in particular on Wyclif's massive *postilla* on the entire Bible. Though long known to scholarship, this work has been unfortunately neglected, in part because it has inaccurately been taken as deriving, in its entirety, from a few major works composed earlier in the century (especially Nicholas of Lyre's literal postils), and in part (and relatedly) because it is considered juvenilia, growing out of compulsory university exercises and not representative of its author's mature thought or priorities. This chapter corrects these long-standing misconceptions, focusing in turn on the postils on the Psalter and Matthew to argue that Wyclif was thoughtfully engaged with a variety of sources – leading to his own attempts at balancing hermeneutic commitments – and that he continued to revise portions of his postils throughout the remainder of his career.[62] (The extent of his engagement with earlier sources is made clear in the topical indexing system to his Psalter commentary, discussed in Appendix A.) While seeking to reconcile the competing theories of his different sources, however, Wyclif sets himself apart from the commentators discussed in Chapter 1 by virtue of his relative lack of interest (at least in his postils) in parsing the senses of Scripture – that is, in determining whether a gloss is literal or spiritual. These aspects of hermeneutic theory seem to have been less urgent than his larger understanding of the text's subject matter (*materia*), and he was willing to give priority to readings that matched this understanding, regardless of the *sensus Scripturae* to which they pertained. His hermeneutic eclecticism has affinities with some of Wyclif's later theoretical statements, but, more importantly, this chapter shows that it also corresponds to the priorities found in the other major surviving work of Oxford biblical exegesis from this decade, the unfinished Matthew commentary of William Woodford OFM. The hermeneutic agreement of these opposing controversialists should reinforce the notion that even the most persistent and pervasive interpretive theories, including the senses, were subject to competing trends and traditions.

Expanding our view beyond Oxford, Chapters 3 and 4 explore the composition of biblical exegesis outside the university and the influence of these extramural productions on the creation of new works within the university as well. Moving back to the 1330s and 1340s, Chapter 3 begins with Rolle's *Latin Psalter*, a text which (as seen above) blends material drawn from standard sources with its author's novel interpretations, reading psalms in terms of Rolle's idiosyncratic ideas of the contemplative life. The result is certainly a *scholastic* commentary, one which could appropriately be studied alongside the various Oxford productions discussed in Chapter 1, but one which also appears to have been aimed at meeting the devotional and (more modest) scholarly needs of clerical readers with, like the commentator himself, a limited university education.[63] The text is an act of *translatio*, then, insofar as it makes the basic interpretive offerings of the schools (especially the Lombard's *Glosatura*) available in a more succinct form, and with Rolle's particular "mystical" additions. Indeed, Rolle devoted considerable attention to this Latin commentary, apparently revising it at least once in its entirety (as Appendix B reveals), and we will see that his *English Psalter* should be considered yet another attempt to revise this earlier Latin work. In the *English Psalter*, however, Rolle places more sophisticated intellectual and interpretive demands on his readers, reflecting his growing confidence in his authority as a glossator as well as his awareness that the exegesis he provides in the vernacular is likely *all* the scholastic commentary that these readers will ever encounter. The hermit's experiments with the Psalter – undoubtedly the most widely copied texts discussed in this book – were uniquely influential on later commentators, and the final sections of this chapter trace the variety of uses to which the *English Psalter* in particular was put: by imitators who adapted the commentary-translation form to create exegetical poetry, by Wycliffite revisers who sought to update Rolle's works to reflect their own commitments, and, finally, by an Oxford exegete who looked to Rolle as an authoritative reader of Old Testament poetry. This chapter, in sum, argues for the importance of the hermit's work with scholastic commentary to his broader authorial *persona*, in Latin and English alike.

The importance of the Psalter in the liturgy and in private devotion, as well as its crucial role as a source of theological insight – the Lombard called it the "consummation of the whole theological page" ("consummatio ... totius theologicae paginae") – make it almost inevitable that the expansion of scholastic commentary into English would begin with this particular biblical book.[64] But vernacular commentators did not stop there, and Chapter 4 takes up two major commentary-translations of the Gospel of Matthew, at once allowing for more sustained consideration of the hermeneutic priorities specific to that book (and the other gospels) and also revealing how vernacular biblical commentary could develop when Rolle's influence was less acute or immediate. The chapter begins with some consideration of an unstudied commentary-translation of Matthew produced in the North of England in the second half of the fourteenth century, likely the work of Durham Benedictines. This text echoes material from Rolle's *English Psalter* in its prologue before going on to adapt and translate a twelfth-century Latin commentary that was at the same time being put to a quite specific use in Durham Priory. (The vernacular commentator's dependence on this Latin text is established by the material edited in Appendix C.) This commentary-translation introduces a major formal innovation, the citation of the patristic and early medieval authorities whose glosses are compiled in its immediate source, and this interest in citation also appears in the text discussed next, the Wycliffite *Glossed Gospels*, focusing especially on the different versions of English Matthew commentaries produced by this team of exegetes. Here we will see some of the clearest signs of vernacular exegesis as experimental literature – with authors beginning their work without fully knowing what the final product would include or what it would look like – and, as a result of this experimentation, these texts also depart significantly from Rolle's style, offering a compilation of discontinuous glosses rather than the continuous prose of other vernacular commentaries. At the same time, the author of their prologues still makes it clear that these texts are meant to support (studious) devotional reading.

By way of conclusion, the Epilogue considers the fate of vernacular biblical exegesis in the English Reformation. In contrast to the works discussed in Chapters 3 and 4, the major reformist commentators of the early sixteenth century saw English exegesis as an alternative to (and indeed a rejection of) scholastic interpretation. More precisely, these authors tend to reverse the theoretical paradigm discussed above, treating exegesis as a function of translation rather than translation as a form of commentary. By aligning their work with Protestant efforts at biblical translation, reformist exegetes are able to deemphasize the degree to which their commentary-translations are, in fact, commentaries. This shift is matched by the treatment of Middle English biblical exegesis in the hands of sixteenth-century bibliographers, and in particular John Bale, who (insofar as he mentions them at all) tends to treat medieval vernacular commentaries as simple biblical translations, even as he misattributes them to Wyclif and thereby presents them as nascent critiques of scholastic exegesis. Bale's approach to medieval works severs vernacular commentaries from the larger discourse of scholastic exegesis, rewriting the history of these texts as the earliest stirrings of English Protestantism.

Undoubtedly, the desire of fourteenth-century writers to make Scripture available in the vernacular is an important antecedent to the English Reformation, and it seems likely to have been driven by similarly demotic pastoral commitments. Further, insofar as Tudor translators may have been familiar with (and even drawn on) Middle English biblical versions, the historical continuity between these moments in religious and literary history is indeed real.[65] Yet, as made clear above, this sense of continuity has too frequently resulted in a misunderstanding of fourteenth-century vernacular biblicism as either wary of or, in some cases, overtly hostile to the intellectual program of scholastic exegesis. As the chapters that follow will make clear, to see Middle English biblical translations as so many attempts to shake off the oppressive yoke of scholasticism would be to accept too readily the narrative of Tudor reformers seeking to claim these texts as authoritative precedents for their work. The Middle English texts themselves – in their adaptation of exegetical material, in the formal conventions they borrow from Latin commentaries, and in their attempts to broadcast the interpretive approaches of the universities to a broader audience – resist such historiographical appropriation, and more careful consideration of their creation and use reveals the widespread appeal of scholastic hermeneutics in later medieval England. At the same time, the Latin glosses on which the fourteenth-century translators drew, as well as the Latin exegetical texts composed contemporary to these commentary-translations, are hardly tedious or intellectually repressive tools of clerical control. The recovery of a complexly plurilingual program of scholastic biblical commentary – and, with it, a richer history of the Bible in English – must therefore begin with a fuller understanding of the innovative, creative, and experimental quality of Latin biblical commentary itself.

CHAPTER I

Interpretive Theories and Traditions

In the middle decades of the fourteenth century, Henry of Kirkestede OSB (d. *c.* 1378), librarian and later prior of Bury St. Edmunds, compiled his *Catalogus de Libris Autenticis et Apocrifis*. Now preserved only in Thomas Tanner's seventeenth-century transcription, the *Catalogus* is an alphabetic listing of nearly seven hundred classical and medieval authors, their works, and a selection of the English libraries in which those works could be found. Following the catalogue proper, Henry includes an index recording the "nomina doctorum qui scribunt super Bibliam" ("names of doctors who write about the Bible"), essentially a listing of commentaries organized, generally, by biblical book (Fig. 2).[1] For each book, Henry seems to have assembled an initial list of commentators drawn from the catalogue, with additional names appended out of alphabetical order at the end of each list, perhaps indicating that the index, like the catalogue itself, was a work-in-progress. Indeed, Henry must have updated the index and catalogue independently of one another, since some of the authors added to the index do not appear in the catalogue, and many exegetes noted in the catalogue are omitted from the index.[2] An invaluable bibliographical resource, the *Catalogus* indicates how widely different texts circulated in fourteenth-century England,[3] and the index in particular records (albeit imperfectly) the range of biblical commentaries on which later medieval English exegetes could draw. At the same time, in the way its offerings are organized, the index can help to illustrate an important and largely unappreciated aspect of medieval commentary – namely, the range of distinct interpretive priorities and practices that developed surrounding different books of the Bible.

It has become customary, following the work of Beryl Smalley, to discuss the history of medieval biblical scholarship in terms of the varying fortunes of the literal and spiritual senses, with Smalley's narrative of the rise of literalistic exegesis challenged (though not, I think, overturned) by Henri de Lubac's insistence on the continued importance of mystical meanings.[4] This emphasis on general interpretive theories, however, shared by Smalley and de Lubac,

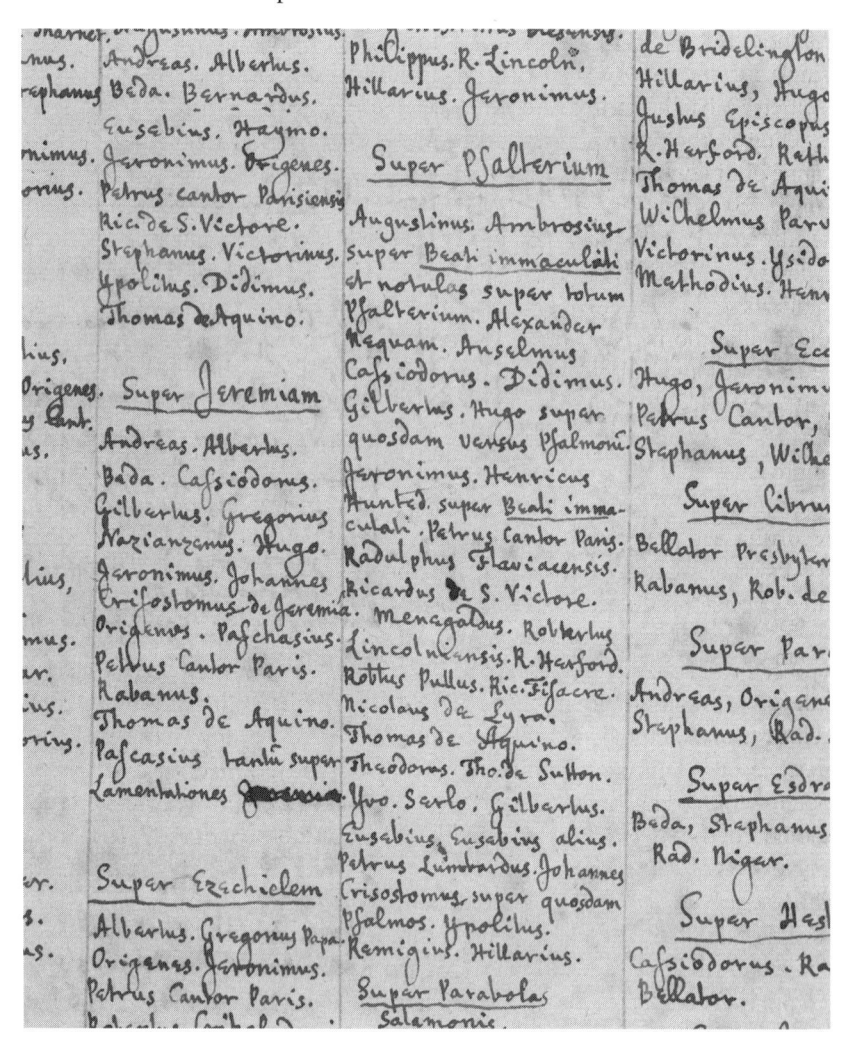

Figure 2 CUL MS Add. 3470, p. 150 (detail).

has the potential to obscure the complex hermeneutic variety witnessed in the commentaries themselves. As will become clear in the examples discussed throughout this study, medieval exegetes worked with sometimes radically different ideas of what constituted the literal meaning of a biblical book, and by focusing on *the* literal sense, in contrast to, say, *the* tropological sense, we run the risk of effacing these disagreements and the divergent interpretations they supported. Further, even when they agreed on one or another definition of the scriptural senses, medieval commentators only rarely insisted that a single interpretation exhausted the possible meanings of a passage, and as Gilbert Dahan has noted, they often seem to delight in piling up alternatives, reveling in the richness (literal and spiritual) of the text they glossed.[5] The range of different theories underpinning scholastic biblical exegesis, what we might call the variegation of scholastic hermeneutics, in large part reflects and results from the practice of commentary in the medieval schools and universities, where exegetes tended to focus their interpretive energies on individual biblical books. Not only did these different books require the consultation of different authoritative patristic sources – composed in various circumstances to meet various local needs, none neatly anticipating the scholastic classroom – but, as we will see, medieval commentators also recognized the formal diversity of Scripture *qua* compilation, and they developed different interpretive approaches to find meaning in these diverging textual forms. Certainly, beginning late in the eleventh century, exegetes increasingly turned to a recurring set of interpretive categories, identified by Richard Hunt and discussed by Alastair Minnis as some of the hallmarks of scholastic literalism – now-familiar headings such as the *intentio auctoris* and *modus procedendi* – but the commentators' use of these terms can vary considerably, often depending on the interpretive history of the specific scriptural text they seek to gloss.[6] Likewise, the interpretive theories advanced in thirteenth- and fourteenth-century *summae* and *quaestiones*, presented as applying to any biblical book, in practice only served to introduce more hermeneutic variety, more ways of potentially reading the same text. And even as they seem typically to have thought of themselves as working within a commentary tradition specific to a single book, commentators were certainly aware of the priorities and approaches on offer in the interpretive histories of other parts of Scripture, divergent hermeneutics which, like other new sources of exegetical insight, could allow them to present their own new interpretations.

On the one hand, then, focus on the *sensus Scripturae* can have the unfortunate effect of making medieval biblical commentary appear totalizing or reductive, with commentators striving to reach a single meaning, or at most, with four senses, four related and mutually informing meanings.[7] The tralatitious or accretive nature of these commentaries, on the other hand, their tendency to quarry glosses from the authoritative sources of late antiquity, can support a misunderstanding of medieval exegesis as plodding, dull, or derivative, so many theories attempting to justify predetermined interpretations, even when that interpretive inheritance is acknowledged as diverse and contradictory. The commentaries themselves tell a different story, especially when they are read as part of the longer interpretive history of specific biblical books.[8] Commentators viewed their task as at once preserving the best interpretive offerings of their forebears – a priority which could lead them to read deep into their book's exegetical history, consulting patristic *originalia* and various earlier medieval commentaries and compilations – and finding new ways to open the text to new meanings, bringing new sources and different interpretive theories to bear on an inexhaustibly significant text.

One way to identify these understandings of the task of scholastic exegesis is to look to the surviving commentaries, to consider their engagement with their interpretive antecedents and their efforts to find meaning in the text they glossed. Such an account forms the core of this chapter, focusing on three little-studied Latin commentaries on the Psalter by English writers in the late 1310s and 1320s. Before turning to these works, however, it will be useful to consider in more detail the contours of the tradition in which they wrote and the range of interpretive approaches available to them, at least partially sketched in Henry of Kirkestede's index.

The interpretive histories preserved, almost like a fossilization, in Henry's lists provide a striking visualization suggesting how these commentary traditions formed, and how they were received by scholastic writers.[9] His unusually full listing of Psalter commentaries, reproduced in Figure 2, reveals the successive stages of interpretive activity surrounding this specific book, with at least some of the works produced at every stage available to one or another exegete in fourteenth-century England.[10] The earliest major authorities are the commentaries of Augustine (d. 430), originating as a series of sermons, and Cassiodorus (d. *c.* 585), who made an initial attempt to refine Augustine's interpretations in light of the formal insights about psalmic poetry he found in the writings of Jerome (d. 420).[11] The commentary attributed to Jerome on Henry's list is actually a pseudonymous early medieval production, but it too exercised considerable influence on later writers, as did Ambrose's (d. 397) gloss of Ps. 118 (the long acrostic *Beati immaculati*) and other selected psalms. In contrast, the late addition of Hilary of Poitiers (d. 368) at the very end of Henry's list is fitting, since his work seems to have been only infrequently consulted by medieval commentators.[12] The selective compilation of these early glosses then fell to exegetes of the ninth century, such as Remigius of Auxerre (d. 908), who added abundant interpretations of his own, typically reflecting ways of reading borrowed from his work with Servius's treatment of Virgil.[13] Remigius's approach was further refined by the bevy of exegetes active in the late eleventh and twelfth centuries, who continued to compile patristic glosses, as well as glosses from Remigius and other earlier medieval writers, supplemented with their novel interpretations and increasingly elaborate prologues. Especially influential was the *Magna glosatura* of Peter Lombard (d. 1160), which became a standard text and was, in turn, supplemented by more selective treatments, such as the partial commentary by Robert Grosseteste (d. 1253), through the early decades of the next century.[14] At this point, it is easy enough to discern a clear set of priorities developing in the tradition of Latin exegesis on the Psalms, with commentators increasingly seeking ways to describe and interpret the text's poetic qualities, and in particular its status as a collection of lyric poems (*lyrica carmina*, variations on which occur throughout these works).[15] The details of this approach will be described at length below, but for now we should simply note how significantly it diverges from the interpretive priorities that had by the same time come to the fore in commentaries on, for example, the Gospel of Matthew. Not only did the patristic authorities (e.g., Augustine's *Quaestiones in Evangeliorum* and *Quaestiones XVI in Matthaeum*) and early medieval compilations (e.g., Hrabanus Maurus's careful marginal accounting of his patristic sources) differ in kind from pre-scholastic sources on the Psalter, but the gospel's narrative of Levantine history drove commentators to different extra-exegetical works (e.g., Josephus's *Antiquities*) and focused their attention on very different literary interpretive issues, especially the status of parables.[16] Through the twelfth century, producing commentaries on the Psalms and Matthew were distinctive, though of course not wholly unrelated, interpretive undertakings.

Such efforts only become more complicated in the thirteenth century, when, in addition to the continuing influence of these book-specific traditions, exegetes were increasingly presented with general statements of hermeneutic theory that seemingly applied to the whole of Holy Writ. At least in part, scholastic theorists recognized the hermeneutic diversity of earlier book-specific traditions, and some attempted to accommodate their differing demands when formulating their general statements of scriptural interpretation.[17] Beginning in the eleventh century, as noted above, commentary prologues included some consideration of a biblical book's *modus procedendi*, accounting for the particular "stylistic and rhetorical qualities of the authoritative text."[18] (This understanding of *modus* should be distinguished from its use as an equivalent to *forma tractatus* or the structure of the text, e.g., *modus bipartitus*.) In the thirteenth century, this range of book-specific prologue discussions was incorporated into accounts of exegetical theory more generally, such as the *Summa Alexandri* assembled by the students of Alexander of Hales OFM (d. 1245). On the question of whether the mode (*modus*) of the Old Testament is uniform or manifold, Alexander favors multiplicity:

> In Lege est modus praeceptivus, in historicis modus historicus, exemplificativus, in libris Salomonis modus exhortativus, in Psalmis modus orativus,

> in Prophetis modus revelativus. Relinquitur ergo non esse modum uniformem in libris Veteris Testamenti.[19]

> In the Law the mode is preceptive, in histories the mode is historical [or/and?] exemplary, in the books of Solomon the mode is exhortative, in the Psalms the mode is prayerful, in the Prophets the mode is revelatory. It therefore follows that there is not a uniform mode in the books of the Old Testament.

This list was later expanded in the *Breviloquium* of Alexander's fellow Franciscan, Bonaventure (d. 1274). After praising the profundity of its mysteries, Bonaventure addresses the question of Scripture's mode:

> In tanta igitur multiformitate sapientiae, quae continetur in ipsius sacrae Scripturae latitudine, longitudine, altitudine, et profundo, unus est communis modus procedendi, authenticus videlicet, intra quem continetur modus narrativus, praeceptorius, prohibitivus, exhortativus, praedicativus, comminatorius, promissivus, deprecatorius et laudativus. Et omnes hi modi sub uno modo authentico reponuntur, et hoc quidem satis recte.[20]

> In the manifold complexity of the wisdom contained in the width, length, height, and depth of Holy Scripture, there is one common mode of proceeding, namely the authentic, within which are contained modes that are narrative, preceptive, prohibitive, exhortative, predicative, threatening, promising, prayerful, and laudatory. And all of these modes come within the one authentic mode, and this rightly enough.

The "authentic" *modus procedendi* used in Scripture serves to distinguish it from other texts that employ logical reasoning (*ratiocinationes*) and proceed by definition, division, and inference (*definitivum, divisivum, et collectivum*).[21] Within this general mode are many different *modi*, which can easily be identified with different biblical books, especially insofar as Bonaventure's list overlaps with Alexander's. In light of this multiplicity, it should be unsurprising that Bonaventure goes on to assert that "Scriptura in his locis variis non est uniformiter exponenda" (207: "Scripture should not be interpreted uniformly in these different places"). By acknowledging the different modes of biblical books, as well as the different exegetical strategies required by this modal variety, Bonaventure can advance a general hermeneutic theory that leaves room for the range of approaches developed in the interpretive histories of specific books.

Thomas Aquinas appears to agree with Alexander and Bonaventure regarding the diversity of biblical modes, and in the preface to his commentary on the Psalms – included on Henry's list – he briefly contrasts the "mode of praise and prayer" ("modum laudis et orationis") used in that book with the narrative, admonitory, exhortative, preceptive, and disputative modes found elsewhere in Scripture.[22] In his general discussions of biblical hermeneutics, however, those found in the *Summa Theologiae* (1a.1.10) and among his quodlibetal questions, Thomas does not once mention the notion of *modus*. Instead, his focus is on the four senses of Scripture, emphasizing in particular the literal sense. He thus explains, in what has become a classic formulation, that the literal or historical meaning of the text is "illa ... qua voces significant res. ... Illa vero significatio qua res significatae per voces iterum res alias significant dicitur sensus spiritualis, qui super litteralem fundatur et eum supponit" ("that ... whereby the words signify things. ... That meaning, however, whereby the things signified by the words in turn also signify other things is called the spiritual sense; it is based on and presupposes the literal sense").[23] This notion of the senses works especially well when interpreting books that narrate Old Testament history, as Thomas acknowledges in his quodlibet (7.6.a2 ad 5); in such cases, literal interpretation is focused on recovering the actions of historical figures, while spiritual meanings inhere *in* those figures and actions.[24] At the same time, Thomas notes the uneven applicability of this scheme, observing that some biblical books treat on their literal level what appears to be proper to allegory, and these books thus do not have a discrete allegorical sense, while others "que moraliter dicuntur secundum sensum litteralem, non consuerunt exponi nisi anagogice" ("which are spoken morally according to their literal sense, can typically only be expounded anagogically").[25] By this last statement, Thomas appears to mean that, when a text's literal sense is taken up with tropologies, the anagogical is then the only spiritual sense that remains for the exegete to explore: there is no allegory, and there is no tropology apart from what is contained in the literal sense. At this point, some reconciliation of the theories of mode and sense appears possible, since it could be inferred that, for example, something written in the *modus exhortativus* would, according to this scheme, be expounded tropologically according to its literal sense.[26] But Thomas ignores such questions, and he is therefore able to avoid the hermeneutic complexity that the issue of modes would introduce, offering instead a general theory of interpretation that purports to apply, without variation, to any scriptural text.[27] Further, though the caveats in his quodlibet imply a need for different approaches to different biblical books, we will see that, in his later commentaries, Thomas tends to read even the Psalter in a way that emphasizes its relation to biblical-historical narrative.

These totalizing commitments are taken further by one of Thomas's most prolific and influential followers, Nicholas of Lyre OFM (d. 1349), whose name appears immediately before Thomas's on Henry's list of Psalter commentators. Writing in Paris early in the fourteenth century,

Lyre first commented on the literal sense of the Bible in its entirety (his literal postils, composed 1322–29), and he subsequently glossed the text again, producing a much briefer commentary on its moral sense (1333–39).[28] In the general preface to the first of these works, Lyre is at pains to emphasize the novelty of his undertaking, quickly dismissing the efforts of his exegetical forebears: "Licet multa bona dixerunt, tamen parum tetigerunt literalem sensum: sensus mysticos in tantum multiplicauerunt, quod sensus literalis inter tot expositiones mysticas incertus, partim suffocatur" ("Although they have said many good things, yet they have touched the literal sense too little, and they have multiplied the mystical senses to such an extent that the literal sense, uncertain among so many mystical interpretations, is somewhat suffocated").[29] This wholesale criticism of earlier exegetes, which retrospectively (and misleadingly) classifies their interpretive priorities as non-literal, appears to signal Lyre's affiliation with the relatively recent Thomistic formulation of the literal sense. These postils will be literalistic, that is, because they will conform to Thomas's theories of interpretation – but they will also extend them. At least with regard to the Old Testament, Lyre declares that he will be able to offer a more accurate reading of the literal sense by having recourse to Hebrew manuscripts (*ad codices Hebraeorum*), and he further notes his intention "non solum dicta doctorum Catholicorum sed etiam Hebraicorum, maxime Rabbi Salomonis, ... [ad] declarationem sensus literalis inducere" ("to include for the declaration of the literal sense ... not only the sayings of Catholic but also of Hebrew doctors, and especially Rabbi Solomon [i.e., Rashi]").[30] Though Thomas lacked Lyre's facility with the language, this interest in a literal sense grounded in the Hebrew text is already evident in his work on the Psalms, where Thomas routinely draws variants from other Latin translations in an attempt to get closer to the original.[31] As his prologue suggests, then, Lyre's postils attempt to show how Thomas's general interpretive theories can indeed be applied in commentary on all books of the Bible.

Very few later exegetes were as thoroughly Thomistic as Lyre, however, even when Thomas's commentaries figured among their major sources. Instead, most fourteenth-century scriptural glosses, whether in Latin or the vernacular, represent a negotiation of the hermeneutic priorities suggested in Henry's lists, on the one hand, and, on the other, those proposed by Thomas and exemplified in Lyre's literal postils. In many cases, it could be that the choice between these interpretive approaches was made without much thought, as a commentator either responded to what he found in his antecedents or simply favored what was convenient, because his interests in writing a commentary were not wholly motivated by questions of hermeneutic theory. But at least some exegetes actively and intentionally sought to grapple with the problem of reconciling recent scholastic interpretive theories with the book-specific traditions within which they wrote. For these writers, decisions regarding their interpretive approach could be motivated by intellectual allegiances, expectations of their audience's interests or abilities, a desire to represent a range of interpretive options, or perhaps even by an aspiration to academic prestige and professional preferment.

In the late 1310s and 1320s, at almost the same time as Lyre was at work on his postils, three English exegetes faced these problems of hermeneutic reconciliation in their commentaries on the Psalms.[32] In a way that seems to repeat the overshadowing of contemporary exegesis after the success of the *Glossa ordinaria* in the twelfth century, the works of Henry Cossey OFM (d. 1336), Nicholas Trevet OP (d. *c.* 1334), and Thomas Waleys OP (d. *c.* 1349) were all relative failures compared with the wide dissemination of Lyre's postils, and none survives in more than a handful of manuscripts.[33] Yet, in their differing responses to recent developments in interpretive theory, these exegetes help to illustrate the continuing importance of book-specific interpretive traditions, an importance which Lyre's success has largely effaced. All three claim to comment on the Psalter's literal sense, presenting varying understandings of literalistic exegesis that reflect the interpretive priorities found (sometimes implicitly) in earlier commentaries as well as those advanced in generalizing scholastic theories. And all three offer ideas of the Psalter's literal sense that depart, sometimes significantly, from Lyre's more popular postils.

Of the three, only Waleys wrote his commentary outside of England, preparing it in the course of his duties as lector to the Dominican *studium* in Bologna, beginning in 1326.[34] The survival of four English copies, however, suggests that Waleys put the work into circulation after his return to Oxford, *c.* 1342.[35] This incomplete commentary, which ends in the course of glossing Ps. 38.2, provides a useful starting point, in part because, though he may have been familiar with Aquinas's gloss on the Psalter, Waleys prefers to follow the approach to the literal sense found in, especially, the Lombard's mid-twelfth-century *Magna glosatura*. His work therefore presents an opportunity to consider in more detail the tensions between the priorities of this source and more recent Thomistic literalism. Waley's preference for the literalism of the older *Glosatura* should not be taken as a sign that his glosses are boringly derivative, however, and we will see that he is committed to discovering new ways to read these psalms.

His innovations simply avoid matters of interpretive theory, and his hermeneutic conservativism is a matter of convenience.

The Indifferent Conservative: Thomas Waleys

After comparing earthly liturgical singing to "the spiritual incense of the angelic hosts" ("exercituum celestium spiritale thimiama"), the Oxford-trained Dominican Thomas Waleys concludes the prologue to his Psalms commentary with a prayer for his students and readers:

> Huius operis et exercituum non solum participes sunt verba Dauid in ecclesiis c[a]nti[ta]ntes, sed in scholis eadem legentes et audientes, vt merito sperare possint illud quod eis promittitur, Apoc. 1: *Beatus qui legit et qui audit verba prophetiae huius*.[36]
>
> Not only those who sing David's words in churches, but also those who read and hear them in the schools partake in this work and are fellows of these [angelic] hosts, so that they might rightly hope for what has been promised to them, Apoc. 1.3: *Blessed is he who reads and hears the words of this prophecy*.

Assuring his audience that their study of the Psalter will be met with the same heavenly reward as the text's regular devotional recitation, Waleys seems to acknowledge that these two activities are somehow distinct, that study and prayer involve different approaches to the Psalms. As Monika Otter describes it, devotional reading or singing, whether in private or as part of a liturgical performance, depends on an appropriation of a psalmic voice "that is both intimate and public," at once an expression of the individual's private prayers and potentially shared with other readers.[37] In this regard, the Psalms are "the definitive form" of what David Lawton has called "public interiorities," presenting "the voice of another, available to others to voice, and an address to God that may be limitlessly personal."[38] As we will see, the question of voice, and even the cultivation of a voice potentially appropriable by other readers, factors prominently in scholastic Psalter exegesis, but commentators approach this issue as part of a larger consideration that begins, primarily, with a specific understanding of the authorship and composition of the Psalms. That is, scholastic exegetes like Waleys sought to recover the potential meanings of the Psalms as texts composed under specific historical circumstances by their prophetic human author, and it is insofar as the Psalmist designed his texts with later readers in mind that, according to these exegetes, they support the creation of prayerful public interiorities.

The Psalmist, Peter Lombard writes, was the most outstanding of prophets (*eximius prophetarum*), a writer who "digniori atque excellentiori modo ... quam alii prophetavit" ("prophesied in a more worthy and excellent way than others").[39] While other prophets describe visions or record angelic messages without necessarily grasping their import, David was able to perceive and meditate upon the details of future salvation history. As another early scholastic commentator notes, "Diuina inspiratione dominicam incarnationem praeuiderat et humani generis reparationem et ediderat scriptam" ("With divine inspiration he foresaw the Lord's incarnation and the restoration of the human race, and he committed it to writing").[40] But the Psalmist did not simply write prosaic descriptions of his prophetic insights. Rather, with the details of Christ's life and humanity's salvation in mind, he composed the Psalter as a series of lyric poems, concealing his knowledge behind a screen of literary conventions. This notion of the Psalter's poetic qualities led commentators to adopt a variety of interpretive strategies, including invoking different literary devices (aposiopesis, apostrophe, hendiadys, litotes, polyptoton, etc.) to explain certain details of the text. Likewise, commentators gave particular attention to the identification of the voice (*vox* or *persona*) they believed David to assume in each psalm, frequently suggesting that he wrote entire psalms in the voice of the prophesied Church or, indeed, of Christ. The Psalter's Christological content could thus be recovered as part of the meaning intended by its human author.

This book-specific approach proved difficult to reconcile with the general theories of interpretation described above, those advanced by Thomas Aquinas and his followers.[41] Though Thomas praises David for the glorious clarity (*gloriosa claritas*) of his prophecy, he also describes the Psalter's prophetic content in a way that limits the human author's involvement. In the preface to his commentary, Thomas writes that the Psalms

> sunt exponendi de rebus gestis ut figurantibus aliquid de Christo vel ecclesia. ... Prophetiae autem aliquando dicuntur de rebus quae tunc temporis erant, sed non principaliter dicuntur de eis, sed inquantum figura sunt futurorum, et ideo Spiritus sanctus ordinavit quod quando talia dicuntur, inserantur quaedam quae excedunt conditionem illius rei gestae, ut animus elevetur ad figuratum.[42]

> ought to be expounded about things done as figuring something about Christ or the Church. ... Prophecies are sometimes said about things which were then present, but they are not principally said about these things, but only inasmuch as they are figures of future things, and the Holy Ghost then

ordained that when such things were read, something would be planted which would exceed the condition of the thing that was done, so that the mind would be elevated to the thing that was figured.

According to this view, echoing Thomas's earlier theoretical discussions, the human author of the Psalms seems to have written about contemporary events (*res gestae*) – and, in his glosses, Thomas does tend to identify the events of David's life as the subject matter of the Psalter's literal sense. It is only because of the divine inspiration guiding the text's composition that figures of Christ and the Church can be discerned in the Psalmist's accounts of these events. Certainly, Thomas does not claim that David was unaware of the Psalter's prophetic prefigurations, but such awareness would seem to be unnecessary in the hermeneutic scheme he describes. There is thus a potential disconnect in Thomas's prologue between the considerable prophetic knowledge enjoyed by David, who had been taught about the truth without mediation (*nude doctus fuit de veritate*), and the composition of his text, where this knowledge is almost inconsequential and the guiding influence of the Holy Ghost comes to the fore.

Though his time in northern Italy, where Thomas's commentary entered circulation and is preserved today, may have allowed Waleys to become familiar with his predecessor's work, the English exegete nevertheless favors the older approach to the Psalter, identifying the prophetic content of the text as the human author's primary intended meaning.[43] In his preface, Waleys twice quotes from the prologue to the Lombard's *Magna glosatura* (which he simply calls a *glosa*), praising David's preeminence among prophets:

> Dicitur in glosa: Alii prophetae per quasdam imagines rerum atque verborum integumenta, scilicet per somnia, visiones, facta, et dicta pr[o]phetauerunt. Dauid autem solius instinctu Spiritus sancti, sine exteriori adminiculo, suam edidit prophetiam. Ad cuius euidentiam sciendum quod prophetia est idem quod visio et propheta idem quod videns. Visio autem triplex est, scilicet corporalis, imaginatiua seu spiritualis, et tertia quae est omnium certissima et clarissima, scilicet intellectualis. Et ideo sunt totidem genera prophetandi. Omnes igitur alii prophetae vsi sunt quandoque primo genere vel secundo. ... Dauid autem solus vsus est genere prophetandi tertio, propter quod et inter prophetas tantam habet excellentiam, vt secundum glosam cum dicitur Propheta sine additione nominis proprii intelligitur Dauid. (sig. A1[rb])

> The gloss says: Other prophets prophesied through certain images of things and coverings of words, as through dreams, visions, deeds, and speeches, but David composed his prophecy with the inspiration of the Holy Ghost

alone, without any external means. As proof of this, it should be known that prophecy is the same thing as seeing, and a prophet is the same as a seer. Now vision is threefold, i.e., bodily, imaginative or spiritual, and a third way which is the most certain and brilliant of all, i.e., intellectual. And therefore there are just as many types of prophesying. All other prophets, then, made use sometimes of the first, sometimes of the second type. . . . But David alone made use of the third type of prophesying, and he therefore has such excellence among the prophets that, as the gloss says, when we say "the Prophet" without adding a proper name, David is understood.

According to Waleys, the Psalmist did not "see" in the same way as other prophets, who were either confronted with marvelous events (*facta*), recorded divine or angelic speech (*dicta*), or had their imaginative faculties stimulated with divinely inspired dreams or waking visions (*somnia seu visiones*). Instead, David's prophetic sight was wholly intellectual, allowing him simply to know all that the Holy Ghost wanted him to know.[44] Waleys acknowledges that it may seem strange for David to have enjoyed such divine favor, since he was a murderer and adulterer (*homicida et adulterus*), but the sincerity of his penance "ad cernenda diuina misteria oculum mentis acuit et disponit" (sig. A1^{va}: "sharpened and prepared his mind's eye to perceive these divine mysteries").[45] And it is because of his apparently unique ability to perceive prophetic truths that "recipienda sunt verba prophetiae Psalmiste non superficialiter, vt solum aures vel linguam occupent, sed vt ad cordis interiora descendant et penetrent" (sig. A1^{va}: "the words of the Psalmist's prophecy should not be received superficially, so that they only occupy the ears and tongue, but so that they descend and penetrate even to the heart's innermost depths").

After describing David's prophetic acuity in such effusive terms, Waleys goes on to gloss the first two nocturns of the Psalter in a way that emphasizes the craftedness of the text as prophecy and poetry.[46] Introducing Ps. 7, for example, he elaborates upon what he found in the *Glosatura*, a note deriving ultimately from Augustine's *Enarrationes*, and claims that David intends "agere gratias Deo pro reuelatione silentii, id est sacri secreti Dei super salutem generis humani" (sig. E4^{va}: "to give thanks to God for the revelation of silence, i.e., of the holy secret of God concerning the salvation of humankind").[47] Likewise, at the beginning of his gloss on Ps. 12, Waleys writes, "Iste psalmus compositus est in persona humani generis suspirantis et desiderantis Christi aduentum" (sig. L2^{va}: "This psalm is written in the *persona* of humankind sighing and longing for the advent of Christ"), then adding a second interpretive option: "Potest exponi vno modo in persona humani generis seu aliter in persona patrum antiquorum desiderantium Filii Dei incarnationem, qui se dicunt obliuioni traditos propter incarnationis dilationem" (L2^{vab}: "It can be expounded in one way in the *persona* of humankind, or alternatively in the *persona* of the ancient fathers longing for the incarnation of the Son of God, those who say that they have been forgotten because of the delay of the incarnation"). Again, Waleys is building on the Lombard, who himself appears to be adapting Cassiodoran interpretations by way of Remigius of Auxerre.[48] A similar gloss can likewise be found in Aquinas's commentary – but Aquinas specifies that this is an allegorical interpretation of the text, while the psalm's literal meaning concerns "historiam David, qui diu est persecutus a Saule" ("the story of David, who for a long time was persecuted by Saul").[49] By identifying the adoption of an imagined voice (*persona*) as integral to the text as the Psalmist composed it, then, and treating the prophetic content of that voice as part of David's intended meaning, Waleys signals his preference for a pre-Thomistic set of interpretive priorities.

Yet it would be wrong to take the hermeneutic conservativism of his commentary as evidence that Waleys had serious objections to more recent trends in the interpretation of the Psalms. Instead, it seems more likely that he followed and elaborated on the Lombard because the *Magna glosatura* was convenient and uncontroversial, an authoritative work that allowed him to devote greater attention to other aspects of his commentary. Indeed, while his literal (prophetic, often Christological) glosses are relatively brief, Waleys also consistently includes lengthy allegorical or moral readings, with *exempla* drawn from a wide range of sources to illustrate his interpretive claims.[50] It is in the compiling of these stories that Waleys must have expended most of his exegetical energies.

It is also in the compilation of his *exempla* that Waleys reveals his affinities with Smalley's classicizing friars, the early fourteenth-century English theologians who pursued newly recovered sources on Roman antiquity and (in her somewhat exaggerated phrase) preferred "to write about ancient gods and heroes instead of the Bible."[51] Though at the beginning of his commentary Waleys tends to draw his *exempla* from standard scholastic sources – such as his gloss on Ps. 24.9, citing Aristotle to claim that the elephant is "domestior et obedientior omnibus animalibus agrestibus" (sig. Bb4^{vb}: "more domestic and obedient than all the wild animals") – as his work continues he increasingly turns to classical mythography and history. His ancient sources include the then-obscure *Ab urbe condita*, the first surviving commentary on which was composed by Trevet (on whom, more below) a decade earlier.[52] Waleys most likely encountered Livy's history in Bologna, perhaps only after he had begun his work on the Psalms, and the range of his quotations suggests his careful study of this text.[53]

Especially in the later portions of the commentary, as his classical *exempla* proliferate, Waleys can at times appear to be more interested in antiquity for its own sake than in using these sources to expound the Psalms. He begins his gloss of Ps. 23, for example, by indicating that the text may be divided into three portions, again assigning Christological prophecy to the literal sense: "Primo enim agit de terre formatione, secundo de lucis a tenebris separatione spirituali, tertio de Christi resurgentis glorificatione" (sig. Aa2[va]: "First he treats the formation of the earth, secondly the spiritual separation of the light from the darkness, and thirdly the glorification of the risen Christ"). Ps. 23.2 belongs to the first portion, and Waleys presents its literal sense as comparatively straightforward, requiring only a paraphrase and slight clarification of prepositions: "Terra est fundata *super maria,* id est iuxta maria, et orbis terrae praeparata est *super flumina:* accipitur enim 'super' hic pro 'iuxta'" (sig. Aa3[rb]: "The earth is founded *upon the seas,* i.e., beside the seas, and the compass of the earth is prepared *upon the rivers:* here 'upon' is used instead of 'beside'"). With its literal meaning easily established, Waleys goes on to offer an elaborate allegory, reading the *terra* founded *super maria* as the Church founded upon two women named Mary (*super Marias*), the one an innocent and the other a penitent. He then turns to his classical sources:

> Narrat Titus Liuius primo volumine, lib. 2, et idem narrat Valerius, de Coriolano Romano, quod cum ipse propter persecutiones sibi factas exularet, mouit bellum contra vrbem, et in tantum eam humiliauit et terruit, quod cum armis viri vrbem defendere non possent, mulieres precibus lacrimisque defendebant, scilicet mater ipsius exulis et vxor, quae pacem vrbi lacrimis et precibus impetrabant. (sig. Aa3[vb])

> Titus Livy (Volume 1, Book 2) and Valerius relate the story of Coriolanus Romanus, describing how, persecuted and driven into exile, he fomented war against the city and brought it so low and terrified it to such an extent that, since the men could not defend it with arms, the women defended it with prayers and tears – namely, the exile's mother and his wife, who procured peace for the city with their tears and prayers.

The story of Coriolanus may seem to have little to do with the allegorization that Waleys has just offered, but he insists on its relevance.[54] This Roman general, he argues, may be read as a type of Christ, who is exiled from his Church and consequently punishes it with tribulations, and it is only through the prayers of his mother and the tears of Mary Magdalene that mercy may be obtained.⁵⁵ This extended rehearsal of classical material carries Waleys far from the literalistic parsing with which his treatment of the verse began, and it may indeed be the case that his discovery of this story motivated the creation of the allegorical gloss in its entirety. Yet the violent, bloody tale of Coriolanus certainly makes the otherwise-conventional allegory all the more vivid and memorable, and, here as elsewhere, Waleys seems to delight in the slippages between psalm text and *exempla*, in this case with the Magdalene's copious salty tears potentially evoking the seas of Ps. 23.2.⁵⁶

Other instances of classicism in his commentary have a direct bearing on Waleys's literal glosses. In the third portion of the same psalm, describing the "glorification of the risen Christ," Waleys again invokes Livy, but now without introducing an allegory or moralization. In a conventional move, he presents Ps. 23.9 as a description of the ascension, written "in persona angelorum Christum praecedentium" (sig. Aa6^{vb}: "in the *persona* of the angels preceding Christ [i.e., into heaven]"), and he then turns to Livy to provide an earthly analogue explaining why this form of triumphant entry was appropriate.

> Et merito debebatur Christo victori triumphalis gloria. Dicit enim Titus Liuius lib. 3 primi voluminis quod apud Romanos pro integra victoria triumphum petere voluerunt. Pro dimidia vero victoria, quae scilicet exercitum hostium fugauerunt, verecundum iudicabant hoc facere, ne scilicet impetrasse magis hominum quam meritorum ratio habita videretur. Constat autem quod Christus ante passionem crebram de hostibus obtinuit victoriam, sicut in expulsione demonum patuit, sed erat victoria quasi dimidia, et ideo ad hoc triumphum non petiit. Sed in passione non tantum dimidiam sed integram victoriam reportauit, et ideo non solum ex fauore gratiae, sed ex debito iustitiae sibi concessus est a Patre honor ille. (sig. Aa6^{vb}–Bb1^{ra})

> And rightly was this triumphant glory owed to Christ the victor. For Titus Livy (Volume 1, Book 3) says that, among the Romans, a triumph was sought when there was a complete victory. When the victory was only partial (when, that is, they put the army of their enemies to flight) they considered it shameful to do this, so it would not seem that more attention was being paid to the men than to their merits. Now, it is clear that Christ obtained numerous victories over his enemies before his passion, as is apparent in the expulsion of demons, but these were something of an incomplete victory, and therefore he did not seek a triumph for them. But in his passion he won not a partial but a complete victory, and therefore the Father granted him that honor not only as a gesture of his favor but as something justly due.

Here Waleys is drawing on Livy's account of the consuls Horatius and Valerius, who refused the honor of a triumph after defeating the Aequi and Volsci (III.lxx.15). Unlike the earlier example of Coriolanus, however, the historical details that Livy offers are now inconsequential, and Waleys instead derives from them a larger insight about the customs of antiquity, allowing him to explain the literal meaning of the biblical text. Again, the basic interpretation of this verse as describing Christ's entry into heaven may be found in the *Magna glosatura* and, further back, Augustine, but the extensive elaboration of Waley's twelfth-century source depends upon a decidedly fourteenth-century interest in the classical past.[57]

Though his favoring of a more traditional approach to the Psalter's literal sense may reflect his relative indifference to recent developments in hermeneutic theory, this use of Livy should indicate that Waleys was not simply reiterating well-established interpretations. We have seen that he adds to the glosses he found in the Lombard, and at least some of his additions were motivated by his research into classical antiquity. His notion of literalistic Psalter exegesis may be conservative, then, and his commentary may be indebted to the larger tradition of exegesis on the Psalms, but Waleys nevertheless contributes to the ongoing development of that tradition, attempting to push it in new directions. Indeed, his interest in writing glosses derived from newly available classical texts may have encouraged him to favor the form of literalism he found in the *Glosatura*. It could be that by relying on these well-established and authoritative approaches and avoiding the potentially contentious innovations of Aquinas, Waleys considered himself freer to pursue his classicism and, in particular, to experiment with the possible relevance of this material to the study of the Bible.

Interpretive Innovation: Nicholas Trevet and Henry Cossey

For Nicholas Trevet, his older contemporary at Oxford, the kinds of interpretations that Waleys borrowed from the Lombard certainly had value, but they should not be confused with the text's literal meaning or with the intentions of its human author.[58] Commissioned *c.* 1317–20 by John of Bristol, the Prior Provincial of the English Dominicans, to compose a commentary on the literal sense of the Psalms, Trevet positions himself with respect to earlier exegetes in a way that signals his preference for Thomistic hermeneutics:

> Quia uero omnes prisci temporis doctores circa allegoriarum misteria profunda perscrutanda totis studiis occupati, aut neglexerunt aut perfunctorie tetigerunt uelut abiecta testa, nuclei dulcedinem consectantes, postulauit a me uestra paternitas, ut quo clarius pateret spiritualis propheticusque intellectus qui littere ueluti basi innititur, Psalterium exposicione litterali et hystorica illustrarem.[59]

> Since all the doctors of former times devoted their efforts wholly to studying the profound mysteries of allegories and therefore either neglected or gave only perfunctory treatment to it [i.e., the literal meaning] like a lowly covering, seeking instead the sweetness of the kernel, you, father, have asked me to elucidate the Psalter with a literal and historical exposition, thereby making clearer the spiritual and prophetic understanding which rests upon the letter as though on a foundation.

Claiming, conventionally enough, that he will be content with the husk rather than the kernel, Trevet attempts to convey the modest scope of his work compared with the long line of writers who have plumbed the Psalter's "profound mysteries." As would later be the case with Lyre's prologue (see above, 28), however, Trevet's assertion of humility also serves to dismiss these commentaries as inadequately representing the text's literal meaning.[60] Compared with Waleys, it is immediately clear that Trevet is more interested in taking up questions of interpretive theory, but rather than trying to reconcile these different approaches, Trevet presents Thomistic hermeneutics as offering a literal supplement that consigns earlier exegetical undertakings to the realm of the spiritual senses.[61]

By collapsing the "spiritual and prophetic understanding" into a single category, defined against the "literal and historical exposition" of the text, Trevet's interpretive approach clearly follows the precedent set by Aquinas, revealing his indebtedness to Thomistic theory if not to the text of Thomas's Psalter commentary itself.[62] He goes on to explain that this "literal or historical" meaning of the text is "quiduis ipsa uerborum de prima intentione auctoris fuisse pretendat, qualeque per os eius Spiritus sanctus misticis sensibus prestruxit fundamentum" (f. 1rb: "whatever it is in the words that [the Holy Ghost] puts forward according to the first intention of the author, and what through his mouth the Holy Ghost prepared as a foundation for the mystical senses"). Echoing his own account of the literal meaning as a foundation or pedestal (*basis*), Trevet agrees with Aquinas that the divine author is responsible both for the text's prophetic content and for a later reader's ability to discover that prophecy amid the more immediate historical referents intended by the human author. As in Thomas's prologue, here too it is unclear whether the Psalmist (as Prophet) was aware of these other senses.

As noted above, this approach curtails the human author's role in the creation of the Psalter's meaning, and yet it is precisely this more restricted authorial ambit that Trevet seeks to elevate and explain. At least in part because he reads the Psalms as evoking specific events in the life of their author, the understanding of David as a writer cultivated over the course of Trevet's commentary is, in some ways, more sophisticated than that of earlier exegetes. Trevet focuses persistently, and in considerable detail, on the Psalms as the written expressions of their human author. This valuing of the Davidic text helps to explain Trevet's decision to gloss not the Gallican translation of the Psalms, the version used commonly in the liturgy, but rather the Hebraicum Psalter, which he believes to have been translated directly (*immediate*) from Hebrew into Latin, as well as his consultation (whether for himself or through intermediaries) of medieval Hebrew exegesis.[63] His understanding of David's authorial control may also account for Trevet's unusual discussion of the Psalter's structure, including his confusing comparison of what was commonly seen as a collection of lyrics, not to Horace,[64] but to the narrative epic of Virgil:

> In Psalterio non ponuntur Psalmi secundum ordinem continuum hystorie, sed carptim interponendo que postea contingerunt, nunc econtra secundum quod deuocio psallentis consurgebat in Dei laudem. Et iste est proprius modus eorum qui scribunt carmina, quod non secundum ordinem hystorie sed carptim scribant. Sic Vergilius enim a medio hystorie incipiens in libro tercio redit ad principium. (f. 2[rb])

> In the Psalter the Psalms are not arranged in a continuous historical order but rather disconnectedly, interposing things that happen later, and now, on the contrary, according to what the devotion of the singer stirs up in praise of God. And this is the proper mode of those who write poems [or songs: *carmina*], that they do not write according to the order of history but rather disconnectedly. For thus Virgil, having begun in the middle of his story, in Book Three returns to the beginning.

Unlike earlier commentators, such as the Lombard, who maintained that the authorial ordering of the Psalms as a collection had been lost during the exile in Babylon and that the current state of the text reflects its reconstruction by the prophet Ezra, Trevet here implies that this apparent disorder is the result of its author's poetic design.[65] In part, the need to explain the Psalter's ahistorical arrangement may be motivated by Trevet's unusual insistence on reading the text *historialiter*, but he moves away from history by describing the affective response – the feelings of devotion that the sequence of the Psalms can help "stir up" – apparently anticipated by the human author. The Psalmist may not have intended all of the

Christological meanings that other commentators attributed to him, but he is still a poet who shaped his whole composition with care.

Throughout his work, then, Trevet presents the literal sense of the Psalter as describing events in the life of its author. Yet his insistence on distinguishing between the "historical" and "prophetic" meanings of the text does not prevent Trevet from claiming that at least some psalms contain prophecy in their literal sense. In these cases, his focus on David as a historical figure persists, and he tends to interpret such prophecy as predicting other events in the Psalmist's life. These prophecies can thus be part of the "first intention of the human author" while also continuing to provide the "foundation prepared for the mystical senses." This treatment of prophecy as part of a heightened interest in the life of David can be seen, for example, in Trevet's gloss of Ps. 6. This is the first of the Penitential Psalms, and its place in this sequence led even Aquinas to read it apart from the narrative of David's life, claiming that "videtur hic psalmus exprimere affectus hominis qui pro peccatis castigatus et in manibus inimicorum datus, poenitentia peracta liberationem obtinuit" ("this psalm seems to express the feelings of a person who, punished for his sins and given over into the hands of his enemies, has won freedom with acts of penance").[66] Trevet rejects this sort of generalizing move, which would make the devotional adoption of the psalm's *persona* part of its author's designs, and instead favors historical specificity: "Orat Dauid petens a Domino liberationem a persecutione inimicorum suorum" (f. 13[rb]: "David prays, asking God for freedom from the persecution of his enemies"). The particular identity of those enemies soon becomes clear:

> Increpat ergo inimicos et hostes suos dicens, *Recedite a me*, id est desiste a me persequendo, *omnes qui operamini iniquitatem*, scilicet consenciendo iniquis operibus Absolon. Hec increpacio prophetica est, et ideo exponend[a] est. *Recedite*, id est recedetis, quod factum est post mortem Absolon restituto Dauid in regnum. Deinde cum dicit, *Quia exaudiuit*, huius increpacionis prophetice causam subiungit, dicens quod oracio pro liberacione sua fuit exaudita a Domino. Et hoc primo insinuat dicens, *Quoniam exaudiuit*, quasi dicat: Ideo dico quod recedetis, *quoniam exaudiuit Dominus uocem fletus mei*, id est mei flentis. Secundo, versus ix, cum dicit *audiuit* ex uehementi gaudio hoc idem iterum ac tercio replicat. Cum dicit, *Audiuit Dominus deprecationem*, ecce iterum, *Dominus orationem meam suscepit*, ecce tercio idem replicat. Et est poliptodon. (f. 14[ra])

> He therefore rebukes his enemies and the hostile peoples, saying, *Depart from me*, i.e., stop pursuing me, *all you workers of iniquity*, i.e., joining in the unjust works of Absalom. This rebuke is prophetic and therefore must be

interpreted. *Depart*, i.e., you will depart, which indeed happened after the death of Absalom, when David was restored to power. Then when he says, *For he has heard*, he prophetically adds the cause of this rebuke, saying that the prayer for his freedom has been heard by the Lord. And he first suggests this, saying, *For he has heard*, as though he said: For this reason I say that you will depart, for the Lord has heard the voice of my cry, i.e., of my crying. Secondly, when he says, *He has heard*, out of his wholehearted joy he repeats it a second and third time. When he says, *The Lord has heard my prayer*, this is the second time, and he repeats it a third time: *The Lord has received my prayer*. And this is called polyptoton.

Though this identification of a literary device reveals an understanding of the text's poetic quality shared by the commentary tradition on this book more generally, his interpretation of the psalm in terms of Davidic history sets Trevet apart from other exegetes. Waleys insists, for example, that David is speaking here "in persona paenitentis, pro suis et aliorum delictis deprecantis" (sig. D6[v]: "in the *persona* of a penitent, praying for his faults and those of others"). In contrast, Trevet believes that the Psalmist was describing recent events, and, in keeping with this historical focus, the scope of his prophecies is limited, in this case predicting Absalom's death and the restoration of his kingdom. Neither offering Christological prophecy nor anticipating the adoption of his lyric *persona* by future readers, Trevet's Psalmist writes songs of his own experience.

Perhaps in part because his attempt to extend Thomas's theoretical innovations overlapped with Lyre's more comprehensive project, produced a few years later, or simply because he chose to interpret a translation of the Psalter not used in liturgical devotion, Trevet's commentary appears not to have enjoyed a wide readership.[67] It did, however, attract the attention of one of Trevet's younger contemporaries, Henry Cossey, master of the Franciscan school at Cambridge, *c.* 1325–26.[68] In his own commentary, likely produced during a stint at Oxford following his regency, Cossey extends many of the interpretive priorities that he found in Trevet's gloss, as well as in the literal postils of Nicholas of Lyre, both of whom he cites by name, and he works to develop their interest in the Hebrew text of the Psalms and in the interpretations offered by medieval Jewish writers.[69] Indeed, a note on Hebrew prepositions occurring at the end of Cossey's work suggests that he had acquired at least a rudimentary understanding of the language, a conclusion reinforced by his frequent habit of presenting a transliteration of the Hebrew text in the body of his commentary.[70] Even as he embraces some of their methods, however, Cossey is critical of the way Trevet and Lyre dismiss their exegetical forebears and distinguish between the prophetic content of the Psalms and their human author's intentions. In Cossey's view, earlier commentators were often right to find Christological prophecy as the text's literal meaning, and his task was therefore to assess how these earlier understandings might be refined, though not rejected, in light of Trevet's and Lyre's Thomistic innovations.

Of course, as we have seen, Trevet was in complete agreement that the Psalms could be read as prophecy of Christ, but, unlike Trevet, Cossey insists that this prophecy is part of their human author's intended meaning. As had pre-Thomistic commentators, Cossey imagines the moment of prophetic insight to be the same as the moment of poetic inspiration, describing how "totum nempe quod Psalmista Deo inspirante concepit vt prophetando prediceret, psallere voluit et cum ympnis et canticis inspiratoris laudi tribuere" (f. 1^r: "all that, with God's inspiration, the Psalmist understood himself able to predict in his prophecy, all of this he wished to sing in psalms and to offer in praise of his inspirer with hymns and songs"). In what could be an oblique response to the application of Thomistic theories to non-narrative books, Cossey goes on to observe, "Modus enim tradendi istam propheciam non est simplici narracione sed psalmodia et decantacione, vt duriora corda que verbis non compunguntur modulacionis suauitate moueantur" ("The mode of conveying this prophecy is not with simple narrative, but with psalmody and song, so that harder hearts, which were not pricked by words, would be moved by the sweetness of the melody"). Indeed, Cossey is less surprised by the notion that David could have intended to write prophecies about Christ than he is that the rustic monarch and military leader was able to compose such sophisticated poetry:

> Sed mirum est quomodo ipse Dauid, de post fetantes assumptus et postea per totam vitam suam in actibus bellicis occupatus, sciuerit versificare. Sed in lingua materna eciam laici sciunt versificare. Verumptamen ipse Dauid literatus fuit: dicunt enim Hebrei, et recitat Ysidorus, libro 6 *Ethimologiarum*, quod Dauid scripsit vltimam partem libri Samuelis vsque ad calcem. (f. 3^r)

> But it is astonishing to think how David, taken from the sheepfold [cf. Ps. 77.70] and, later, occupied with warfare throughout his life, knew how to write poetry. But even the laity are able to write poetry in their mother tongue. Yet David was literate, for the Hebrews say, and Isidore repeats (*Etymologies*, VI.ii.10), that David wrote the last part of the book of Samuel, up to its conclusion.

It is precisely the actions of the embattled David that Trevet had taken to be the subject matter of much of the Psalter, but Cossey maintains that the

Psalmist was able to compose his prophetic poetry *despite* the amount of time he spent on the battlefield. In Cossey's commentary, as in the earlier exegetical tradition on this book more generally, the Psalms present their human author's attempt to express his divinely given knowledge and to use literary language and form to move his readers with his prophetic message.

Earlier commentators had praised the Psalmist for his uniquely extensive knowledge of the incarnation, an appraisal we have seen repeated by Thomas Waleys. Though Aquinas had similarly recognized the "glorious clarity" of David's foresight, the historical focus of Thomistic exegetes like Lyre and Trevet cast doubt, if only implicitly, on the Psalmist's prophetic preeminence. Cossey takes up this question as part of his discussion of the *genus prophetiae* to which the Psalter belongs, and, though he finally agrees with the earlier tradition, his engagement with the Thomists results in a tortuous and caveat-ridden line of reasoning:

> Valde difficile est homini cognoscere quis prophecie gradus perfeccior sit, et valde difficilius quis prophetarum habuerit illum gradum post Christum. Et dicit Lira quod Dauid non fuit perfeccior propheta quam Apostoli, quia ipsi plenius acceperunt graciam Spiritus sancti. ... Quamuis Apostoli fuerunt viri perfecciores quia et viderunt corporaliter Messiam et alia de quibus Dauid prophetauerat, non propter hoc sequitur quod fuerunt perfecciores prophete, nec quod habuerunt perfecciorem gradum prophecie: ymmo raro leguntur prophetasse, nisi Iohannes in Apocalipsi. Dico ergo quod propheta excellit prophetam vel propter maiorem certitudinem et euidentiam rerum sibi reuelatarum, vel propter maiorem dignitatem rerum ipsarum, vel maiorem multitudinem reuelatorum, vel propter concursum omnium istorum, et iste est perfectissimus gradus qui excellit in omnibus istis. Sed quando vnus propheta excellit in vno et alius in alio, quis est perfeccissimus gradus difficile est dicere (nisi Deus reuelet), et quia omnes prophete in celo sunt vnanimes de eorum excellenciis, non disputemus in terris. Tamen Dauid potest dici prophetarum eximius qui suo tempore prophetabant secum, vel etiam quia rex erat, vel quia suam propheciam metrice et ympnidice concinebat, vel aliis de causis quas Deus nouit. (f. 9ʳ)

> It is very hard for people to know which degree of prophecy is more perfect, and, especially after Christ's incarnation, it is harder still to know which of the prophets attained to that degree. Lyre says that David was not a more perfect prophet than the Apostles, since they received the grace of the Holy Ghost more fully. ... Yet, though the Apostles were more perfect men (since they saw the Messiah in the flesh, as well as other things about which David prophesied), it does not follow from this that they were more perfect prophets, nor that they had a more perfect degree of prophecy – no, rather, with the exception of John in the Apocalypse, they are rarely said to have

> prophesied. I say, therefore, that one prophet excels another either on account of the greater certainty and evidence of the things revealed to him, or on account of the greater dignity of those things, or the greater number of his prophecies, or on account of the coincidence of all of these things, and this is the most perfect degree, which excels all the others. But when one prophet excels in one regard and another in another, it is difficult to say which is the most perfect degree (unless God reveals it!), and since all the prophets are in agreement about their excellence in heaven, let us not argue about these things on earth. Nevertheless, David can be said to be the most outstanding of the prophets who prophesied in his lifetime, either because he was the king, or because he sang his prophecy metrically and hymnically, or because of some other causes known to God.

As happens elsewhere in his prologue, here Cossey comes closer to offering a deconstructive reading of earlier commentaries than any positive interpretive claim of his own. At least part of his difficulty can be explained by the different ways of classifying prophecy that had developed in the commentary traditions specific to different biblical books. While exegetes of the Psalter had tended to follow the Cassiodoran distinction of prophecy by words, events, images, and "hidden inspiration," the prologues to Apocalypse commentaries, for example, generally framed their discussion in terms of the three modes of sight adapted from Augustine's *De Genesi ad litteram*, though there was considerable disagreement regarding whether John saw in the second (spiritual) or third (intellectual) modes.[71] Increasingly through the thirteenth century, however, commentators attempted to find ways to reconcile these disparate accounts of prophecy. We have seen that Waleys, for example, perhaps following Aquinas, included both the Cassiodoran and Augustinian schemes as part of his praise of the Psalmist. Even as he refutes the specific comparison (found in Lyre) of David to the Apostles, Cossey seems to be expressing his general anxiety concerning the impossibility of the sort of reconciliation and comparison Lyre had attempted.[72] Since "one excels in one regard and another in another," it would be foolish for an exegete to insist on the exceptional status of any single prophet, unless that exegete were himself to receive some prophetic insight on the matter. After this equivocation, Cossey is finally able to affirm the praise of David found in the *Glosatura*, maintaining that the Psalmist was the most outstanding of prophets (*prophetarum eximius*), but he can only offer this encomium with a string of qualifiers. David was the greatest prophet "in his own day," and even in this more restricted sense, the Psalmist's greatness apparently has less to do with his prophetic knowledge and more with political power or literary merit.[73] Cossey is trying to salvage a pre-Thomistic understanding of the Psalter, but the complications introduced by more recent commentators compel him to present that understanding in an especially attenuated form.

Though his qualified praise of the Psalmist indicates the extent to which new developments in general hermeneutic theory could complicate book-specific traditions, at other points in his commentary Cossey is able to dismiss Thomistic approaches with confidence and apparent ease. At the opening of his gloss on Ps. 29, for example, he cites and quickly sets aside Trevet's non-Christological reading of the text:

> De materia psalmi dicit Triuet quod est regraciatorius pro reditu de captiuitate Babilonica, et cantabatur in templi dedicacione, et sic tractat totum psalmum, et quod infra dicitur, *Domine eduxisti ab inferno*, exponit de ergastulo Babiloniorum. Sed si iste psalmus sit propheticus, sicut oportet secundum istam exposicionem, et prophecia Dauid fuit de Christo maxime, sicut testatur Regum [23], multo melius videtur de Christo exponere ad literam. (f. 41^v)

> Concerning the subject matter of this psalm, Trevet says that it is an offering of thanks for the return from the Babylonian captivity, and it was sung at the dedication of the temple. And he interprets the entire psalm in this manner, and what is said below, *Lord, you have brought [my soul] from hell* [Ps. 29.4], he expounds as concerning the prison of the Babylonians. But if this psalm is prophetic, as it ought to be according to this exposition, and David's prophecy is especially about Christ, as II Reg. 23 makes clear, it would then seem much better to expound it as being literally about Christ.

According to Cossey, Trevet had conceded that the human author's intentions in Ps. 29 were, in a limited way, prophetic, insofar as David foresaw the reconstruction of the temple that would take place after the captivity in Babylon, and he composed this psalm to be sung at its dedication.[74] Identifying an apparent weakness in Trevet's (and Thomas's) theory of prophetic authorship, Cossey insists that, if Trevet is willing to identify some prophecy as the literal sense of the psalm, then he should admit that the Psalmist could also have intended to express his prophetic foreknowledge of Christ. To support this claim, he refers to II Reg. 23.1–2, the last words of David, in which the king claims to speak with divine inspiration, and which Cossey had quoted in his prologue, arguing that "quandoque psalmus est principaliter prophecialis, et hoc de Christo sicut sunt multi" (f. 1^v: "sometimes a psalm is principally prophetic, and, indeed, in many cases about Christ"). The reference in Ps. 29.4 to being raised from hell does not need to be treated as a metaphor for the Babylonian captivity, then, but can instead be read, literally and prophetically, in the *persona* of Christ. This reasoning allows Cossey to offer an interpretation of the psalm which is much closer to what he found in the *Glosatura*, where it is said to describe Christ's passion and resurrection.[75]

Affirming that Christological prophecy is essential to the literal meaning of the Psalms, Cossey is critical of the interpretive theories underpinning the work of Thomists like Trevet and Lyre. In other cases, however, it is his facility with Hebrew that allows Cossey to find fault with these exegetes, who, he says, fail to pursue their newer interpretive priorities with sufficient rigor. In other words, though he disputes their theory of authorship, Cossey wholly supports some of their other interpretive innovations, especially their recourse *ad codices Hebraeorum* to determine the meaning of the text as composed by its human author. At the beginning of his gloss on Ps. 76, for instance, Cossey notes, "Dicit Triuet quod istud, *Asaph Psalmus*, in veris exemplaribus non habetur: sed istud est mirabile, cum in vtroque psalterio, quorum vnum erat diligentius scriptum et quo correctum, planissime scribatur" (ff. 122^v–123^r: "Trevet says that this, *A Psalm of Asaph*, is not to be found in the best copies: but this is very strange, for in both of my psalters (one of which was quite diligently copied and therefore correct) it [i.e., the title] is written clear as day"). The two psalters mentioned here are invoked throughout Cossey's commentary, and these repeated references make it clear that they are copies of the Hebrew text. Cossey seems to have acquired one of them from a Jewish convert, while he likely encountered the other in the library of the Oxford Greyfriars, part of the Grosseteste bequest.[76] Here we learn that Cossey thinks one of these manuscripts (though which one is unclear) to have been written with considerable care, and he therefore considered it all the more valuable as a witness to the Hebrew.[77] Since both of his Hebrew manuscripts contain the reference to Asaph in the title of Ps. 76, Cossey finds it perplexing (*mirabile*) that Trevet would claim that the phrase lacks the support of "true exemplars," suggesting either that Trevet's sources were faulty or that his skills as a textual critic were, in this case, deficient. Rather than rejecting Trevet's interpretive priorities, Cossey is pursuing them with greater acuity and accuracy.

Cossey's scholarly work with the Psalter, along with his critique of Trevet, extended beyond the initial drafting of his commentary. In the only surviving copy of the work, Cambridge, Christ's College MS 11, the scribe has included a series of marginal notes tied to specific points in the text, some consisting of only a single sentence and others filling the margins of both pages in a single opening (Fig. 3). The length of some

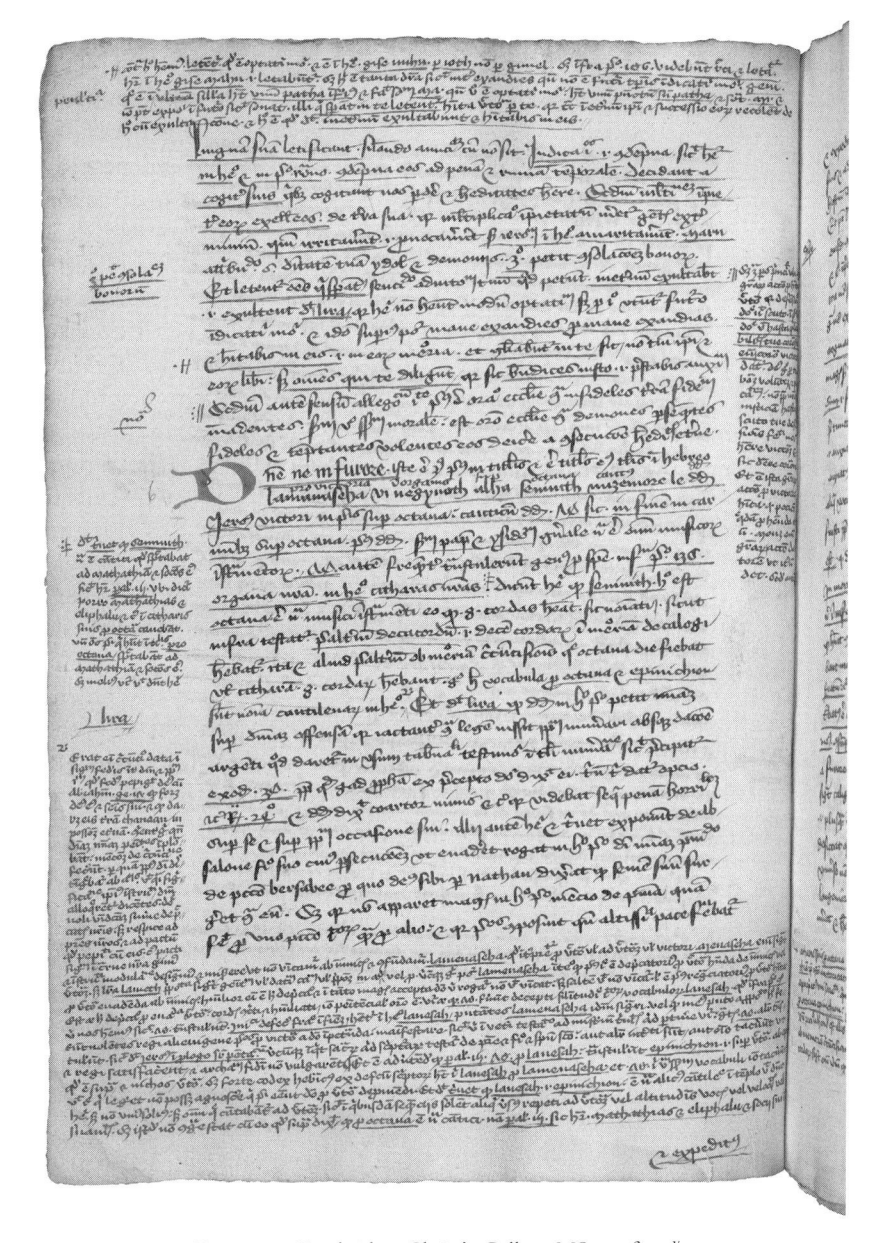

Figure 3   Cambridge, Christ's College MS 11, f. 21ᵛ.

examples makes it unlikely that these notes represent an attempt to correct errors in the copying of the text. Instead, they seem to have been positioned as the scribe found them in his exemplar, reproducing, in other words, notes added to supplement the main text in Cossey's working copy.[78] This impression is reinforced by their content: the shorter notes often add contrary opinions attributed to single authorities, while the longer ones reflect more substantial work with numerous sources. Cossey appears to have extended his discussion of the transliterated Hebrew title of Ps. 6, for example, with material borrowed from Trevet, visible in the middle of the left margin in Figure 3.

> Dicit Triuet quod *seminith* nomen est cantici quod spectabat ad Mathathiam et socios eius, sicut habetur Paral. 15 vbi dicitur: *Porro Mathathias et Eliphalu* etc. *in citharis suis pro octaua canebant.* Vnde omnes psalmi qui habent in titulis *pro octaua* spectabant ad Mathathiam et socios eius. Sed melius videtur vt dicunt Hebrei. (f. 21ᵛ)

> Trevet says that *shemineth* is the name of a song pertaining to Mathathias and his companions, as in I Chron. 15.21: *And Mathathias and Eliphalu*, etc., *sang for the octave on their harps*. And therefore all the psalms which have *for the octave* in their titles pertained to Mathathias and his companion. But it seems better, as the Hebrews say.

The seemingly fragmentary ending of this gloss allows the added passage to flow seamlessly into the preexisting text in the body of the commentary, which, immediately after the *signe de renvoi*, reads, "Dicunt Hebrei quod *seninith*, hoc est *octaua*, est nomen musici instrumenti eo quod octo cordas habeat sic nominati" ("The Hebrews say that *shemineth*, i.e., *octave*, is the name of a musical instrument, so called because it has eight strings"). Cossey then returns to Trevet's suggestion in a longer addition, copied in the lower margin spanning ff. 21ᵛ–22ʳ, and he offers further evidence from the Hebrew text of the psalm and of I Chron. 15, as well as from Jerome, to support the conclusion that "adherendum est illis Hebreis qui dicunt quod *seminith* est nomen instrumentorum illorum que octo cordis tangebantur" ("we should keep to the opinion of the Hebrews who say that *shemineth* is the name of instruments that are played with eight strings").[79] Again, the end of the marginal note, "Et dicit Lira, etc.," repeats the beginning of the next sentence in the main text ("... et dicit Lira quod Dauid in hoc psalmo ..."), allowing Cossey's exposition to continue. Additions like this one may seem oddly unnecessary, offering a long detour that simply allows Cossey to affirm his original position and refute an alternative from a source he had to hand when first writing the commentary, and which, at the time, he decided not to include. Indeed, this is not the only series of marginal additions in which Cossey names sources cited throughout his gloss, indicating that the inclusion of these notes was not always motivated by the discovery of new material.[80] These additions, then, may point to the troublesome diversity of Cossey's sources, as well as their persistent disagreements, which he struggled to reconcile throughout his exegetical undertaking. They also reveal the persistence of his efforts, his willingness to entertain the possibility that Trevet may have been right and to carry out further research to ensure that his own Hebrew sources had not led him astray.

Though Cossey clearly found some newer interpretive trends to be quite compelling, he also seems to have recognized the challenges that these approaches posed for the long tradition of commentaries on the Psalms. Unlike Waleys, he does not favor earlier approaches because they are convenient and their authority is established. He seems, instead, to have been committed to testing the strengths and limits of the theories underlying the commentaries on which he and Waleys drew. This commitment also sets him apart from Trevet, since he appears interested in the hermeneutic developments represented in Trevet's commentary chiefly insofar as they could help him refine and revise the interpretations that he found in works like the *Magna glosatura*. Trevet was ready to reclassify this earlier tradition, claiming that it focused wholly on the Psalter's spiritual senses, and to present his work (however humbly) as the first thoroughly literal reading of the text. Cossey, in contrast, insisted on innovating from within the tradition. Elaborating upon the Lombard's description of the Psalter as the summation of all theology (quoted above, 18), Cossey praises the biblical book's lofty subject matter, which, he says, "deissima est et tocius theologie finem continuere videtur, qui in diuinis laudibus et contemplacione diuinorum existit" (f. 12^{rv}: "is godly and seems to contain the end of all theology, consisting of divine praise and the contemplation of divine things"). The theological profundity of this book is, Cossey insists, part of its human author's design, and he embraces hermeneutics specific to the Psalter as well as general scholastic interpretive theories in his ongoing attempt to draw out those meanings in all of their richness.

Interpreting Solomon's observation in Eccles. 12.12, "Of the making of many books there is no end," Bonaventure laments, "Curiosi nunquam tot habent, quin volint audire plures, quia nunquam volunt audire vetera sed semper nova" ("Curious people never have enough, but they want to hear more, and they never want to hear old things but always new ones").

Yet, though he criticizes idle curiosity as a great affliction (*afflictio magna*), he is not willing to condemn all bibliographic proliferation, to which his own writings obviously contribute. By maintaining that "scientia semper quodam modo renovatur" ("knowledge must always in some way be renewed"), Bonaventure points to the way in which, in almost all cases, the work of exegetes builds on and extends the interpretive efforts of earlier writers.[81] Of the making and revising of commentaries, no end is in sight.

The idea of progress suggested by Bonaventure is developed in much greater detail in the *Summa Quaestionum Ordinarium* (VIII.6) of another Parisian master, Henry of Ghent (d. 1293). Against the claims of the Joachimites, Henry insists that all truth is contained in the Old and New Testaments, and all that remains is for the proper understanding of the canonical Scriptures to be made known.[82] This understanding, for Henry, takes three forms: disseminating the text throughout the world, responding to it with acts of penance and worship, and, finally, glossing it. He considers the first two of these acts already accomplished, but the last will continue until the end of time:

> Sic ergo vult Dominus vt quilibet de suo offerat, vt sic totum aedificium continue crescens tandem perfectum fiat, et hoc tam cognitione doctrine quam opere vite. ... Vnde cum non solum predicatum fuerit euangelium per orbem vniuersum Christi nomen diuulgando, quod impletum fuit tempore Apostolorum, sed etiam cum effectu poenitentiam recipiendo, vt in omni gente ecclesie aedificentur et ab aliquibus in illis colatur Christus, quod nondum erat factum tempore Augustini, vt dicit in epistola ad Esichium, quod forte impletum fuit postmodum conuersis temporibus beati Gregorii Pape insulis oceani – cumque non solum hoc factum fuerit, sed etiam expositum et opere impletum quod restat exponendum et implendum, tunc erit consummatio et finis mundi. Citra autem continue augmentatur sacre Scripture intellectus et expositio. (sig. 15^v–6^r)

> The Lord therefore wishes that everyone contributes his own offering, so that the whole edifice, continuously growing, may finally be perfected in the knowledge of doctrine and in the conduct of life. ... Thus, not only when the gospel has been preached throughout the whole world, spreading abroad the name of Christ, which was fulfilled in the time of the Apostles, but also when this preaching has led to penance, so that churches are built in every nation and Christ is worshiped in them, which had not yet happened in the time of Augustine, as he says in his letter to Esichius, but which was perhaps fulfilled later, when the islands of the ocean had been converted in the time of Pope Gregory – when not only all this is done, but also when what remains to be expounded and fulfilled has been expounded and fulfilled, then the consummation and end of the world will

come. Until then, the understanding and exposition of Holy Scripture will be increased continuously.

"The end of time," as Dahan explains, "will make the work of exegesis unnecessary. But that has not yet come, and so writers must continue to construct the hermeneutic edifice, generation by generation and brick by brick."[83] In some cases, more commentaries will be needed because earlier exegetes left lacunae, failing to gloss every word or phrase in the text, but the formulation of new hermeneutic theories will also allow for new interpretive insights. As Henry notes elsewhere in his *Summa* (IX.2), Scripture was written by human authors who, he claims, "regulas artis huius quam conscripserunt perfectissime intellexerunt" (sig. i7[v]: "perfectly understood the rules governing the art that they composed"), and new ways of analyzing these compositions will yield new understandings of their meaning.[84]

Apparently sharing this sense of exegetical progress, Trevet and Cossey seem to have approached their task as commentators with the aim of building on the work of their predecessors and offering new understandings of the Psalms in light of recent hermeneutic innovations. Though they disagree about whether the tradition of Psalter commentaries was focused on the text's literal or spiritual meaning, both necessarily position their interpretations in relation to the work of earlier exegetes, contributing however many more bricks to the "hermeneutic edifice" of scholastic interpretation. In this edifice there were many rooms. Many of the points on which Trevet and Cossey disagree – in particular the place of Christological meaning in the Psalms and the ways in which an exegete is to draw out that meaning – reflect interpretive priorities that were specific to the Psalter and that had developed in one Psalter commentary after another over the course of centuries. Though they could certainly have some bearing on the interpretation of other books, questions of how poetic voice and literary devices could be used to enrich (or perhaps disguise) prophetic foreknowledge had especial urgency in the case of this particular text, and it is to these questions that their major antecedents, especially the *Magna glosatura*, drew Trevet's and Cossey's attention. Commentators tended to define their interpretive priorities in terms of traditions specific to individual biblical books or, in some cases, groups of books, and it was largely in terms of these book-specific traditions that hermeneutic progress was made.

At the same time, it was their differing responses to recent general interpretive theories, especially those propounded by Aquinas, that led

Cossey to disagree with much of what he found in Trevet's commentary. Presented as applying to the Bible as a whole, Thomas's theories of the scriptural senses were formulated, it would seem, without much concern for the specific interpretive demands of non-narrative books like the Psalter, and, though his own commentary offered one model of how these competing priorities could be reconciled, other exegetes could very well disagree with his solution and propose one of their own, as the case of Cossey in particular makes clear. Cossey's work also indicates that other methodological priorities often associated with Thomistic commentators, especially the consultation of Hebrew manuscripts in the case of Old Testament books, could be taken up without causing as many problems. The Thomistic toolkit could be drawn on selectively, and, indeed, some of these methods could be used to reinforce the authority of long-standing (book-specific) interpretations. The negotiation of different interpretive theories could result in varying degrees of methodological piecemealism and further hermeneutic variegation.

Late medieval biblical commentaries were more intricately and diversely experimental than the familiar narrative of the rise of the literal sense would suggest, complicated by the continued importance of book-specific traditions of exegesis. This complexity makes it less useful (for the modern critic) to discuss medieval biblical hermeneutics as a single unified field, since the theories underpinning different commentaries varied greatly depending on the biblical book in question, and it is only by gaining a familiarity with the shape of a book-specific tradition as it developed over the course of centuries that, in many cases, we will be able to discern how later medieval commentators responded to the challenges posed by general scholastic hermeneutic theories. Then again, precisely this sensitivity to the shape of the long tradition of Psalter commentaries can be seen, to varying degrees, in the work of Cossey, Trevet, and even Waleys. Cossey in particular has shown himself to be an astute reader both of earlier approaches to the Psalms and of newer interpretive theories.

Recognizing the continued influence of these early scholastic (and pre-scholastic) interpretive traditions is especially important in the case of the Psalter, since, though they are focused on recovering the *intentiones* of the book's author, the priorities and procedures found in works like the *Glosatura* hold open the possibility of bridging academic and devotional modes of reading. While we have seen that, in the prayer concluding his prologue, Waleys distinguishes between "those who sing David's words in churches" and "those who read them in the schools," his (and, indeed, Cossey's) approach to the Psalter's literal sense points to some continuities between the two activities. That is, by following the Lombard and claiming that the Psalmist's prophecies include texts written in, for example, "the *persona* of a penitent, praying for his faults and those of others," Waleys appears to be suggesting that the Prophet intended to write at least some psalms in a way that anticipated their re-voicing by later (Christian) readers.[85] In these cases, the meaning of the text as it is "sung in churches" is, at least in theory, precisely what the schoolmen are studying, and we will see that this connection between the psalms' literal sense, as understood in this book-specific interpretive tradition, and their devotional performance will be crucial to the development of scholastic Psalter exegesis, in Latin and English alike.

This overlap in the devotional and scholastic reading of the Psalter is largely effaced in the approaches favored by Aquinas, Trevet, and Lyre, for whom the book's literal sense describes or reflects on the historical narrative of its author's life, and what Trevet calls the "profound mysteries" of these devotional re-voicings are consigned to the spiritual senses. We have seen that Lyre's Psalter postil reached England quickly enough to be used as a source of Christian Hebraism in Cossey's commentary, and, though Cossey was critical of Lyre's (and Trevet's) repositioning of earlier scholastic Psalter exegesis, this Thomistic approach would become a new standard, as Lyre's postils gained the status, like the *Glossa*, of a basic exegetical reference work. "By the mid-fourteenth century," as Deeana Klepper notes, Lyre "had come to serve as the Christian Bible commentator of first resort, based in large part on his perceived mastery of the Hebrew Bible."[86] Lyre's success no doubt contributed to the limited circulation of the three contemporary Psalter commentaries discussed here. Yet the pre-Thomistic interpretive tradition on which Cossey and Waleys drew was still available to new exegetes, and, as we will see, the next major attempts at Anglo-Latin biblical exegesis, undertaken at Oxford during the career of John Wyclif (d. 1384), show their continued appeal, even as they also illustrate the newly won authority of Lyre's undertaking. The next clutch of English exegetes would have to negotiate the same competing claims of interpretive history and scholastic theory.

CHAPTER 2

Eclectic Hermeneutics: Biblical Commentary in Wyclif's Oxford

While English exegetes of the early fourteenth century responded in different ways to trends in scholastic interpretive theory developed on the Continent, the final decades of the century saw new theories coming from Oxford itself. Among the most sustained explorations of scholastic hermeneutics, John Wyclif's *De veritate sacrae Scripturae* (c. 1377–78) addresses a wide range of familiar theoretical issues, including the senses of Scripture, figurative language, authorial intention, and textual criticism, before coming, in later books, to focus increasingly on polemical priorities less immediately germane to exegesis.[1] Throughout *De veritate*, however, and quite startlingly in light of the careful attention which he clearly devotes to issues of biblical interpretation, Wyclif suggests that the importance of Scripture *qua* text is relatively limited. This devaluing of the biblical text is expressed perhaps most starkly in his account of the different stages through which, he believes, a theologian advances in scriptural studies:

> Sicut puer primo discens alphabetum, secundo sillabicare, tercio legere, et quarto intelligere, habet in quolibet istorum graduum sensum suum distincte intentum circa illud quod primo discit, et posterius propter confusionem excutit primum sensum, sic theologus post doctrinam gramatice discit secundo gramaticam Scripture, aptatam ad sensum relicta priori, tercio relictis signis sensibilibus attendit ad sensum autoris, quousque quarto viderit sine velamine Librum Vite. (I.iii, ed. Buddensieg, I, 44)

> Just as when he first learns the alphabet, then to spell, third to read, and fourth to understand, a child has in each of these steps a sense applying to it in particular, which he first has to learn and which later, on account of confusion, he casts off, so too does the theologian, after learning grammar, then learn the grammar of Scripture, adapted to its sense and leaving behind what came before, and then, third, leaving behind sensible signs, he attends to the sense of the author, until, fourth, he may see the Book of Life without a veil.

Not only is the biblical text, in the form of its inscribed *signa sensibilia*, left behind rather quickly in this process, but the force of the comparison itself heightens the contrast between biblical studies, on the one hand, and, on the other, anything having to do with reading or the interpretation of texts. Though there is apparently some overlap between the activities of the child and those of the theologian, insofar as the former in the third stage learns to read (*legere*) and the latter begins by studying grammar (*doctrina grammaticae*), by comparing one process with the other Wyclif effectively emphasizes their differences. The first aspires, at most, to understand written human *relicta*, and the other ideally ends with an act of contemplation that sounds almost like mystical rapture.[2] Toward the beginning of what Alastair Minnis has called "his masterpiece of hermeneutic theory," Wyclif appears to be indicating that the interpretation of texts is at best a secondary concern.[3]

The treatment of the scriptural text at this point in *De veritate* is consistent with the positioning of biblical codices just a few chapters later. In what has become a well-known distinction, Wyclif enumerates five grades (*quinque gradus*) of Holy Scripture, the highest being the "Book of Life ... [which] cannot be destroyed" (I.vi, ed. Buddensieg, I, 108–109: "Liber Vite ... [qui] non potest solvi"). Biblical codices, in contrast, make up the fifth and lowest grade, mere "signs for someone remembering the prior [i.e., higher] truth" (108: "signa memorandi veritatem priorem"). Here, in other words, the notional ascent of *De veritate*, I.iii, is given in reverse, with both accounts ranging, though in different directions, from written *signa* to the Book of Life. The same range, though divided into only three grades, appears in Wyclif's *Trialogus*, III.xxxi, where "Phronesis" identifies Scripture as, primarily, the "Book of Life, in which every truth is written" ("Librum Vitae, in quo omnis veritas est inscripta"), and only in its lowest sense as the various "books of God's Law" ("ex codicibus legis Dei") and "bare material writing" ("nudum scriptum materiale").[4] It should be unsurprising, then, that Wyclif maintains that the Christian faith would persist even if all biblical codices were "burnt up or otherwise destroyed" (*De veritate*, I.x, ed. Buddensieg, I, 238: "combustis vel aliter pereuntibus"), or that one of his followers was willing to extend this argument, claiming that even "ȝif Holy Wryt on the þridde manere be brent or cast in the see," the truths contained and signified therein "may noȝt faile."[5] In light of this dismissive treatment of the written text of Scripture, Kantik Ghosh seems fully justified in claiming that, for Wyclif, the biblical "book itself is quite irrelevant."[6]

The dismissiveness of *De veritate* and *Trialogus* is all the more remarkable in light of one of Wyclif's other major works, his now-fragmentary *postilla* on the entirety of the Bible.[7] In these lengthy and still largely neglected commentaries, based on lectures that Beryl Smalley thought would have taken as many as six years to deliver, we can see Wyclif working carefully to interpret Scripture's *scriptum materiale*.[8] Indeed, noting that "lectures even on single books of the Bible had become scarce at Oxford" in the decades following the careers of the writers discussed in the previous chapter, Smalley concluded that Wyclif must have "toiled at his desk and in his classroom" to make biblical exegesis his "special subject."[9] All of which is hard to reconcile with the devaluing of irrelevant *signa sensibilia* in his theoretical and polemical works.

At least in part, Smalley also suggested a way in which this apparent tension could be resolved. Emphasizing the "derivative nature" of Wyclif's postils, she claimed that their interpretations were taken "from just the kind of works that one would expect," and that they offered only "elementary and generally conservative" glosses.[10] We return, in other words, to too-familiar descriptions of commentary as dull and unoriginal. It seems to be this assessment on which Mary Dove draws to claim that "biblical commentary is not an ideal mode" for Wyclif, and that, rather than worrying much about the interpretation of individual verses, "his chief concern" in the postils "is with interpretive issues relating to the Bible as a whole."[11] If his glosses are cursory and derivative, then perhaps he was not especially interested in the fifth grade of Scripture after all. At the same time, Dove cautions against exaggerating the dismissive attitude toward the biblical text evident in *De veritate* and *Trialogus*, noting that, in these moments, it seems to her simply "that he protests too much."[12] So too Ian Levy, who reads the passages quoted above as indicating that, for Wyclif, "manuscripts are valuable, . . . but their status must not be inflated."[13] For his apologists, then, the troubling inconsistencies in Wyclif's treatment of Scripture can be minimized by insisting that he is neither adventurous in his exegesis nor particularly radical in his hermeneutic theories.

Yet it is hard to avoid the sense of a contradiction here. Wyclif, after all, authoritatively cites the written text of Scripture to support his argument about the relative unimportance of that same written text.[14] Ghosh attributes this tension to *De veritate*'s positioning on "an uneasy interface between the academic and the revelatory," and he describes how, repeatedly in the treatise, "Wyclif seems to be laying down coherent intellectual, 'sciential' strategies to make sense of the biblical text, only to leave this academic discourse behind suddenly, without warning, and launch into full, revelatory flight into the mind of God."[15] It is tempting to consider Wyclif's postils as the sustained expression of the "academic" and "sciential" side of this binary, the result of a "coherent intellectual" approach to the fifth grade of Scripture. Such an understanding would not be wholly misguided, but, as will become clear in what follows, these commentaries also bear the traces of their author's "revelatory flight into the mind of God," his "idiosyncratic and highly polemical interpretations" of the mystical Book of Life.[16] Rather than simply resting on one side of the "interface" identified by Ghosh, the postils themselves present their own iteration of the same inconsistencies. To put it another way, the exegetical content of the postils also reflects a tension between interpretations derived from detailed consideration of Scripture *qua* text, on the one hand, and, on the other, interpretations reflecting Wyclif's seemingly magisterial judgment of what he calls, in the passage quoted above, the *sensus auctoris*. This tension results in what could be considered hermeneutic inconsistency or, perhaps more positively, hermeneutic eclecticism: with baffling unpredictability, Wyclif adopts a range of different theoretical approaches even in his commentaries on single biblical books, all in an apparent attempt to match their texts to his meanings.

The persistent dismissal of the *postilla* as "derivative" and "conservative" has hindered the recognition of this tension, a problem exacerbated by the continued reliance, in those few studies to discuss the commentaries, on selections printed by Smalley and, following her, Gustav Benrath.[17] Though I am by no means arguing that Wyclif's postils present consistently new and wholly original interpretations, it will quickly become clear that he does engage thoughtfully with a range of exegetical sources – including some quite unusual ones – in a way that has gone unappreciated. His postil on the Psalter offers a crucial example of this work, in part because of the dense and complicated tradition of commentaries on that book, discussed in the previous chapter, and in part because the status of the Psalter as itself a compiled collection of texts presents immediate challenges to Wyclif's generalizing theoretical tendencies. After assessing his treatment of the Psalms, this chapter will then turn to consider, by way of comparison, the exegetical priorities of his work on a very different kind of biblical book, the Gospel of Matthew. And this new focus will allow us to explore, finally, the possibility that Wyclif's eclectic hermeneutics, including his approach to his major sources, were shared by other Oxford exegetes active in the 1370s.

Hermeneutic Eclecticism and the Structure of the Psalter

For Smalley, Wyclif's approach to the Psalter, and in particular to the question of the Psalter's attribution to David, provides a clear example of his general lack of interest in the kinds of intricate interpretive issues that had developed in recent scholastic commentaries.[18] Treating the topic in the prologue to his Psalter commentary, Wyclif first cites Augustine's belief that David was responsible for the book in its entirety, and, though he acknowledges the existence of dissenting opinions, Augustine's authority ultimately proves more compelling.

> Secundum Augustinum omnia contenta in libro Psalmorum erant Dauid reuelata. Alii vt Ieronimus et Hillarius et multi doctores Hebreorum (minus probabiliter michi) dicunt quod tantum psalmi intitulati "Dauid" erant sibi reuelati, licet, vt dicunt, Esdras reparans bibliam post eius combustionem a Caldeis congregauit ex omnibus autoribus vnum librum et propter maiorem partem ac digniorem intitulauit eos "Dauid" et psalmis titulos apposuit. Ponit autem Ieronimus in prologo decem fuisse autores Psalmorum: Dauid, Moisen, Salomonem, tres filios Chore, Asaph, Echam et Eman et Ytidum. Rabbi Salomon ponit decem, sed loco Eman et Echam ponit Melchisedech et Abraham. Sed non video quid obest cor Dauid fuisse tactum in eadem prophecia quam habuerunt prophete priores, et cum immediate habuit propheciam a Deo, totum sibi ascribi vt organo. Ideo teneo sentenciam Augustini quousque video oppositum probatum a sanctis doctoribus.[19]

> According to Augustine the whole content of the Psalter was revealed to David. Others, such as Jerome, Hilary, and many Hebrew doctors, maintain what seems to me a much less likely position, that the only psalms revealed to him are the ones entitled "of David," even though, as they say, reassembling the Bible after the Chaldeans had burnt it up, Ezra brought together in one book materials by all the authors and, on account of the larger or better portion of them, called them all "of David," and he also added titles to psalms. In his prologue, Jerome asserts that there were ten authors of the Psalms: David, Moses, Solomon, the three sons of Core, Asaph, Ethan, Eman, and Idithun. Rabbi Solomon also says that there were ten, but he names Melchisedech and Abraham in place of Eman and Ethan. But I do not see what prevents the heart of David from having been touched with the same prophecy as the prophets had before him, and since he received his prophecy from God without mediation, I do not see what prevents them all from being ascribed to him as the mouthpiece [i.e., of the Holy Ghost]. And so I hold to the opinion of Augustine until such time as I see the opposite proved by holy doctors.

Certainly, as Smalley noted, almost all of the details of this passage have been quoted or adapted from Nicholas of Lyre's literal postils, specifically his prologue to the Psalms and the opening of his exposition of Ps. 1.[20] Wyclif is, however, unwilling to agree with Lyre's conclusion about the Psalter's mixed authorship, following instead the "opinion of Augustine" that all of the Psalms represent prophecy revealed to David – though by maintaining a cagey distinction between authorship and revelation, Wyclif may hold open the possibility of multiple authors. When he says that the Psalmist could have been "touched with the same prophecy" as earlier prophets, Wyclif seems to be acknowledging that the names listed by Jerome and Rashi ("Rabbi Solomon") appear in the titles of various psalms, in positions that may look like authorial attributions. Yet these, he suggests, simply register where Davidic prophecy (which is, in any event, superior because unmediated) overlaps with the foresight also granted to the named figures. And by dubbing David the mouthpiece or instrument (*organum*) of the divine author, Wyclif effectively minimizes the urgency of the question.[21]

Though this preference for a single author marks Wyclif's approach to the Psalms as less overtly Hebraizing than Lyre's, it need not be taken as a sign that he is shying away from interpretive complexity. Among the English exegetes discussed in Chapter 1, for example, Nicholas Trevet similarly persisted in treating the Psalter as the work of David, despite his considerable indebtedness to Thomistic theory.[22] And Wyclif does not simply raise these issues in a cursory attempt to demonstrate his awareness of them. As his prologue continues, he returns to Lyre's claims about the post-exilic compilation of the Psalms, and he maintains that some meaning may be located in the present arrangement of the biblical book:

> Nec solicitor multum de diuisione libri nec contendo quod psalmi n[unc][23] sequuntur ordinem temporis vel composicionis, sed quod positi sunt secundum ordinem quo inuenti vel compilati, aliqui ab Esdra et alii ab aliis prophetis quorum nomina ignorantur. … Diuiditur iste liber in prohemium, in primo psalmo qui ascribitur Esdre, et in partem tractantem de regno Christi, vsque ad psalmum 109, et tercio in partem tractantem de sacerdocio Christi, a psalmo *Dixit Dominus* vsque in finem. (f. 109ᵛ)

> I do not trouble myself much with the book's division, and I do not contend that the psalms now follow a chronological order or the order in which they were composed, but that they have been arranged in the order in which they were discovered or compiled, some by Ezra and others by other prophets whose names are unknown. … This book is divided into a preface (in the first psalm, which is attributed to Ezra), and into a part about Christ's kingship (up to Ps. 109), and third into a part about Christ's priesthood. (from the psalm beginning *The Lord said* [i.e., Ps. 109] until the end)

Though he claims to have little interest in the subject, here Wyclif offers a three-part division of the Psalter, drawn, again, from Lyre's postils.[24] Unlike Lyre, however, Wyclif apparently attributes this arrangement to the text's post-exilic compilers, who gathered the psalms into two uneven groups based on common (and very general) subject matters, with the first psalm then composed by the chief compiler, Ezra, specifically to serve as a preface to the whole collection. The two alternatives he presents to describe this ordering, however, *inventi vel compilati*, indicate that, apart from Ezra's prefatory psalm, the pattern seen by Wyclif (following Lyre) could be either adventitious or intentional, and the claim that he has not troubled himself much with it may be motivated by doubts about how much purchase this possibly fortuitous *divisio* can offer for his interpretation of the text.

Since the arrangement of the psalms reflects neither a chronological-historical narrative nor the order of their composition, and since their compilers' arrangement may have been similarly unplanned, it falls to the commentator to bring some order to this haphazard collection. Wyclif therefore provides two ways to read the Psalter discontinuously, or, to put it another way, he gives two different systems for identifying and interpreting significant groupings of nonadjacent psalms. The first is taken from one of his major sources on the generic or formal classification of biblical texts, Peter Auriol's *Compendium sensus litteralis totius divinae Scripturae* (1319). It was from Auriol, as Smalley noticed, that Wyclif borrowed the eight-part division of his postils on the whole canon of Scripture.[25] The Psalter begins the fourth part in Wyclif's version of this arrangement, the "hymnic and as it were poetic" books (f. 108^v: "hymnidica et quasi poetica"), and, more specifically, it presents "songs of joy" ("carmina que sunt cantus leticie"). The other two types of poetry, according to Wyclif following Auriol, are elegies (*elega*) and dramatic poems (*dragmata*), represented in Scripture by the Lamentations of Jeremiah and the Song of Songs, respectively.[26] Continuing to draw on Auriol, Wyclif claims that every psalm may be categorized as either an *alleluia, canticum, oratio, intellectus, psalmus,* or *titulus*. The kind of descriptive work done by these categories varies, including historical-contextual claims (e.g., the *cantica*, which were sung by the Levites and priests of the Jerusalem temple), as well as issues of subject matter (e.g., the *intellectus*, in which the Psalmist offers especially profound prophecy of Christ).[27] Quite conveniently, all but one of the classificatory terms used by Auriol and Wyclif are taken from the titles or superscriptions which appear at the beginning of psalms (and which, as we have seen, Wyclif attributes to Ezra), with the sole exception being psalms that lack a superscription but begin with the word *alleluia*. Since, in any case, these terms appear in prominent positions in the first lemmata at the beginning of each psalm, it is easy enough to flip through Wyclif's commentary in Oxford, St. John's

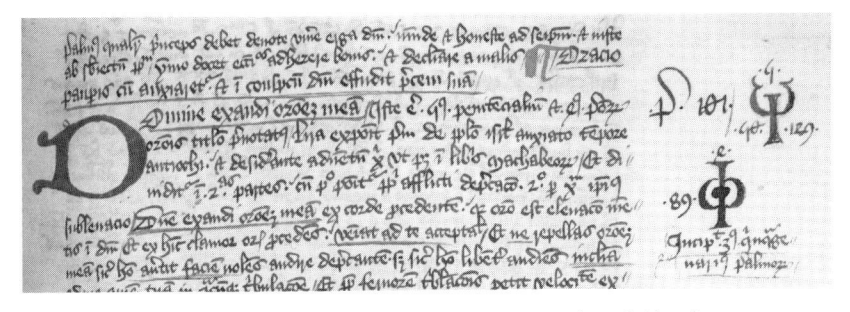

Figure 4   Oxford, St. John's College MS 171, f. 241ʳ (detail).

College MS 171 (the only surviving copy) and locate all the psalms pertaining to each category. Alternatively, it is possible to refer back to the prologue's account of the significance of these words at the start of any psalm.

Of course, since he has taken the three-part division of the Psalter and this system for grouping psalms from Lyre's postils and Auriol's *Compendium*, respectively, these borrowings could simply be further illustrations of the "derivative" nature of Wyclif's commentary. The divisions and groupings described in the prologue, however, are complemented by yet another organizational system copied in the margins of St. John's 171, one drawn from a far less familiar source. In Gilbert of Poitiers's mid-twelfth-century *Media glosatura*, a work complexly related to the *Glossa ordinaria* on the Psalter and the Lombard's *Magna glosatura*, a series of twelve distinct symbols appears in the margins at the beginning of roughly a third of the psalms, identifying either a formal characteristic or a subject matter discussed in Gilbert's preface to that psalm.[28] Above the symbol, Gilbert includes a Roman numeral specifying the psalm's position in the sequence represented by the symbol, and underneath he provides another numeral identifying the next psalm in the sequence. Though it has not previously been noted, Wyclif has borrowed Gilbert's indexing symbols in his own Psalter commentary.[29] In the case of Ps. 101, for example, reproduced in Figure 4 and the only psalm in these commentaries to be assigned to two sequences, the symbol topped with an Arabic numeral 5 indicates that this is the fifth Penitential Psalm, and the other, with a 4 written above it, signals that it is the fourth psalm with the word *oratio* in its superscription. Wyclif has moved the indication of the next psalm in the sequence to the right of the symbol: Ps. 129 is the next Penitential Psalm, while, since Ps. 101 is the last in the *oratio* sequence, the space to the right of the second symbol is blank. Further, Wyclif has added, to the left, a reference *back* to the previous psalm in the sequence (in this case, Pss. 50 and 89), improving on Gilbert's system by allowing sequences of psalms to be read backward as well as forward.[30] In the body of the commentary included in Figure 4, Wyclif has quoted from the *Media glosatura* to explain (albeit indirectly) the significance of the symbols, and this double indebtedness to Gilbert – in the margins and the text of the commentary – makes it all but certain that the indexing symbols are included as part of Wyclif's design for his work.[31]

Wyclif's adaptation of this indexing system is presented in greater detail in Appendix A, but the fact of the borrowing is itself remarkable. Mary and Richard Rouse note that Gilbert's marginal symbols were generally "too eccentric" to be used by other exegetes, and that by the thirteenth century they tended not to be included in new copies of the *Media glosatura*.[32] Indeed, Wyclif is now the first commentator known to have adopted this system in his own work, and his favoring of a source that was, by the end of the fourteenth century, relatively obscure – not at all a standard exegetical reference text like the Lombard's *Glosatura* – emphasizes his interest in redressing the disorder he found in the Psalter *qua* compilation.

Beyond providing Wyclif with an "eccentric" way of bringing order to the Psalter, the *Media glosatura* also served as an authoritative source of glosses focused on the text's Christological subject matter. Wyclif does, of course, often turn to Lyre's literal postils in his reading of various psalms, adhering to what Smalley described as his "simple recipe for postillating."[33] He thus follows Lyre in reading Ps. 107, for example, as the Psalmist's expression of "thanks for the restoration of the kingdom of Israel ... in the time of David" (f. 254^r: "graciarum accio de restitucione regni Israel ... tempore Dauid").[34] Wyclif continues to draw on Lyre and offer a historicist account of each verse in the psalm, after which the scribe of St. John's 171 inserts a thick paraph mark. Rather than ending there, however, the commentary continues with what might be called a spiritual postscript: "Glosa exponit psalmum mistice de Christo, cum sit sextus psalmus agens de duplici natura Christi" (f. 254^r: "The gloss interprets this psalm mystically as being about Christ, since it is the sixth psalm treating Christ's double nature"). The *glosa* invoked here is Gilbert's *Media glosatura*, with the relevant indexing symbol dutifully copied in the manuscript's outer margin alongside this passage.[35] Thereafter, though he does not comment a second time on every verse, Wyclif does draw on the *Media glosatura* to offer some general Christological readings.[36] Wyclif's gloss of Ps. 54 likewise brings together material from these two sources, though in this case he begins by identifying both the literal and mystical-Christological ways of reading the text, attributed respectively to Lyre and the *glosa*, and he then moves verse by verse, alternately providing what each commentator has to say about each lemma.[37]

In these examples, Wyclif describes the material taken from Gilbert as interpreting the text *mystice*, and he thus appears to be in agreement with Lyre's (and Trevet's) claim, discussed in the previous chapter, that earlier scholastic commentaries on the Psalter were in general focused on the book's spiritual senses.[38] But Wyclif refuses to be so consistent. His treatment of Ps. 81, for example, at least superficially appears to conform to the model of his gloss of Ps. 107, with an initial (and substantial) Lyran reading followed, after a paraph mark, by interpretations drawn from the *Media glosatura*, and, again, Gilbert's indexing symbol is only copied in the margin as this second portion of the gloss begins. Yet it is not at all clear that Wyclif intends this alternative reading to be a spiritual supplement to Lyre's literalism. According to Wyclif, "Lyre and other Hebrew and Latin doctors" offer literal readings of this psalm as being "against wicked judges" (f. 214^{rv}: "Lira et alii doctores Hebreici et Latini applicant exposicionem et sensum huius psalmi ad litteram contra peruersos iudices").[39] In contrast, as he notes at the start of his second gloss of the psalm, "glosa et aliqui doctores Latini exponunt hunc psalmum de Christo arguente Synagogam quia eum presentem non agnouit" (f. 214^{v}: "But the gloss and some Latin doctors interpret this psalm as being about Christ, who reproves the Synagogue for not recognizing him when he was present").[40] To be sure, Wyclif does not overtly identify this approach as being, like the first, *ad litteram*, but neither does he say that this group of authorities interprets the text *mystice*, and the parallel citation suggests that this reading may indeed simply be an alternative to Lyre's, with the Christological content intended, prophetically, by the Psalmist. Here, in other words, Wyclif is able to draw on the Christological content of the *Glosatura* without clearly relegating it to the register of the spiritual senses.

The example of Ps. 81 raises the possibility that Gilbert could serve, compared with Lyre, as an equally authoritative source on the literal sense of the Psalter, and it also illustrates Wyclif's willingness to entertain varying (and contradictory) interpretations of the biblical text. Arguably the highpoint of authoritative Gilbertine literalism in Wyclif's commentary comes in cases like Ps. 18, where, again, the interpretations of Lyre and Gilbert are initially put side by side, but now with a different outcome:

> *Celi enarrant* etc. Titulus huius psalmi dicit secundum Hebreos quod Dauid fecit hunc psalmum in laudem Dei pro legis dacione, ostendens

> primo magnitudinem diuine sapiencie ex celestibus creaturis. Sed nos dicimus quod materia huius est laudare Deum pro eius incarnacione et diaboli superacione, que nouissimis temporibus facte sunt. Et ad istum sensum allegat Apostolus hunc psalmum, Ro. 10. Et sic est primus psalmus agens de primo aduentu Christi. (f. 124ᵛ)

> *The heavens declare*, etc. According to the Hebrews, the title of this psalm indicates that David wrote it in praise of God for the giving of the Law, first showing by means of heavenly creatures the greatness of divine wisdom. But we say that its subject matter is the praise of God for his incarnation and for defeating the devil, which will take place at the end of time. And it is with this meaning that the Apostle cites this psalm (Rom. 10.18). And so it is the first psalm to treat Christ's first advent.

Though he names neither of his major authorities in this passage, it should be clear that Wyclif is first identifying an interpretation of Ps. 18 that he has found in Lyre's postils and then offering the Christological reading of the *Media glosatura*.[41] Not only does he *not* call this second interpretive option "mystical," but his emphatic use of the first person (*Sed nos dicimus*) indicates that he favors the *Glosatura*'s reading as the primary sense of the passage. Unlike Ps. 81, then, this is not a case of two equally plausible alternatives, and Lyre's interpretations are simply ignored for the remainder of Wyclif's commentary on Ps. 18.[42] The refusal to name his authorities at the start of this psalm may indicate that Wyclif is self-consciously deviating from his standard practice, perhaps encouraged by his familiarity with Paul's Christological allusion to Ps. 18.8, but the effect of this repression is to attribute Lyre's Davidic reading exclusively to non-Christian (Hebrew) interpreters and to present Gilbert's Christological-prophetic gloss as the only acceptable reading of the psalm.[43]

As these examples indicate, Wyclif moves rather freely between his two major sources, and his commentary on the Psalter thus presents an unusual and inconsistent hermeneutic blending, bringing together earlier interpretive approaches and more recent scholastic understandings in a way that is more complex than Smalley's "simple recipe" would suggest. At least in part, these inconsistencies appear to be a response to the Psalter's messy textual history, as discussed in Wyclif's preface. If all of the surviving psalms were discovered and compiled by Ezra (and others) and the ordering of the text is consequently haphazard, then each psalm needs to be approached as a discrete unit within the compilation, and an exegete's interpretive methods may not be consistent from one psalm to the next. It is only by means of organizational systems imposed by the commentator – Gilbert's indexing symbols and Auriol's account of the types of psalms – that patterns can be found in the larger compilation. All of this reflects Wyclif's careful consideration of the Psalter *qua* text and his use of what Ghosh calls "'sciential' strategies to make sense" of Scripture.[44] At the same time, it is impossible to predict the specific hermeneutic priorities with which Wyclif will approach any particular psalm – whether, that is, he will prefer one source or another, whether he will treat Gilbert as providing a mystical interpretation or a literal one, whether he will adopt Lyre's literalism or reject it with some magisterial fiat. His approach to each psalm does not appear to be determined, in any consistent way, by the details of the biblical text. Here, then, is the "idiosyncratic" interpreter described by Ghosh, an exegete enjoying "various sapiential liberties" that almost seem to derive from his "revelatory flight into the mind of God."[45] This is the figure whom Smalley backed to win the title of "the most arbitrary interpreter of biblical texts of the Middle Ages."[46]

Yet there is one crucial point on which this "arbitrary interpreter" is consistent. In his prologue, as we have seen, Wyclif identified the subject matter of the psalms as being either the kingship or the priesthood of Christ. To be sure, he took this classification from Lyre, but his source had equivocated considerably, going so far as to claim that on some occasions "various subjects are treated in one and the same psalm" ("aliquando in eodem psalmo de diuersis materiis agitur").[47] Wyclif omits this hedging, and though he expresses doubts about whether the division between the psalms on Christ's kingship and those on his priesthood was intended by the book's compilers, he does not seem to have any reservations about the Psalter's generally Christological character. Throughout his commentary, then, Wyclif finds a way to identify the Christological content of every individual psalm, to show how each psalm can be read either literally or spiritually *de Christo*. At least in part, this persistent interest in Christological readings may reflect his engagement with the *Media glosatura*, where the subject matter of the entire Psalter is identified as "Christus integer, caput cum membris" (MGT 488, f. 3[ra]: "The whole of Christ, head and members").[48] But, as we have seen, Wyclif by no means simply follows the *Glosatura*'s Christological interpretations. Instead, this understanding of the Psalter's *materia* seems to have encouraged his development of an interpretive eclecticism, drawing on one or another source and favoring one or another hermeneutic scheme throughout his exegesis.

The consistency with which he includes Christological interpretations of every psalm, whether literal or spiritual, suggests that, for Wyclif, these interpretations may be a higher priority, they may matter more, than determining the intentions of the historical human author. In this regard, his eclectic approach to the Psalter is surely related to Wyclif's larger theoretical claims about the nature of Scripture, which is, in its primary sense, "Jesus Christ, the Book of Life, in whom every truth is written" (*Trialogus*, III.xxxi, ed. Lechler, 238: "Iesum Christum, Librum Vitae, in quo omnis veritas est inscripta"). And it may be related, too, to what Ghosh has identified as Wyclif's unusual understanding of "the 'literal' as that sense intended by God in all its 'spiritual' fullness."[49] But the Psalter commentary by no means perfectly reflects (or anticipates) these later theories. Simply because Christ is Scripture in a primary sense need not mean that all of Scripture in its written form is *about* Christ, and, likewise, though Wyclif consistently includes spiritualizing interpretations of psalms when that is where he can locate their Christological content, he does not identify these "mystic" meanings with the text's literal sense. (These instances should not be confused, of course, with those cases where Wyclif, following one or another source, determines that Christological prophecy *is* the literal sense of a psalm.) In his Psalter commentary, as in his later writings, Wyclif attempts to negotiate seemingly contradictory interpretive commitments, to Scripture as a written text and as a theoretical ideal. He offers careful analysis of the Psalter as a text with a complex history of composition and compilation, all of which matters for its interpretation. Yet such details are of secondary importance compared with the necessity of reading the divinely intended – and magisterially intuited – *sensus auctoris*.

His use of the *Media glosatura* does more than merely indicate that the "simple recipe" which Smalley believed to have yielded Wyclif's postils is overly simplistic. More importantly, it illustrates Wyclif's willingness to engage with interpretive approaches that had developed in exegetical traditions specific to individual biblical books, and that he could draw on his familiarity with these interpretive histories to complement or contradict his more recent scholastic sources. His weighing of different sources and his appreciation of the history of commentary reveal that his postils are not as "conservative" and "derivative" as earlier critics have believed, just as his persistent use of Lyre and Auriol across different biblical books should not be taken as signaling a thoughtlessly uniform hermeneutic. Wyclif's treatment of the Psalter reveals that his postils, though far from the most innovative or sophisticated exegetical offerings of the fourteenth century, are neither cursory schoolroom exercises nor the derivative afterthought of a master whose mind was elsewhere.[50]

Private Glosses

In all likelihood, Wyclif died in the midst of writing biblical exegesis. The unfinished *Opus Evangelicum* is a sprawling commentary in which he proposes to go "beyond the letter and the common interpretation" ("supra litteram et exposicionem communem") of two lengthy selections from the Gospel of Matthew (5–7 and 23–25) as well as a third from John (13–17).[51] Both surviving English copies of the *Opus* end with a colophon suggesting that Wyclif was still at work on this text at the time of his death: "Autoris vita finitur et hoc opus ita" ("The author's life is finished and so [too is] this work").[52] The position of this commentary at the end of Wyclif's career should, generally, indicate the prominence of scriptural criticism in his corpus, alongside his earlier philosophical, theological, and polemical writings. But the *Opus* also reveals, more specifically, the continued and perhaps heightened importance of his postils after his forced retirement to Lutterworth in 1381. Early in the work, explaining the meaning of the lamp (*lucerna*) not to be hidden under a bushel (Matth. 5.15), Wyclif first offers lengthy quotations from Augustine's *De sermone Domini in monte* (which, as he does frequently in the *Opus*, Wyclif then glosses) and from Ps.-Chrysostom's *Opus Imperfectum*. These authoritative statements are followed by a longer series detailing the lamp's possible spiritual meanings, a passage which he attributes to "a certain private gloss" ("quedam … glossa privata").[53] This "private gloss" is almost certainly Wyclif's *postilla* on the gospels, in this case specifically Luke 11.33, where the entire passage appears verbatim (BodL MS Bodley 716, f. 43[rab]). Earlier in the *Opus*, glossing Matth. 5.13, Wyclif likewise attributes a lengthy account of the properties of salt to "a certain gloss" ("quedam glossa"), a passage corresponding to his postil on the same verse.[54]

These substantial quotations from his earlier commentary are perhaps startling, especially if they would implicitly – in line with the intentions laid out at the start of the *Opus* – categorize the postils' interpretations as "beyond the common exposition." That kind of conventionality is, after all, what the postils are now generally said to represent, and it is undeniable that, even compared with his treatment of the Psalter, Wyclif's postillation of Matthew – and the gospels in general – is relatively brief and heavily reliant on Lyre's literal glosses. Yet these borrowings appear to indicate that, already in his earlier university exegesis on the gospels, Wyclif was attempting to go beyond (*supra*) interpretive approaches he considered both literalistic and conventional, and this in turn begs the question not just of what counts as "common exposition," but also of how he conceptualized the gospels' literal sense. As we will see, here too Wyclif works at least in part within the bounds of established scholastic theory (especially as defined by Lyre) while also venturing, idiosyncratically and perhaps inconsistently, beyond recent understandings of literalism.

In order to address these hermeneutic issues, however, we must first resolve some textual problems presented in Wyclif's commentaries on the gospels – specifically, how it can be that he describes these postils, presumably delivered like all the others as a series of university lectures, as constituting a *glossa privata*. Indeed, when she first noted this description, Pamela Gradon expressed her doubt that Wyclif meant to refer to his earlier commentary, suggesting instead that the phrase would "more naturally" denote "provisional glossing such as might be written in the margins ... in his own Bible." Such "less formal" annotations, she ventured, could have provided a common source for both the postils and the *Opus*.[55] The sheer size of the passages noted above, however, makes this scenario unlikely: the description of the properties of salt and their spiritual significance, for example, fills almost forty lines of heavily abbreviated text in Bodley 716, ff. 4vb–5ra, and it is hard to imagine this material fitting in the margins of a small pandect. Further, as we saw in his Psalter postil's citations of the *Media glosatura*, Wyclif uses the word *glossa* (or *glosa*) to refer to a commentary rather than an individual annotation, and the correspondences noted above would indicate that the commentary quoted in the *Opus* is indeed his postil on the gospels.[56] Yet it remains unclear why he would describe this work as *privata*, suggesting (as Gradon indicates) a kind of personal volume that readers of the *Opus* would not be able to consult.

Fortunately, compared with the patchier survival of his Old Testament postils, Wyclif's commentaries on New Testament books are somewhat better attested, preserving details of a complex textual history that can both account for this description and, further, reinforce the importance of the postils – especially those on the gospels – in Wyclif's larger authorial program. In addition to Bodley 716, the gospel postils survive in a second English manuscript, Oxford, Magdalen College MS lat. 55, and a Bohemian copy, Vienna, ÖNB MS 1342.[57] Smalley noted some significant variations in the prologue to Matthew in the two Oxford manuscripts, on the one hand, and, on the other, in Vienna, discrepancies that she attributed to "two abbreviators ... working on the same original."[58] According to Smalley, each version of the Matthew prologue contains substantial passages omitted in the other version, leading her to suppose that a single fuller source (now lost) was subjected to two different stints of abbreviating and adaptive copying. This is a sensible enough explanation for the situation she describes, but in fact the differences between the two versions of the prologue to Matthew (and, indeed, of the Matthew postil generally) are more complicated than Smalley's account of scribal selectivity would suggest.[59]

Not everything that Smalley considered an omission is simply cut from one or the other version of Wyclif's prologue to Matthew. Vienna, for example, contains a passage apparently acknowledging that, at a point where a reader might expect a fuller treatment of the gospel's *divisio textus*, the commentary will proceed instead to consider its *materia*, derived from Auriol:[60]

> Dimissa diuisione huius libri, ne videar frustra verba in vanum profundere, mox me ad materiam intentam conuertam. Vnde ergo quam omnes quattuor ewangeliste principaliter intendunt est ista: homo iste qui dictus est Iesus fuit Christus uel Messias in lege promissus, rex et Dominus omnium, saluator hominum et Filius Dei naturalis, quam singulus istorum testium testatur. (ÖNB 1342, f. 2ra)

> Lest I appear to spew words in vain, I forgo the division of this book and now turn to consider its intended subject matter. All four of the evangelists principally intend to convey that this man, called Jesus, was the Christ or Messiah promised in the Law, the king and Lord of all, the savior of humanity and the natural-born Son of God. Each of these witnesses testifies to this.

Taking *dimissa* to indicate a refusal to copy existing material, Smalley read the first sentence of this passage as the scribe commenting on his treatment of his exemplar, "a note to the effect that the omission is deliberate."[61] And, at this point in Bodley and Magdalen, there is indeed a passage detailing the gospel's *divisio*, beginning with a close borrowing from Lyre and ending with an apparently original subdivision of what both exegetes identify as the text's second part, beginning at Matth. 4.12.[62] This departure from Lyre, along with the identification of Matth. 1.1 as a "proem" written "in the manner of scribes" ("more scribencium ... prohemium"), echoing his account of Ps. 1, would indicate that the *divisio* is the work of Wyclif and not some scribal invention.[63] But that need not mean that the sentence occurring at this point in Vienna is written in the voice of a scribe who refused to copy it. We have already seen Wyclif declaring his lack of interest in the *divisio* of the Psalter ("Nec solicitor multum ... ": see 59), and it seems much more likely that the shorter passage in Vienna is also Wyclif's work, presenting his desire to press on quickly to the (for him) more important topic of the gospel's subject matter. The inclusion of the *divisio* in Bodley and Magdalen, then, could represent an attempt at revision, supplying material that the exegete did not provide in his initial treatment of this biblical book.

Revision, rather than scribal omission, could also account for the major discrepancies in the opening of the prologue in these two versions, substantial variations that, before Smalley, impeded the identification of the Oxford copies as Wyclif's work. Manuscripts of the *Glossa ordinaria* tend to include two prefaces before Matthew – the so-called Monarchian preface (attributed spuriously to Jerome) and a second that may be original to the *Glossa* – and it had become standard practice for schoolmen to comment on these prefaces at the start of their lectures on the gospel.[64] In the Vienna copy of his postil, Wyclif appears to do the same. He begins in Vienna by quoting the Monarchian preface, attributing it to Jerome, and dividing it into four parts; thereafter, short lemma-like quotations from both prefaces appear throughout the prologue, framing Wyclif's remarks as though he were commenting on that material.[65] Despite these appearances, however, in practice these quotations do little more than punctuate Wyclif's prologue, breaking his introductory discussion of Matthew's gospel into discrete sections in which (as he had for the Psalter) he addresses fairly conventional topics, such as the intentions of the evangelist and the gospel's structure and subject matter.[66] After offering his *divisio* of the Monarchian preface, for example, Wyclif immediately sets out in another direction, discussing the order in which the canonical gospels were composed and arranged by the compilers of the New Testament.[67] Wyclif thus appears to treat these prefaces with relative indifference in the Vienna text, including them rather perfunctorily to satisfy the expectations of a university lecture on Matthew. In the Oxford manuscripts, all pretense of adhering to this convention is dropped: the prologue begins with a revised account of Matthew's intentions and the ordering of the four evangelists in terms of Ezechiel's vision of the four-headed animal, and all of the lemmata drawn from the Monarchian and *Glossa* prefaces, as well as the account of the first preface's *divisio*, disappear.[68] Smalley is therefore right to say that the Oxford version "omits the opening lines" of the Vienna text, but, rather than a scribal innovation, this seems to be part of the exegete's larger effort to revise the prologue and shed unwanted vestiges of its origins in the classroom.[69]

Another detail at once supports this notion of revision and indicates how it might, in part, have been carried out. In both Oxford copies, the margins of the gospel postils (and of Matthew in particular) contain a variety of substantial notes providing further interpretations, as well as other, less strictly exegetical content that may still be related to the biblical text at hand. These marginalia often conclude with an attribution – "Hec Lyra"

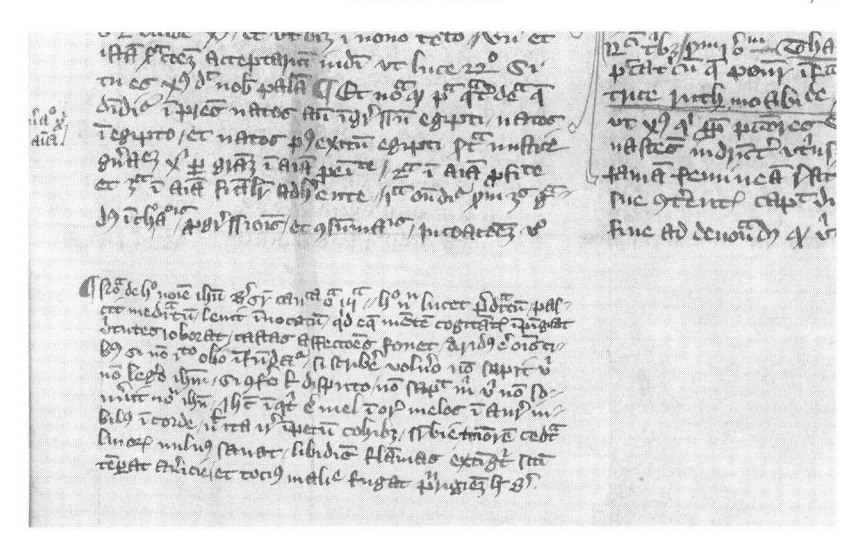

Figure 5   BodL MS Bodley 716, f. 2ʳ (detail).

("These words are Lyre's") is the most frequent, and Augustine and Bernard are also cited – though, unlike the marginal additions to the Christ's College copy of Henry Cossey on the Psalms, discussed in the previous chapter, no substantial effort has been made to indicate that these passages should be brought into the text of Wyclif's commentary at specific points (Fig. 5).[70] The presence of at least some of these notes in both Bodley 716 and Magdalen lat. 55, as well as the observation that, in both cases, they are copied in the same hand as the commentary, strongly suggest that they were present in Bodley's and Magdalen's common exemplar, and, further, that the scribes of both manuscripts regarded them as in some way authoritative and worthy of preservation.[71] While the revisions described above would necessarily involve the cancellation of existing material in the author's working copy and potentially the interleaving of *schedulae* to support substantial new passages, these shorter marginal additions seem likely to reflect Wyclif's attempt to supplement his glosses as he found new material, or even as familiar material (e.g., previously overlooked glosses from Lyre) struck him as newly relevant.[72] Anne Hudson considers Bodley and Magdalen to be "credibly of Oxford origin," and, based on this likelihood, it seems that the common exemplar of these surviving Oxford manuscripts was made, in turn, from this authorial working copy, available at the university before Wyclif's retirement.[73] Further, to return briefly to the *Opus Evangelicum*, it may now be possible to explain the presence of passages in that text that are cited as though drawn from Wyclif's postils, but which are *not* present in the

Oxford copies of his commentaries. It could be that Wyclif continued to annotate his working copy of the postils after the exemplar of the surviving copies had been made.[74]

This, then, is Wyclif's *glossa privata*, a well-worn working copy of his gospel postils, marked with years of revisions and supplementary annotations such that he could no longer be certain of the accuracy of citing his circulating commentaries. Taking this copy with him to Lutterworth gave Wyclif ready access to the patristic and scholastic interpretive material he had assembled over the course of perhaps a decade, and, since it was clearly not the only book he had in his retirement, he may have annotated it further. Recovering some of the history of his *glossa privata*, and with it Wyclif's continued interest in his gospel postils, challenges the dominant narrative of his commentaries as early and perfunctory productions.[75] Indeed, the task he set for himself in the unfinished *Opus Evangelicum* – assembling further interpretations of passages glossed in the postils – was in some ways an extension of this ongoing supplementation, overflowing beyond (*supra*) that *glossa* in the creation of a new text.

Uncommon Exposition

This link between the *Opus Evangelicum* and Wyclif's postils, and especially the possibility that one could represent a kind of exegetical outgrowth of the other, raises a variety of questions about Wyclif's understanding of the status of earlier commentaries and the hermeneutic theories underpinning their approach to Matthew's gospel. As noted above, the *Opus* begins with an expressed desire to offer interpretations going beyond both the letter ("supra litteram") and conventional scholastic glosses ("exposicionem communem"), a formulation that seems to identify literalism as the standard fare of scholastic commentary while, implicitly, coming down in favor of spiritual exegesis.[76] Almost certainly, the unstated object of Wyclif's criticism at this point in the *Opus* is Lyre's now widely used *Postilla litteralis*, on which (as we have seen) Wyclif drew in his own postils. Yet, perhaps counterintuitively, though Wyclif's early commentary on Matthew depends heavily on Lyre's, it also shows signs of the same desire to get beyond conventional literalism. Though Lyre's text must have been open before him at almost every point in the preparation of his Matthew postil, Wyclif does not adapt this source with any consistency, and the variations in his treatment of Lyre appear to reflect Wyclif's engagement with hermeneutic challenges specific to the gospels.

Certain chapters of Matthew prompt from both Lyre and Wyclif the kind of literal-historicist approach to Scripture that was, above all, the focus of Smalley's intervention. As narratives of the life of Christ, the gospels are by and large written in what Alexander of Hales called the *modus historicus* and Bonaventure the *modus narrativus*. In the prologue to his commentary on Luke, Bonaventure used both terms ("historicus et narrativus") to describe that book's *modus*, while Thomas Docking, lector to the Oxford Franciscans in the 1260s, notes that the *causa formalis* of all four gospels "appears to be narrative, since the evangelical text is historical" ("videtur quod narratiuus, quia tractatus euuangelicus est historicus").[77] Understanding the literal meaning of a text in this mode requires an exegete to recover details of (as Docking says) its *res gestae*, the events, people, and locations it describes, and to account for these details in terms of a coherent and consistent historical narrative.[78] Smalley's work revealed that this approach was already being practiced in the twelfth century, and later scholastic exegetes continued to develop it, producing an ever-wider range of sophisticated historiographical sources, materials (such as encyclopedias and universal histories) that would give them access to more details of the Roman-occupied Near East of the early first century.[79] Glossing these chapters, Wyclif apparently supplemented his reading of Lyre with one of the standard textbooks on this subject, Peter Comestor's *Historia Scholastica* (c. 1173), itself the object of scholastic commentaries.[80] He cites Comestor's work by its title ("vt dicitur in *Historia Scholastica*"), and his consultation of this source helps to explain interpretations that do not correspond to what he found in Lyre's glosses, such as the specification that, when Herod burned the ships of Tarshish (fulfilling the prophecy of Ps. 47.8, a detail included by Lyre), he did so "in transitu suo versus Romam" ("on his journey to Rome"), presumably to settle his dispute with his sons.[81] Similarly, Wyclif's different ways of understanding the appearance of the star and the journey of the Magi, whom he calls "philosopher kings" (*philosophi regnantes*), may reflect his reading of the *Historia*. Lyre's simpler account of the journey's duration – it took only thirteen days, since the Magi were coming from the homeland of Balaam, close to Judea – becomes the last of Wyclif's three explanations.[82] Some, he says, maintain that the star appeared a year before Christ's birth and that the Magi traveled throughout that time, others that it appeared only at his birth and that the kings followed it for a year afterward, and still others (including, apparently, Lyre) that it appeared at his birth and that the journey took only thirteen days.[83] Wyclif does not specify which of these interpretations he thinks to be more likely, but his decision to furnish different options may indicate that he found Lyre's explanation unsatisfying.[84] Even when he is moving quickly through the biblical text, then, Wyclif reveals his attentiveness to the ambiguities of biblical history.

But these historicist approaches have a limited utility, even in the recovery of the gospel's literal sense. Other chapters of Matthew present extended episodes in which Christ conveys moral teaching, passages where, returning to the Thomistic distinction, the literal sense of the text was tropological or, to use Bonaventure's terms, where the gospel contains, within its historical narrative, material written in the *modus exhortativus* or *praedicativus*. Much of this moralism takes the form of parables, where narrative-focused historicist approaches may, in an attenuated form, still be useful.[85] Other passages present moral teaching apart from any inscribed narrative, though the continued use of figurative language in many of these instances (e.g., Matth. 7.13, "Enter ye in at the narrow gate") led exegetes to describe them as parabolic, and in this regard, as we will see, Wyclif was no exception.[86] In such cases of non-narrative tropology, while some reference to the historical audience may still prove useful, both Lyre and Wyclif place greater emphasis on abstracting general moral principles from Christ's teaching.[87]

In light of the attention he would later give to these moralistic passages in the *Opus*, it may be unsurprising to find Wyclif departing from Lyre with greater frequency when glossing them in his postil, where he provides his own more sustained interpretations. Many of these innovations match the general quality of the tropological exegesis seen in Lyre's literal postils, translating Christ's preaching into relatively abstract moral principles. Glossing Matth. 7.16–20, for example, Wyclif introduces a distinction between two metaphorical meanings of "fruit," the *fructus viae* and *fructus patriae*, arguing that here Christ intends to refer to the former. This "fruit of the way" describes a person's actions, the "final operation compared to the intention and quality from which it proceeds," and whoever is lacking in this good fruit will be condemned as a barren tree and cast into fire.[88] In such cases, Wyclif's departure from Lyre seems to arise from similar motives as his historicist glosses, whether he seeks to introduce further interpretive possibilities, or he simply disagrees with his source's reading, or (as apparently in this case) he thinks that Lyre treated a passage too quickly.[89] But at other times Wyclif appears to intervene out of some dissatisfaction with the generality of this literal moralism. That is, he wants to interpret the biblical text as it applies, more specifically, to the lives of his commentary's contemporary readers, and he therefore includes a variety of what might be called presentist asides at the end of glosses adapted from Lyre. For example, after elaborating on Christ's command to "judge not" (Matth. 7.1–2) by condemning judges who "sin doubly by obdurately continuing in sin and therefore ceasing to prosecute people committing crimes," Wyclif adds, "So too the preacher in a similar circumstance" ("durans in peccato et cessans ex hoc arguere delinquentes, peccat dupliciter, sicut et predicator in casv consimili"). Likewise, soon after this gloss, he supplements another Lyran borrowing about casting pearls before swine (Matth. 7.6) by noting that Christ's admonition can "be interpreted likewise concerning ecclesiastical benefices" ("et idem interpretatur de beneficiis ecclesiasticis").[90]

The presentist (almost polemical) priorities suggested in these short asides come to the fore in Wyclif's postil on Matth. 5, where he departs from Lyre to offer his own sustained moral interpretation of the opening of the Sermon on the Mount. At least at the start of the chapter, Wyclif builds, though loosely, on what he found in Lyre's postils, and his glosses maintain a historicist focus on Christ's original act of preaching.[91] Referring to him as the "prudent law-giver" (*prudens legifer*), Wyclif notes that Christ's ascent up the mountain signifies both his efficacy in imprinting (*imprimendum*) the law and the heaven-inspired excellence of the law itself, with only this last detail corresponding to material in Lyre's postil.[92] The notion of Christ "imprinting" his teaching is developed almost immediately, when Wyclif contrasts this scene with the giving of the law in the Old Testament, a passage which quickly departs from its starting point in Lyre:

> Quod Christus *ore suo* docuit istam legem signat eius excellenciam super Vetus Testamentum, quod datum est per angelum, Act. 7. Cum enim lex vetus fuit disponere malis ad legem nouam, decuit ministrum illam imprimere et architectorem formam inducere, vt in artificibus docetur, primo Methafisice. Nec scripsit in tabulis lapideis vel pellibus mo[r]tuorum, sed in animabus hominum, vnde Gal. 3 dicitur lex vetus pedagogus. (Bodley 716, f. 4ᵛᵃ)

> That Christ taught this law *with his mouth* signifies its excellence compared to the Old Testament, which was given by means of an angel. (Acts 7.38) For since the old law had been given to prepare the wicked for the new law, it was fitting for a minister to imprint it and for the architect to confer its form, as is taught about craftsmen in the *Metaphysics*, Book 1. Nor did he [i.e., Christ] write on stone tablets or on the skins of dead things, but on human souls, and for this reason the old law is called a teacher. (Gal. 3.24)

Though Lyre had noted the contrast between Christ's unmediated words and the ministering work of angels, Wyclif adds the citation of Acts and, more significantly, all of the discussion that follows.[93] The angel who gives the law on Sinai becomes an intermediary servant imprinting that law on tablets and, at the same time, an architect providing the outline or form of the new law conveyed by Christ (now writing on human souls).[94] So far, though Christ is clearly enacting a long-prophesied fulfillment of the law, Wyclif's focus has remained on his historical act of preaching, emphasized by the exegete's continued use of the past tense (*docuit, decuit, scripsit*) to describe Christ's actions. This focus seems to continue when Wyclif begins his interpretation of the moral teaching of Matth. 5.13 ff., which he says was given in figurative language "quia Palestini intenti sunt parabolis" ("because people living in Palestine were attentive to parables"). This historicist account of Christ's rhetorical approach, echoed in a marginal note in the Bodley copy of the postils, explains why "he compares them" (that is, apparently, his historical audience) "to salt, light, a city, and a lantern" ("comparat eos sali, luci, ciuitati, et lucerne").[95] Wyclif focuses on the first of these comparisons, noting the various uses of salt in Scripture and then listing some of its properties – it renders land barren, pickles foods, can be used to dry and preserve meat – and he then explains their significance:

> Et omnia ista cum suis consequentibus debent mistice prelatis competere. Ad hoc enim a puro sole sunt eciam sic sapide coagulati vt terram, id est terrenis inhiantes faciant sterilescere quoad secularia desideria in radice corosa sale desiderii celestis iuxta illud Titum 2, *Apparuit gracia Saluatoris* etc., et euellant plantas inutiles iuxta illud Ier. 1, *Ecce constitui te super gentes* etc. Omnem doctrinam, que est cibus spiritualis, spes celestis premii sapidam reddit iuxta illud Ps. 18, *Iusticie Domini recte* etc. (Bodley 716, ff. 4vb–5ra)

> And all of these [properties], with the things that follow from them, should be applied mystically to prelates. For to this end they are by the bright sun thus prudently given solid form, so that they might make the earth, i.e., those who desire earthly things, grow sterile with regard to worldly desires when their root has been worn away by the salt of heavenly desire, as in Tit. 2.11, *The grace of the Savior has appeared* etc., and so that they might pluck out all useless plants, as in Jer. 1.10, *Lo, I have set you over the nations* etc. Every teaching, which is our spiritual food, is made flavorful by the hope of heavenly reward, as in Ps. 18.9, *The justices of the Lord are right* etc.

Evidently it is not just the residents of ancient Palestine but also modern-day clerics who can fruitfully be compared to salt. By claiming that this comparison should be made *mystice*, Wyclif suggests that his interpretation is shifting from a literal to a spiritual register, a move reinforced by the consistent present tense of his verbs (*debent, faciant, euellant*). No longer just brief notes added at the end of Lyre's more general literal tropologies, Wyclif is now offering substantial and sustained presentist interpretations of Christ's moral teaching.[96]

The comparison of priests to salt represents an ideal, but Wyclif evidently feels that most of his contemporary clergy are better described as "salt that has lost its savor," denoting their inability or refusal to carry out their task of flavoring the food of spiritual teaching. He then takes up some of his favorite critiques of the clergy, drawing in other biblical instances of ineffectual salt to develop his argument:

> Vnde radicalis causa regnacionis diaboli est peccatum superiorum Ecclesie. Deficit enim inter Deum et populum mediator, pro peccato populi satisfactor, et ignorancium informator cum nullus laicus est sacerdote plus secularibus inuolutus. Istud inquam sal sic infatuatum per aspectum retro ad temporalia versum est in statuam salis, que non est sal viuum terre vel lapidum sed fatuum simulacrum, patet historia Gen. 19. Et Veritas meminit ita dicens, *Mementote vxoris Loth*. (f. 5[ra])

> The radical cause of the devil's rule is the sin of superiors in the Church, for the mediator between God and the people, who makes satisfaction for the people's sins and informs their ignorance, fails when no layman is enveloped in more worldly matters than a priest. Such salt, I say, thus made ineffective through its backward glance toward temporal affairs, is turned into a statue of salt, which is not fresh salt of the earth or of rock but a foolish likeness, as is clear in the story of Gen. 19. And the Truth itself recalls this, saying thus, *Be mindful of the wife of Lot*. [Luke 17.32]

At the same time as Christ points (mystically) to the failure of the clergy, Wyclif also believes that he has indicated how their corruption can be resolved, glossing the assertion that the salt should be "cast out" (*mittatur foras*) with the note that "it would indeed be meritorious and charitable to cast our prelates out of temporal offices" ("Meritorium quidem esset caritatiue expellere nostros prelatos a temporalium dignitate"), and he claims specifically that "it is valid for those who pursue divine justice, whether popes or princes, to throw out such ineffective salt" ("Valet igitur exequentibus diuinam iusticiam, siue pape siue principi, mittere foras salem sic fatuum"). By now the basic parameters of his spiritual interpretation have been established, but Wyclif is not yet ready to move on to the next verse. Instead, perhaps reflecting his belated consultation of further sources, he introduces yet more details of the properties of salt, allowing him to continue his attack on clerical corruption. Such prelates, he says,

> iniuriantur autem maxime toti Ecclesie, cum secundum Ysidorum, 16.2, sal sit maxime necessarium ad cibarii condimentum, in tantum quod oues et pecudes inmixtum pabulo prouocat ad edendum et per consequens ad impignandum. Vnde columbe affectant lapidem salis in columbari, cum caliditate et siccitate stomacum iuuat et digestionem confortat. Est enim calide nature et sicce. Vnde secundum Auicennam habet virtutem dissoluendi, mundificandi, et consumendi. (f. 5rb)

> are especially injurious to the whole Church, since, according to Isidore, XVI.ii.6, salt is especially necessary as a seasoning of foods, so much so that when mixed in with their fodder it encourages sheep and other beasts to eat and so to become fat, and therefore doves desire a rock of salt in their dovecotes, since it aids their stomach with heat and dryness and strengthens their digestion. For it is of a hot and dry nature, and therefore according to Avicenna it has the ability to dissolve, to purify, and to wear down.

Perhaps because he has already devoted so much space to this tropology, Wyclif does not elaborate on the significance of salt's ability to encourage the appetites of livestock, though it is easy to see how this could be tied to his earlier comment on priestly teaching as spiritual food. It is healthy to grow fat on such fare. He focuses instead on the notion of salt as a digestive aid, reflecting, he notes, its ability to maintain the body's proper humoral balance. This is the kind of balancing force that he says a prelate should have in his community, and he ends this lengthy passage by asking, "Why, therefore, when the salt is willingly neglecting these good acts and thus causes injury to God, to himself, and to his people, does the whole world not fight, along with God, in seeking retribution for such enemies?" ("Quare ergo cum sit sal voluntarium hec bona necligens et sic Deo, sibi, et populo iniurians, non pugnaret cum Deo orbis terrarum in vlcionem talium inimicorum?"). In total, Wyclif devotes a third of his commentary on Matth. 5 to this tropological discussion of salt, without saying anything about its more general moral applicability or its specific connotations for the historical audience of Christ's teaching, intent as they might have been on parables. Though this is evidently not the literal or historical meaning of the text, it is the one that Wyclif, even early in his career, felt most urgently needed to be expressed.

His focus on this kind of moralism – a distinct tropological sense, as opposed to literal tropology – continued after the composition of his Matthew postil, indicated in Bodley and Magdalen's marginal notes, which (as we have seen) apparently preserve material added to his working copy. While generally reflecting his efforts at revision, it is possible that some of these notes were actually included as Wyclif wrote the commentary, since, in a few cases where his interpretations depart significantly from Lyre, he includes bits of Lyre's glosses in the margin.[97] (Perhaps, even as he decided to offer his own readings, Wyclif thought it best to keep the opinions of this major source readily accessible for future consultation.)[98] Other marginalia reflect his reading of additional sources. One such annotation, quoting Augustine's letter *ad Januarium*, is tied by a later reader to the end of Wyclif's Lyre-derived gloss on Matth. 23.4, building on the commentary's suggestion that heavy burdens (*onera*) are imposed by certain "feigners of goodness" (*fictores bonitatis*), who derive them from their own traditions rather than from divine law. Certain people, according to Augustine, weigh down Christianity with "servile burdens" (*servilibus oneribus*) far beyond the small number of true sacraments. Here the relevance of Augustine's writing to the commentary is obvious, and even the saint's specific choice of words could have recalled this particular passage of the gospel. Other connections are less clear, suggesting that Wyclif was reading at least a selection of Augustine's letters with an eye to how they might apply to his exegetical program. Above the parable begun in Matth. 13.3, for example, which Wyclif says concerns "the state of the Church from now until the end of the age" ("statum Ecclesie ab hinc vsque ad finem seculi"), he adds a passage from Augustine's letter *ad Valerium* about the difficult, laborious, and perilous work of the ordained clergy, while, in the margins of his prologue to Matthew, he adds an excerpt from the letter *ad Vincentium* about the lesser authority of the writings of "holy doctors" compared to Scripture.[99] This last example is a potentially useful point of exegetical theory, the sort of thing that one might look for in a prologue, even if it does not obviously build on anything already in Wyclif's prefatory discussion.[100] The others point to his continuing interest in the tropological application of Matthew's text to the present state of the Church, and, just as importantly, they anticipate Wyclif's turn to patristic authorities, apparently consulted in the *originalia*, to supply more of that tropological meaning – the same authorities who are quoted and glossed at length throughout the *Opus*.

Moving between the literal-historicist approach he takes in other chapters and the moral presentism seen in the postil on Matth. 5, Wyclif places considerable weight on a single adverb, *mystice*.[101] As noted above, the same word is used in his Psalter commentary to indicate a shift in interpretive registers, but there his mystical interpretations were added after glosses on a psalm's literal sense. In contrast, Wyclif interprets Matth. 5.13 *only* according to its mystical meaning. His sense of the overriding significance of this approach to these passages is reinforced in the *Opus*, when Wyclif reproduces his lengthy gloss on this verse, now adding a note not found in the postil: "Tales salis proprietates et multas alias intelligit Patris Sapiencia quando dicit, *Vos estis sal terre*" ("The Wisdom of the Father comprehends such properties of salt, and many others besides, when he says, *You are the salt of the earth*").[102] It is tempting to see in this statement the suggestion that Christ intended to convey the tropological understandings advocated by Wyclif in the historical moment of his preaching, but several details indicate that, here too, Wyclif is maintaining a more traditional distinction between the senses of Scripture. It is not the historical person of Jesus, but rather the more abstract Wisdom of the Father who speaks (*dicit*) this phrase and understands (*intelligit*) these meanings, with this present tense matching the tropological readings in his postils. At the same time, however, his assertion of Christ's intentions elevates the moral reading of this passage above any consideration of its literal sense. Historicist readings apparently matter much less when the exegete can provide divinely intended morality. Again, Wyclif's desire to move beyond the letter ("supra litteram") seems to be a desire to move beyond hermeneutic distinctions, deemed less urgent than the exegete's notion of the overriding meaning of the biblical text.

Perhaps the clearest statement of Wyclif's eclectic approach to Matthew comes in a lengthy passage added to the revised version of his prologue.[103] He begins by repeating some of the conventional material found earlier in the prologue, noting Matthew's particular focus on the humanity of Christ and some of the details of the evangelist's biography included in the Monarchian preface. But, as in his gloss on Matth. 5, Wyclif quickly turns away from (or, perhaps, broadens) this literalistic approach:

> Et sic, si bene consideretur, Matheus primo ostenderet quod animal esset in visione Ezechielis 1, quia, tractando principaliter de Christi humanitate (vt descendit a patriarchis et regibus), ostendit se figurari per faciem hominis. Secundo, si bene consideretur quomodo ex puplicano peccatore factus sit primus euangelista, ostenderet in se opus Dei quod est graciose agere et misericorditer remittere, et non solum in se sed eciam in hiis pluribus peccatoribus de quibus dignatur Christus nasci et eis misereri. Hoc enim est proprium opus Dei et non vindicari. ... Licet enim tractat de Chrsti humanitate narrat tamen miracula de Christo, que solus Deus potest facere. ... Per faccionem miraculorum Christus ostendit se idem cum Patre, quia cum Deus vnus est et solius Dei est facere tot miracula, seminando fidem per paucos simplices tam cito per tantum spacium, ideo relinquitur Christus idem essentialiter cum Patre. In isto ergo euangelio vtile est volentibus Deum cognoscere, vt sic transcurrant per principium, medium, et finem huius euangelii [et] intelligant vocacionem huius

apostoli, solicitudinem huius operis, et dileccionem Dei volentis pro nobis incarnari, que plene tanguntur in hoc euangelio. Sic ergo cognoscent naturam diuinam in qua per vnionem natura humana communis et per consequens omnes homines apprehensi sunt communicatiue, sicut et illam naturam apprehendere cupiunt participatiue.[104]

> And so, if one considers carefully, Matthew first showed what the animal was in the vision in the first chapter of Ezechiel, for, writing principally about Christ's humanity (as he descended from patriarchs and kings), he shows himself to be figured by the face of a man. Second, if one considers carefully how he who had been a sinful publican became the first evangelist, he showed in himself the work of God, which is to act graciously and to forgive mercifully, and not only in himself but even in these many sinners for whom Christ deigns to be born and on whom he has mercy. For this, not vengeance, is the proper work of God. . . . Although he writes about Christ's humanity, he still narrates miracles concerning Christ, and only God can perform these. . . . By performing miracles Christ shows himself to be one with the Father, for since God is one and the performing of so many miracles pertains to God alone, in sowing the faith through such a small number of simple men so quickly and throughout such great territory, therefore it remains that Christ is in essence one with the Father. There is something useful, therefore, in this gospel for those wishing to know God, and so they should progress through the beginning, middle, and end of this gospel and then understand the calling of this apostle, the solicitousness of this work, and the love of God wishing to be made incarnate for us – which are written about fully in this gospel. In this way they will know the divine nature, in which, by union, our common human nature and, consequently, all human beings are assumed by communication, just as they desire to assume that [i.e., the divine] nature by participation.

There is a clear movement from literal to spiritual interpretation in the course of this passage – from what Matthew showed (*ostenderet*) to what Christ shows (*ostendit*) – though the lack of overt references to the senses makes it harder to parse these interpretive registers with certainty. The moral reading of Matthew's conversion, for example, may reflect the evangelist's historical intentions, but it seems more likely to be part of some divinely intended meaning inhering in the events of his life. Intriguingly, while earlier in his prologue Wyclif had followed Auriol and claimed that Matthew's particular intentions led him principally to discuss Christ's generation and humanity (*generationem et humanitatem*), he now reads this focus on the incarnation as pointing to a larger interest in God's love for humankind. This may be as close as Wyclif ever comes to saying he "lered that love was our Lords mening," and it is an understanding that he, like Julian, seems to have reached after years of study.[105] He now expresses this interpretation in terms of its utility to readers of the gospel (and, presumably, his commentary) who "wish to know God," a kind of interpretive presentism that seems at least obliquely related to his habit of glossing the gospel's moral content specifically as it applies to the Church in fourteenth-century England.

This added passage ends with an account of biblical reading that, like the schema from *De veritate* with which this chapter began, ties scriptural study to a kind of mystical experience of union with the divine. Here, however, union is presented only as a desire: just as God has taken on human nature by virtue of the incarnation (which Matthew describes), so too do human beings wish to take on, and participate in, divine nature. The desire for this kind of union should prompt study of the gospel, in which the divine nature can at least be known (*cognoscere*). While the emphasis on divine *dilectio* in this passage may seem to align it with the tropological focus seen in some of Wyclif's more substantial departures from Lyre, it is important to recall that his postil also includes careful consideration of the literal and historical content of Matthew, and that kind of approach therefore appears to be an integral part of coming to know the divine nature as well. To put it another way, insofar as Wyclif's postil furnishes material for the kind of scriptural study that can lead to knowledge of God's nature, then that study consists of an eclectic mix of historical and tropological glosses, a blending of the senses that Wyclif continued to explore, with a particular focus on the Gospel of Matthew, throughout the remainder of his career.

Eclectic Hermeneutics and Belated Exegesis: William Woodford on Matthew

This last example reinforces the notion, suggested at the outset of this chapter, that Wyclif's exegesis is not a simple expression of the interpretive theories advanced in *De veritate*. Instead, faced with the clearly articulated and (more or less) consistently implemented hermeneutics of Lyre's postils, Wyclif had to assess the degree to which this particular brand of scholastic literalism allowed for a satisfying interpretation of the biblical text, and where Lyre's inconsistencies and disagreements with earlier exegetes might indicate the need for reconsideration or correction. The similarities between passages in Wyclif's postils and his later theoretical writings reflect his continued engagement with the tradition of scholastic biblical commentary as he found it in Oxford late in the fourteenth century, and though, as we have seen, the approach to that tradition in his postils at least sometimes reflects Wyclif's intellectual idiosyncrasies, the same need to reconcile the disagreements in this body of texts could have been felt by any contemporary exegete. Arguably more significant than the similarities in his earlier and later works, then, are the attitudes toward Scripture and exegesis that Wyclif's commentaries appear to share with the other major postil produced in Oxford in the 1370s, the incomplete work on Matthew by William Woodford OFM (d. 1397). By way of conclusion, some consideration of this other handling of interpretive history, undertaken by "the first major polemicist" to critique Wyclif's writings, can allow us to distinguish idiosyncrasies from larger trends in late medieval biblical studies.[106]

Though Woodford's writings on scriptural authority have received some critical attention, especially as they compare with Wyclif's theoretical works, his *postilla* on Matthew has been wholly neglected in the almost fifty years since Jeremy Catto's unpublished dissertation.[107] Catto's work remains immensely valuable, providing a detailed description of the single manuscript in which the commentary is now preserved (CUL MS Add. 3571), a summary of the different topics addressed throughout the text, and a careful account of the many sources on which Woodford draws.[108] Yet much more remains to be said, not least concerning how Woodford positions his interpretations in relation to the larger scholastic tradition of exegesis represented in his sources, and how his hermeneutic commitments compare with Wyclif's.

Woodford's postil is incomplete, and the sole surviving manuscript suggests its scribes' uncertainty in the face of a disorderly exemplar.[109] Most obviously, the work, dated by Smalley to 1372 or early 1373, ends in the middle of the exegete's discussion of Matth. 5.46, using only seven lines of f. 244vb, and various references forward, indicating that Woodford intended to return to subjects but did not ultimately do so, suggest that he at least initially planned to comment on the biblical book in its entirety.[110] The scribes of Add. 3571 provide no colophons to begin or end the commentary, and they have made no attempt to indicate the start of new chapters in the gospel (often done with a simple rubricated note in other commentaries) or to set the lemmata apart from the exegetical prose (e.g., with rubricated underlining).[111] Similarly, running headers noting the chapter discussed on a given opening are only added by a later reader. Catto raises the possibility that the scribes, who apparently worked within Woodford's lifetime, may have been copying directly from the exegete's autograph, and certainly at least some of the marginalia they include must have begun as Woodford's notes for revision.[112] In the outer margin of

f. 93ᵛ, for example, alongside an account of John the Baptist as the voice crying in the wilderness, the scribe adds an instruction to "see especially f. 24 of Grimestone's postil, why he is called voice" ("nota optime folio 24 postille Grymmistone, quare dictus est vox"), either providing a citation for Woodford's interpretations or indicating a source that should be consulted to augment the text.[113] The latter is certainly the case with another note, included after Woodford offers a dozen reasons why Christ compares the Apostles to salt (Matth. 5.13), directing someone (likely the exegete himself) to "note what is said about the twentieth property of water in the little book about the properties of the elements, and add it here" (f. 172ʳᵃ: "nota illa que ponuntur in 20 proprietate aque in libello de proprietatibus elementorum et adde hic"). Like the three lines left blank on f. 120ʳᵇ, where the exemplar (and presumably Woodford) provided only the opening of a fuller quotation from Robert Holcot's popular work on Wisdom, these details reveal that Woodford's postil, though still a massive undertaking, remained an unfinished draft, a work-in-progress.[114]

The provisional state of Woodford's commentary makes it harder to interpret the text's unusual opening. As noted above, most scholastic commentaries on Matthew begin with a discussion of one or both of the *Glossa* prefaces. This was the approach adopted, as we have seen, by Lyre and (at least initially) by Wyclif, and it was also how the Carmelite John Baconthorpe began his gloss on Matthew, delivered as lectures at Oxford, *c.* 1336–40.[115] While one of Woodford's major sources, Peter John Olivi OFM (d. 1298), did not follow this practice in his Matthew commentary, he still begins with a standard extrinsic *accessus* in praise of Scripture, opening with a quotation of Ezech. 1.6–7, which, since it was referenced in the Monarchian preface, was discussed in the prologues to the other postils as well.[116] Woodford, in contrast, begins by posing a series of questions about the gospels and their authors:

> *Liber generacionis Iesu Christi, filii Dauid, filii Abraham.* Hic incipit euuangelium secundum Matheum, et est primus liber Noui Testamenti. Antequam ergo descendam ad exposicionem istius littere sunt aliqua dubia premittenda, quorum aliqua in communi pertinebunt ad quatuor euuangelia et aliqua in speciali ad euuangelium Mathei, quod pre manibus habemus. (f. 69ʳᵃ)

> *The book of the generation of Jesus Christ, the son of David, the son of Abraham.* Here begins the Gospel of Matthew, the first book of the New Testament. Before turning to the exposition of this text, a number of uncertainties should be set out in advance, some pertaining commonly to the four gospels and some in particular to Matthew's gospel, the work now at hand.

Woodford enumerates and discusses seven questions about the relationship between the Old and New Testaments and the work of the four evangelists, and he then turns "to investigate some things pertaining in particular to the first gospel" (f. 72rb: "inuestigare aliqua pertinencia in speciali ad primum euuangelium"), amounting to sixteen additional questions, all but the first of which actually deal with the genealogy in Matth. 1.1–17.[117] To be sure, other exegetes include similar *quaestiones* early in their commentaries – Olivi addresses seven after his extrinsic prologue, Baconthorpe three (one in two parts) after glossing the Monarchian preface, and Docking positions five between the extrinsic and intrinsic prologues to his commentary on Luke, another major source for Woodford – but Woodford is unusual in prefacing his postil *only* with such questions.[118]

Considering the commentary's unfinished state, it is certainly possible that Woodford intended to return and supply a standard prologue, and that such a plan, like the continuation of the postil beyond Matth. 5, was never realized. Yet this possibility is made much less likely by the general form of Woodford's exegesis. Beginning with his treatment of Matth. 2.1, for each major section of his commentary Woodford first specifies the portion of the gospel he is about to consider (e.g., f. 86rb: "*Cvm natus esset Iesus in Bethelem* [2.1] ... supponitur textus vsque ibi: *Qui cum recessissent* [2.13]"), and he then discusses the Old Testament prophecies (*conditiones*) fulfilled by this particular passage.[119] (These are taken from Auriol, who had enumerated twenty-two in total across the whole of Matthew, and they appear to have been a popular innovation in fourteenth-century writing on this gospel: Wyclif quotes them in both versions of his prologue, and Baconthorpe elaborates on them to create his own list of twenty-seven *conditiones*).[120] Woodford then offers a detailed and apparently original *divisio* of the specified section of biblical text, accounting for its structure down to the level of individual words or short phrases.[121] Next comes a listing of questions he will address for the given section – ranging from twelve for Matth. 1.18–25 to sixty-seven for 5.27–32 (f. 190ra: "sunt multa pertractanda!") – and his discussion of these questions accounts for the great bulk of his commentary. In this regard, then, though it is perhaps surprising that he does not offer a *divisio* for the gospel as a whole, Woodford's decision to introduce his postil with a series of *quaestiones* is in keeping with his general interpretive practice.

By focusing his work on these questions, Woodford sets his postil apart from earlier commentaries. Catto may be right to note that, compared with the masters of Paris, Oxford exegetes were more likely to include *quaestiones* in their postils – a phenomenon Smalley associated with the influence of Grosseteste among the Oxford friars – but other writers simply do not allow the serial addressing of questions to dominate the content or the structure of their commentaries.[122] Indeed, Woodford's work almost has more in common with Augustine's *Quaestiones XVII in Matthaeum* or Isidore's *Quaestiones* on the Old and New Testaments than with its major scholastic sources, though his inclusion of *divisiones* and *conditiones* indicates that he is also not simply imitating these texts. Here we should recall Smalley's observation about the place of *quaestiones* in scholastic commentaries, such as Bonaventure on Ecclesiastes, where the close parsing of lemmata is interrupted, at uneven intervals, by such questions, "deal[ing] with points arising directly from the text."[123] These *quaestiones* allow the exegete to pursue specific problems in greater detail, or, to put it another way, they presume a text already glossed, anticipating that the commentary's readers will have a basic understanding of how to interpret it, but that more can be said about particular topics or passages. Baconthorpe, for example, after closely parsing Joseph's dreamy revelation in Matth. 2.20, asks why the angel says that *they* are dead who sought to kill Christ, when, earlier in the same chapter, it was specified that Herod sought the boy and that the death of Herod alone had prompted the angelic message.[124] In this case, in addition to considering a single point in greater detail, presenting this discussion in the form of a question allows Baconthorpe to argue for the internal consistency of the whole chapter, referring back to Matth. 2.13 and 2.19, an attention to larger issues that could be discouraged by the phrase-by-phrase glossing of the text.

While Bonaventure and Baconthorpe provide their own expositions, which they then supplement with *quaestiones*, Woodford apparently presumed that an initial interpretation of Matthew's gospel could be sought in another source, and he almost certainly had Lyre in mind. To be sure, Woodford does not overtly describe his text as a supplement to Lyre's literal postils, which he elsewhere praised as a precious work (*opus preciosus*), but the notion of these postils as a necessary antecedent to Woodford's text would go far in explaining the questions that the later exegete decides to pose.[125] In many cases, he explores topics that Lyre had simply failed to address (e.g., why it was a star that guided the Magi), and in others he indicates that Lyre's interpretations are not the only (or the best) way to understand a passage (e.g., why the evangelist included the seemingly gratuitous detail that Jesus "opened his mouth" to preach the Sermon on the Mount).[126] In this last example, Woodford first gives Lyre's answer – that this is done to set the New Law apart from the Old

Law, the latter conveyed (as we have seen) by the intermediating work of angels – noting that this is the "racio doctoris de Lire super hoc textu," before offering different explanations attributed to Chrysostom, Augustine, and the *Glossa ordinaria*, another which he says represents the "communis racio postillatorum" (apparently not including Lyre), and a final account which is unattributed and therefore presumably original to Woodford. In other instances, admittedly, Lyre is one of several authorities who agree on an interpretation that Woodford feels compelled to supplement, as in the early question concerning why Matthew titles his gospel the Book of the Generation of Jesus Christ, rather (Woodford says) than the book of his preaching, passion, or resurrection. Here Woodford appears to be drawing on a variety of sources to form the fullest possible version of their standard answer – that titling a book based on its beginning reflects Hebrew and Greek conventions – and his failure to include attributions for any of his three alternative explanations may indicate that they are all original to him.[127] Rather than simply building on Lyre, then, it may be more accurate to say that Woodford sought to supplement the standard (*communis*) interpretation of the gospel, and that he considered Lyre's postils a convenient starting point for assessing that scholarly consensus. And, of course, though these *quaestiones* dominate his text, Woodford's postil would also enrich Lyre's by including Auriol's prophetic conditions and a much more extensive *divisio textus*.[128]

Since he is not glossing the biblical text but rather asking questions about it, Woodford is generally able to avoid the kinds of hermeneutic problems that, as we have seen, faced other commentators. Though Catto claims that Woodford was especially interested in "posing moral questions" with the larger goal of "summari[zing] the moral wisdom of the Church," in practice the exegete's choice of topics varies from section to section, reflecting the variations in the gospel's content noted above.[129] When discussing the narrative of the Magi (Matth. 2) or the baptism of John (Matth. 3), his questions focus on the historical setting of the events, the different figures involved in them, and why the evangelist chooses to foreground some details rather than others (e.g., What kind of people were the Magi? Why does Matthew bother to specify that the Baptist wore a leather girdle, when such clothing is quite common?).[130] It is only when he reaches Christ's preaching in Matth. 5 that Woodford, like Wyclif, comes to focus on the text's moral teaching (e.g., on the injunction, in Matth. 5.16, to let people see your good works, whether it is really permissible to show off *all* your good works, and whether works performed with the intention of pleasing onlookers can still be considered good).[131]

Yet, even after he has reached this more overtly moral material, Woodford still asks some literalistic questions, just as isolated tropological questions had appeared in earlier sections of his commentary.[132] After discussing the Baptist's upbringing and his decision to preach in the desert, for example, Woodford notes his ascetic camelhair and asks if it is therefore sinful to wear "costly and comfortable clothing" (*vestimenta pretiosa et mollia*). To begin his response, he first quotes from Gregory's homilies, where the example of the Baptist is cited to support the notion that an interest in such clothing is indeed sinful, to which Woodford opposes the practice of bishops and secular lords, before going on to distinguish eleven reasons to wear such clothing, only two of which are necessarily sinful.[133] His decision to take up this question seems to have been motivated by Woodford's particular present-day concerns – he quite clearly feels that it is appropriate for prelates to wear precious robes "propter timorem pariter et honorem" ("on account of holy fear and also honor") and for schoolmen to do so "propter dignitatem gradus sui" ("on account of the dignity of their degree") – as well as by his discovery that one of his authoritative sources had cited this biblical text to condemn the practice. This pair of factors – his own ideas about what would make for an interesting or valuable discussion, and the diverse material, beyond Lyre's glosses, found in his sources – does more to account for Woodford's choice of questions throughout the commentary than his prioritizing of one or another sense of Scripture, or, indeed, his commitments to any particular hermeneutic theories.

Woodford's relative lack of interest in these theories, at least in his postil, is made clear in the few instances where he *does* use the language of the senses. In this regard, his discussion of the Old Testament prophecy fulfilled in Matth. 4.1–12 (the sixth *conditio*) is unusually elaborate. Auriol had maintained that the angels who minister to Christ after his wilderness temptation were predicted in Ps. 90.11, but Woodford finds this reading wholly implausible.[134] Following Lyre, he claims that this psalm, in its literal sense, is about the journey of the Israelites from Egypt to the Land of Promise, and its reference to angelic ministration therefore describes the fiery and cloudy pillar, just as the fear of dashing one's foot against a stone recalls when the Israelites "passed through rocky and dangerous places" ("quando transibant per loca saxosa et abrupta"). He argues, furthermore, that Ps. 90 should not be interpreted as concerning Christ even according to its "farthest prophetic understanding" ("secundum vlteriorem prophetalem intelligenciam"), since Jerome maintains that it refers prophetically "to some other holy man" ("de alio viro sancto"). Finally, Woodford finds it odd that this verse would ever be considered the best prophetic antecedent to Matth. 4.1–12, since the evangelist's principle intention (*principalis intentio*) has nothing to do with angelic ministration, but is instead focused on the devil's temptations and Christ's responses. He therefore suggests that a more germane prophecy would be Ps. 17.30–31, where he claims that David writes "in persona Christi." Woodford's decision to correct Auriol thus makes it clear that he has not borrowed this material thoughtlessly, but his hermeneutic commitments are far from consistent: though he refutes Auriol's interpretation of Ps. 90 with a reference to Lyre, that same source also provides a literalistic and non-Christological interpretation of Ps. 17 (which Woodford neglects to cite), and it is unclear whether Woodford's vague and apparently novel notion of an *ulterior prophetalis intelligentia* refers to a literal or spiritual understanding of the text.[135] In attempting to reconcile Auriol with Lyre and Jerome, he shows himself, again, to be interested less in pursuing questions of interpretive theory, and more in providing exegetical material that reflects as fully as possible the wide range of sources on which he has drawn.

To be sure, Woodford elsewhere devotes considerable attention to hermeneutic distinctions, and Minnis has shown that his criticisms of Wyclif in the *Quattuor determinaciones* (1389–90) are based on a careful delineation of the literal and spiritual senses.[136] In the postil, in contrast, though he sometimes uses the language of the senses, he seems to have thought it unnecessary to consider these hermeneutic issues in any systematic or consistent way. Rather than seeking to craft a thoroughgoing literal or spiritual interpretation of the text, Woodford uses the relative flexibility of his serialized *quaestiones* to address whatever topics strike him as most relevant – most in need of his consideration – for a given passage. In this respect, then, though the styles of their commentaries are quite different, Woodford's work coincides with Wyclif's postils, with both exegetes apparently valuing their own interpretive interests over a clear theory of the senses. The result is, in both cases, what I have called hermeneutic eclecticism, commentaries that include an unpredictable variety of interpretive approaches to a single biblical text.

In both cases, this eclecticism arises as a response to their consideration of a range of earlier commentaries, but especially Lyre's literal postils. Both Wyclif and Woodford clearly hold Lyre in high regard, and their works suggest that they considered his interpretations as *the* standard against which other glosses should be judged. But they also agree that his readings, however authoritative, are far from definitive. On various points, Lyre's glosses need to be reconsidered in light of other sources, inevitably representing other hermeneutic approaches, either because Lyre may have erred in assessing the literal meaning of the text, or because literalism is not the most important approach to a particular passage. They go about this task differently – Wyclif offers a traditional lemmatized commentary drawing on Lyre where appropriate and on other sources where he considers the literal postils to be deficient, while Woodford assumes independent access to Lyre's text, which he augments and corrects with his *quaestiones*, *conditiones*, and *divisiones* – but both exegetes apparently viewed their basic task as supplementing this landmark of medieval biblical scholarship. Their postils, in other words, adopt a posture of belatedness. The careful work of parsing the whole of both Testaments according to the theories of Thomistic literalism had already been accomplished, and these later writers could imagine their own work only in relation to this major source.

The common approach of these Oxford writers with regard to their exegetical sources – to Lyre's postils as well as earlier commentaries – calls for some revision to the narrative of fourteenth-century biblical studies advanced by Smalley and supported, more recently, by William Courtenay.[137] According to these accounts, Wyclif's postils represent a "revival" in the writing of commentaries, following a period of relative inactivity after the works discussed in the previous chapter.[138] Yet, while it is certainly the case that the postils of Wyclif and Woodford indicate their authors' commitment to writing commentaries in a way that had not been seen for several decades, in some respects their works reveal the continuing inability of Latin exegetes to build confidently on (and thus to move beyond) the rigorously applied literalism of Lyre's postils. In retrospect, then, their works might help to explain the decline in production at midcentury. While Smalley points to the stifling effects of the plague and Courtenay to shortened periods of regency and a growing preference for theology based in "logic, mathematics, and physics," one of the principal factors must have been the seeming definitiveness of Lyre's commentaries, so thoroughly successful that, forty years later, exegetes could only see themselves as supplementing this now-standard work.

At the same time, it is significant that their attempts to correct and add to Lyre's glosses involved, to differing degrees, a return to earlier commentaries and the various book-specific hermeneutics that informed them. In this regard, their response to Lyre has much in common with Cossey's earlier set of critiques, discussed in Chapter 1. As we will see in the following chapters, these works by Oxford theologians represent only one facet of the larger enterprise of scholastic exegesis in fourteenth-century England, and the continuing influence of earlier interpretive theories, like the impulse to revisit and revise standard sources, can also be found in commentaries written outside the universities, in English and Latin alike.

CHAPTER 3

Richard Rolle's Scholarly Devotion

The depiction of Richard Rolle, the Hermit of Hampole, in BL MS Add. 37049 seems to capture at once the sources of Rolle's authority and the reasons for his widespread appeal in later medieval England (Fig. 6).[1] The hermit (d. 1349) sits in an elaborate cell, the Holy Name emblazoned on his chest and a book open on his lap, while above him an angelic choir sings its hymn of praise. Rolle's ability to perceive the angels' song is suggested by the trio of words which, together with his cell's spires, bridge the space between him and the heavenly host: *harmonia, odas,* and *canora* (harmony, hymns, and songs), words used in Rolle's writings to denote what he believed to be the pinnacle of mystical experience.[2] Directing his placid gaze outward, Rolle mediates and translates this celestial music for his earthly audience, but the text he offers, rather than simply rendering the angels' Latin or providing some other standard liturgical or biblical phrase, is drawn instead from one of his own lyrics: "I syt and synge of luf-langyng þat in my breste is bred. / Ihesu, my kynge and my ioyinge, when were I to þe ledde?"[3] A strong statement of the authorization, even valorization, of early English poetry, this image presents Rolle's mystical experiences as legitimating his authorial activities in the vernacular, activities meant, in turn, to support the devout practices of his readers.

A similar emphasis on Rolle's rapturous experiences, focusing in particular on his distinctive accounts of divinely granted *fervor, dulcor,* and *canor* (heat, sweetness, and song), has dominated critical assessments of his writings for more than a century, beginning with the studies of Carl Horstman and Hope Emily Allen and continuing in even the most recent work. It is on these experiences that Rolle's authority as a writer is said to rest. In his meticulous and thoughtful account of the hermit's literary career, for example, Nicholas Watson describes Rolle as "determin[ed] to establish and exercise a form of eremitic and mystical authority," and "as a mystical writer whose *materia* was his own experience."[4] Other critics have

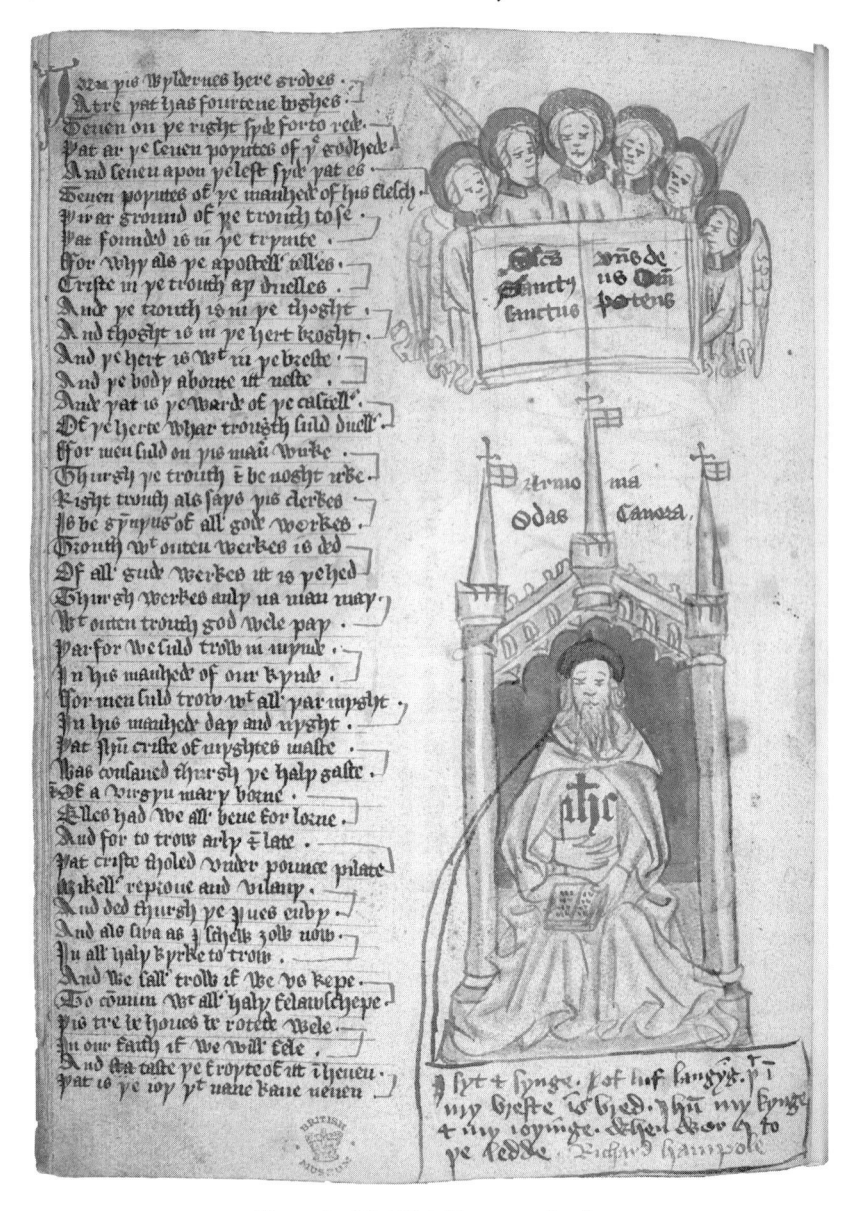

Figure 6 BL MS Add. 37049, f. 52ᵛ.

gone further, seeing in Rolle's experiential authority an "implicit privileging of affect over intellectual ... understanding," one which can be "associated with the anti-intellectual" and "oppose[d] ... to book-learning."[5] These views can perhaps find some justification in late medieval sources, such as the office readings prepared soon after Rolle's death in anticipation of his canonization. Though Rolle spent some time at Oxford, where he was "quite accomplished in his studies" ("ualde proficiens in studio") and even "wanted more fully and deeply to be immersed in the theological teachings of sacred Scripture" ("desiderauit plenius et profundius imbui theologicis sacre Scripture doctrinis"), his decision to leave the university is here described in markedly negative terms. He is said to have fled "lest he be caught in the snares of sinners" ("ne peccatorum laqueis caperetur").[6] While the authority of the exegetes discussed in previous chapters derived from their position in an interpretive tradition grounded in the supreme authority of Holy Writ, Rolle's flight from Oxford could be seen as a rejection of such academic discourses, one that required the development of his experiential *auctoritas*.

Throughout his career, however, Rolle also wrote biblical commentaries drawn from many of the same sources, and in much the same style, as the scholastic exegesis discussed above. The most substantial and among the most widely copied of these undertakings is a Middle English commentary on the Psalms, now called the *English Psalter*, perhaps "the first long biblical commentary ever written in English."[7] In this work, Rolle presents himself not (or not simply) in his more familiar pose as a mystical "purveyor of ecstasy," but as a diligent compiler who has attempted to make the standard fare of the scholastic classroom, along with some glosses of his own devising, available in the vernacular, and specifically for the sake of an ambitiously learned form of devotional reading.[8] More than any other single writer, Rolle can thus lay claim to establishing Middle English scholastic commentary and translation as a distinct category of texts, and, as we will see, English exegetes in the decades following his death looked to capitalize on his success, exploring different ways in which biblical commentary could be made into vernacular literature.

Before he glossed the Psalms in English, however, Rolle had already written a complete commentary on the text in Latin, a work now known as his *Latin Psalter*. It is in this commentary, his most sustained effort in the language and generally copied at the head of anthologies of his collected writings, that Rolle seems first to have developed his distinctive approach to the task of biblical exegesis.[9] Like his contemporaries in Oxford, Rolle turned to standard early scholastic sources, especially Peter Lombard's *Magna glosatura*, preserving and refining many of the interpretations he found there, but he also, again like these other exegetes, attempted to bring something new to this interpretive tradition, to add more bricks to its hermeneutic edifice and extend the project of Latin exegesis in his own idiosyncratic ways. In the *Latin Psalter*, the hermit seizes on some of the approaches and priorities specific to the interpretive history of the Psalms – especially theories of the Psalmist's prophetic authorship and the composition of individual psalms in discrete lyric *personae* – and he adapts them to find, in the case of some psalms, divinely inspired descriptions of the ideal religious life, his own form of living and the ecstatic experiences he associated with it, as the meaning of the text. (We have already seen a brief example of this move, in the passage discussed in the Introduction, 1–3.) The result is a commentary that sits, sometimes uneasily, between the expectations of scholastic exegesis and devotional concerns familiar from Rolle's better-known writings. It is this distinctive blending that he further explores and elaborates with considerable sophistication in his later English commentary.

Though the neglect of his exegetical works has been unfortunate, therefore, it would also be unfortunate simply to posit commentary as a distinct if important mode in Rolle's writings. It would be misleading to present Rolle the exegete as a second authorial *persona* alongside Rolle the mystic.[10] The devotional ends of his exegesis, his efforts to compile and adapt scholastic glosses as the proper reading materials for an aspiring contemplative, point to a subtler and more complicated authorial program, at once focused on the furthest possibilities of affective experience and grounded in the resources of fourteenth-century intellectual life. The hermit remains committed to "book-learning," then, treating it as a rich source of insight into his ecstatic experiences and, at least in mediated form, suitable material for meditative *lectio*, what might be called studious devotion.[11] It is this cultivation of an idiosyncratically blended interpretive program, developed outside the university but drawing on the resources and discourses of the schools, which allowed Rolle to exert such influence on the shape of biblical exegesis in fourteenth-century England, and which helped to make him, as Ralph Hanna has said, "the first real 'author' in Middle English."[12] It also allowed him, finally, to return to Oxford, recognized as an authoritative interpreter of Scripture, in Latin and in English.

Hermit Hermeneutics

The devotional designs of Rolle's exegesis are made explicit at the opening of the *Latin Psalter*, where he describes the Psalms in terms that call to mind the rapturous figure depicted in Add. 37049. The commentary's short preface begins with an encomium suggesting all that can be achieved through pious singing of the biblical text:

> Magna spiritualis iocunditatis suauitas illabitur mentibus cantica psalmorum deuote canencium. Mellita sunt enim dulcedine amoris eterni, et ineffabili elapsu feruoris corda fecundant, discipline recte ostendunt instituta, et nostre tribulacionis prestant consolamen: purgant vicia, inflammant animos, psallentes erigunt in canoram contemplacionem.[13]

> A great sweetness of spiritual delight flows into the minds of those devoutly singing the songs of the psalms. These songs are honeyed with the sweetness of eternal love, and they make hearts fecund with an ineffable occurrence of heat, they reveal the principles of proper discipline, and they offer the consolation of our suffering: they purge vices, enflame souls, and raise singers into melodious contemplation.

Trying to place it early in his career, Allen suggests that the *Latin Psalter* might have begun as a university exercise, but this opening reveals that, at least by the time he completed the commentary, Rolle had a more or less fully articulated understanding of his experiences of *fervor*, *dulcor*, and *canor*, and he was able to account for the place of the Psalms in a devotional program derived from such sensations.[14] The hermit describes those who sing the Psalter devoutly (*devote*) as being led through ever more rarefied states, from the purgation of vices to the heights of sonorous contemplation. The same association of the Psalms with successive stages of spiritual progress also appears in some of Rolle's decidedly late works: in *Ego Dormio*, for example, he commends the reading of the Psalms to those who "forsake al þe world … and folow Crist in pouert." Addressing someone imagined to be in this state, he writes, "Gyf þe myche to say psalmes of the Psauter … in al þe deuocioun þat þou may, liftyng vp þi þoght to heuyn," and he assures her that, through such reading, "þou shalt fynd gret swetness, þat shal draw þi hert vp, and mak þe fal in wepynge and in grete langynge to Ihesu; and þi þoght shal be reft abouen al erthly þynges, abouen þe sky and þe sterres, so þat þe egh of þi hert may loke into heuyn."[15] Here, as in the *Latin Psalter*, the imagery of spiritual progress as an upward movement (*erigere*) is combined with contrary motions downward: in the *Psalter*, sweetness is poured in (*illabi*), presumably from on high, while in *Ego Dormio*, being raised into heaven is matched with a fall into weeping and love-longing.[16] These accounts thus describe an engagement with the biblical text meant to foster a complex range of devotional experiences, an approach for which scholastic interpretation would seemingly have little, if anything, to offer.

With its very next sentence, however, the preface shifts registers, and Rolle turns his attention to the mundane task of parsing the biblical text. Drawing material from the prologue to the Lombard's *Magna glosatura* (on which, see above), he writes,

> Notandum vero est quod in primo huius doctrine, que est de toto Christo, scilicet de capite et corpore quod est ecclesia, subiectum describit et reprobos secernit. Vnde secundum hoc primus psalmus diuiditur in duo, et quia prius est carere malo quam habundare bono, ideo primo Christus distinguitur ab omnibus hominibus per hoc quod caruit omni malo, non pene sed culpe, quod nullus aliorum habuit ad minus propter contractum originalis peccati. Quod autem omnino culpa caruit, ostendit inducendo in triplici genere culpe, que induccio continetur in his tribus negatiuis: *Non abiit, non stetit, non sedit.* (f. 1ra)

> It should be noted that at the beginning of this teaching, which is about the whole Christ, i.e., his head and body (which is the Church), he describes this subject and separates out the reprobate. And therefore this first psalm is divided in two parts, and since lacking wickedness precedes abounding in goodness, he first distinguishes Christ from all men insofar as he lacked all wickedness (not of punishment but of guilt), which, owing to original sin, was true of no one else. He shows that he is entirely free from guilt by introducing three kinds of guilt contained in these three negatives: *He has not walked, he has not stood, he has not sat.*

As he does throughout the commentary, Rolle adapts and abbreviates only a few sentences from what had been a much more elaborate discussion in his source.[17] Taking the account of the Psalter's Christological subject matter from earlier in the Lombard's prologue, Rolle weaves this notion into his explanation of the first psalm, also reflecting (though not explaining) his source's account of this psalm as "something of a title and prologue … of the following work" (60b: "quasi titulus et prologus … sequentis operis"). This subject matter is used to explain the structure of the psalm or its division into parts, again borrowed from the *Glosatura*, and Rolle thereafter transitions to his phrase-by-phrase explanation of the text.

This opening can thus be read as pulling the *Latin Psalter* in two different directions, alternately devotional and scholastic, but such a contrast should not be exaggerated. Indeed, the material presented here as two distinct halves can also be read as a unified whole, and, in his adaptation of his source, there are signs that the hermit sought this sort of reading. Rolle's identification of Christ's body as the Church ("de capite et corpore quod est ecclesia"), while perhaps simply a pedantic clarification added to what he found in the Lombard ("de capite et corpore"), also helps to signal where within the text the devout reader should locate himself. This sense of identity is heightened with Rolle's next addition, namely, the idea that the first psalm is concerned with establishing a distinction between the reprobate and the body of the Church to which the reader belongs.[18] Likewise, the specification that one must lack wickedness before abounding in goodness – again, not found at this point in the *Glosatura* – mirrors the movement from the purgation of vices to heavenly contemplation described earlier in the preface.[19] This more unified reading is supported by Rolle's apparent decision to minimize the amount of scholastic jargon taken over from his source, as well as the elimination of some of the Lombard's common exegetical techniques. Even the preface's *divisio* of Ps. 1 ultimately offers little by way of interpretive insight: though he notes that this psalm may be divided "into two parts," Rolle never specifies where the second half begins or why it should be considered distinct from the first.[20] And while the Lombard goes on to introduce each psalm with some consideration of its *materia*, *modus*, and *intentio*, the hermit does not make substantial use of this technical language.[21] Regardless, Rolle clearly considers at least some scholastic material to be appropriate to his commentary and, presumably, to the kind of devoutly attentive reading enjoined here and throughout his writings.

Even without its technical vocabulary or *divisiones*, Rolle is still able to draw on some of the *Magna glosatura*'s major exegetical strategies, its ways of approaching the text and framing its larger interpretations, and in this regard his handling of the voicing of individual psalms is especially significant. As noted above, identifying the voice (*vox* or *persona*) adopted by the Psalmist was often an essential part of a scholastic exegete's interpretation of each psalm.[22] As a prophet, David could write poetry in his own voice or in that of some future figure (such as Christ or a faithful Christian), and, since the Psalter was seen as a collection of lyric poems, the voice of each psalm would very likely be different from those coming before and after it. An exegete's interpretation of a psalm could thus cohere around what he identified as its distinctive voice. Throughout the *Latin Psalter*, after first quoting the opening of a psalm and sometimes offering his gloss on the quoted text, Rolle provides a brief prefatory discussion that often includes an account of the voice in which he believes the psalm was written.[23] In many cases, he simply borrows this material from the Lombard, as when he says of Ps. 25, "Vox est Prophete in persona perfecte anime" (f. 11[ra]: "This is the voice of the Prophet in the *persona* of a perfect soul"), or when he hears in Ps. 68 "vox Christi in passione" (23[rb]: "the voice of Christ in his passion").[24] For other psalms, Rolle can either subtly refine or refocus what he found in his source, such as when he identifies the speaker of Ps. 42 as a *vir sanctus*, which seems simply to be more specific than the Lombard's ecclesial *corpus Christi*, or when he specifies that Ps. 142 "attribuitur penitenti oranti pro remissione ... peccatorum" (f. 44[va]: "is attributed to a penitent praying for the remission of his sins"), even though the Lombard had held open the possibility of reading this psalm in the voice either of a penitent Christian or of Christ himself.[25] Such attention to the voicing of different psalms allows Rolle to present the Psalter as a complex assembly of texts potentially suiting a variety of devotional needs, whether providing phrases (and exegetical paraphrases) with which the reader can express his penitence or elaborate meditations on Christ's suffering on the cross or his love for humanity. Rolle transforms this scholastic interpretive category for the sake of meditative reading.

Further, in his most elaborate departures from the *Magna glosatura*, Rolle claims that certain psalms are not simply spoken in the voice of a generic devout reader, but, more specifically, in that of a soul pursuing the hermit's idiosyncratic vision of the contemplative life. In his introduction to Ps. 83, for example, the Lombard does not actually identify a voice, stating instead that the psalm describes both the suffering of Christ on the cross and the persecution of the Church in the present age.[26] The hermit seizes on this omission as an opportunity to give his own reading, suggesting that this psalm contains the words "contemplatiue et amore Christi ardentis anime, que solum Christum sapiens et pre nimio amoris feruore pene moriens ac deficiens ait: *Nunciate dilecto quia amore langueo*" (f. 29[rb]: "of the contemplative soul aglow with the love of Christ, which soul tasting Christ alone and nearly dying and collapsing from love's excessive heat, says: *Tell my beloved that I languish with love* [cf. Cant. 5.8]").[27] Even when the *Magna glosatura* includes notes on the voicing of a psalm, Rolle can disagree. Thus, while the Lombard writes that, in Ps. 9, "hic loquitur in persona Ecclesiae" (130b: "here he [i.e., the Psalmist] speaks in the *persona* of the Church"), Rolle offers his own interpretation:

> Vox est perfectorum, qui nullis mundanis cogitacionibus vacillant sed toto desiderio ad Deum tendentes Deum perfecte laudant. Intendit monere homines vt nichil casu sed iusto Dei iudicio omnia in mundo credantur

fieri. Quidam enim videntes affligi eque bonos et malos, ignorantes cur fiat, detrahunt Deo, putantes que diuina sunt administracione casuum temeritate contingere, et hii in parte cordis laudant, quia quedam opera Dei approbant, quedam blasphemant. Sed ego qui cerno occultas causas quibus hic iuste facit, *in toto corde* laudo, qui omnia recte disponi sencio, *narrabo omnia mirabilia tua.* (f. 3vb)

This is the voice of the perfect, who do not hem and haw in any earthly thoughts, but rather striving toward God with all their desire, they praise him perfectly. He intends to admonish them to believe that nothing happens by chance, but rather all things in the world happen by the just judgment of God. But seeing that the good and the wicked suffer equally, and being ignorant of why this is so, some blame God, rashly thinking that this is brought about by some divine plan. These people praise God in a portion of their heart, for they approve of some of God's works, and with another portion they blaspheme. But I who discern the hidden causes by which this justly happens, I praise him *with my whole heart,* and I who sense all things to be properly ordained, *I will tell all your wonders.*

Though Rolle has borrowed some phrases from the *Glosatura* (including a rare occurrence of *intendere*), other glosses in this passage are new, reflecting his belief that David wrote this psalm in the voice of perfect men and women.[28] Particularly suggestive is the omission of the Lombard's explanation that the Church praises God with its whole heart "quia in nullo de providentia Dei dubito" (130d: "because I [i.e., the Church] have no doubt in God's providence"), for which Rolle substitutes the claim that the *perfecti* can "discern the hidden causes" of apparently unjust suffering in the present life.[29] The strong implication here is that Rolle should be numbered among these *perfecti*, just as he is surely the burning contemplative soul (or, at least, one of them) imagined to speak in Ps. 83. These accounts of voice thus allow Rolle to take on the authority of the psalmic speaker, and to present the biblical text as, in some way, written to be spoken specifically by him.[30]

The hermit's assumption of a psalmic voice – or, more precisely, his glossing of certain psalms as prophetically anticipating his recitation – becomes especially clear when he reads phrases in the biblical text as alluding to his distinctive experiences of mystical ecstasy, the heat, sweetness, and song for which he is now so well known. After the initial reference to the psalmic speaker's *fervor amoris*, for example, his discussion of Ps. 83 continues: "*Cor meum* mellitum amoris dulcedine *et caro mea*, etsi grauiter, id est exterior homo consenciens et condelectans suauitatis interne *exultauerunt* hic" (f. 29rb: "*My heart,* honeyed with the sweetness of love, *and my flesh*, albeit heavily, i.e., the outer person joining in the sensation and delight of internal sweetness, *has exalted* here"). Similarly, as part of his gloss on Ps. 38, identified indirectly as written in the *persona* of the just and perfect, Rolle offers a startling interpretation of the spiritual fire the Psalmist describes.[31]

> *Concaluit cor meum intra me* zelo animarum, vt darem cibaria conseruis, *et in meditacione mea* que de eterno amore et vita celesti est, *exardescet ignis* id est feruor perfecte dileccionis, vt vere non ymaginarie sentirem ignem Spiritus sancti vrentem cor meum. (f. 15vb)

> *My heart was hot within me*, with the zeal of souls, that I might give nourishment to my fellow-servants, *and in my meditation*, which is of eternal love and the heavenly life, *the fire flared up*, i.e., the heat of perfect love, so that, indeed, not imaginarily, I felt the fire of the Holy Ghost burning my heart.

After what is itself an arresting account of his writings sharing in the cure of souls, a gloss which seems to inscribe an audience of readers with similar pastoral responsibilities, the remainder of this passage presents a clear statement of Rolle's contemplative priorities and ecstatic experiences.[32] The quick reference to his meditation *de eterno amore* neatly sums up his other writings, and the description of divinely granted *fervor* accords perfectly with the accounts of that sensation in his better-known works. In particular, this passage shares language with arguably the most famous sentence in the hermit's Latin corpus, the opening of *Incendium Amoris*, where he writes, "Admirabar [amplius] quam enuncio quando siquidem sentiui cor meum primitus incalescere et uere non imaginarie [sed] quasi sensibil[i] igne estuare" ("I cannot find the words to express how I wondered when I first felt my heart grow hot and, indeed, burn not imaginarily but with, as it were, perceivable fire").[33] Elsewhere in his treatment of Pss. 38 and 83, Rolle diligently adapts material from the *Magna glosatura*, but he supplements such received readings with these original glosses, presenting the psalms as describing – at once validating and perhaps prophesying – the specific sensations he claims to have experienced, and which he elsewhere suggests are only available to those who live, like himself, as solitaries.[34] Of course, the conventions of the commentary form allow Rolle to offer these glosses without overtly claiming that they describe him, or that the text is uniquely or specifically intended to anticipate his own prayerful reading. He is simply providing a paraphrase of the Psalmist's lyric utterance, and as such his voice as commentator can blend into the voice in which (he thinks) the text was written.

In one of the few moments in the *Latin Psalter* when his own voice can be distinguished clearly from his ventriloquized psalmic voice, after glossing the word *solitudo* in Ps. 54.8 as "me segregans a turba terrenorum desideriorum" ("separating myself from the crowd of earthly desires"), Rolle insists that he has preferred this figurative reading of solitude "ne videar statum meum superexaltare, quia solitarius sum [qui] hanc breuem exposicionem compilaui" (f. 19[va]: "lest I seem inordinately to exalt my own state, for I who have compiled this brief exposition am a solitary"). Such momentary humility notwithstanding, it should be clear enough that the hermit's glosses do sometimes focus not just on the contemplative life, but specifically on his own understanding of its perfect form. Yet Rolle does not at all suggest that these readings are a radical departure from, or rejection of, the early scholastic tradition represented in the Lombard's text. Instead, he seems to position his readings within the framework he found in the *Glosatura*, using these inherited interpretive categories to carve out a space for his own glosses, and in many cases he revises and adapts preexistent material as part of this effort. In this regard, at least, he works very much like the Oxford exegetes discussed in previous chapters, but, rather than drawing on knowledge of Hebrew or innovative theories of the literal sense, Rolle turns to his ecstatic experiences of divine love to find new meanings in individual psalms. The careful balance that he achieves between the learned habits of scholastic exegesis and his desire to describe the ideal life of contemplation is an essential element of the hermit's hermeneutic in the *Latin Psalter*, as he strives to create a biblical commentary that fits his vision of proper devotional reading.

Rolle's approach to this balance, his notion of what should be included in this new type of commentary, apparently continued to develop as he composed the text, and, beyond that, across his career. Though, as noted above, Rolle generally seems to have considered the detailed discussions (of *modus*, *intentio*, etc.) found in scholastic *accessus* to be unhelpful to his devotional-exegetical program, he was ultimately unwilling to omit this material entirely. At the end of his commentary on Ps. 150, but before his glosses on the six ferial canticles (on which, more below), Rolle presents a compilation of general insights on the Psalter drawn (as in his preface) from the prologue to the *Magna glosatura* (f. 46[rb–va]). Here, in what the text's early modern editor labeled its epilogue (*epilogus*), Rolle notes that "apud Hebreos … [psalmi] sunt metrice scripti, quod in translacione seruari non potuit" ("among the Hebrews the psalms are written metrically, which could not be preserved in translation"), and he offers an account of David as the book's author and the role that his unmatched prophetic insights played in its composition ("modus excellencior quo Dauid istam edidit propheciam"). As Wyclif would later note in his postils (discussed above), Rolle also specifies that the present arrangement of the Psalms is not authorial, since "Esdras propheta, qui Psalterium et totam bibliotecam a Baboloniis combustam instinctu Spiritus sancti reformauit, eodemque Spiritu reuelante psalmos ita disposuit, eisdemque titulos apposuit" ("the prophet Ezra, who guided by the Holy Ghost restored the Psalter and the whole collection that had been burnt up by the Babylonians, under the guidance of the same Spirit put the psalms in their present order and affixed titles to them").[35] Positioned as they are at the end of the *Latin Psalter*, it is unclear what sort of use Rolle expected to be made of these considerations of the Psalms' composition and history.[36] He seems to have felt that these notes could in some way help to inform a proper understanding of the biblical text, but he evidently supplied them almost as an afterthought, suggesting that the information they offer is not utterly essential.

Likewise, if less securely, it seems that Rolle also held back but ultimately included another of his sources, a short pseudo-Augustinian tract in praise of the devotional efficacy of the Psalms.[37] With its listing of the benefits of psalmic reading ("Canticum psalmorum corpus sanctificat, animas decorat," etc.), this text may have inspired the similar though briefer list in the *Latin Psalter*'s preface, quoted above ("purgant vicia, inflammant animos," etc.), and, as we will see, Rolle certainly had it to hand at some point, since he translated a portion of it in his *English Psalter*. The text appears immediately after the *Latin Psalter*'s treatment of the ferial canticles in three insular copies, as well as in a clutch of closely related Bohemian witnesses, and though it seems to be the perfect candidate for copying as a bit of filler, several details argue against its chance inclusion by a later scribe.[38] The text's appearance in the same form and position in manuscripts from divergent branches of the commentary's transmission indicates that it must have been added very early in the *Psalter*'s history, likely omitted in some of the major anthologies of Rolle's Latin because it is overtly attributed to another writer, Augustine.[39] Further, unlike other copies of the tract, the Rollean version does not end with praise of the biblical text, but instead with yet more material apparently adapted from the prologue to the *Magna glosatura* (or perhaps another related commentary) and not included in Rolle's epilogue.[40] It would seem, then, that the hermit continued to compile material he considered potentially relevant to the work of his commentary, deferring any decisions about *how* all of this should relate to his exegetical project.

That project continued after the initial composition of the *Latin Psalter*. As the material gathered in Appendix B indicates, Rolle appears likely to have undertaken a systematic revision of his commentary, moving the text further away from the *Glosatura* and introducing more readings that reflect his understanding of the Psalms as describing his experiences of the contemplative life. Though the identification of this revision as Rolle's must, for now, remain tentative, it is far from the only evidence of the hermit's desire to revisit and refine the hermeneutic blending developed in the *Latin Psalter*. Indeed, as we will see, there is good reason to think of his other major work on the Psalms, an English commentary almost certainly composed toward the end of his life, as yet another revision of this initial effort. Reflecting his growing confidence in his status as an authoritative reader of Scripture, these revisions also point to his changing ideas of how the exegetical resources and interpretive strategies compiled in the *Glosatura* could be made to serve the needs of a studious form of devotion.

The Invention of Commentary-Translation

Rolle appears to have begun writing vernacular works only late in his career, and this shift in languages brought with it (or perhaps was prompted by) a shift in his audience. His three English letters of spiritual counsel were addressed, in the first instance, to female religious readers, while the verse prologue found in a single copy of the *English Psalter*, BodL MS Laud. misc. 286, names Margaret Kirkeby, a Hampole nun and later anchoress, as the original recipient of that commentary.[41] Though this last identification should be regarded with greater skepticism than it has generally received, the notion that the *English Psalter* was aimed at an audience of female religious (perhaps the Hampole community as a whole) is still quite likely.[42] These early readers of the *English Psalter* would presumably be almost wholly unfamiliar with the interpretive norms of scholastic exegesis, and Rolle might therefore be expected to adjust his hermeneutic priorities and present a simpler mode of interpretation than he had in the *Latin Psalter*.[43] Yet Rolle frustrates any such expectations, offering instead both more fervent devotional language and more sophisticated scholastic interpretive techniques. The distinctive hermeneutic of the *Latin Psalter* is thus amplified in the English commentary, demanding a more rigorous response from its readers.

This amplification is already evident at the start of the *English Psalter*'s lengthy prologue. The text opens with an elaborative translation of the first portion of the preface to the *Latin Psalter*, describing the ecstatic joys that await the devout singer (or, Rolle now adds, reader) of the Psalms:[44]

> Grete habundance of gastli cumforth and ioy in God cummes in-to þe hertes of þame þat saies or synges deuouteli þe psalmes of þe Sauter in louing of Ihesu Crist. Þay drop suettnes in mans saule and helles delite in-to þaire thogehtes and kindilles þaire wylles with fyre of louf, makand þaim hote and brynand with-in and faire and luffli to Cristes eghen. And þay þat lastes in þaire deuocioune þai raise þaim in contemplatif lyffue and oft sithes [in] soune and mirth of heuen. (HM 148, f. 23ra; Bramley, 3)

Rolle promises the same experiences here as he had in his Latin text, making use of the same sense of contrary vertical motion (*þay drop swettnes ... þai raise þaim*), but the English text is more expansive, transforming, for example, the Latin preface's *corda fecundata ineffabili elapsu fervoris* into wills enkindled "with fyre of louf" and made "hote and brynand with-in." This initial eruption of praise is then extended in the English prologue, as Rolle selectively translates from the Ps.-Augustinian text appended, very likely by the hermit himself, to the end of his Latin commentary (see above). "Þe sang of salpmes," he proclaims, "[chases] fendes, excites aungels till oure helpe, it dos awaye sine, it pleses God, it infourmes perfyttnes, it dos awaye and dystroies noy and angire of saule, and makes pes bitwix body and saule, it bringes desire of heuen and dispit of erthli þyng."[45] Apparently finding this litany insufficient, the hermit then turns to the prologue to Cassiodorus's Psalter commentary, paraphrasing Song of Songs 4.12–13 and describing this biblical book as a "garth[en] enclosede, welle ensaled, paradise ful of alle apils," and noting that, when we sing the psalms, "with aungels whaim we may noght here we meng wordes of lofing."[46] In light of the fervor with which the *English Psalter* opens, then, Margaret Deanesly is quite right to say that Rolle's "aim was increase of devotion."[47]

This heightened emphasis on devotion is matched, as the prologue continues, with an equally elaborate introduction to the Psalter drawing on the conventions of scholastic commentary. Here Rolle provides some of the material from the preface to the *Magna glosatura* which he had reserved for the appended epilogue in the *Latin Psalter*, including the notion that "þis buke is distinguid in thris fifti psalmes, in þe whilke thre states of Cristen mens religioune is signified."[48] Further, he now makes use of the scholastic jargon avoided in his earlier text, translating from the Lombard to identify the Psalmist's "entent" (*intentio*), the "mater of þis boke" (*materia libri*), and its "ma[n]er of lare" (*modus tractandi*).[49] Hanna calls Rolle's use of these terms "deliberately parodic and disordered," yet they function here much as they would in any scholastic commentary, and the hermit continues to invoke them (especially *entent*) in his discussions of individual psalms, suggesting their importance to the *English Psalter*'s hermeneutic program.[50]

This indebtedness to scholastic interpretation and theory continues in the final portion of the prologue, a comparatively brief account of Rolle's priorities as a translator that obviously has no precedent in his Latin work. Rolle indicates that the *verbum pro verbo* style preferred in his translation should assist in reading the Vulgate, and he argues that his interpretations are authoritative because they have been drawn from saintly sources:

> In þis wirke I seke no straunge Ynglisch, bot þe liʒtest and comunest, and swilke þat is most like to þe Latin, so þat he þat knaus not þe Latin bi þe Ynglisch may come till many Latene wordes. In þe translacione I folow þe letter als mykyll as I may, and þaire I fynde no propere Ynglisch I folow þe witt of þe worde, so þat þaim þat sall rede it þare not drede erringe. In expowndyng I folow hali docturs, ffor it may cum in some enuyouse manns hand, þat knaus not what he suld saye, þat will say I wist noght what I sayde, and so do herme till him and till oþere, if he dispice þe wirk þat is profytubell for hym and for oþere. (HM 148, f. 23[vab]; Bramley, 4–5)

By addressing in turn his techniques as a translator and an exegete, Rolle anticipates the structure he has given to the work that follows. For each verse of the Psalter, he first provides the relevant Latin text, then his close translation, and finally a sometimes quite lengthy passage of interpretation. Claiming that he has sought to avoid "straunge Ynglisch" even as he favors words that are "most like to þe Latin," Rolle describes an ideal that he was rarely able to realize, and his translation tends to favor the Latin in its choice of words and its phrasing. The result is a rendering that has been criticized for its "awkwardness and stiffness" and described as "reflecting the syntax of its original so closely as to be nearly incomprehensible."[51]

As has long been recognized, this preference for the close translation of a biblical text had an important precedent in the work of Jerome, who abandoned his usual *sensus de sensu* style when faced with the task of translating the Bible, "ubi et uerborum ordo mysterium est" ("where even the order of words is a mystery").[52] Considerably less attention, however, has been paid to the ways in which the style of the *English Psalter* reflects current scholastic theories of translation. Indeed, Rolle's preference for awkward literalism was shared by the great majority of academic translators rendering Greek and Arabic theological and scientific texts into Latin beginning in the twelfth century, "even at the expense of elegant Latin style."[53] Introducing his translation of Chrysostom's homilies on John, for example, Burgundio of Pisa (d. 1193) explains his fear that "si sentenciam huius sancti patris commentationis assumens meo eam more dictarem, in aliquo alterutrorum horum duorum sapientissimorum virorum sentenciis profundam mentem mutarem" ("if I were to take up the meaning of the text of this holy father and declare it in my own manner, I would in some way change the profound intention in the opinions of either of these two most wise men [i.e., Chrysostom and the evangelist]"). Therefore, Burgundio says, "Difficilius iter arripiens et verba significatione eadem et stilum et ordinem eundem qui apud Grecos est in hac mea translatione servare disposui" ("I took the harder path and decided to preserve in my translation both words with the same meaning and the same style and order as the Greek").[54] As Charles Burnett observes, such literal translation "became the norm" in thirteenth-century universities, apparently "chosen out of respect for the authors of the works and out of an almost religious compunction not to impose anything of oneself onto the translation."[55]

Yet the *English Psalter* does not consist simply of a close translation, and the hermit's compunctious literalism extends only to the text of the Psalms, not to the interpretive selections from the "hali doctus" which form the bulk of his work. In those expository passages, Rolle's close translation is divided and rearranged to furnish the lemmata for his commentary, and these more idiomatic glosses can help to resolve any ambiguities in the translation at the same time as they provide further interpretive content. With this blurring of commentary and translation into a single hermeneutic project, the *Psalter* fits with yet another trend in scholastic theory. According to Huguccio of Pisa (d. 1210), whose *Derivationes* is one of several scholastic reference texts which Rolle appears to have known either directly or indirectly,[56] translation is best defined as "expositio sententie per aliam linguam" ("the exposition of meaning through another language"), a notion reiterated and developed by a range of later writers.[57] Thus, in his early fifteenth-century *determinatio* on the translation of Scripture into English, the Oxford theologian Richard Ullerston writes,

> Dicuntur "translatores" qui vnam lingwam alteri coaptant seu proporcionant aut vnam per aliam exponunt. Et sic loquendo de "transferre" accipitur pro "interpretari," quod est vnam lingwam per aliam exponere, et "translator" pro "interprete" sumitur. Vnde et "translatores" dicuntur "interpretes" et econtra, quamuis lacius "interpretes" et "interpretari" sumantur. Sumitur enim "interpretari" aliquando per exponere, reuelare, explanare, seu reserare sensum in verbis latentem.[58]
>
> They are called "translators" who adapt or apportion one language to another or expound one language through another. And speaking in this

way, "to translate" is taken to mean "to interpret," that is, to expound one language through another, and "translator" is taken to mean "interpreter," whence "translators" are called "interpreters" and vice versa, although the words "interpreter" and "to interpret" may also be taken more broadly. For "to interpret" is at different times taken to mean to expound, to reveal, to explain, or to unlock the meaning hidden in words.

Following Huguccio's definition, Ullerston ties translation to the exegetical activities of the universities. To translate is, he says, to gloss. By referring to the "broader" meanings of "interpreter" and "to interpret," Ullerston appears to be suggesting that, while "to translate" does mean "to interpret," the latter can refer to many more things than just translation, and the list of synonyms with which this passage concludes thus provides a fuller sense of what it means for a translator to be an interpreter. Later in the *determinatio*, Ullerston praises Rolle as someone who "totum Psalterium transtulit in uulgare" ("drewe oon Engliche þe Sauter," as the Middle English translation of the *determinatio* has it), suggesting that he recognized the *English Psalter*'s affinities with these scholastic theories of translation.[59] Ullerston, in other words, saw Rolle as someone who at once, and as part of a single coherent project, translated and glossed the Psalms.

To be sure, the observation that Rolle's work makes use of scholastic terms and is in line with contemporary theories does not guarantee that the early readership of his *Psalter*, presumably without Ullerston's extensive university training, would have been aware of this academic pedigree. If they were indeed among the first to read Rolle's commentary, the nuns of Hampole would almost certainly be unfamiliar with Burgundio's translations and the conventions of scholastic prologues. Yet these scholarly affinities are also signaled by the visual arrangement of the earliest extant manuscripts of the text, copied either in Yorkshire or the Midlands, with the commentary's *mise-en-page* also being adapted (or, perhaps better, translated) from the *Magna glosatura*.[60] In many manuscripts of the Lombard's commentary, each verse of the Psalter is first presented in a distinctive larger script, followed by expository passages in a smaller minuscule, with the lemmata often underlined in red when they reappear in these glosses.[61] Similarly, almost all early manuscripts of the *English Psalter* set the Latin apart (sometimes along with the close English translation) by the use of a larger or more formal script, thereby at once affirming the authority of the Latin and, more pragmatically, allowing the reader to find specific verses with greater ease.[62] In one clutch of manuscripts, the translation is underlined, typically in red, to distinguish it from the commentary (Fig. 7), and this format would seem to support Rolle's

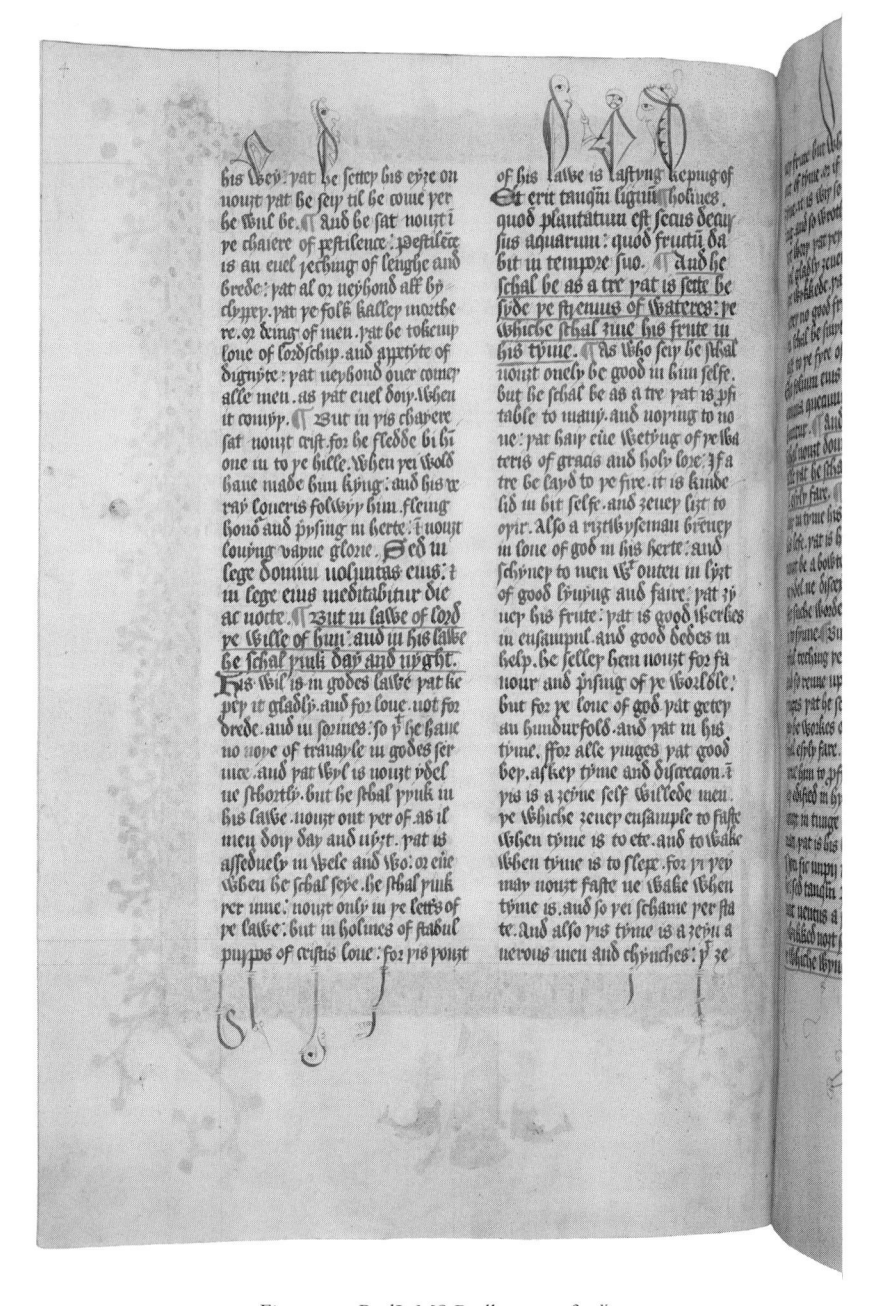

Figure 7   BodL MS Bodley 953, f. 2ᵛ.

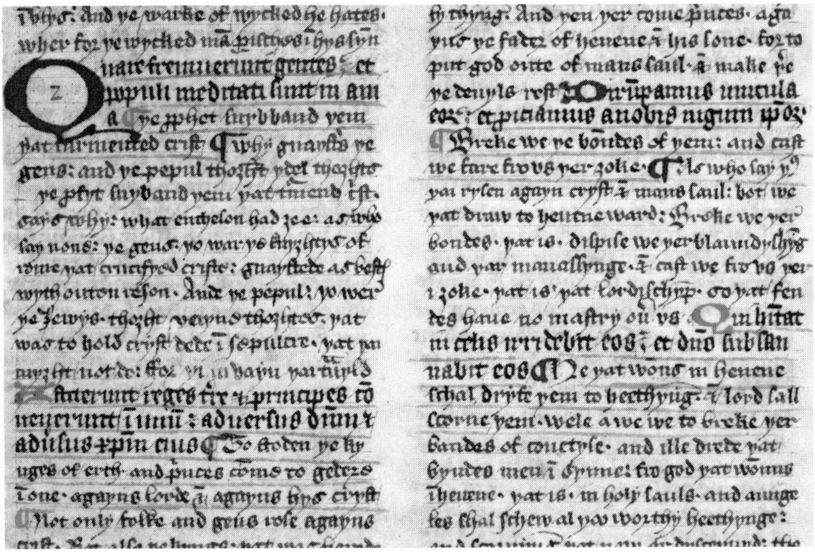

Figure 8   Aberdeen Univ. Lib. MS 243, f. 3ʳ (detail).

aim, articulated at the end of his prologue, that "he þat knawes not þe Latin bi þe Ynglisch may come till many Latene wordes."[63] In another early group, rubricated underlining extends beneath both the Latin and the close translation (Fig. 8).[64] In these cases, though the hierarchy of scripts distinguishes between the two registers of underlined text, the more extensive underlining seems to indicate that the Latin and the translation provide, as a unit, the object of the exposition that follows, a bilingual issue that is, of course, without precedent in Latin commentaries. These modes of presenting the *Psalter* make it appear more obviously scholarly than contemplative or devotional, and though they are clearly meant to facilitate the *use* of the text, they also suggest that even readers unfamiliar with the nuances of Latin exegesis could imagine themselves participating, however generally, in the scholastic enterprise of interpretation.[65]

The augmentation of the hermit's distinctive hermeneutic, at once adding richer accounts of the biblical text's devotional possibilities and demanding more complex engagement with the interpretive priorities of scholasticism, continues throughout the *English Psalter*, informed by Rolle's return to the *Magna glosatura*. In some cases, his fresh consultation of the Lombard leads Rolle to back away from material presented in his earlier commentary, such as the elaborate identification of Ps. 83 as the words of a burning contemplative soul, replaced in his English work with several glosses translated from the Lombard and the claim (not found in the *Glosatura*) that "þis is þe voice of a holy saule."[66] In many more instances, even when he is drawing on the Lombard, Rolle adds discussion of a variety of concerns familiar from his other writings, condemnations of those who love worldly goods rather than God, or attacks on the "bakbyters" who harass anyone leading a life of pious devotion.[67] He continues to identify psalms – indeed, many more than in the *Latin Psalter* – as spoken in the *persona* of a "haly mane," "rightwise man," or "perfit man," and he remains eager to find references to his favored contemplative experiences in the words attributed these speakers.[68] Rolle reads Ps. 12, for example, as "þe voice of holy men, þat couaites and ȝernes þe connyng of Ihesu Cryst, þat þai myȝt liue with hym in ioye," explaining that "þese wordes may none say suthli bot a perfyt mane or womman þat has gedyrde togedyre all þe desyres of þaire saules and with þe naile of lufe festend þaim in Ihesu Cryst." Glossing Ps. 12.6, then, though he draws some phrases from the Lombard, Rolle develops an elaborate description of the lofty experiences of heavenly song for which such a "perfyt mane or womman" longs:

> Þou sall not anly make me bryght and brynand in luf ffor me, bot also . . . *my herte sall ioy in þi hele*, þat is in Ihesu wham I behalde in thoght, and to hym *I sall synge* in gladnes of saule. When all the myȝtes of my herte are raysyde in-to þe soune of heuen, þan may I synge with ioye and woundyrfull noyse.[69]

Likewise, though Rolle still interprets Ps. 38.4 as describing experiences of *fervor* familiar from his other writings, he does not simply translate his earlier gloss (quoted above). Instead, he now specifies that Ps. 38 is written in the voice of a "holy man," and he includes more references to truly ("verraly") feeling sensations of divinely granted heat:

> *My hert hetid within me, and in my þinkinge bren sall fyere*, þat is *my hert* verraly *hetide* with þe fire of Cristes lufe so þat my þoght was holy taken til þe ioy of God, *and in my þinkinge*, þat is in meditacioun of Criste and of heuen, *bren sall fire* of perfit luffe, so þat I fele þe brynyng in my herte. (f. 84[vab]; Bramley, 142–43)

Perhaps most revealing, Rolle's earlier hesitancy to gloss *solitudo* in Ps. 54.8 as describing the physical solitude of his eremitic lifestyle has disappeared, and his interpretation of the verse now presents a full-throated endorsement of his chosen way of life:

> *Lo I lenghed* fro ille men *fleand* þere liffe, þat I were not like þaim, *and I wonnede in only-stede* of þoght, whore none is with me bot Gode, whore is

rest in Gods luf, and no man lettes. In onely-sted a man may fynd his vertu and take tent til hymselfe, ffor only-sted is able for praynge, for gretynge, for þinkynge, for studiyng, and for spekynge tille his frende, and for brynand luffynge and wittynge of Gods priuety. (f. 79rb; Bramley, 195)

While "only-stede of þoght" preserves the *Latin Psalter*'s "solitudo mentis" (Bodley 861, f. 19va), the remainder of the gloss appears to refer to the more literal life of a hermit, with its *otium* affording time for prayer, study, and (ideally) mystical insight into divine privities. In all of these examples, then, Rolle finds new ways to read these psalms as describing his vision of the contemplative life, and as written to be recited by "a perfyt mane or womman" like himself.

At the same time as he finds more opportunities to read the biblical text in these overtly devotional terms, however, Rolle also adds more (and more detailed) accounts of the Psalter as the carefully crafted prophetic expression of its historical author, often written in David's own voice. Some of these discussions are translated directly from the *Magna glosatura*, such as his introduction to Ps. 86, where Rolle writes, "Þe Prophete, cytisyn of þe gostly cyte, as he had in hymselfe þoght thare-of, he brestes in voice and sayis … ."[70] In Ps. 13, in contrast, while the Lombard claims that the Psalmist is prophetically chastising the Jews after the resurrection, Rolle insists that "þe Prophett" is actually "blamande þaim þat giffes þaim to all þe lust and likyng of þaire bodys and þis werld, so þat þai hafe forgeten God and his domes."[71] That is, this psalm is meant to admonish the same lovers of the world who are so frequently the object of hermit's own scorn. These overt references to David's prophetic vision and moral teaching continue throughout the *English Psalter*, serving as constant reminders that (as he says at the beginning of Ps. 44) the author of the Psalms was a historical figure who foresaw "þe weddyng of Cryst and his spouse, Holykirke," and who was left, in the past, "ȝernand to cum in-till þis wedding."[72]

Various other details could be marshaled to demonstrate the heightened complexity of the *English Psalter* compared with Rolle's earlier commentary. While in the *Latin Psalter*, for example, he had tended to present only a single interpretive option for any given verse, the hermit now offers alternative readings, and he sometimes supplements what he takes to be the Lombard's literalism with "gastely" glosses of his own devising.[73] To some degree, certainly, the decision to add more material to this commentary must have been a function of language. While any readers of the *Latin Psalter* who wanted more exegesis could at least potentially turn to another commentary, including Rolle's ubiquitous source, there were simply no other texts like the *English Psalter*, and the hermit surely knew that what he provided in this work would be the only scholastic interpretation of the Psalms available in this vernacular. Just as important, though, is Rolle's evident confidence in his exegetical authority, made clear both in his more substantial discussions of his ecstatic experiences and in his handling of his scholastic source. All of this comes across clearly in the hermit's dazzling gloss on Ps. 26.11. (Here small capitals set off the initial Latin quotation of the verse, with its close translation given in roman type and subsequent quotations in italic.)

> CIRCUIUI ET IMMOLAUI IN TABERNACULO EIUS HOSTIAM UOCIFERACIONIS. CANTABO ET PSALMUM DICAM DOMINO. I vmeʒed and I offird in his tabernacle þe host of heghyng of voice. I sall synge and psalme I sall say to Lorde. *I vmeʒed*, that is I gedird in my þoght his beneficeʒ þat he has don to me, and vnkynd I was not, bot *I offird in his tabernakill*, þat is in holy kyirke, *þe host of heghing of voice*, þat is of gastly criynge and louyng in wondirfull ioye. Þat ioy and þat criyng is when a holy saule is fillid with Cristes luffe, þat makes þe þoght to ryse in-to þe soune of heuen, or þe soune of heuen liʒtes þere-in, and þan þat man may loue Gode in *heghynge of v[o]ice*. Alle þe clerkes in erthe may ne ymagyne it ne witte what it is bot þat haues it, and in þat *I sall synge* in delittabillte of contemplacioun. Þus is sayde in þe glose: *And I sall say psalme to Lorde*, þat is I sall shew gud dede to his honoure. (f. 56[vab]; Bramley, 96)

Much of this passage is borrowed and translated from the *Magna glosatura*: the circling as recalling the benefices given by God (272a: "omnia beneficia ... pertractavi"), the "tabernakill" as "holy kyirke" ("*in tabernaculo eius*, id est ecclesia toto orbe diffusa"), and even the vociferous offering as a kind of spiritual singing ("*vociferationis* vel iubilationis, id est laudis ineffabilis, ut deficiente sermone sola iubibilatio restet"). But Rolle adds his own account of the experience of heavenly song, including, again, contrary upward and downward motions (*risen*, *lighten*), and now insisting that this song must be experienced to be imagined. By singling out "clerkes," who presumably seek knowledge in texts, as those whose imaginations will fall short, Rolle may be indulging in a kind of anti-intellectualism, but this is undercut by his almost immediate citation of his own clerkly source, the "glose" or *Glosatura*. Book-learning, though insufficient on its own, is evidently an important part of the hermit's religious program.

The purpose of this citation is itself ambiguous. This is one of only two instances in the *English Psalter* where Rolle names the *Magna glosatura*, though for other psalms he makes use of the system of marginal citations evidently contained in his copy of the *Glosatura* to attribute readings to the patristic and early medieval authorities on which the Lombard drew.[74] This reference to the "glose" appears to indicate that Rolle's *Glosatura* lacked a citation for this particular interpretive phrase, but, of course, he evidently felt no need to draw attention to this fact in his earlier borrowings in the passage.[75] It would seem that this attribution serves, instead, primarily to divide Rolle's interpretation of most of the verse from his reading of its final phrase, *et psalmum dicam Domino*, and not because his source has shifted, but because his preferred interpretation of these words moves away from the focus on the contemplative life around which his treatment of the rest of the verse has cohered, pointing now to the need for good works, a robust and virtuous *vita activa*. That is, the citation acknowledges the seams in Rolle's commentary, indicating that, rather than trying to craft a single continuous and consistent reading of each psalm, he is compiling received glosses, quarried from the "hali doctures" and supplemented by his own interpretations. In his treatment of Ps. 26.11, then, Rolle presents himself as both an authoritative practitioner of the contemplative life, able to imagine heavenly song because he has heard it, and as a confident wielder of the Lombard's glosses, a solitary with ample time for the "studiyng" needed to gain familiarity with the interpretive tradition represented in this text.

The creation of the *English Psalter* was thus the result of (at least) a double impulse, at once supplying material for readers, in all likelihood female religious, who would otherwise have been unable to study biblical exegesis for themselves, and also meeting Rolle's apparent desire to reconsider and revise his earlier efforts at interpreting the Psalms. The *Psalter* continues Rolle's earlier project of, as it were, writing his idiosyncratic experiences of heat, sweetness, and song into the tradition of commentaries on the Psalter and at the same time authorizing those experiences by finding them as the meaning of the biblical text. But it also results in something wholly new, a translation of a biblical book together with a sustained English commentary drawn primarily from a source that was, as we have seen, still being used as a basic interpretive reference work within the universities.[76] The *English Psalter* opens that interpretive tradition to a broader readership, inviting less well-educated men and women to find material for study and models for their own contemplation in the Psalms. Without major English antecedents, this project could have taken any number of forms, and it is therefore especially significant that Rolle demanded an elaborate response from his audience, the careful weighing of multiple interpretive options and the consideration of the Psalmist's role in the crafting of his richly prophetic texts. It is significant, too, that Rolle chose to pair vernacular commentary with close translation, and to have his exegesis emerge from this translation, with the Latin included on the page as well. As we will see, this specific multilingual form proved to be incredibly influential, and along with his blending of learned and devotional priorities, it constitutes Rolle's major contribution to the interpretive history of the Psalms.[77] Neither simply a rendering of the Latin nor a vernacular gloss, this form necessarily carries out both of these functions at one and the same time, and it should be described in a way that reflects that duality, Rollean commentary-translation.

The School of Rolle

The clearest sign of the *English Psalter*'s innovative quality is the variety of responses it prompted in the second half of the fourteenth century, when a host of other writers extended, imitated, and elaborated on Rolle's project of making biblical exegesis available in the vernacular. In this regard, the hermit's most devoted readers were surely the team of revisers who methodically worked through the *Psalter*, refining Rolle's translations and rewriting his glosses in ways that indicate their Wycliffite sympathies.[78] These revisers also supplemented the *Psalter* with more material. While the hermit had included, after his treatment of Ps. 150, glossed translations of the six Old Testament canticles sung at Lauds on ferial days, as well as the *Magnificat* (Luke 1.46–55), recited daily at Vespers, the Wycliffite redactors added translations and commentaries treating five more Office texts: the *Benedicite* (Dan. 3.57–88), *Te Deum*, *Benedictus* (Luke 1.68–78), *Nunc dimittis* (Luke 2.29–32), and *Quicumque vult* or Ps.-Athanasian Creed.[79] This revised version of the *English Psalter* was then itself subject to further revision, apparently without reference to Rolle's original.[80]

Clearly, the Wycliffite revisers valued Rolle's work as an important precedent for biblical translation and vernacular commentary, but they seem to have been much more ambivalent about the place of his ecstatic experiences in this exegetical program. Though the opening promise of sweetness, heat, and heavenly song remains largely untouched in the revised prologue (I, 3), other references to Rolle's distinctive experiences are either minimized or, in some cases, metaphorized and made to support the revisers' more overtly pastoral commitments. Of the various vernacular glosses discussed above, for example, the claim that Ps. 26.6 describes the fantastic "lighting" of heavenly song into the soul is replaced with a more straightforward account of Christ's love causing "þe þouȝte to rise in-to þe soune of heuene, desiryng þat Goddes wille were fulfilled in erþe as it is in heuene" (I, 311; cf. Matth. 6.10), and though, in Ps. 38.4, the speaker's heart is still said to be "þurghly heted wiþ þe fier of Cristes loue," this burning is now glossed as a reference to "perfite charite, þurgh þe which I shal laste in his loue and in my neiȝebores" (II, 428). In both of these examples, the revisers preserve some material that can be construed as describing Rolle's experiences, but they back away from his most audacious claims, tempering these descriptions with gestures toward the active life. Elsewhere, Rolle's accounts of his experiences are excised completely. The hermit had read the inflamed heart of Ps. 72.21, for example, as another clear reference to the fire of divine love, translating and elaborating on material first developed in his *Latin Psalter*:

> *Quia inflammatum est cor meum* igne diuini amoris ita vt sentirem illud ardens et conuersum in flam[m]am, *et renes mei commutati sunt* id est mutata temporalium voluptate totus factus sum castus desiderio eternorum. (Bodley 861, f. 25[rb])

> *For my herte is enflaumed* with fiere of Cristes luffe, þat I file it brenand and turned in-til flawme, *and my neres are chaungid*, þat is, my fleschely lustes are chaunged in-till gostly delytes of haly luf, so þat my saule is mad all chaste in ȝernynge of heuen. (HM 148, f. 113va; Bramley, 261)

The revisers replace the bulk of this gloss with one focused on an idealized concern for one's fellow Christians, an imagined spiritual community which Fiona Somerset has identified as a major preoccupation of Wycliffite writers.[81] "Feiþful men," they maintain,

> may not þenke on þe goodenes of God, doon to his puple, ne on þe vnkyndenes of his creatures, but if þei inwardli sorowe in her *herte*, where-inne his loue as fier brenneþ, *and þe neeres* of hem *ben togyder-chaunged*, þat is, þe moost priuey þouȝtes þat letteþ grace to þe profit of commune helþe of Cristes chirche. A trewe louere chaungeþ in-to vertuous desire, þirstyng aftir grace, wherbi alle fleisheli lustes and veyn desires ben wasted wiþouten eny mynde to be punyshed. (II, 662–63)

Rolle's experience of burning love becomes a simile ("loue as fier brenneþ"), and though his typical interest in conversion from worldly love to love for God is preserved, this turning is now framed as necessary specifically to allow one to focus on the "commune helþe" of the Church. The experiences of contemplative ecstasy favored by Rolle are, for his revisers, simply less important than this love for other Christians, and at least some references to them should therefore be removed if vernacular commentary is to support the spiritual reforms they envision for the English Church.

These changes do not reflect any uncertainty about Rolle's authority, however, or about his claims of experiencing bodily heat or heavenly song, and the revisers are sometimes eager in their added glosses to cultivate a sense of Rolle's performance of the psalms. In his relatively brief discussion of Ps. 33.4, for example, glossing the Psalmist's command to magnify and exalt the name of the Lord, Rolle had claimed, "Þis he says of" (that is, on account of) "b[yrn]ynge of luffe: hegh we his name Iesu in hert and ded" (HM 148, f. 64rb; Bramley, 118). Certainly, compared with the passages discussed above, this invocation of *fervor amoris* is relatively restrained, but in this case, since he does not identify the psalm as spoken in the voice of a perfect or holy man, it would seem that Rolle believes David to have written it in response to his own sensations of burning love, similar to those experienced by the hermit.[82] Instead of eliminating this reference, the revisers elaborate on it, offering a fuller account of the *persona* that speaks here, as well as a fuller paraphrase of the material attributed to this voice.[83]

> Þis is þe uoyce of him þat brenneþ in perfite loue, desyring þat oþere were liȝtned wiþ þe same charite, seiyng, "Hiȝe we þe name of Iesu in oure herte, for it is blessed and uertuous abouen alle names, and þenke we þat we ben nouȝt of oureself . . . . Forþi preye we deuoutly to þat hiȝe holy name þat he reule oure þouȝte to þenk on him enterly, and oure wordes to looue him mekeli wiþoute pride, and oure werkes to serue him lastingly wiþoute veynglorye." (I, 368)

The speaker burning with perfect love is surely Rolle himself, a notion reinforced by the paraphrase's focus on his favored devotion to the Holy Name.[84] Indeed, with their pairing of this ecstatic experience and devotional interest, the revisers have created a much more fully defined, almost overdetermined *persona*, more like the identifications of psalms spoken in the voice of Christ than the generalized (and potentially appropriable) attributions to a "rightwise man" or "perfit man" discussed above. At the same time as the Wycliffite revisers seem to share Rolle's belief that he could indeed be an ideal speaker of the biblical text, however, they also restrict this imagined performance to an isolated gloss, and by crafting this distinctly Rollean *persona*, they could be seen as holding his claims to perfect love apart from the more pastorally minded concerns found in their other glosses. Their Rolle revels in his ecstatic experiences, and he even encourages others to cultivate the same heat, but many of the glosses in which he describes his experiences are removed, and by the end of this paraphrase even this Rollean speaker has arrived at a focus on the proper "werkes" of the active life. The hermit remains an authoritative figure in the revised *English Psalter*, then, and perhaps in part because that authority is already established, the revisers are free to build on his work and find other meanings in the biblical text.

While the Wycliffite revisers worked to produce new versions of the *English Psalter*, ones with glosses more closely reflecting their own priorities, other writers seized on the basic form developed in Rolle's commentary-translation, replicating the *Psalter*'s shift from Latin biblical text to close English translation to expansive English gloss, as well as the blurring of the commentator's voice with that of the biblical author. They thus present their writing as the possible meaning of one or more psalms, even as their works transform biblical commentary to create new kinds of vernacular religious literature. Compared with the Wycliffite revisers, these writers rarely demonstrate their direct dependence on Rolle's *Psalter* – in part because they were perfectly capable of generating their own translations of psalms, and in part because they drew on different sources and put forward their own interpretations – but, even if they were somehow unfamiliar with his widely circulating text, their focus on the Psalter and their adaptations of Rolle's commentary-translation form indicate at least their indirect dependence on the model he provides. Just as much as the revisers, then, these more experimental writers should be considered part of the school of Rolle.

Creative engagement with the commentary-translation form can readily be seen in the work known as *Qui Habitat*, an extensive treatment of Ps. 90 tentatively attributed to Walter Hilton (d. 1396).[85] While he agrees with the hermit's general understanding of the text, in which (Rolle says) the Psalmist describes the proper religious life to a "man þat lastis in Godes luffe" and "þat has al his hope sett in God" (HM 148, ff. 138ra and 137rb; Bramley, 332 and 330), Hilton transforms this basic idea into an expansive vision of religious progress, from a person's initial resolution to "forsakeþ himself and secheþ help of God" (a decision which, for Hilton, apparently entails entry into some form of vowed religion), to the attainment of contemplative rapture, with "ure Lord ... wonderfulliche openyng þe siȝt of þi soule in-to biholdyng of him, tenderliche touchinge þe affeccion of þi soule þorw swetnes of his loue, schewyng to þe in gret reuerence þe siȝt of his priuitees" (2, 14). Hilton, in other words, uses the commentary-translation form to present a narrative of spiritual development abbreviating what he offers, much more fully, in Book Two of the

Scale of Perfection.[86] In this progressive narrative, Hilton's quotations and translations of the psalm's verses have less of an indexical function – that is, it seems unlikely that a reader would consult this work to find how Hilton interprets a single verse in isolation – and they instead come to mark new stages in the development he seeks to describe. After devoting his treatment of Ps. 90.5-7, for example, to the temptations assaulting a would-be contemplative, Hilton turns to describe the experiences awaiting those who persevere in their devotions, with the move to a new verse marking this pivot in his discussion (here with the close translation and subsequent lemma in italic):

> ȝif þou stonde stiflich in þi purpos and trist fulliche in help of þe hiȝest . . . , with þe scheld of soþfastnes for þi defense, alle heore temptacions, as mony as þer ben on boþe sydes of þe, schal falle from þe, and þin enemy schal not neiȝe þe. VERUMPTAMEN OCULIS TUIS CONSIDERABIS ET RETRIBUCIONEM PECCATORUM VIDEBIS. *Soþliche with þin eȝen þou schal be-holden, and þe ȝeldyng of synnes þou schalt sen.* Whon þou art turned from loue of þe world to þe loue of God and, þorw long exercise in preying and þenkyng on God, þou felest þi concience muche i-clansed . . . from . . . þi fleschlich desyres, þat þou felest hem lasse miȝti þen þei ware, þen schalt þou be-holden with þin eiȝe. What? Soþly, God. (25–26)

To read Ps. 90 with Hilton is thus to move through the different experiences, the perils and rewards, that await an aspiring contemplative, with the persistent future tense – in psalm and commentary – suggesting that Hilton's "louere of God" is at the earliest of the stages he describes (36). Hilton finds justification for this model of religious development by identifying it as the meaning of the psalm, an interpretive claim enabled by his adaptation of the commentary-translation form.

A very different kind of transformation was undertaken by Richard Maidstone OCarm (d. 1396), who evokes the features of the Rollean form in his versification of the seven Penitential Psalms, rendered as a series of eight-line tetrameter stanzas.[87] For each verse of these psalms, the Oxford-trained Maidstone first quotes the Latin, presents his close translation in two to four lines, and then devotes the remainder of the stanza to its exposition (see Fig. 9).[88] Like Rolle, who generally presents these psalms as written in "þe voice of hym þat dos penaunce for hys synne" (HM 148, f. 83ra; Bramley, 138), Maidstone suggests that his stanzas are by and large meant to serve as prayers that can be taken on and performed by any penitent reader, what Annie Sutherland describes as the "direct devotional appropriation of the penitential voice of the Psalmist," resulting in an "intercessory monologue."[89] In this regard, Maidstone's treatment of Ps. 31.4 is typical:

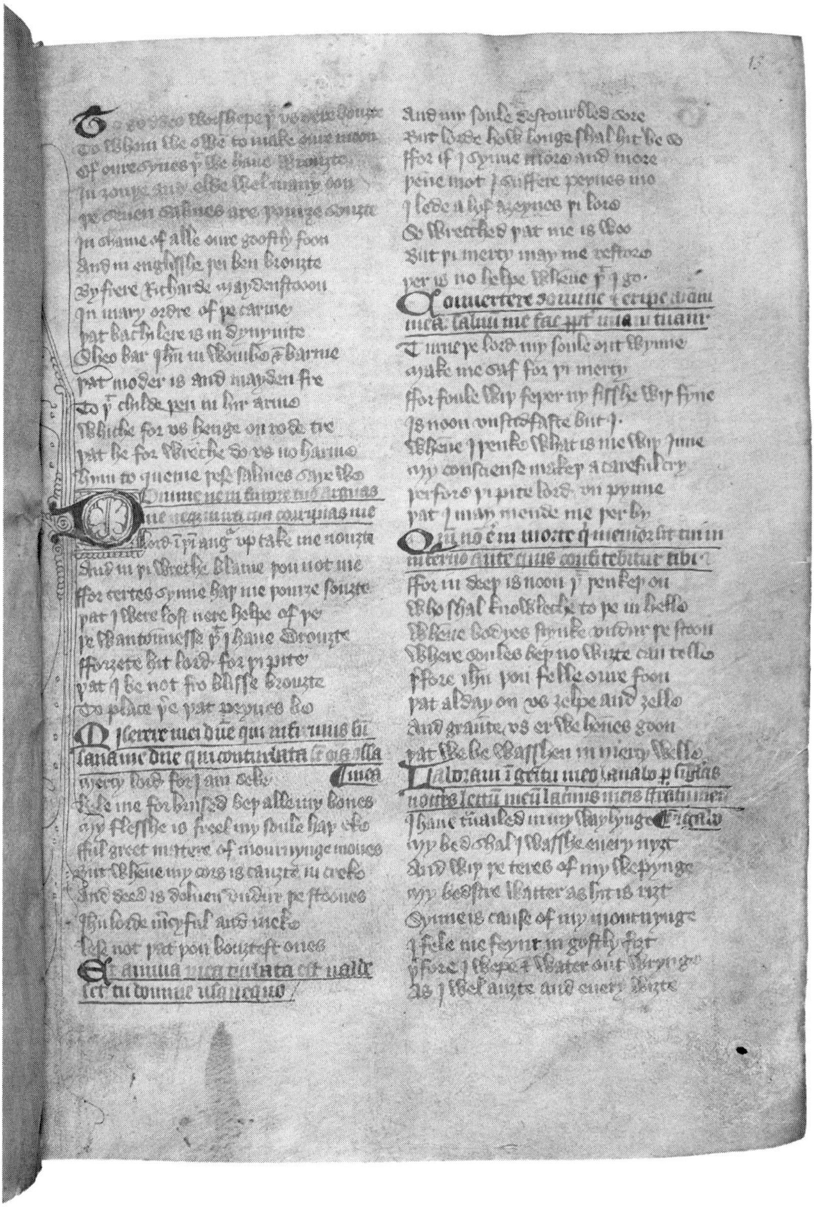

Figure 9   BodL MS Rawl. A. 389, f. 13ʳ.

> QUONIAM DIE AC NOCTE GRAUATA EST SUPER ME MANUS TUA:
> CONUERSUS SUM IN ERUMPNA MEA, DUM CONFIGITUR SPINA.
> For boþ day and nyȝt also
> On me þi honde liþ heuyly,
> And I am turned in my woo,
> Whil þorn it prickeþ greuously.
> Þer prickeþ me perelouse þornes two,
> Of synne and payne, þis fele wel I!
> Þerfore, Lorde, whil it is so,
> I putte me holly in þi mercy. (113–20)

The first four lines of the stanza translate the quoted Latin, with only two words (*also* and *heuyly*) added for the sake of the meter and rhyme, and while the rhyme scheme reinforces the sense of the English material as a single coherent unit, the sentence break helps to locate the shift between translation and gloss. Maidstone is able to do only so much in four lines of commentary, and here he focuses on the Psalmist's metaphorical thorn (*spina*), defining it as sin and pain (presumably, *culpa* and *poena*), before exemplifying the plea for divine mercy that should follow meditation on these failings. With its persistent first-person pronoun, this example clearly supports Sutherland's claim, but at times Maidstone's handling of psalmic voice is more elaborate than her description would suggest. Rendering Ps. 101.4, for example, he writes,

> QUIA DEFECERUNT SICUT FUMUS DIES MEI,
> ET OSSA MEA SICUT CREMIUM ARUERUNT.
> For my lyfdayes like þe smoke
> Han fayled and awaywarde hyed,
> My boones beþ dryed and al þourȝe soke
> Like a þing þat is forfryed.
> Wel miȝt Crist þis word haue spoke,
> Þat on þe cros was don and dryed,
> For whenne his blessed breste was broke
> For drouȝte and þirste ful loude he cryed. (569–76)

Even as the reference to "þis word" reinforces a sense of the first four lines as a discrete unit within the stanza, the expository section overtly identifies this verse as spoken in the voice of Christ, apparently at the crucifixion.[90] Maidstone continues to read Ps. 101.5–12 in this voice, and yet, while his focus remains on the crucifixion, it is not always clear that this speaker is actually imagined on the cross. Glossing the next verse, for example, Maidstone's Christ explains, "I sawe my cosyn Ion mournyng, / I saw my modur in swonyng synk," concluding that "I wepte as childe of ȝeres ȝing / On þis myscheef whenne I gan þinke" (587–88, 591–92). As with the previous stanza's "was don and dryed," the tense of these lines suggests a speaker recalling his experience of the crucifixion, thus creating a kind of devotional tableau on which Maidstone's reader, together with Christ as speaker, is encouraged to look. As Maidstone later writes, "vche man is þe" (that is, to Christ) "þe leuer / Þat þis matere haþ wel in mynde" (647–48). Though his exposition can be somewhat simplistic, then, by focusing on the different possibilities of psalmic voicing, Maidstone turns the commentary-translation form into poetry that can, at times, demand a complex and considered response.

Further, as the examples from his treatment of Ps. 101 should already suggest, Christ and the generalized penitent are not the only ones whose voices can be heard in Maidstone's poem. Phrases addressing the reader and encouraging him or her to have "þis matere ... wel in mynde," and identifying verses as appropriately spoken by Christ on the cross – that is, phrases that provide instruction on the interpretation and, more generally, proper use of the poem – could be understood as written in a third voice, perhaps that of Maidstone himself, especially in manuscripts that name him as responsible for translating the psalms: "... in Englisshe þei ben brouȝte / By frere Richarde Maydenstoon."[91] More precisely, though, since they appear exclusively in expository passages and (as we have seen) comment on the psalm text as a distinct object, a lemma, it is better to consider such passages as written in the voice of a commentator, an authoritative guide to the biblical text and its meaning. A similar voice may be found in other works in the school of Rolle, with these different writers most frequently adopting this exegetical pose to present themselves as intermediaries, standing between a reader of the vernacular and a large body of specialist knowledge otherwise preserved in Latin. In the revised *English Psalter*, for example, this intermediating position is clear when the commentators describe material as what "clerkis seyn," most frequently in the course of providing details of the natural world, animals, and heavenly bodies typically found in scholastic encyclopedias.[92] The same reference to what "clerkes calle" natural phenomena occurs at one point in Maidstone's poem (748). In *Qui Habitat*, in contrast, the material available to the commentator and provided (or denied) to his anglophone audience is not Latin scholarship but rather – in a way that is still in keeping with Rolle's *Psalter* – accounts of contemplative ecstasy, as when Hilton avers that "what maner beholdyng a louere of God schal haue in God, mai I not telle þe, but þis I sigge ... ." Even here, though, the ability to interpret Scripture is at stake, since, whatever he refuses to tell the would-be contemplative, Hilton promises that someone who "haþ his biholdyng with swetnes of loue in gostly good" will have "þe wordes of Holi Writ... opened to his siȝt, boþe morali and mistili."[93] In addition to offering limited descriptions of the experiences that await his readers, then, in this instance Hilton could be seen as affirming his own status as a "louere of God," familiar with this kind of "beholdyng" from his own experience and thus enabled to interpret the words of the biblical text.

As these examples indicate, the *English Psalter* did more than model the handling of translation and exposition relative to scriptural Latin, what I have called the Rollean commentary-translation form. It also offered a way for writers to position themselves in relation to the authority of the biblical text, and to present their own writings as authoritative insofar as they both convey the meaning of that text and, in doing so, draw on and mediate a specialized and typically Latinate body of knowledge. As this formulation should suggest, the two – the form and the authorization of vernacular literary activity – are necessarily related, with the commentator's English glosses following from, and depending on, the biblical Latin and its sometimes awkwardly close translation. These writers were eager to explore the potential of Rollean commentary-translation, to find new ways to adapt and build on the precedent of the hermit's work, and, as Maidstone's deployment of psalmic and exegetical voices makes especially clear, their efforts seem primarily to reflect a desire to supply material for devotional reading that, as in the *English Psalter*, required sophisticated intellectual engagement with the text and interpretation of the Psalms. The different works in the exegetical school of Rolle point to the hermit's increasingly widespread appeal, and with it his considerable authority, in the decades following his death. The nature of that authority, the contours of his reputation as an author and commentator, can be seen more clearly by considering texts that quote his works and cite him by name.

Rolle in Oxford, Again

Though he had purportedly fled its sinful snares after only a brief period of study, Oxford proved to be an important center for the dissemination of Rolle's writings and the promotion of what Vincent Gillespie has called his "textual cult."[94] As Anne Hudson notes, it was most likely in the university that the Wycliffite revisers undertook their work on the *English Psalter*, and other evidence points to the ready availability of a clutch of exemplars supporting the copying of his Latin, including the *Latin Psalter*, in the final decades of the fourteenth century and into the fifteenth.[95]

Further, beyond simply reading and copying his texts, Oxford writers began to treat Rolle as an *auctor*, as someone whose weighty opinions could be invoked in support of their arguments and, importantly, as an authoritative interpreter of the Psalms.

It is in this authoritative role that the hermit's name appears in the writings of Richard Ullerston (d. 1423), a career theologian associated with Queen's College, Oxford, from 1391 until his retirement in 1416.[96] One of his citations of Rolle has already been quoted, with Ullerston pointing to the precedent of the *English Psalter* to support his argument in favor of the translation of Scripture into the vernacular.[97] Later in the same *determinatio*, Ullerston turns to Rolle in an attempt to characterize churchmen who argue against the validity of an English Bible, a passage included in the Wycliffite translation of Ullerston's work:

> Sed eo deterius eis contingit, quod bene notat Ricardus Hampole super isto uersu Ps. 118[.43], *Ne aufferas de ore meo uerbum ueritatis vsquequaque*, ubi sic scribit: Nonnulli sunt qui pro Deo uolunt sustinere uerbum falsitatis, sciencioribus et melioribus credere nolentes, similes amicis Iob, quia cum Deum deffendere nitebantur, offenderunt. Tales inquit si occidantur, quamuis miracula faciant, sunt tamen (ut uulgus dicit) fetentes martires. Hec Ricardus.

> But wel touchiþ þis holi man Richard Hampol suche men, expownyng þis tixte, *Ne auferas de ore meo verbum veritatis vsquequaque*, þer he seiþ þus: Þer ben not fewe but many þat wolen sustene a worde of falsenes for God, not willing to beleue to konynge and better þan þei ben. Þei ben liche to þe frendes of Iob, þat wiles þei enforsiden hem to defende God þei offendeden greuosly in hym. And þouȝ suche ben slayne and don myracles, þei neuerþeles ben stynkyng martirs.[98]

Here it is not Rolle's ability as a translator but rather his attack on those who have only the outward appearance of piety and refuse to defer to the judgments of "the more knowledgeable and better" members of the Church, presumably the spiritual elite like himself, that leads Ullerston to quote from the *Latin Psalter*.[99] A similar view of Rolle as an authoritative critic of common spiritual shortcomings appears in Ullerston's defense of clerical endowment, the *Defensorium Dotationis Ecclesiae*, though in this case he names and quotes from the hermit's *Emendatio Vitae*.[100]

> Vide quid dicat Ricardus Hampol, dictus Heremita, in libello suo qui intitulatur *De emendacione vite* seu *Regula viuendi*, capitulo de paupertate, vbi ad propositum ita scribit: Non inquit omnes qui sua derelinquunt Christum sequuntur, nam nonnulli sunt peiores post desercionem quam ante fuerunt.[101]

> See what Richard Hampole, called the Hermit, says in his little book called *Emendatio Vitae* or the *Rule of Living*, in the chapter on poverty, where he writes: Not all who forsake their possessions follow Christ, for more than a few are worse after that forsaking than they were before.

Again, Ullerston turns to Rolle for his ability to identify those who properly "follow Christ," and to distinguish them from those who are only feigning true devotion. In his two major early works, then, both originating in university lectures given in 1401, Ullerston presents Rolle as an authority on ideal religious living, and he appears especially drawn to the hermit's often acerbic – and perhaps folksy ("ut uulgus dicit") – attacks on the moral failures he sees in the world around him.[102]

A much more elaborate engagement with Rolle's writings appears in Ullerston's final work, a commentary on the ferial canticles based on lectures given (according to its colophon) at Oxford in 1415.[103] Of course, it is unlikely that Ullerston devoted a whole course of lectures to six canticles, and instead he seems to have glossed them, as Rolle had, after treating the Psalter in its entirety. So much is suggested in his commentary's brief preface, which begins:

> Finita vtcumque exposicione Psalterii Dauitici, superest per Dei graciam aggredi exposicionem breuem eorum que dicuntur cantica, que nostro Psalterio vsuali sunt annexa. Quod quidem opus eo difficilius est assumere quo pauci hec cantica ad sensum litteralem exposuerunt, ad quem sensum intendimus ea exponere modo quo Psalterium exposuimus. Et quia compositor Nicholaus, quem doctorem de Lira appellamus, hec omnia ad litteram exponit iuxta sensum a Domino sibi attributum, hinc est quod sue exposicioni intendo ut plurimum inniti in hoc opere.[104]

> Having finished an exposition of the Davidic Psalter, it remains through the grace of God to attempt a brief exposition of what are called the canticles, which are typically appended to our Psalter. This task is harder to undertake, since few people have expounded these canticles according to their literal sense, and it is according to this sense that we intend to expound them, as we have expounded the Psalter. And since the author Nicholas, whom we call the doctor of Lyre, expounds all of them literally, according to the sense assigned to them by the Lord, I therefore intend, like most people, to depend upon his exposition in this work.

Ullerston claims to have expounded the Psalms, but in each of its surviving manuscripts his work is preceded instead by the Psalter commentary of an older contemporary, Peter of Herentals oPraem (d. 1391).[105] In all likelihood, Ullerston adhered to the increasingly common practice of lecturing *secundum alium*, drawing his lectures on the Psalms from

Herentals's copious assemblage of patristic and earlier medieval sources, and he therefore did not produce a Psalter commentary of his own.[106] Herentals had not glossed the ferial canticles, however, and Ullerston therefore had to consult other sources for interpretations of these texts, resulting in one or more lectures that were subsequently published as a discrete commentary. In his preface, Ullerston points to Lyre as his major authority, but elsewhere he invokes Rolle. He ends his gloss on Deut. 32.1–43, for example, with what amounts to an advertisement for, presumably, the *Latin Psalter:* "Cui vero placet moralis instruccio huius cantici, videat exposicionem venerabilis viri Ricardi Hampollis, qui eleganter exposuit ista cantica" (f. 215[ra]: "He who desires the moral instruction of this canticle, let him see the exposition of that venerable man, Richard Hampole, who has elegantly expounded these canticles"). A similar citation appears at the end of his gloss on Ex. 15.1–19, where he notes that Rolle has interpreted the text brilliantly (*luculenter*) according to its moral sense.[107] Since he claims to have limited his glosses to the literal sense of the canticles, Ullerston must point elsewhere for a reading that focuses on their moral teaching, and, as in his earlier writings, he continues to treat Rolle as an authority on this topic.

While this fulsome praise for Rolle's moral teaching has led Jeremy Catto to suggest that Ullerston intended his commentary as "a literal companion to [Rolle's] moral exposition," other references to Rolle reflect a much less straightforward arrangement.[108] Even in his treatment of Deut. 32, Ullerston draws on the *Latin Psalter* to furnish readings he presents as comparable to Lyre's postil, apparently offering an interpretation of the biblical text according to its literal sense. He gives three ways of reading Deut. 32.6, for example, glossing the incredulous question Moses poses to the "wicked and perverse generation" named in the previous verse:

> *Heccine* questio *reddis,* vi[c]issitudinem per oppositum, tu *popule stulte,* credens vtile quod non est, *et insipiens,* non cognoscens vtilitatem vbi est? Sic exponit Nicholaus. Vel sic: O *popule stulte,* qui non attendis in quantis malis es, *et insipiens,* qui non precaues in futurum. Sic enim exponit Ricardus. Vel sic: O *popule stulte,* qui te extollis secundum propriam voluntatem, licet scias (aut scire debeas) quod Deus contrarium diffiniuit, *et insipiens,* qui non sapis ea quae Dei sunt aut in lege eius sunt sanccita. (f. 211[vab])

> *Is this* the question *you return,* i.e., vicissitude for its opposite, you *foolish people,* believing to be useful what is not so, *and you senseless people,* not recognizing usefulness where it does exist? Thus Nicholas expounds it. Or

thus: Oh *foolish people*, who pay no attention to how wicked you are, *and senseless people*, who do not prepare yourselves for the future. For thus Richard expounds it. Or thus: Oh *foolish people*, who extol yourselves according to your own will, even though you know (or you ought to know!) that God has ordained to the contrary, *and senseless people*, who do not understand the things of God or what has been decreed in his law.

Ullerston draws the first of these interpretive options from Lyre and the second from the *Latin Psalter*, while the third is apparently original to his commentary.[109] Though he again turns to Rolle for his condemnation of worldly wickedness, Ullerston presents this criticism as a potential reading of the verse's literal meaning, in line with the larger hermeneutic priorities governing his commentary. Indeed, a bit later in his gloss on this canticle, at Deut. 32.33, Ullerston provides only one way of reading the text, a gloss he borrows from the *Latin Psalter* and attributes to Rolle: "*Venenum aspidum insanabile*, quia, vt dicit Ricardus, maliciam incorrigibilem in se retinent ne salutis medicinam recipiant et si quandoque corripiuntur deteriores fi[u]nt" (f. 214[ra]: "*The incurable venom of asps*, for, as Richard says, they keep incorrigible wickedness within themselves even when they receive the medicine of salvation, and if they are ever corrected, they simply become worse").[110] Certainly, this condemnation of those who refuse the benefit of spiritual medicine appears to be more moral instruction, but Ullerston's presentation of it in isolation, without any other interpretive options, suggests that this verse presents an instance of literal moralism, that it is (though he does not use this language himself) tropological according to its literal sense.[111] However they appeared in the context of the *Latin Psalter*, Ullerston is thus able to offer these glosses as fitting in his avowedly literalistic project, and the positioning of the hermit's work alongside Lyre's literal postil reflects a high estimation of his authority as an interpreter of Scripture.[112]

Though he names only Lyre at the start of his commentary, then, Ullerston appears to have had regular recourse to Rolle's *Latin Psalter* as he prepared his work on the canticles, and though the hermit's moral teachings sometimes fell outside the purview of his own gloss, at least some were judged suitable for the scholastic classroom. One citation of Rolle in Ullerston's commentary, however, cannot be explained as a reference to the *Latin Psalter*. Toward the beginning of the song of Anna, I Reg. 2.1–10, when the biblical author praises the "God of all knowledge," to whom all thoughts (*cogitationes*) are prepared, Ullerston writes,

> Vt enim notat hic Ricardus, quinque sunt que reperiuntur in homine, videlicet cogitacio et affeccio, intencio, opus et locucio. Quapropter inquit sit cogitacio sancta, affeccio munda, intencio recta, opus iustum, et locucio moderata. (f. 208rb)
>
> As Richard notes here, five things are to be found in a person, i.e., cogitation and affection, intention, work, and speech. And so, he says, cogitation should be holy, affection clean, intention upright, work just, and speech moderate.

Like a citation *ad loc.*, the specification that Rolle provides this definition *hic* (here) indicates that Ullerston is quoting from his gloss on this particular verse, but nothing like this discussion appears at this point in the *Latin Psalter*.[113] Instead, Ullerston has translated this passage from the *English Psalter*, where Rolle writes, "Fife thingis are fundyn in a man: þoght, affeccioune, entent, werke, and speche. Þe þoght be holy, þe affeccioune clene, þe entent right, þe werke rightwis, þe speche atempre."[114] Intriguingly, then, though his translation of the gloss obscures this difference, Ullerston apparently compared the treatment of the ferial canticles in the *Latin Psalter* with the fuller exposition offered in the *English Psalter*, and here he draws on that later work for what he presents as part of his literal exposition. In light of this borrowing, it becomes much harder to know which of Rolle's commentaries Ullerston had in mind when he enjoined his readers to turn to the hermit for moral instruction, and it even seems possible that he considered the two *Psalters* as part of a single interpretive project, recognizing the vernacular work as a revision of the Latin.

For Ullerston, then, Rolle is an authority on the proper religious life and the many ways lovers of the world have persistently failed to meet this moral standard. Writing with elegance (*eleganter*) and rhetorical brilliance (*luculenter*) in both Latin and English, Rolle offers commentaries that are sometimes moralizing supplements to the standard source of scholastic literalism, Lyre's postils, and sometimes persuasive accounts of the biblical text's literal sense. In this regard, it is significant that in writing his commentary Ullerston does not turn to Rolle's other works, such as *Emendatio* or *Contra Amatores Mundi*, in which the hermit expresses similar views on the subject of worldly immorality. It is, at least in part, because Rolle expresses these views in the course of writing biblical commentaries, identifying them as the meaning of the sacred text, that Ullerston is able to incorporate them so readily into his own scholastic project. Rolle is a moral authority, therefore, describing his own form of living, but he produces texts that resemble the works of university writers, sharing their form and at least some of their hermeneutic commitments even as he develops them in new ways. The hermit returns to Oxford as both an elite practitioner of the contemplative life and an authoritative exegete.

That is, as we have seen, the writerly pose that Rolle cultivates in his commentaries. He insists that he is a mere *compilator* of authoritative exegesis, a mode of scholastic authorship that would put his *Latin* and *English Psalters* on a level with the assembly of patristic material in the *Magna glosatura* or, for that matter, in Herentals's Psalter commentary, printed in 1480 with the accurately descriptive title *Collectarius super librum Psalmorum*. And by adapting some of the Lombard's general interpretive strategies, especially his understanding of the composition of psalms in distinct and sometimes prophetic *personae*, Rolle repeats and develops hermeneutic categories that continued to be explored in scholastic exegesis.[115] He wields patristic glosses as easily as any other late medieval commentator, and he assembles this material in ways that reflect common scholastic understandings of the Psalter. At the same time, when he is not compiling material from the *Glosatura*, Rolle devises glosses that describe, sometimes in striking detail, his own ideas and experiences of perfect contemplation, and especially the ecstatic sensations of heat, sweetness, and heavenly song enjoyed by true lovers of God, like himself. Introducing both of his Psalter commentaries, Rolle holds out these experiences as the goal toward which his readers should strive by devoutly (*devote, deuouteli*) attending to the details of the biblical text. To put it another way, Rolle presents his exegesis as material for ruminative reading, with this careful parsing of the text – its figurative language and its various *personae* – meant for those who seek (as he says elsewhere) "to studie and rede in Holy Scripture" specifically in order "to come to the love of God and to have a love brennyng in-to hevenly blisses."[116]

By rewriting scholastic exegesis to serve the needs of devotional reading, Rolle expands the potential audience of commentary beyond that of the academic authors discussed in the previous chapters, and, crucially, his understanding of who should be pursuing this program of devout "studie" includes aspiring contemplatives with limited or no knowledge of Latin. His decision to revise his *Latin Psalter* in English can therefore be seen as an almost natural extension of his larger experiment in the interpretation of the Psalms. Certainly, Rolle was not the only early fourteenth-century English author to seek a broader audience for the modes of writing cultivated within the universities. In this regard, his work on the Psalter bears comparison with Robert Holcot's wildly popular commentaries on

Wisdom and Ecclesiasticus, or Thomas Ringstead's companion piece on Proverbs, as well as, a bit further afield, Thomas Bradwardine's *De causa Dei contra Pelagium*, with which Rolle's *De amore Dei contra amatores mundi* shares a titular allusion.[117] While the works of Holcot, Ringstead, and Bradwardine at least began as university lectures, however, Rolle wrote as a religious solitary and elite practitioner of the contemplative life, and at the same time as his works draw on the interpretive resources of scholastic exegesis and engage with some of their priorities, they are also clearly written from outside the university and aimed at readers with, at most, a limited university training, comparable to the hermit's. Though Ullerston's use of the *Latin* and *English Psalters* reveal that these works were eventually brought into the scholastic classroom and regarded as, at least obliquely, part of the same interpretive tradition as Lyre's postils, such treatment came only *after* the *English Psalter* had been established, outside Oxford, as an important source and model for devotional literature. This move epitomizes what Ian Doyle termed "vernacular theology," the development of trends and priorities in religious writing outside of the Latinate discourses of the university, and their eventual influence on (or appropriation by) university writers.[118] This more demotic and devotional view of commentary is certainly present in the *Latin Psalter*, but as the examples discussed above have indicated and as the next chapter will further reveal, it was especially through the *English Psalter* and its commentary-translation form that Rolle came to shape ideas of biblical exegesis in later medieval England.

This blend of devotional and scholastic commitments seems to have informed, finally, the work of the scribe and illuminator of BL Add. 37049, with whose portrait of the hermit this chapter began (see above, Fig. 6). This image of Rolle appears as part of the Middle English *Desert of Religion*, and related portraits are included at the same point in two other extant copies of the poem.[119] In one, BL MS Cotton Faustina B. vi (part 2), f. 8^v, Rolle is similarly presented with the Holy Name on his chest and a book on his lap, while angels gather above him singing their heavenly *Sanctus* (Fig. 10). Here, however, Rolle's white habit and tonsure suggest a monastic identity, similar to the figure in BodL MS Eng. Poet. a. 1, f. 265^{rc}, which Wendy Scase has tentatively identified as another attempt to depict the hermit.[120] The figure in Faustina is labeled "Richarde Heremite," and, though the verses surrounding him are not taken from one of Rolle's poems, they nevertheless borrow a phrase from the authentic lyric included in Add. 37049 (emphasis added):

Figure 10   BL MS Cotton Faustina B. VI (part 2), f. 8ᵛ.

A solitari here, hermite life I lede,
For Ihesu loue so dere, all flescli lufe I flede,
Þat gastili comforthe dere, *þat in breste brede*,
Might me a thowsand zeere, in heuenly strenghe haue stedd.

These verses, identifying the figure as "a solitari," are repeated in a third copy of the *Desert*, BL MS Stowe 39, f. 16ᵛ, but rather than striking the pose of a contemplative reader, this figure is seated at a writing desk with a

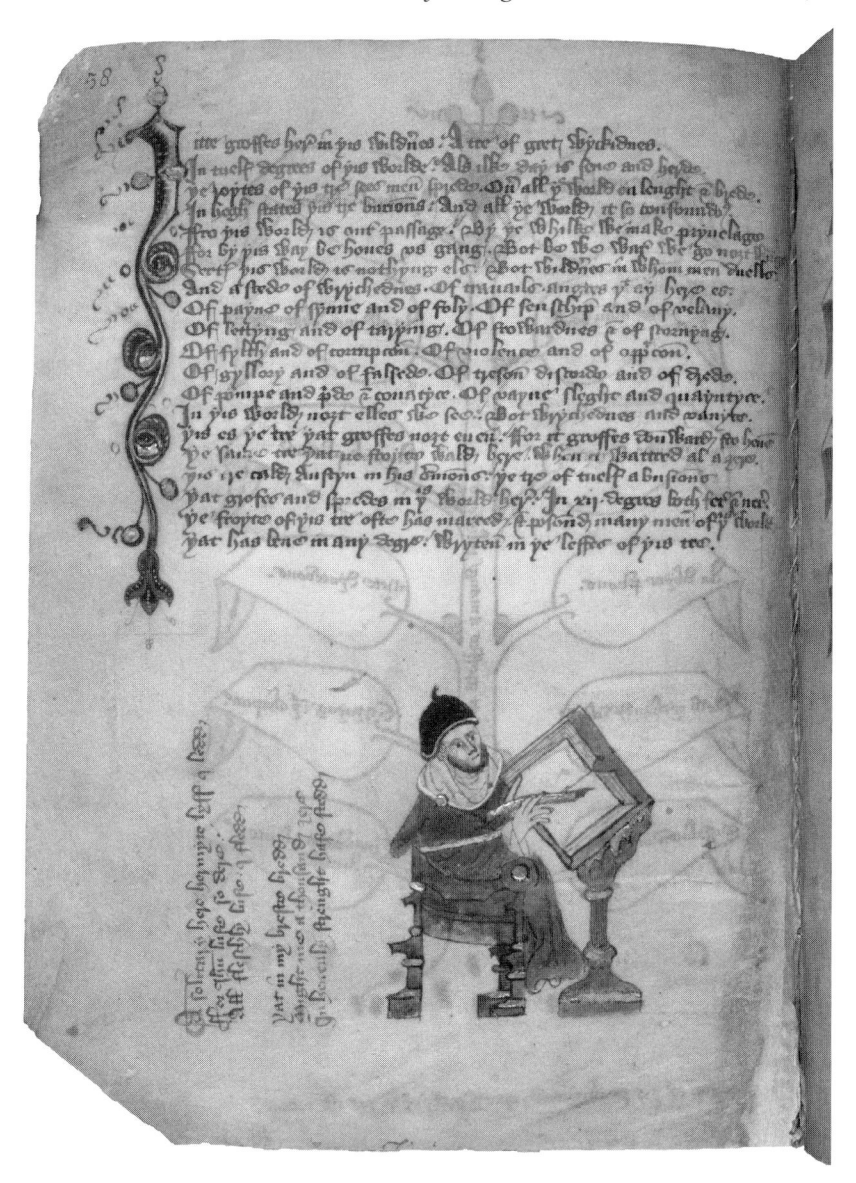

Figure 11   BL MS Stowe 39, f. 16ᵛ.

stylus in his hand, an image more typically associated with university masters (Fig. 11).[121] While this could be an attempt to present the hermit (unnamed here) in a more scholastic guise, other details of Stowe's execution suggest that instructions on the arrangement of the text and its program of illuminations reached the scribe and artist in a confused or ambiguous form, and it is possible that a direction to depict a *solitarius* was mistakenly read as describing a *scholaris*.[122] Regardless, the similarities between the Faustina and Additional portraits make it clear that these two copies depended on a common exemplar, but the scribal artist responsible for the Additional portrait apparently tailored his image to fit his understanding of the hermit. Perhaps because he recognized the allusion in the Faustina/Stowe verses, for example, the Additional scribe replaces that poem with a selection from Rolle's authentic lyrics ("I syt and synge of luf-langyng ..."), copied elsewhere in the manuscript, and he also moves the hermit indoors, potentially evoking the chapel in which, as he writes in *Incendium*, he first heard heavenly song.[123] Likewise, the scribal artist replaces Faustina's tonsure with the same sort of scholar's cap as depicted by the apparently confused artist of Stowe.[124] That is, the Additional scribe/artist presents Rolle as dressed, at least in part, like a university master. With this minor detail, he appears to nod toward the crucial role of book-learning in Rolle's authorial program, reflecting a recognition of the hermit's indebtedness to the discourses of the schools even as he celebrates his ecstatic experiences of contemplation.

CHAPTER 4

Moral Experiments: Middle English Matthew Commentaries

> And certis ȝe schal not be excused be vnkunnynge of Goddis lawe, for ȝe myȝten knowe it ȝif ȝe wolden axe it of God by tru deuocion and good lyuynge, bi þe kyndely resoun þat God haþ writen in ȝoure soulis. Also, ȝif ȝe wolden seke to be tauȝte of trwe prestis dredynge God as bisily as ȝe seken worldely goodis of worldly pepel. Wherfore eche Cristen man and womman besi hem wiþ alle her myȝtis to lerne and kepe Goddis comandementis, and ocupie þei her wittes boþe bodily and gostly in þinkynge, lernynge, and spekynge Cristis gloriose gospel, for þerynne is al counfort and sekernesse to come to þe blysse of heuene.[1]

This vision of lay biblicism appears in the tenth of the *Twelve Cambridge Tracts*, a collection of short texts preserved in CUL MS Ii.6.26, here ff. 50[v]–51[r]. The compiler of these *Tracts* was, in Anne Hudson's phrase, "anxious to assemble as many documents to support the legitimacy of vernacular Scriptures as possible," a concern indicated by some of the descriptive titles he apparently composed to head individual texts: e.g., *Tract* ii: "Þis preueþ þat þei ben blessed þat louen Goddis lawe in þere owen langage," and *Tract* iv: "Anoþer sentens comendynge þe gospel in our moder-tunge."[2] Yet, as Mary Dove observes, though they all support a model of lay piety centered on biblical teaching, eight of the twelve do *not* directly advocate scriptural translation.[3] *Tract* x falls into this latter category: the claim that "eche Cristen man and womman" should learn the gospel through the teaching of "trwe prestis" does not require biblical translations, though such texts would presumably aid in that teaching. The pedagogical scene imagined here thus resembles the fourth of six stages of scriptural study described in *The Holi Prophete Dauid*, a contemporary tract not included in Ii.6.26, according to which "Cristene men shulden ... enquere mekeli of euery lerned man, and speciali of wel-wellid men and weel-lyuynge, þe trewe vndirstondyng of Hooli Writ."[4] In these accounts, access to biblical material, whether in Latin or English, is mediated through the figure of the learned teacher.

133

Like many (if not all) of the other texts in this collection, *Tract* x has been taken from a preexisting source, and in its other manuscript setting the notion of lay biblical study evoked by this passage shifts significantly.[5] The compiler of the *Cambridge Tracts* has excerpted this text from the epilogue to the longer version of the vernacular Wycliffite commentary on Matthew, part of the group of texts known collectively as the *Glossed Gospels*.[6] As part of this epilogue, though they do not specifically describe the reading of exegetical material, or even of Scripture, these references to "lern[ynge] and kep[ynge] Goddis comandementis" and to "þinkynge, lernynge, and spekynge Cristis gloriose gospel" would seem necessarily to refer back to the commentary that they follow. The approach to biblical material imagined in this passage would now appear to have more in common with the fifth and sixth stages of study described in *The Holi Prophete*: "The fifþe tyme, rede þei besili þe texte of þe Newe Testament.... The sixte tyme, þei shulden see and studie þe trewe and opyn exposicioun of hooli doctours and oþere wise men, as þei may eseli and goodli come þerto."[7] It may still be necessary (as the epilogue earlier maintains) for a "lerned man" to correct the occasional "defaute in þis glos," but this vision of lay biblicism now presumes direct engagement with the scriptural text and its commentary tradition, all in English.

The adaptation of the Matthew epilogue to serve as a more or less freestanding polemical tract is a comparatively limited example of the complex textual history of the *Glossed Gospels*. Rather than a single set text or work, the *Gospels* were a developing project, the effort of a team (or, indeed, perhaps several teams) of scholars active in the final decades of the fourteenth century, either working at Oxford or at least with a close connection to the university.[8] Variations in some of the essential elements of the *Gospels* across their different versions – such as the use of Latin sources, the methods and priorities of compilation, the arrangement of lemmata and commentary on the manuscript page, methods of citation, and the handling of marginalia, prologues, and epilogues – reveal changes in the commentators' idea of vernacular exegesis, with the *Gospels* team learning from their own undertaking and making changes to their practice as their project progressed. Owing to this complexity, Hudson has discussed the *Gospels* as an example of a "variable text," and, while this description is certainly appropriate, they might also usefully be considered an experimental text, one in which, lacking sufficient immediate precedents, the shape of the final product is not fixed (or even known) when composition begins.[9]

In this regard, the *Glossed Gospels* continue the work of vernacular exegesis begun in Rolle's *English Psalter*, which, in light of its multiple Wycliffite revisions, was very likely known to the *Gospels* team.[10] Yet, as we will see, the *Gospels* were a far more ambitious project, in part surely reflecting the resources available to, and expectations for, exegetes working within a major university. To put it another way, just as Ullerston presented Rolle's *Latin* and *English Psalters* as authoritative exegetical sources in his university lectures, comparing them with Lyre's postils and his own literalistic interpretations, so too was the whole enterprise of English exegesis, begun by Rolle outside of Oxford, brought into the university and, in the process, remade as a more obviously scholastic undertaking. In addition to advancing the work of biblical interpretation in Latin, at least some scholastic exegetes now devoted themselves to compiling material from the long tradition of gospel commentaries *and* making their findings available in the vernacular. And, especially as this massive project continued, their commentary-translations became increasingly more elaborate than the offerings in the *English Psalter*.

The *Glossed Gospels* also depart from the *English Psalter* in their hermeneutic, their interpretive approach to the biblical text. As I argued in the previous chapter, Rolle's typical hermeneutic reflects and adapts the prophetic-literalistic emphasis of the scholastic commentary tradition on the Psalms, and literalism is also the interpretive priority that has, until quite recently, been most closely associated with Wycliffite writings. The *Gospels* in particular have been seen, very generally, as meant to "facilitate the understanding of the literal sense" and "to make available in English authoritative commentaries that elucidate the 'literal sense' of Scripture."[11] Certainly, as we will see, there is some attention to biblical historicism in the *Glossed Gospels*, the kind of literalistic priority which (as shown in Chapter 2) informed both Wyclif's and Woodford's near-contemporary commentaries on Matthew. Yet this literalism is matched, and quite often eclipsed, by the vernacular exegetes' overriding interest in the gospels' tropological or moral meaning, regardless of whether that tropology is part of the literal or spiritual sense of a particular passage.[12] This interest in moralism, already suggested by the epilogue's references to "good lyuynge" and the need "to lerne and kepe Goddis comandementis," coincides with what Fiona Somerset has identified as a Wycliffite commitment to "instill[ing] a disposition toward personal and communal amelioration in their readers," one which runs counter to the usual portrayal of Wycliffites as "fleshly adherents to the letter of the biblical [text]."[13] In the case of the *Glossed Gospels*, however, this blurring of literal and spiritual for the sake of moral meaning should not just be seen as a Wycliffite priority. Instead, it reflects another long-standing interpretive tradition specific to the gospels, one which also found expression in both Latin and non-Wycliffite English writings.

The differences between the *Glossed Gospels* and the *English Psalter*, though many, should not be exaggerated. As in the prologue to the *English Psalter*, the long Matthew commentary's epilogue holds out the possibility of reaching "þe blysse of heuene" by studying glossed vernacular Scripture, and, though this promised rest is less sensational than Rolle's account of celestial song, its expression nevertheless seems to signal a broader, shared understanding of the function of biblical commentary in English.[14] In the *Gospels* as in the *Psalter*, reading exegesis to help one arrive at heavenly bliss, reading as a sign of what the epilogue calls "tru deuocion," involves putting scholarly interpretive techniques to devotional ends.

Of course, begun outside the university, the work of vernacular biblical commentary continued to develop in the hands of non-university writers as well, with some turning their attention to the same biblical books as the Wycliffite team. Before considering the *Glossed Gospels* – their manuscripts, prologues, and the content of their glosses – in detail, then, it will be useful to recover some of the priorities common to these different post-Rollean texts by giving attention to yet another work of English exegesis, one which can be seen as coming (conceptually, if not more concretely) between the *Psalter* and the *Gospels*.[15] This almost unstudied commentary-translation of Matthew, though lacking any signs of Wycliffite affiliation in its origin or reception, shares with the *Gospels* an interest in formal experimentation (though comparatively restrained), as well as an interpretive program blurring literalism into tropology. At the same time, it is also more clearly indebted than the *Gospels* to the precedent set by the hermit's *Psalter*. This non-Wycliffite Matthew commentary can thus reveal how the *Psalter*'s example was developed beyond the Psalms in the second half of the fourteenth century, an effort at innovation taken even further by the writers of the *Glossed Gospels*.

"Not of Myne Hede Nor of Myne Owne Fantasy"

Though its author's familiarity with the *English Psalter* cannot be established with utter certainty, the late fourteenth-century commentary-translation of Matthew now preserved in BL MS Egerton 842 and CUL MS Ii.2.12 seems aimed at cultivating a similar sense of scholarly devotion. Affinities between the two texts are evident already in the commentator's preface, in which he offers a defense of what may at first (he claims) seem like the unfortunate awkwardness of his prose:

> In þe whilk oute-draghyng I sette not of myne hede nor of myne owne fantasy, bot as I fond in oþer expositores. . . . Also in þis drawyng, for cawes

> þat I wold not presume of myn owen wytt, I haf to þe Latyne and to the sayghis of þe doctours als euyn proporcyond þe English as I kouth, for þe tyme and as grace was gyfen me . . . , þat bacbyteres sulde haf no cawse of chalyngyng. Wherfor to some I suppose it wyll beseme þe more vnsafery in þe redyng, bot I suppose if þei wyll not our-ryne bot esely take with hem þe sentence, þei sall fynde gostely edyfycacion þer-in, and no mater of ill spekyng.[16]

At least in part, the commentary-translation's "vnsafery" style can be explained as a precaution against the critical judgments of "bacbyteres," imagined readers who recall the hermit's anxiety that his *Psalter* may fall into "some enuyouse manns hand." This writer's consequent proportioning of the English "als euyn" as possible to the Latin, and especially his avowed reliance on what he has "fond in oþer expositores," also seem to echo Rolle's paired claims: "In þe translacione I folow þe leter als mykyll as I may, and . . . in expowndyng I folow hali doctours."[17] Whether in deliberate imitation of Rolle or simply as the result of a shared deference to the Vulgate and to his exegetical sources, the Matthew commentator goes on to offer a work that closely resembles the *English Psalter*, with quotations of Latin verses, distinguished in both manuscripts by the use of a larger or more formal script, followed by close translations of the biblical text and vernacular glosses (Fig. 12).[18]

This Matthew commentator also shares with the hermit a similar approach to his sources, his means of locating the "sayghis of þe doctours." Though, as noted above, Rolle drew the great majority of his glosses from Peter Lombard's mid-twelfth-century compilation, he could nevertheless be confident that he was following the interpretations of "hali doctours," since most manuscripts of the Lombard's *Glosatura* (apparently including Rolle's) feature marginal citations indicating the patristic or earlier medieval sources from which the glosses ultimately derive.[19] Likewise, even as his claim to have "fond" his glosses "in oþer expositores" suggests the consultation of a range of sources, the Matthew commentator depended almost entirely on a single antecedent, a twelfth-century Latin commentary now preserved in its complete form uniquely in Durham, Cathedral Library MS A.I.10, ff. 1ʳ–169ᵛ.[20] Like manuscripts of the *Glosatura*, the Durham text includes marginal citations (copied in red) identifying the sources of various glosses. Yet, while Rolle apparently made no effort to reproduce the Lombard's apparatus in his *English Psalter*, the Middle English Matthew commentary does include at least some of the Durham text's citations. In Figure 12, for example, references to Hilary and Augustine float in the margin of Egerton 842, f. 14ᵛ, naming the authorities whose opinions are

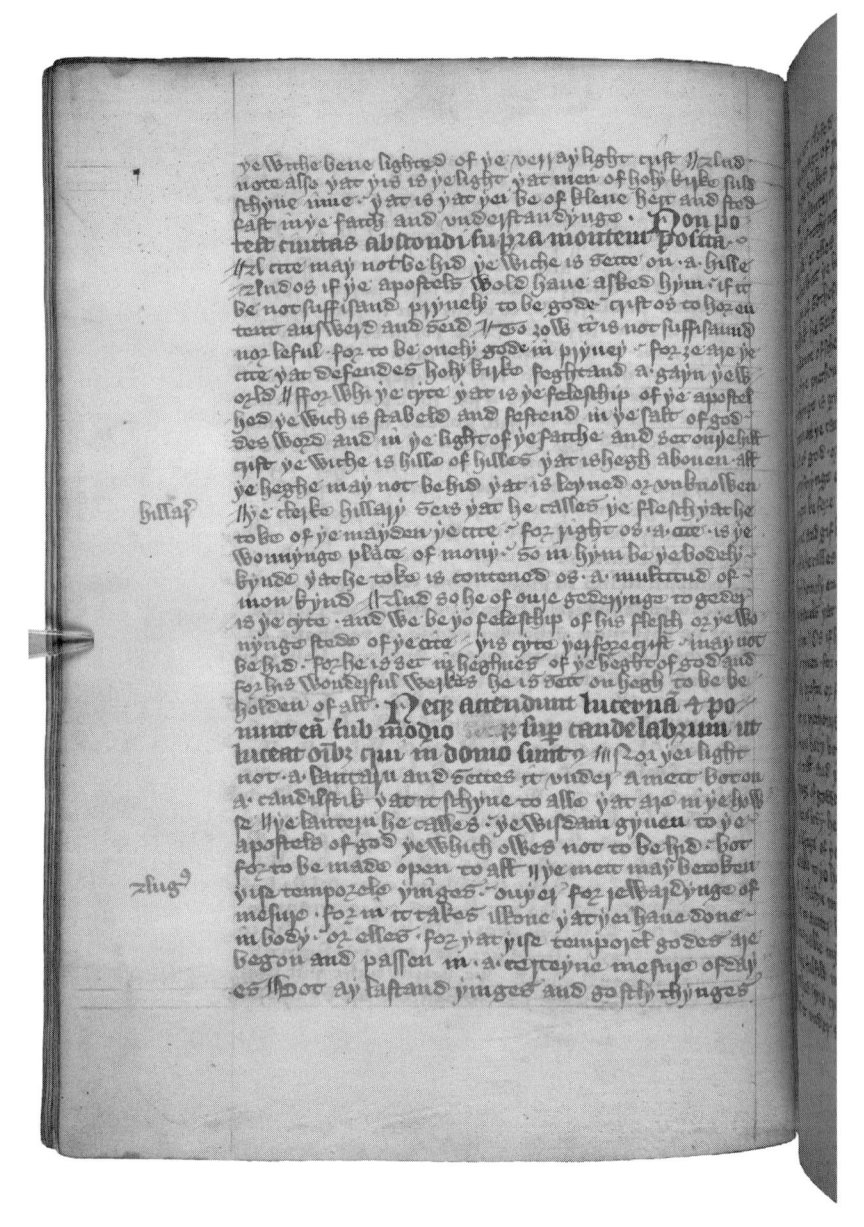

Figure 12 BL MS Egerton 842, f. 14ᵛ.

represented in the commentary on Matth. 5.14 and 15. The same citations appear at this point in the Latin text in Durham, f. 43ʳ, in the inner margin.[21]

As with the hermit's use of the Lombard, the writer responsible for the Middle English Matthew commentary preserves many of his source's hermeneutic priorities, and these tend (as we will see) to be specific to the gospels.[22] In particular, the Middle English commentator takes up his Latin source's interest in exploring the tropological or moral meaning of the biblical text, though these spiritualizing concerns do not always come at the expense of literalism. A considerable portion of his discussion of Matth. 26.2, for example, is devoted to distinguishing between that verse's use of *pascha* and the reference to the *festus* (or *dies*) *azymorum* with which the same scene is introduced in Mark 14.1 and Luke 22.1 (cf. also Matth. 26.17).

> Betwene þis word "paske" and "aȝyme" is þis dyfference: þat þis word is sett only for þat day, in þe whiche day at euyn þe lomb was slayn, þat is in þe fourtenth lune of þe first monethe, and þe fyftenth lune or day when þe childir of Israel went oute of Egipte was callid aȝime in seuen dayes, þat is to þe one and twentye day of þe same moneth at euyn.[23]

At least at first, this careful Hebraism may appear to be driven by a desire to position the gospel's narrative in Levantine antiquity, a historicizing impulse similar to that seen in the commentaries of Wyclif and Woodford, discussed in Chapter 2. Such apparent continuities are undercut, however, when the English commentator goes on to assert that, across the different gospels, "indifferently þo ton is sett for þat oþer, for þe dayes of paske are celebrate in aȝyme."[24] Instead, following his Latin source, the commentator has introduced these Hebrew terms chiefly to support a lengthy moralization:

> In one day at euyn þe lombe sacrifysed, seuyn dayes of aȝyme folowys. For oure lorde Iesu Crist ones for vs suffyrd in his flesch in þe ende of tymes; be all þe tyme of þis world þat god abouthe be seuyn dayes, he byddys vs to life in aȝyme of clennesse and sothfastnes and euer to fle þes wordly desyres as þe agey[n]holdyngys of Egipte. And he amonestys for-to take þe way of vertues, þat is þe wyldernesse for barayne fro yuel and departyd fro þe wordly lyfyng....[25]

The tropological gloss continues at some length, but its basic terms are already apparent. The single day of the *pascha*, "in þe whiche day at euyn þe lomb was slayn," finds it fulfillment in the singular event of the crucifixion, while the seven-day *festus azymorum* corresponds to the subsequent (and consequent) need for Christians to live in "clennesse and sothfastnes," with the ideals of that form of living illustrated by the barrenness of the Egyptian desert. Indeed, the drive to moralize is dominant throughout this commentary, and, in this regard, what began here as a literalistic distinction between Hebrew terms seems to be little different from the straightforward tropological claim, just a bit later in the commentary, that the Magdalene's ointment "betokyns þo deuocyon of þo feith, þo whiche takes boþe togedyr, þo manhede and þo godhed of Crist."[26]

Such spiritualizing interpretations apparently do not to depend on the intentions (as the commentator understands them) of either the evangelist or the historical actors whose story the gospel narrates. This hermeneutic decoupling is especially clear in the Christological reading of the Magdalene's ointment, where the commentator asserts that "þof ho were ignorante, ȝit ho schewis his [i.e., Christ's] passion."[27] Yet not every case is quite so unambiguous. As Beryl Smalley noted with regard to gospel exegesis in the first half of the twelfth century, including texts related to the English commentary's source, "a zone of uncertainty" often exists "in the demarcation of the literal and spiritual senses."[28] This uncertainty, Smalley observed, was inherited from patristic glosses but made more pointed by the growing scholastic interest in distinguishing between senses, and it was complicated further by Christ's apparent awareness of the spiritual significance of his words and deeds, as well as "the problem of the evangelists' participation in the divine secrets which they revealed to their readers."[29]

The same problems may be found throughout the English commentary, where the exegete presents Christ at once as a historical actor within the narrative and as controlling all levels of that narrative's meaning. At Matth. 26.6–7, for example, we are told that "Crist comys to Bethanye þat þo vpraysyng of Laȝar þat was late done schulde faster be in mynde" at the time of his own death and resurrection.[30] In this case, Christ's (fore)-knowledge within the narrative would still seem to be separable from the subsequent moral reading, namely, that the house he enters in Bethany "mystyly signyfyes þat partye of þo pupyl þat thoro þo fayth was obediente to Crist and thoro obedience is helyd."[31] Other moments in the commentary, however, present a more thorough blurring of Christ's intentions as historical actor or speaker and the larger moral understanding of the biblical text. At Matth. 20.26, for example, when Christ declares that "who-so wil a-monge ȝowe be made more (þat is, in vertus), be he ȝour mynyster or ȝour seruande," the most obvious historical or literal referents of these words are the quarreling disciples.[32] The commentator therefore seems to be offering a non-literal interpretation when he writes, "Be we þerfor warre þat þer be no strife amonge vs of prelacie and of dignite, ffor if þe apostles couettid or hadden enuye amonge hem, it is not for vs to excusacion, but raþer if we so do, to þe acusynge aȝens owre siilfe." Yet he then ties this moral point to the form of the text as Christ spoke it: "To all is saide one forme of sentence, þat þer be no striuynge for prelacy but of meknes."[33] Christ's words, spoken (apparently by design) in a universalized form, apply just as fully to the disciples as they do to readers of the commentary, and the distinction between literal and moral meaning is therefore difficult to define. As the exegete says in a different context, "Crist . . . wust þat his gospel schuld be spredd thoro alle þo world," and he could choose his words in light of this exceptional knowledge.[34]

Then again, Christ may not always be responsible for the "forme" of the words attributed to him. As Smalley noted, early twelfth-century exegetes often suggest, in their glosses if not in their overt theorizing claims, that the evangelists were aware of the "divine secrets" hidden beneath the covering of their words, and in this way the human authors of the gospels could contribute to the creation of their texts' spiritual significance. This may be especially true of John, who, as the English commentator reports in his prologue, wrote for those who are "more sotel of vnderstandyng," but his glosses suggest that it applies to Matthew as well.[35] A particularly intricate example of these overlapping authorial agencies comes at Matth. 26.18, when Jesus sends the disciples "into þo cyte, to som man" (*in civitatem ad quemdam*). The command is presented as direct speech, prompting the commentator to explain its apparent vagueness:

> *Some certayne man*, whom of his [i.e., Christ's] persone spekand þo ewangelist ryghtly schuld hafe sett, but now whene he sette þo wordys of Crist among hem he sette þis worde, *to som man*, not for Crist seid þis, but þat he schuld schew to vs holdande stylle his name þat þer was som in þo cyte to whom þei were sente. In þis þat he seis þis, *to som man*, of hymself and not of þo persone of Crist, þis Seynth Mathew dyd for cause of schortnesse, betokynand þo same þat Mark callys *þo lorde of þo house* [14.14], and Luke *þo husbondeman* [22.11]. Or þerfor he expressyd not þo name of þo man, for ȝitt was not þo honour of Crysten name gyfen to men þat trowde.[36]

Though most of the verse presents "þo wordys of Crist," Matthew has substituted the indefinite pronoun (*quemdam*) in place of the proper name that Christ presumably supplied. Noting a similar refusal to name this man in Luke's and Mark's accounts, the commentator suggests that Matthew favored this phrasing because of its comparative brevity, and he also presents the possibility that all three synoptic gospels avoid identifying him because he did not have a Christian name. (The implication seems to be that, by the time the evangelists were writing, converted believers adopted Christian names, and the lack of such a name in the case of this early believer would lead to confusion.) Introducing the notion that the evangelist could refashion Christ's words to match his writerly intentions, to this point this gloss has remained wholly literal or historical. As it continues, however, this literalism is left behind:

> Warly also are þo namys of þe berers of þo watyr and of þo maystyr of þo howse not expressyd, þat it be schewyd þat who so redye þe veray pask and coueyte for-to be fulfyllud with þo sacramentys and coueyte to hafe Crist in þo herberogh of his sowle, he may, and to none þat will it is denyed.[37]

Without any of the words (e.g., *mystyly*, *betokyns*) he usually employs to set spiritual interpretations apart from literal ones, the commentator suggests that the evangelist substituted *quemdam* better to allow faithful readers to imagine themselves, tropologically, in the position of "þo maystyr of þo howse," welcoming Christ into the "herberogh" of their souls through the sacrament of the altar. By mingling his own words with those of Christ, the evangelist enables a wide range of interpretations, at least some of which conform to the commentator's moralizing priorities.

Indeed, rather than theorizing the competing claims of authorial agency and intentionality raised in glosses like these, the English commentator seems more interested in taking advantage of this complexity, Smalley's "zone of uncertainty," and using it to generate as many moral readings as he can.[38] In this regard, he bears out Vincent Gillespie's claim that an exegete's understanding of authorial intention is often "deduced from [his] inductive understanding [and] his subjective projections of those understandings onto a text."[39] Though he maintains that Matthew wrote, in the first instance, for "þem þat receyfid þe circumcysyon," and though he can certainly interpret the text in terms of this historical audience, the commentator is primarily interested in identifying the gospel's tropological import, and he will find that moral meaning as readily in the intentions of Christ as in those of the evangelist, or in a superadded spiritual register.[40] He inherits this focus on moralism (and its consequent hermeneutic heterogeneity) from his twelfth-century source, but, as we will see below, he was not the only Middle English exegete to favor this approach to the gospel.

This exegete thus extends – whether intentionally or not – the project of Rolle's *English Psalter*, outfitting the commentary-translation form with maringal citations and making a new set of interpretive priorities, surrounding a different biblical book, available in the vernacular. Yet he remains anonymous, even compared with the Oxford-based team of (at least some) Wycliffite writers responsible for the *Glossed Gospels*, discussed below. Like the *English Psalter*, this work was apparently a local production, based on sources available to hand, to meet a perceived need on the part of specific known readers. Before turning to consider the *Glossed Gospels* and their development of vernacular exegesis within the university, then, it will be useful to recover as fully as possible, if still tentatively, where this comparatively "unprofessional" effort at English exegesis was carried out. Fortunately, compared with the late medieval ubiquity of the *Magna glosatura*, the Matthew commentary's major Latin source is exceptionally obscure, and careful consideration of its somewhat messy textual history can therefore help to tie the English work, if not to a specific author, then at least to a community with an apparent interest in vernacular exegesis.[41]

The Latin commentary in Durham A.I.10 is a revised version of a more widely circulating work on Matthew, attributed in one early copy to the well-known master Anselm of Laon (d. 1117).[42] As part of his augmentation of "Anselm," the Durham reviser turned to a second commentary, attributed in some manuscripts to (the comparatively little-known) Geoffrey Babion (fl. 1103–c. 1110), and this work is itself a revision of the earlier "Anselm" commentary.[43] The reviser apparently had both of these commentaries more or less constantly open before him, supplementing "Anselm" when "Babion" offered material not in the earlier text, and sometimes comparing passages shared by both of his sources, alternately adopting the phrasing of one or the other. These compilational strategies are evident already in the Durham commentary's prologue, edited in Appendix C.[44]

Though it is possible that a finished copy of the resulting compilation reached Durham, where Michael Gullick has placed the copying of A.I.10, c. 1115–30, it is just as likely that the work of assembling the commentary from its two major sources was undertaken at the cathedral priory itself.[45] That is, this text could have been a local production. It certainly seems to have had a limited influence beyond Durham: aside from A.I.10 and, of course, the Middle English commentary, its only surviving witness is an early thirteenth-century miscellany, BodL MS Laud. misc. 5, ff. 109^v–113^v, which excerpts the bulk of its prologue. As the textual notes in Appendix C indicate, this portion of Laud. misc. 5 may have been copied directly from A.I.10, or at the very least from an exemplar closely related to the Durham manuscript.[46] Similarly, there is evidence to suggest that, in selectively adapting and translating his Latin source, the Middle English commentator was working directly from the surviving Durham

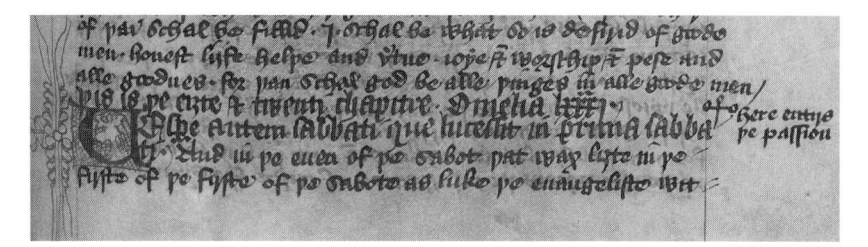

Figure 13   BL MS Egerton 842, f. 200ʳ (detail).

copy. As Richard Gameson has observed, annotations in A.i.10 indicate that it was the object of some interest in the fourteenth-century Durham priory, and these markings include a description written across the top of f. 1ʳ: "Omelie super euangelium Mathei" ("Homilies on the Gospel of Matthew"), echoed in the priory's 1395 catalogue: "Omelie excerpte de diuersis doctoribus super ewangelium Mathei per totum" ("Homilies drawn from various doctors on the Gospel of Matthew in its entirety").[47] The description of the commentary as a series of *homeliae* appears to refer to its division into one hundred sections, which only imperfectly align with the twenty-eight chapter divisions of the gospel itself. The A.i.10 rubricator labels these sections as *capitula*, and a list of them is presented, in the hand of the manuscript's main scribe, on f. 1ʳᵛ.[48] This *divisio textus* is unusual in twelfth-century commentaries: while the great majority of commentators – his immediate sources included – seem to have been content to let the chapter divisions of the biblical text structure their expositions, the Durham reviser prefers to divide his work into more or less even units, such that, e.g., eight chapters of the commentary are devoted to Matth. 5, with the last covering Matth. 5.43–6.9a.[49] This unusual *divisio* is reflected in the commentary's English adaptation. Though, unlike the Durham manuscript, both copies of the Middle English text do note the beginning of each chapter of Matthew (called *capitula* or *chapitres* and identified marginally or in the text, before a decorated initial), the English exposition itself is divided into eighty-two numbered sections labeled *homeliae* (Fig. 13).[50] The shared preference for this latter term (at least, in the case of the Latin manuscript, by its fourteenth-century readers), together with the correspondences in their marginal apparatus of citations, their evident textual affinities, and the limited circulation of the Latin source, strongly suggest that the Middle English work was prepared from A.i.10, either at Durham priory or by someone with access to the priory's books.[51]

Though speculative, a Durham origin would be consistent with what little we know about the English commentary's production. The most straightforward piece of evidence, though unfortunately vague, is a note that the main scribe of Ii.2.12 has added in the upper margin at the beginning of the text: "A man of þe north cuntre drogh þis into Englisch" (f. 4ʳ).[52] Since, as Ralph Hanna notes, Ii's dialect is localizable to central Nottinghamshire, the scribe would seem to be "engaged in 'north-midlandising' something otherwise foreign, from somewhere in those wilds north of Doncaster."[53] At the same time, the translator's account of how he came to undertake the work of writing the commentary, and of the support he received throughout the project, could be read as suggesting his position within a community like Durham priory. He writes,

> Þis werk som-tyme I was styrde to begyne of one þat I suppose veraly was Goddys seruant and oft tymes prayd me þis werke to begyn, seyand to me þat sethyn the gospell is rewle be þe whilk ich Cristen man owes to lyf, and dyuers has draghen into Latyn, þe whilk tung is not knowen to ilk man bot only to þe leryd, and many lewd men are þat gladly wold kon þe gospell if it were draghen into Englisch tung, and so it suld do grete profete to man saule, about þe whilk profete ilk man þat is in þe grace of God and to whome God has sent konnyng owes hertely to bysy hym. Wherfor I þat þurgh þe grace of God began þis werk, so styrd as I haf seid befor be sich word, thoght in my hert þat I was holden be charyte þis werke to begyn, and so þis werke I began at þe suggestyon of Goddys seruant, and gretly in þis doyng I was comfortid of oþer Goddys seruantes dyuers, to sich tyme þat þurgh þe grace of God I broght þis to ane ende.[54]

In light of such analogues as Trevisa's dialogue between a lord and clerk or the "prologue" to the Anna Paues biblical version, it is tempting to understand the figure who "oft tymes prayd" the translator as being among the intended readers of the English commentary.[55] Like the petitioning figures in these dialogues, this "seruant" may have been dependent on the linguistic expertise of the translator if he (or she) was to gain access to the material in the Latin text. Then again, this "seruant" could instead be another educated cleric, sharing with the translator both a familiarity with this Latin commentary and a pastoral commitment to helping "lewd men" who "wold kon þe gospell." Likewise, rather than referring to prospective readers of the vernacular commentary, "Goddys seruantes dyuers" could be fellow members of a monastic community encouraging and "comfort[ing]" the translator in his "oute-draghyng." At roughly the same time that the Middle English commentary was prepared, A.1.10 was kept among the books read during meals in the Durham refectory, and, as Alan Piper notes, "it was chiefly the novices who would have been fed this good solid diet of patristic and other authorities."[56] That is, as an assemblage of early and authoritative interpretations, the Latin text seems to have been deemed an appropriate entrée into the commentary tradition for the new Durham monks, and its translation could have been considered a useful way to extend this essential exegetical material to a broader, though similarly elementary, audience.

To be sure, there is no other surviving evidence of an interest in scriptural translation among the Black Monks of Durham. Yet the very novelty of Middle English biblical commentary in this period means that, unless it can – like the hermit's *Psalter* – be tied to the larger program of an individual author, any commentary-translation is likely to appear atypical and unprecedented. In this regard, then, Northern Matthew could be considered an expression of the Durham community's preaching interests, which included, as Margaret Harvey has observed, a regular course of sermons aimed at lay audiences and delivered in the vernacular.[57] Just as importantly, a Durham origin for the commentary could tie it, indirectly, to other English exegesis of this period, since the Durham monks benefited from having their own college at Oxford. Indeed, R. B. Dobson has maintained that "the exposure of large numbers of Durham monks to Oxford learning, Oxford scholastic techniques, and Oxford academic society was the greatest single cultural influence on the convent" in the two centuries before the Dissolution.[58] If this exposure and influence included an awareness of the biblical translations underway at Oxford in the final decades of the fourteenth century, it is just conceivable that such university activities could have encouraged the creation of the commentary-translation at Durham.

Though its origin in Durham remains speculative, this Middle English Matthew commentary should still be seen as speaking at once to the great precedent for vernacular exegesis, Rolle's *Psalter*, and to more recent (perhaps contemporary) trends in Oxford, the work of Wycliffite writers. Like the *Psalter*, the commentary-translation of Matthew demonstrates an interest in vernacular exegesis in the North of England, and it meets this interest with a formal presentation that, perhaps by design, matches the *Psalter*'s. Likewise, both Rolle and the author of Northern Matthew turned to twelfth-century sources, and they seem to have favored these texts not because they were "spiritual classics," as Giles Constable has argued of other twelfth-century writings that gained popularity in the fourteenth century, but because they were convenient compilations of authoritative exegesis, an authority reinforced by the marginal apparatus of the Matthew text.[59] At the same time, if he was writing with Rolle's model in mind, the Matthew commentator's inclusion of these citations would indicate his interest in experimenting with the commentary-translation form of the *Psalter*, experimentation which would be taken much further in the Wycliffite *Glossed Gospels*.

"Þis Scribeler Hadde Travelid wiþ Fals Bookis"

What is by now the familiar presentation of biblical translation and commentary in the Wycliffite *Glossed Gospels* might immediately undercut the notion that this group of texts is any more elaborately experimental than the hermit's *Psalter* or the Northern commentary-translation of Matthew. Consider, for example, BodL MS Bodley 143, a copy of the short recension of the commentary on Luke (Fig. 14).[60] Blocks of biblical text in the Early Version Wycliffite translation are written in a more prominent script on every other line, and the commentary follows as a series of discrete glosses in a smaller script, beginning with a lemma drawn from the block of biblical text and set off with underlining in the text ink. Each gloss concludes with a note identifying its patristic or medieval source, copied in the text and repeated, in red, in the margin. This form thus presents little that could be considered new. Though, for example, the placement of citations in the text is distinctive, their inclusion in the margins is anticipated by Northern Matthew. Indeed, the most significant formal departure may not be what the *Gospels* include but what they omit, namely, the Latin biblical text that had preceded the close translations in both Northern Matthew and the *Psalter*. It is tempting to read this omission in light of the Wycliffite view, expressed in the Prologue to the Later Version Bible and discussed in greater detail below, that the "sentence" of the biblical text could be "as opene or openere in English as in Latyn."[61] Then again, the use of the Early Version translation here, with its close adherence to the vocabulary of the Vulgate, foregrounds its dependence on a Latin source almost as clearly as the inclusion of Latin in the other commentary-translations.[62]

Despite its familiarity, however, this *cannot* be considered the standard or inevitable way of presenting the text of the *Glossed Gospels* on the manuscript page. Only three of the nine surviving medieval copies of the *Gospels* follow this arrangement, and the remaining copies are far from uniform.[63] At least in part, these different *mises-en-page* correspond to different versions of the text: the commentaries on Matthew and Luke are

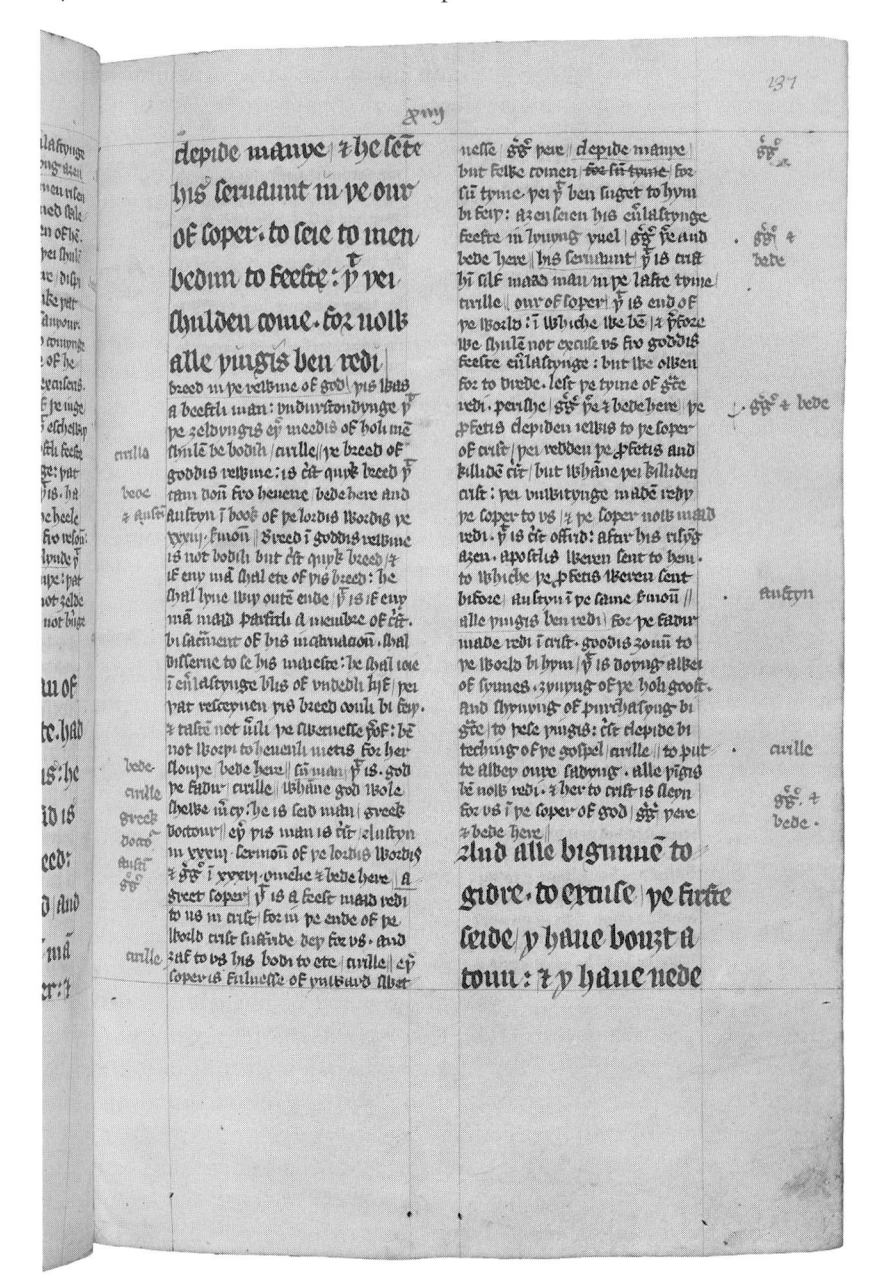

Figure 14   BodL MS Bodley 143, f. 137^r.

preserved in both longer and shorter recensions, and it seems that one way of arranging the text was deemed suitable for the longer versions but not the shorter ones.[64] But even these cases can contribute to a more general sense of the *Glossed Gospels* as an experimental text, with the commentators' developing ideas about their vernacular exegetical project finding expression in a similarly developing range of scribal handlings. As we will see, even the most deluxe copies of the *Glossed Gospels* offer evidence of the degree to which the text was unfixed and not fully known to the scribes who began copying it.

By first attending to the various and provisional scribal handlings of the *Glossed Gospels*, it becomes possible to recover a sense of the experimental quality of the *Gospels* project as a whole, a sense of the degree to which the compilers of the *Gospels* were making decisions about the shape of their work while it was still in progress. Further, just as scribes developed strategies to disguise this uncertainty, at least one of the *Gospel* compilers appears to have offered a different kind of patch, writing a more or less uniform series of prologues that retrospectively give the appearance of consistency to the work as a whole. After considering the various manuscripts of the *Gospels*, therefore, our attention will turn to these prologues, and from there it will be possible to investigate the interpretive content of the commentaries themselves as similarly suggesting the gradual development of this vernacular exegetical project.

In many respects, the organizational priorities of Bodley 143 can also be found in the long recension of the *Glossed Gospel* of Luke in CUL MS Kk.2.9 and the long recension of Matthew in BL MS Add. 28026.[65] Though the scribes responsible for these copies did not employ a hierarchy of scripts, they still worked to maintain a distinction between translation and commentary, consistently setting the translation apart with red underlining. This gives the pages of these manuscripts a generally more compressed aspect, a level of workmanlike informality that seems not unrelated to the compression of the script in which they are written. Like Bodley 143, Add. 28026 includes citations both in the text itself and in the margins, where, again, they are copied in red. Or, rather, they are copied in red when, like the Bodley marginalia, they identify an authority by name alone. Less frequently, but still throughout the manuscript, the scribe of Add. 28026 has copied some marginalia in text ink, apparently at the same time as he copied the text itself, and these marginal notes provide fuller, more specific citations than those embedded in the text.[66] Since they offer information that could not be derived from the text itself, these detailed citations indicate not only that the marginal apparatus was present in Add. 28026's exemplar, but also that it was in some way intrinsic to the long recension of the Matthew commentary at the time of its compilation. This makes the absence of such marginalia in Kk.2.9 all the more intriguing. Certainly, as noted above, these peritextual citations are particularly prone to scribal tampering, and it could be that their absence in the sole surviving copy of the long Luke commentary should be attributed to such scribal interference.[67] Yet the work of copying Kk.2.9 seems to have been shared by four different scribes, and their consistent omission of such marginal citations would in turn indicate either that citations were absent in their exemplar or that, if present, all four scribes received some direction not to copy them.[68] This inconsistency between the long versions of Matthew and Luke could thus indicate some change in the commentators' practice.

Another minor detail in Kk.2.9 suggests something about the process by which this manuscript (or perhaps its exemplar) was assembled. Throughout the stints of all four scribes, in addition to the use of red underlining, the shift between commentary and translation has been given even greater prominence. The scribes sometimes add the word *text* at the conclusion of a run of glosses, either in the text itself or in the margin, and the passage of biblical lemmata that follows is then set apart by a partial box in text ink, extending down the left column of the translation, underlining the end of the passage, and extending two or three lines back up the right margin (see Fig. 15). A similar system appears in Cambridge, Trinity College MS B.1.38, a smaller and comparatively informal copy of the short recension of glossed Matthew and John. Like Kk.2.9 and Add. 28026, the scribe of B.1.38 does not use a hierarchy of scripts to distinguish between the translated biblical text and the gloss. Here, however, the partial boxing and "text" label are much more important for the proper parsing of the *Glossed Gospels*, since almost no rubrication has been added to set the biblical translation apart from the commentary (see Fig. 16).[69] It seems likely, then, that Kk.2.9's exemplar looked more like B.1.38, a rougher copy that adopted this text-ink boxing out of necessity, and that the scribes of Kk.2.9 repeated this system in their more formal copy, perhaps without realizing (or caring) that their underlining would make it superfluous.

B.1.38 also contains a significant scribal error that points to the process by which the *Gospels* were compiled and copied in an apparently early form. The scribe of B.1.38 begins copying the short recension of glossed John at the top of f. 99ʳ, but he provides only the short-form lemmata and the bank of glosses. That is, he omits the longer passages of translated biblical text. He continues writing only the short lemmata and glosses

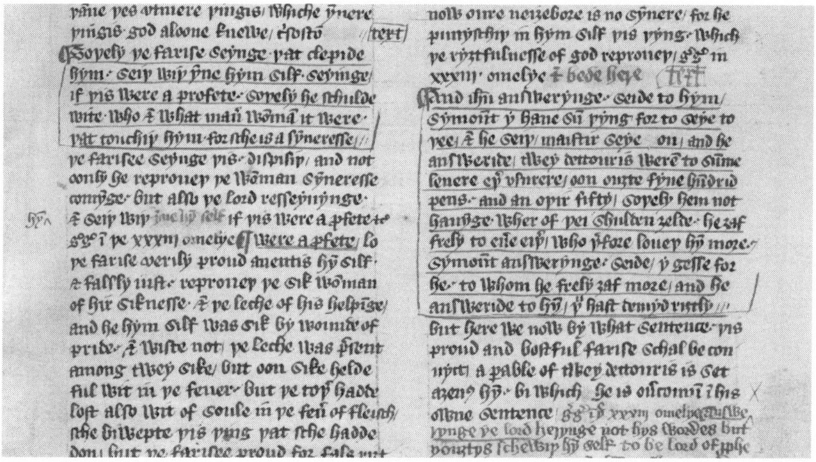

Figure 15   CUL MS Kk.2.9, f. 73ᵛ (detail).

through the bottom of f. 102ᵛ, covering John 1.1–3.21, when he seems to have noticed (or been informed of) his error. He then starts over, on f. 103ʳ, this time beginning with the prologue to short John and (after his first "text" label) the Early Version translation of John 1.1–5, before finally repeating the glosses with which his first attempt had mistakenly begun.[70] While other explanations are certainly possible, this error was most likely the result of the scribe's need to assemble the full form of the *Glossed Gospels* from multiple exemplars, drawing the passages of biblical translation from a copy of the Early Version of John and his exegesis from a catena of short lemmata and glosses resembling what he copied on ff. 99ʳ–102ᵛ.[71] Additionally, the prologue to the short commentary on John seems to have reached the Trinity scribe apart from his manuscript of the glosses, either copied together with the Early Version translation or (more likely and more ephemerally) as a distinct unit, a loose sheet or single bifolium. The scribe apparently learned from his mistake, and his stint copying the short commentary on Matthew – originally a discrete unit but now bound together with short John – begins with what he calls "Þe prologe of þe schorte exposicioun on Matheu," filling f. 1ʳ and followed immediately, at the top of the verso, by the alternating sequence of translation and commentary.[72] In light of the error in the commentary on John, however, this comparative tidiness could disguise the scribe's compilation of short Matthew from a similar variety of books, booklets, and parchment pieces.

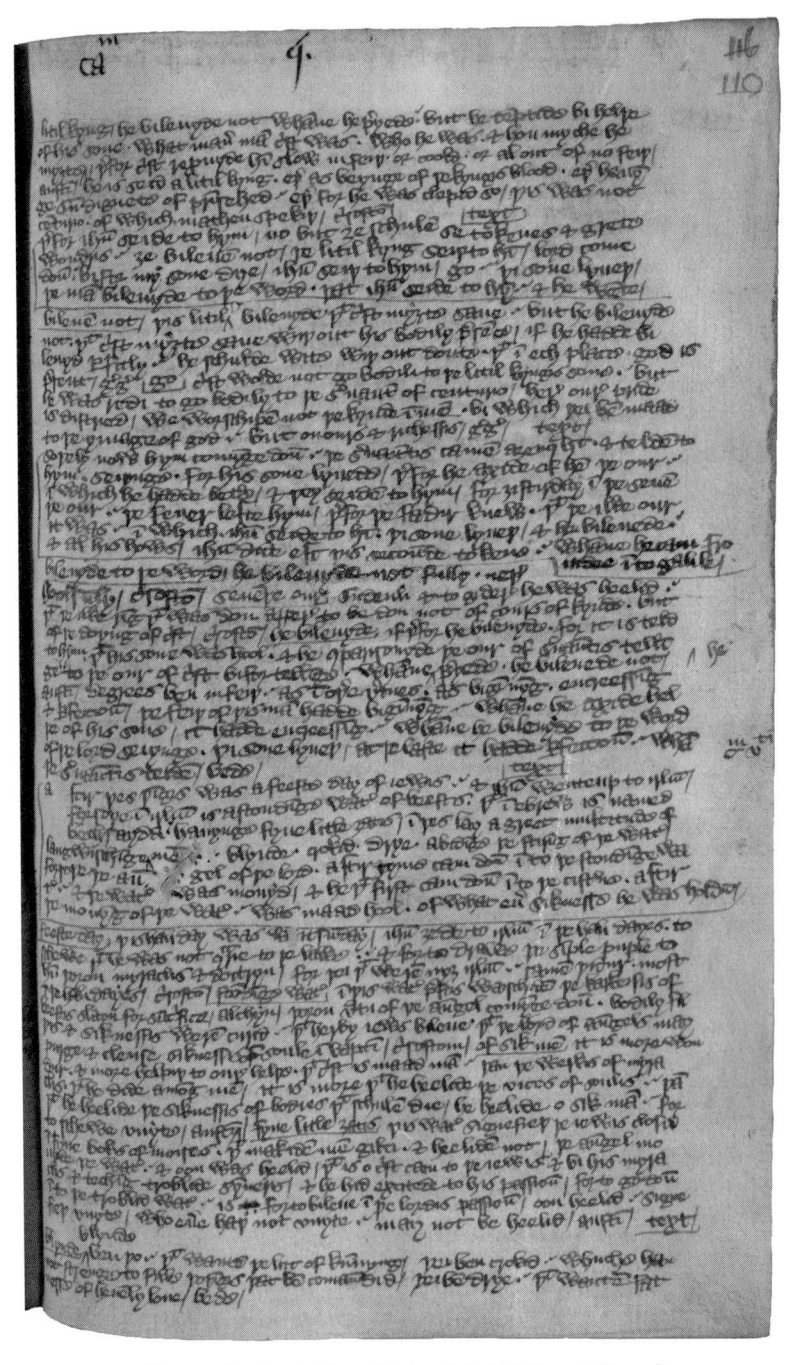

Figure 16 Cambridge, Trinity Coll. MS B.1.38, f. 110ʳ.

B.1.38's generally unpretentious execution might make this messy start to John less surprising, but evidence of piecemealism – of scribes depending on different exemplars for different pieces of the text – can be found even in deluxe copies of the *Glossed Gospels*. BL MS Add. 41175 and BodL MS Bodley 243, for example, now form a two-volume set containing the short recension of the commentaries on all four gospels, copied by a single scribe in what were originally four distinct booklets.[73] All four texts adopt a uniform mode of presentation: the translation is written in a larger script on every other line and underlined in red, and the same red underlining is used for the shorter lemmata in the gloss, with each lemma prefaced by alternating red and blue paraphs. (Unlike Bodley 143, in Fig. 14, these copies do not include marginal citations of authorities.) Though he apparently planned the copying of the commentary and translation with care, however, it seems that this scribe did not know all of the details of the text's final shape when he started to write. That is, he apparently obtained exemplars of the prologues only after he had copied the commentary-translations, and he seems not to have acquired a full set, since his volumes lack the prologue to Luke (found in Bodley 143) and to Mark (which, if it ever existed, does not survive).[74] The prologues that did reach him, on Matthew and John, had to be fit into the material that he had already produced. He copied the first of these onto the verso of single sheet (f. 1^v) now bound before the first full quire of Add. 41175, and he added the much briefer prologue to John on what had been a blank sheet at the end of the final quire of Luke (now Bodley 243, f. 115vb), positioned so that, when the two texts were bound into a single volume, the prologue would face the opening of the John commentary on 116^r. Similar evidence of the independent and somewhat belated circulation of prologue material appears in Bodley 143, where the prologue to short Luke has been copied in a single bifolium with smaller dimensions than the rest of the book and bound before the commentary-translation proper (ff. iii^{vb}–iv^{va}). The prologue is written in red and in a hand that appears to be distinct from that of the main text.[75] Intriguingly, this scribe had initially begun to copy the prologue on the recto of the flyleaf, before breaking off and starting again on the verso. This is another suggestive error, perhaps reflecting the scribe's desire to have the prologue face the opening of the commentary-translation, as in Add. 41175 and Bodley 243. (Alternatively, the scribe may have wanted to protect the text from unnecessary wear.) It is possible, then, not only that this prefatory material reached these scribes after they had already begun copying the *Gospels*, but also that it came with instructions on how the added texts were to be positioned in relation to what the scribes had already produced. The author (or at least the disseminator) of the short-recension prologues may have foreseen the trouble caused by the piecemeal diffusion of the text and therefore offered guidance to the scribes.[76]

The various ways of handling the text in these manuscripts – with differing uses of marginalia, hierarchies of script, underlining and boxing, and rubrication – thus reflect more than just the preferences of their scribes. They are signs of a text that circulated in pieces, one which at least some scribes had to assemble from multiple exemplars, with different iterations of the text responding in different ways to a common and consistent set of priorities, most basically how to distinguish between biblical text and commentary and how to cite exegetical authorities. Some of these decisions may be attributable to the scribes, but others, such as Add. 28026's use of marginal references to supplement the naming of authorities within the commentary, must derive from the compilation of the commentary itself. Scribes and compilers together, that is, seem to have contributed to the developing sense of what the *Glossed Gospels* should contain and how they might best transmit their vernacular exegetical offerings.

As distinct units added, at least in the case of the short recension commentaries, after the copying of some or all of the main text, the prologues appear to be attempts in some way to settle the unfixity and experimental quality of the *Gospels*. They are, as Hudson suggests, "retrospective" accounts that speak univocally and thereby bring order to the complex and collaborative process of creating the commentary-translations.[77] But, of course, this retrospective positioning means that they can only function descriptively – they are responding to the state of the *Gospels* as much as (or more than) theorizing how such a text should ideally be constructed – and, in this regard, their ability to convey a sense of uniformity and a pre-planned design is rather limited. To stay, for the moment, with only the short recension of the text, the prologues suggest the uniformity of the commentary-translation project by having, themselves, something of a set form. Each of them moves, in the same order, through three distinct sections. The prologue-author first invokes biblical precedents, which in some cases he glosses and reads with the aid of patristic exegesis, emphasizing the need for clergy to teach Scripture to the laity or, more generally in the John prologue, to fulfill "þe lawe of Crist, that is, of charite."[78] These different articulations of a related pedagogical mandate are then taken, in a second section, as motivating the creation of the *Glossed Gospels*, with the prologue-author seeming to assume responsibility for the entirety of the project. As he puts it in the prologue to short Luke,

> Herfore a pore caityf, lettid fro prechyng for a tyme for causis knowun of God, writiþ þe Gospel of Luk in Englysh wiþ a short exposicioun of olde and holy doctouris to þe pore men of this nacioun whiche kunnen litil Latyn eþer noon, and ben pore of wit and of worldli catel and neþeles riche of good wille to plese God.[79]

The reference to the author's temporary inability to exercise his preaching office, an apparent biographical detail that has been used in attempts to identify him with known Wycliffite authors, more importantly contributes to the sense that there is a single writer responsible for the whole of the *Glossed Gospels*.[80] Here he calls himself "a pore caityf," while in the Matthew and John prologues he is "a symple creature," and, in either case, this self-styling conveys the sense that these massive books have been produced by a lone humble cleric simply seeking to perform his pastoral duties.

This fiction of authorship continues in the final section common to the three prologues, passages in which the prologuer describes how to parse the different registers of commentary-translation. His instructions for reading, which Rita Copeland describes as "a technical manual to the method of exposition" in the commentary, are presented as a narrative account of the text's composition, with the prologue-author suggesting that he is himself responsible for its shape.[81] To continue quoting from short Luke:

> First þis pore caitif settiþ a ful sentence of þe text togidre, þat it may wel be knowun fro þe exposicioun. Aftirward he settiþ a sentence of a doctour declarynge þe text, and in þe ende of þe sentence he settiþ þe doctouris name, þat men mown knowe verili hou fer his sentence goiþ.[82]

Startlingly, the prologue-author presents the longer biblical translations and the citations of authorities as though they were included simply to help in parsing the commentary. The translations are included as "a ful sentence" so that, when they are broken up in the short-form lemma, the biblical text can be distinguished ("knowun") from the gloss, while the names of authorities function not as citations but as punctuation, allowing one gloss to be distinguished from the next.[83] (Intriguingly, in light of the foregoing discussion of the text's variable *mise-en-page*, none of the short prologues mentions underlining, rubrication, or a hierarchy of texts.) The prologuer's claims cannot, of course, be taken as exhaustively defining the purposes of the different parts of the text. As in any medieval biblical commentary, visually prominent quotations of lemmata aid in the location of specific biblical passages within the bulky volume, while the calquish Early Version has very likely been preferred to the Later Version because it is closer to the Vulgate, and therefore, as in Rolle's *Psalter*, "he þat knawes not þe Latin bi þe Ynglisch may" thereby "come till many Latene wordes."[84] Likewise, in the short Matthew and Luke prologues, additional instructions on how to parse the citations – e.g., "Whanne Y seie 'Ierome here,' Ierom seiþ þat sentence on Matheu on þe same texte" – suggest that at least some readers were expected to be able to make sense of them as citations (more on this below).[85] For the short recension of John, in contrast, where authorities are cited by name alone, without any further note of the works in which their interpretations appear, the prologue-author explains that these sources are named "in general . . . , remytting to þe grettir gloos writun on Ioon where and in what bokis þes doctours seyen þes sentences."[86] These prefatory descriptions thus suggest the experimental newness of commentary-translation as an English literary form, at once revealing the prologuer's perceived need to bring some measure of uniformity to these complex and inconsistent texts, and indicating his belief that at least some English readers will be wholly unfamiliar with the norms of exegetical prose.

But not all of the prologues function as patches, disguising the seams of these composite works. Unlike the prologues supplied for the short recensions, the prologue and epilogue associated with the long *Glossed Gospel* of Matthew reveal the commentators' changing sense of what was needed – or what was possible – in these peritextual pieces. It could be that no substantial prologue was originally planned for long Matthew, which, as Hudson has shown, seems to be the earliest of the *Glossed Gospels*.[87] In BL MS Add. 28026, this work begins with only a short account of its major exegetical sources, part of a rubricated incipit:

> [Þ]is is a schort gloose on Matheu for lewid men for-to vndirstonde þe text, and onely Holi Writ [and] holy doctouris, specially Seynt Ierom, Seynt Ioon Crisostom, and Gregory and Austyn and Bernard, and Rabanus aleggynge holy doctouris, ben set in þis glosse. (f. 2ra)

The modest (and misleading) description of this 189-leaf manuscript as bearing a "schort gloose" seems to suggest that the shorter commentary-translation of Matthew (similarly described, as we have seen, in Trinity College B.1.38 as a "schorte exposicioun") had not yet been undertaken, and perhaps it was not yet even planned. As in Rolle's *Psalter* and the Northern Matthew, here too the writer has felt it important to insist that he is providing only Scripture and authoritative exegesis – a wariness of interpretive novelty that, in the other works, was tied to concerns about the status of biblical literature in the vernacular.[88] If this was indeed all that the commentator (or commentators) first included at the beginning of the text, by the end it clearly struck him as an insufficient account of his purpose, for he went on to offer a substantial epilogue, more than twice as long as the prologues to short Matthew and Luke. The content of this epilogue is, however, quite different from what we have seen in those prologues. It ends with a long meditation on the failures of the age and the need for devoted scriptural teaching, material that would be excerpted to create *Cambridge Tract* x, quoted at the beginning of this chapter.[89] Before that, the commentator again insists that he has translated only Scripture and standard exegetes, asking that "if ony lerned man in Holy Writ fynde ony defaute in þis glos, sette he in þe trewe and cler sentence of holy doctouris, for þis is þe grete desire of þis pore scribeler."[90] Again, he seems to have concerns about the questionably authoritative status of biblical texts and commentary in the vernacular.[91]

Between the opening invitation to correction and the concluding call for more biblical teaching, the writer's preoccupation with authority causes the epilogue to move in a series of unusual and perhaps unexpected directions. The uncertain status of one of his sources, Hrabanus Maurus, was already suggested in the incipit to Add. 28026, where the ninth-century monk is invoked not as an authority in his own right, but as someone "aleggynge holy doctouris." This qualification is developed further in the epilogue:

> Wondre not, lewide men, þouȝ Rabanes be myche alleggid in þis glos, for he was an old doctur, almest six hundrid ȝeeris agon, and hadde plente of olde docturis whiche he rehersiþ in his book þorou-out, and litil seiþ of himsilf, and ȝit he touchiþ no but pleyn mater which may lyȝtly be prouyd by Holy Writ and resoun.[92]

While he seems to presume that the other expositors cited in his commentary – "Austyn, Crisostom, Ierom, Gregorie, Ambrose and such olde seyntis" – should be familiar, the presence of Hrabanus requires explanation.[93] His potential lack of authority, at least compared with the patristic exegetes, is explained by identifying him as a compiler, but the epilogue-author does not let the matter rest there. While Hrabanus's value seems to come from his access to the writings of "plente of olde docturis," the epiloguer still insists that he was "an old doctur" himself, and while he only infrequently offers his own interpretations ("litil seiþ of himsilf"), what he does say appears to have some authority, easily "prouyd by Holy

Writ and resoun." Exegetical authority is proving to be a thorny issue, but the epiloguer does not shy away from the complexity. He immediately goes on to offer three criteria for judging the authority of exegetes and their interpretations: their "oldenesse and holynesse," their learning and long-standing approval "of holy Chirche," and ("moste of alle") that they never compel agreement with their views but invite readers to see how they "weren wel groundid in Holy Writ expresly, or in pleyn and sufficient resoun."[94] At which point, to support especially the third of these criteria, the epiloguer provides a lengthy catena of substantial quotations from various writings of Augustine and Jerome, all on the subject of biblical and exegetical authority. The epilogue becomes, in effect, a short treatise on medieval literary theory.

More will be said below about these notions of interpretive authority and the exercise of the reader's "resoun" in assessing the merits of different glosses. For the moment, it should be noted that the epilogue-author has seized on the basic compilational method of the *Glossed Gospels* – the assembly of a catena of patristic opinions – and extended it, using the epilogue as an opportunity to include patristic opinions on the theoretical underpinnings of the kind of text that has just concluded, a biblical commentary. A similar motivation and method stand behind the opening of the prologue found in another copy of the long recension of Matthew, BodL MS Laud. misc. 235, ff. 1ra–2vb.[95] In this copy, the rubricated list of sources that begins Add. 28026 has been expanded considerably and repositioned in a text that resembles, in its basic form, the three-section prologues discussed above. The list now appears as part of the prologue's second section, when the writer turns to describe the commentary which he claims to have created:

> For þis cause a synful caytif, hauynge compassioun on lewed men, declariþ þe Gospel of Mathew to lewid men in Englische, wiþ exposicioun of seyntis and Holy Writ, and alleggiþ onely Holy Writ and olde doctours in his exposicioun, as Seynt Austyn, Seynt Ierom, Seynt Gregorie, Seynt Ambrose, Seynt Crisostom, Seynt Bernard, Grosted, and olde lawes of seyntis and of holy Chirche, wel groundid in Holy Writ and resoun, and alleggiþ also Rabanes on Mathew, an olde monk and doctour, rehersynge copiously olde holy doctouris for hym, as Austyn, Gregorie, Ambrose, Bede, Illarie, Crisostom, Ierom, and many mo.[96]

As in the opening to Add. 28026, the imagined audience of the commentary-translation is identified as "lewed men," and, again, Hrabanus is set apart at the end of the list of authorities, now more overtly identified as a compiler who "rehers[iþ]" the interpretations of other "holy doctouris." This is followed by an explanation of the text's format similar to those appearing in the short recension prologues, though in this case the prologuer does make reference to the scribal handling of the text, specifying that the short lemmata beginning each gloss are "vndir-drawen" or underlined.[97] Then comes a detailed discussion of citational conventions, in particular (as in the short recension prologues) explaining that the adverb *here* is being used with the force of *ad loc.*, and finally (as in the epilogue and, to a lesser extent, the short prologues) a critique of the evils of the age, condemning especially those "sotil enmyes and weiward eretikis" that would "letten Cristen peple to knowe, here, rede, write, and speke Holy Writ in Englisch."[98]

In all of this, then, the long prologue corresponds to the kind of material found in the shorter prologues, suggesting its importance in establishing the form used in those presumably later texts. Where it departs from them, however, is in its handling of the first section, the justificatory "cause" of the commentary predicating the passage quoted above. As we have seen, in the shorter prologues this rationale is made up of collections of scriptural and exegetical material of various lengths, all underscoring the need for capable clerics to fulfill the "lawe of charite." In the Laud. misc. 235 prologue, in contrast, this first section consists of another catena of patristic quotations, as in the epilogue, but this time focused on basic interpretive theory.[99] Much of this is drawn from Augustine's *De doctrina Christiana*, and especially his rehearsal of the Tyconian rules, and much of it, intriguingly, overlaps with quotations assembled in the General Prologue to the Later Version Wycliffite Bible, though arranged in a different order and with significant variations in wording.[100] The organization of these quotations appears to be purposeful, with the lengthy passages on proper interpretive technique followed by shorter accounts of the complexity and, at times, the opaqueness of Scripture, apparently justifying the need for the foregoing discussion.[101] The final excerpt in the sequence, from Gregory's *Moralia*, then extols the value of commentary, comparing meticulous study of Scripture to more and more finely ground and therefore flavorful spices, in the process introducing a pun that is absent in the *Moralia*'s Latin, while also transitioning to the rationale for the commentary-translation's creation (as quoted above):

> Seynt Gregorie seiþ (in þe xxix book of *Moralys*, vij cº) þat Goddis wordis ben as pyment or precious spycerie. Hou myche spicerie is more powned [Latin: *teritur*], bi so myche vertue is encressed in pyment: so hou myche we pownen [*conterimus*] more Goddis spechis in expownynge [*exponendo*], by þat we, herynge as drynkynge, ben more holpen. For þis cause a synful caytif, ...[102]

In contrast to the duty-bound teachers evoked in the short prologues, this passage presents exegesis as a pleasurable sensory experience, a rich and heady brew that should be available to readers in English as it is in Latin. The opening catena may read awkwardly, made up of disconnected excerpts held together only with additive conjunctions ("Also ... Also ... Also ... Also"), but as he moves to his original prose, the prologue-author seamlessly yokes his interpretive project to these patristic authorities, suggesting that the *Gospels* are a kind of studious and devotional delight to the senses.[103]

Though there is thus no sign of a break between the catena of patristic theory and the prologuer's original prose in Laud. misc. 235, this collection of excerpts *did* circulate as a discrete text, compiled – like the portion of the epilogue included in the *Cambridge Tracts* – as part of a series of short writings relevant to the translation and interpretation of Scripture. The full catena, from the opening of the Laud. misc. prologue through the *Moralia* excerpt, appears as an additional preface in various manuscripts of *Oon of Foure*, copied between two other short tracts, *In þe Bigynnyng of Holi Chirche*, arguing that the primitive Church offers a precedent for the translation and glossing of the gospel "in comwne langage," and *Cambridge Tract* ii, a lengthier polemical piece favoring study of Scripture in the vernacular.[104] In one such copy, BL MS Arundel 254, ff. 9^r–12^v, these three texts form a distinct quire (copied in a distinct script), perhaps indicating that their persistent co-occurrence was supported by their circulation together in booklet form.[105] Similarly, the Laud. misc. catena and *Cambridge Tract* ii appear together as a sequence of prefaces in two copies of the (unglossed) Later Version translation of the New Testament, again possibly having been drawn as a set from a loose booklet.[106] Hanna has emphasized the advantageous "flexibility" afforded by such single-quire booklets, noting that texts copied in this form "can potentially be fitted into nearly any context" in larger scribal productions.[107] Indeed, whether such discrete quires were "fitted into" the fuller manuscript (as in Arundel) or simply served as an exemplar for an anthology of prefatory tracts, the copying of this catena in such a flexible form appears to reflect its potential applicability (and utility) in numerous settings. The newness of vernacular biblical translation and commentary as a field meant that this collection of patristic excepts could be a useful accompaniment to many different texts. Wycliffite writers seem to have made good use of such fascicular flexibility, seen most clearly in the General Prologue to the Later Version translation, which (despite its editorial title) can easily stand on its own as a useful summary of the Old Testament and a treatise (including a catena) on theories of translation and exegesis – as it essentially does in Oxford, University College MS 96.[108] In other cases, pieces of the General Prologue could be excerpted to serve as prefaces to specific biblical books, e.g., in BL MS Add. 10046, which takes the description of the four senses of Scripture found in chapter 12 of the Prologue as a preface to the Later Version Psalter (with ferial canticles), or in Lincoln College MS lat. 119, which excerpts the Prologue's summaries of different Old Testament books, presenting them each as prefaces to those books in the Later Version translation.[109]

This penchant for practical adaptation and repackaging also appears to lie behind the catena in Laud. misc. 235, making the creation of the prologue to the long glossed Matthew somewhat uncertain. That is, while the seamless transition from the catena to the prologue's original prose suggests that the catena was prepared specifically for this prologue, it is also possible that the prologue-author found the catena in a preexisting booklet and crafted his text as a continuation of it, making its patristic excerpts serve the ends of his particular exegetical project.

If a copy of the Laud. misc. prologue was ever a part of Add. 28026, it must have been as a discrete singleton or bifolium, as in the case of the short prologues in Add. 41175, Bodley 143, and Bodley 243, and it has since been lost. As Hudson notes, the explicit to long Matthew in Add. 28026, occurring between the end of the commentary and the epilogue, identifies its glosses as taken from "holy doctoures ... as is teld in þe firste prologe" (ff. 185^v–186^r), and this seems more likely to refer to the passage from Laud. misc. quoted above than to Add. 28026's shorter opening rubric.[110] In either case, this prologue would appear to be a late addition to the project, one judged necessary only after some of the work of compilation had been completed, and which, therefore, would at least at first have to be supplied as a separate bibliographical unit. In contrast, though the inclusion of an epilogue could also have been devised after the process of compilation had begun, the decision to include it seems at least to have been made before the long glossed Matthew was complete, and it could therefore be copied straightaway at the end of that text. Once it was created, the long Matthew prologue seems to have provided the basic form followed by the three surviving short prologues, but this consistency then makes the separate circulation of the short prologues all the more curious. If the inclusion of these kinds of peritexts had been established with the long commentary, why were they apparently neither planned nor included as part of the short recensions from the outset? Perhaps they were, but they were simply copied and circulated apart from the compilation of glosses, leading to the multiple exemplars needed by the scribe of copies like Trinity College B.1.38. Then again, the prologue to short Luke could suggest a different scenario. Perhaps, that is, when the prologue-writer says he has been "lettid fro prechyng for a tyme," he is also indicating his inability to participate in the process of compiling some (or all?) of the short-recension glosses, only able to contribute his prologues after that compilation was completed.[111] Turning from these prologues to consider the commentaries themselves, we will see that such potential changes in the commentators contributing to the project are matched by changing compilational practices. The move from the fuller and more theoretically sophisticated material of the long Matthew prologue to the comparatively humble how-to guide of the shorter prologues corresponds to the compilers' developing sense of the kinds of glosses that should be offered in the vernacular, and how those glosses should be arranged.

As part of a seemingly conventional gesture of humility, the author of the Laud. misc. epilogue avers, "Þis scribeler hadde trauelid wiþ fals bookis," and therefore, he says, in a passage quoted above, "If ony lerned man in Holy Writ fynde ony defaute in þis glos, sette he in þe trewe and cler sentence of holy doctouris, for þis is þe grete desire of þis pore scribeler."[112] In the context of the epilogue, this is a clear reference to the compilers' need to draw on a great number of exegetical texts, and the problem of "fals bookis" suggests the consultation of multiple copies of the same works to find the best possible text.[113] The problem of laboring with a potentially confusing array of books – catenas of glosses, parchment pieces with different prologues, and Early Version Bibles marked for division into lemmata – was one the compilers passed on to the earliest "scribelers" of their text. At least in part, their preference for copying in pieces reflects the uncertain and experimental quality of the text they were creating, a newness that led the compilers to favor the flexibility and open-endedness of booklet production, thereby allowing them continuously to develop and redefine their text.

"As in a Riche Mannes Schoppe"

Arguably the single most significant development in the *Glossed Gospels* project was the decision to make use of a particular source, an important precedent for the compilation of short extracts of patristic exegesis. This source is discussed in the prologue to the short recension of glossed Matthew, part of the writer's explanation of the commentary's citational norms:

> Whanne Y seie "Bede in his omeli" eþer "Gregorie in his omeli" and telle not in what omeli, Y take þat sentence of Alquyn on Matheu. Whanne Y telle in what omeli of Gregorie eþer of Bede, þanne Y mysilf se þat orignal of Gregorie eþer of Bede, and, schortli, whateuer doctour Y allege and telle not speciali where, Y take þat aleggaunce of Alquyn on Matheu, for he hadde many mo originals boþe of Grekis and of Latyns þan I haue now, and I haue manye scharpe doctours whiche he hadde not.[114]

This "Alquyn" is Thomas Aquinas, whose *Catena Aurea* presents what he describes as "a continuous exposition drawn from diverse books of the doctors" ("ex diversis doctorum libris ... expositionem continuam compilavi").[115] By calling it an *expositio continua*, Aquinas is apparently attempting to distinguish his text from the presentation of marginal and interlinear notes found in works such as the *Glossa ordinaria*, though, arguably even more than in that earlier work, the *Catena* simply assembles patristic and early medieval quotations with little adaptation and little effort to sew one excerpt to the next.[116] His compiled glosses are presented as a block of continuous prose, with the relevant biblical text relegated to a narrower flanking column. Each gloss begins with a (typically rubricated) citation identifying its source, and these notes function to divide the individual pieces of the commentary.[117] It was thus an easy enough task for the compilers of short glossed Matthew to select specific interpretations from the *Catena*'s offerings, and, even as he points out that he has consulted some "scharpe doctours" on his own, the prologuer acknowledges the wide range of sources made available in "Alquyn on Matheu."

At least formally, setting aside the question of language, the *Glossed Gospels* and the *Catena Aurea* have much in common, both being extensive exegetical compilations focused on the same biblical texts, drawing on many of the same authorities, and similarly committed to the careful citation of their sources. It should be unsurprising, then, that the compilers of the short recension of the commentary-translation of Matthew drew on the *Catena* from beginning to end, treating it, in Hudson's phrase, as a convenient "starting point" for their project.[118] In contrast, whether through ignorance of its existence or a deliberate decision, the commentator (or commentators) responsible for the earlier, long recension of glossed Matthew made no use of the *Catena*, instead assembling a compilation of English exegesis directly from the sources identified in the Laud. misc. 235 prologue. At the earliest stages of their project of vernacular exegesis, that is, the compilers of the *Glossed Gospels* had to decide for themselves how to assemble their patchwork of interpretive pieces.

Though more complicated than any of the commentary-translations discussed above, the basic method of the long Matthew compilers was still rather straightforward.[119] They worked from a small number of commentaries on the gospel in its entirety, especially Ps.-Chrysostom's *Opus Imperfectum*, Hrabanus's compilation, and Jerome's relatively short commentary, supplementing these with the more selective treatments found in Augustine's and Gregory's homilies, with only isolated readings taken from the other authorities named in the Laud. misc. prologue.[120] Most of these sources, of course, present their interpretations as continuous prose – this is most obviously the case in the sermons, but it is true too for the thoroughgoing commentaries, with the *Opus Imperfectum* organized (like Northern Matthew) into *homiliae*.[121] In creating their vernacular catena, the compilers of long Matthew had to decide how this material would be divided into glosses, and, though they are far from consistent, in practice they appear to have favored whichever source would give them the fullest range of interpretive options in relatively succinct prose. Their discussion of Matth. 2.11b, for example, focuses entirely on the meaning of the Magi's gifts, beginning with a single long gloss. (Throughout the following, lemmata are set off in small capitals and the citations in italic.)

> GOLD, ENCENSE, AND MYRRE. Þe kynges prechen hym by gostly ȝiftis whom þei worshipen: by gold þei prechen hym kyng, bi encense God, by myrre deedly man. Offre we gold to Crist þat we bileeue hym to regne eueryhwere. Offere we encenese to him þat we bileue þat he þat appered in tyme was God byfore tymes (or wiþouten bygynnyng). Offere we myrre, þat we byleue hym dedly in oure fleiche whom we bileuen vnpassible (or þat may not suffre) in his Godhed. Bi gold also heuenly wisdom is vndirstonden, by encense vertu of prayer, by myrre sleewynge of fleische. Þerfore we offren gold to þe kynge boren if we schynen bi clerenesse of heuenly wisdom in his siȝt. We offeren encense if we brennen þouȝtis of fleisch bi holy studies of preieris in þe autter of oure herte, þat we mowe sauere (or make to smelle) to God sum swete þing bi heuenly disir. We offren myrre if we slen vices of fleisch bi abstinence. *Gregor in þe tenþe omely and Crisostom here and Ierom sumwhat on þes wordes.* (Laud. misc. 235, f. 7vb)

Despite the three names given in the citation, this gloss is translated closely from Gregory's homilies, with a bit of original prose (*Bi gold also—sleewynge of fleische*) added to introduce the alternative reading of the gifts found further along in the same source.[122] Ps.-Chrysostom presents a similar (though more diffuse) interpretation of the gifts as denoting the kingship, divinity, and humanity of Christ, and he likewise tropologizes the first two as the "wisdom of faith" (*fidei sapientia*) and "clean prayer" (*munda oratio*). Compared with this, Jerome is indeed only "sumwhat" relevant, quoting from Juvencus' versified gospels to identify the gifts with Christ's kingship, humanity, and divinity, respectively.[123] With this range of readings all translated from a single source, the compilers can then supplement their lengthy gloss with two shorter excerpts, both taken from Ps.-Chrysostom:

> [By] myrre is undirstonden goode werkes: as myrre kepeþ bodies of dede men uncorupt, so good werkis kepen euere Crist crucified in mannes mynde. First it bihoueþ to offere to Crist resonable feiþ, þan clene preyer, in þe þridde place holy werkis. *Crisostom here*. Eche preyer is sike whiche is not kepte bi uertu of almes dedis. *Crisostom here*. (f. 7vb)

Here the compilers translate the portion of Ps.-Chrysostom's moralization that disagrees with Gregory's, and they then append a final note relevant to that specific reading.[124] These glosses are clearly related to one another, and yet the citations serve to divide them into two units. It is tempting to suggest that this division reflects the fact that the compilers have omitted a sentence that comes between the two glosses in the *Opus Imperfectum*, but they showed no such care when condensing the material from Gregory in their longer gloss. Perhaps they simply wanted these two shorter glosses to stand on their own, thereby emphasizing the proverbial force of the final excerpt.

At the same time as such seemingly unnecessary citations give the commentary-translation a more fragmentary quality, however, longer glosses like the one from Gregory cultivate the sense of a more continuous and seamless work. Indeed, it is striking that, unlike the Ps.-Chrysostom glosses, both of which contribute to a single interpretation of the biblical text, Gregory's two different ways of moralizing the same passage are presented as one bout of uninterrupted prose. It could be somewhat misleading, therefore, to treat the compilers' citations as dividing the long recension of glossed Matthew into discrete units, and in some cases their glosses even appear to continue on the other side of a citation. In their lengthy interpretation of the slaughter of the Holy Innocents, for example, they offer two explanations of "Rachel bewailing her children" (Matth. 2.18b), with citations dividing the commentary into three parts:

> RACHEL was buried bysides Betlem in Effrata, and of þis herbore (or byrynge of hir body) sche toke name of moder, *Ierom here*, and þerfore sche is brouȝt in wepyng hir sones. *Crisostom here*. Or for þe lynage of Iuda and Beniamyn of whiche Beniamyn Richel was moder coostiden togidre

and many children of Beniamyn weren slayn, for Eroude kilde in Bethlem and in alle þe coostis þer-of. *Ierom here*. (f. 8va)

The single phrase translated from Ps.-Chrysostom is truly a supplement, necessarily read together with the larger gloss in which it has been inserted.[125] In this case, then, though it may also serve to set the first interpretation apart from the second, the citation of Ps.-Chrysostom seems to have been introduced primarily (and pedantically) to specify that this bit of prose is not taken from Jerome. Reading across the compilers' citations in this manner begins to reveal larger continuities in the commentary-translation. Just to remain with the example of the Innocents, the series of literalistic interpretations from which this quotation has been drawn is followed by two longer passages taken from Hrabanus, and together these final excerpts provide a "gostly" or spiritual interpretation of the same material.[126] The entire passage of commentary, that is, spanning three columns in Laud. misc. 235, can be read continuously as offering a literal and spiritual interpretation of the story of the Innocents.

The tension between fragmentary glosses and through-composed commentary in the long recension is largely absent in short Matthew, at least in part as a consequence of this later text's use of the *Catena Aurea*. The compilers of short Matthew were clearly familiar with the long recension and drew on it extensively – and it is certainly possible that the same writers were responsible for both texts – but the later work eschews long Matthew's tendency toward continuity in favor of discrete glosses.[127] It is, in other words, a true catena. Interpreting the reference to Rachel in Matth. 2.18b, for example, short Matthew provides the same two historicist explanations as the long recension, and it adds a third, but its citations now divide the commentary into more readily isolable units:

> RACHEL. Beniamyn was borun of Rachel, and Bethleem is not in þe lynage of Beniamyn, but for Rachel was biried bisidis Betleem in Effrata, þerbi sche takiþ þe name of modir. *Ierom and Crisostom here*. Eþer for þe lynagis of Iuda and Beniamyn weren ioyned, bicause of Bethleem many children of Beniamyn weren slayn, for Eroude comaundide children to be slayn not oneli in Betleem but also in all coostis þer-of. *Ierom here*. Eþer Rachel þanne biwepte hir sones of Beniamyn sumtyme slayn of oþere lynagis, whanne sche say þe sones of hir sister slayn in siche a cause, þat þei weren eiris of euerlastynge liyf. *Austin in Questiouns of þe Olde and Newe Testament*. (BL MS Add. 41175, f. 7[rb–va])

Though their shared phrasing suggests that the compilers could have been consulting the long recension when they prepared these glosses, this passage is essentially a fresh translation of the *Catena*, where these three glosses appear in the same order, though in slightly fuller forms.[128] Aquinas attributes the first to Jerome alone, and so it would seem that the short recension compilers have added the observation that this interpretation is shared by Ps.-Chrysostom, a point that is suggested, though not made explicit, in the long recension's handling of the same material. This reshuffling of citations results in three discrete glosses, three ways of explaining the lemma quoted at the beginning of the passage. The same move toward patchwork prose can be seen even more clearly in the treatment of the Magi's gift, where the long passage from Gregory is broken into pieces:

> GOLD, ENCENSE, AND MYRRE. Ech of þes þre kingis offriden þre ʒiftis, and ech of hem bi hise ʒiftes prechide him kyng, God, and man. *Remygie*. We offren gold to þe child borun if we schynen in his siʒt bi þe clerenesse of heuenli wisdom; we offren encense if we smellen swote to God bi studies of preieris; we offren myrre if we sleen þe vices of fleisch bi abstynence. *Gregor in his omeli*. Goostli he offreþ gold which ʒyueþ hymsilf ful of wisdom of feiþ to Crist; he offriþ encense to Crist which offriþ clene preier to hym; myrre is gode werkis, for as myrre kepiþ þe bodies of deed men wiþout corrupcioun, so goode werkis kepen Crist crucified euerlastyngli in þe mynde of man and kepen a man in Crist: first offre we resonable feiþ, and þanne clene preier, and holy werkis in þe þridde tyme. *Crisostom here*. (Add. 41175, f. 6va).

Again, the compilers have drawn at least some of this material from the *Catena Aurea*, especially the short Remigian gloss, translated in its entirety, as well as the second gloss, which follows Aquinas's version more closely than Gregory's original.[129] The final gloss, however, does not appear in the *Catena*, and it has been taken instead from the *Opus Imperfectum*, retranslating some material from the long recension, and now, though still selective, providing more of Ps.-Chrysostom's interpretation.[130] In contrast to the long recension, where the compilers apparently noted the overlap between Gregory's and Ps.-Chrysostom's readings of gold as relating to "wisdom" and incense to "preier" and therefore only bothered to add Ps.-Chrysostom's interpretation of myrrh as "holy werkis," the short recension compilers have allowed both of the glosses to stand in more or less complete forms. In other words, the short recension compilers have preferred to offer seemingly self-sufficient glosses, ones that do not depend on the interpretive material that comes before or after them, even if that means repeating some of the same readings.

Although they supplement his attributions and draw some glosses directly from patristic and early medieval sources, the writers responsible for short Matthew adopted Aquinas's general method of compilation, assembling their text as a string of discrete interpretive units. Their commentary may therefore superficially resemble the long recension of the *Glossed Gospel* of Matthew, with passages of exegesis moving from lemmata to gloss to citation, and they may even share some of the same glosses, but the two recensions appear to anticipate different kinds of reading. If the citations in the long recension are treated not as strict divisions between units of text but rather as parenthetical peritexts – which, as we have seen, is how they must be treated in at least some cases – then the commentary's prose can be read almost continuously, an approach also found in Northern Matthew and in Rolle's *English Psalter*. In the short recension, to be sure, there may be some logic to the arrangement of the glosses. In the treatment of the Magi's gifts, for example, it could be that the literalistic specification that they each offered all three kinds of gift was presented first so that each King could better stand in for the tropological subject described in the remaining glosses. But by crafting their glosses such that each can be read as a coherent interpretive whole, the short recension compilers have enabled a kind of discontinuous, disordered, and selective reading that is more difficult (not to say impossible) to undertake in the other commentary-translations discussed in these chapters.[131] Implicit in the compilation's form is the suggestion that the reader can move from one gloss to another, in any order she wants and skipping over any number of intermediating glosses, to study and reflect on different authoritative understandings of the biblical text.

In light of this more piecemeal process of reading, the citations that accompany the short recensions of the *Glossed Gospels*, and especially the marginal citations in Bodley 143, become all the more intriguing (see Fig. 14). According to the prologues, these citations serve to guarantee the authority of the many different glosses that the writers have compiled, part of the insistence on exegetical non-novelty appearing in all of the commentary-translations discussed so far. But, the short recension of John excepted, the compilers of the *Glossed Gospels* have done much more than simply indicating the authoritative sources from which they have drawn their glosses, providing (as we have seen) detailed accounts of where in their sources these interpretations appear. In Latin commentaries, such citations would seem to allow interested readers to locate fuller versions of the same material in the *originalia* from which they have been drawn, but, of course, the compilers of the *Gospels* justify their project by emphasizing that readers of the vernacular are unable to access Latin texts.[132] In part, it would seem that we should not imagine a strictly monolingual readership for these commentary-translations. Perhaps, regardless of what the prologues claim, the compilers hoped that some readers *would* be able to consult the cited sources, though, like Trevisa's lord, not without onerous "studyinge and auysement and lokyng of oþer bokes."[133] But these citations could also potentially help to shape the experience of reading the *Gospels* even when Latin material remained out of reach. They could, that is, provide one way of selecting specific glosses from among the many different interpretations that the compilers have assembled, enabling the recreation of, for example, a specifically Hieronymian, Gregorian, or Augustinian approach to the biblical text. These marginal and underlined notes could thus serve a function analogous to the Porretan indexing symbols used in Wyclif's commentary on the Psalms (discussed in Chapter 2), offering a guide to the discontinuous reading of the short recension's patchwork prose.[134]

The model of the *Catena Aurea* clearly helped to guide the short recension compilers' move away from the kind of continuous commentary still reflected in the long recension of glossed Matthew, and it may therefore be tempting to see the short recension as, in some ways, more "scholarly" and less "devotional" than the earlier examples of vernacular exegesis discussed above. But, though the continuous prose of the *English Psalter* or long Matthew is closer to the kinds of treatises now commonly associated with medieval "devotional reading," by the end of the fourteenth century it was increasingly the case, as Gillespie notes, that such "devotional" texts were "being subjected to new processes of subdivision, compilation, extraction, and anthologizing."[135] At the same time as the discrete glosses of the short recension have, compared with earlier commentary-translations, more in common with scholastic works like the *Catena* or the *Glossa ordinaria*, these differences can also be seen as part of a trend toward selective reading found more generally in vernacular religious literature, allowing the users of these books to attend, in Jennifer Bryan's phrase, "to more localized vicissitudes of taste and feeling, so as to produce more effective personal responses."[136] Indeed, it is precisely this kind of studious devotional reading that the short recension prologuer seems to have in mind when he describes his hope that, through the *Glossed Gospel*, "Cristen puple may haue sikirli þe trewe vndurstongyng of Holi Writ, … and come bi Goddis mersi þerbi to þe endles blis of heuene."[137]

This focus on devotional study, especially as it might be tied to practices of discontinuous reading, can also be seen in a gloss shared by both the long and short recensions of Matthew, the first gloss in both of these commentary-translations. The short recension presents a fuller version of the gloss, explaining the word *book* in the gospel's opening words, "The book of generacioun of Iesu Crist":

> þe book. Þis book is as a schoppe of graces. As in a riche mannes schoppe ech man fyndiþ þe þing þat he sekiþ, so also ech soule fyndiþ in þis book þat þing þat is nedeful to helpe. *Crisostom here.*[138]

At the same time as this gloss points to a single salvific "þing" that can be found in Matthew, the comparison of the "þis book" – most obviously the gospel, but also perhaps the *Glossed Gospels* – to a "riche mannes schoppe" suggests the need to consider and choose from an assortment of objects, and it is hard to resist the identification of these "þing[es]" with the different glosses that the compilers have assembled. The simile of the shop, in other words, could be a version of a more widespread trope of selective reading, also exemplified in the translator's prologue to the *Orcherd of Syon*, where the "religiouse sustren" are told to "walke aboute where ȝe wolen wiþ ȝoure mynde and resoun" and "taste of sich fruyt and herbis resonably aftir ȝoure affeccioun, and what ȝou likeþ best, aftirward chewe it wel and ete þereof."[139] If the image of the "riche mannes schoppe" was meant to describe the weighing of different glosses in the commentary-translation of Matthew, then it is striking that it appears at the start of both of the recensions. Perhaps because their approach to vernacular exegesis was informed by earlier works like the *English Psalter*, or perhaps because they lacked a model for this kind of catena, the compilers of the long recension of Matthew produced a text in which their different glosses, though appearing to be discrete "þing[es]," frequently run together as continuous prose. With Aquinas as guide, then, the short recension compilers succeeded in assembling their "schoppe" of glosses. Experimenting with literary forms for which there were few clear precedents in English, the compilers of the *Glossed Gospel* of Matthew had to work through multiple versions before crafting a text that fully supports the kind of reading imagined in this gloss.

"Pleyn Mater"

As the various examples discussed above should indicate, the compilers of both recensions of the *Glossed Gospel* of Matthew attempted to do more than "facilitate the understanding of the literal sense."[140] Though their historicizing interpretations of Rachel certainly reflect literalistic interpretive priorities also found in the commentaries of Wyclif and Woodford (as discussed in Chapter 2), these are balanced by a tendency toward tropology like that seen in Northern Matthew. To the examples of the moral reading of the Magi's gifts, found in both the long and short recensions of glossed Matthew, and the "gostly" interpretation of the slaughter of the Innocents that concludes the bevy of glosses in the long recension, could be added instances in which the compilers of the *Glossed Gospels* favor tropology in their readings of the biblical text's literal sense. Explaining why, for example, the cry of the Innocents' bereaved mothers is said to be heard "in Rama" – which in Hebrew "is interpretid 'an hiȝ'" – the short recension compiler writes,

> Þerfor þis vois was herd an hiȝ, for it was sent of þe deþ of innocentis. Whanne a pore man suffriþ violence of a myȝti man, his pryue cry is herd an hiȝ, þouȝ he dore not crie opynly, for not gret cri but iust is herd of God. (Add. 41175, f. 7rb)

Shifting away from the feminine gender of "þe modris," the generalized "pore man" of this gloss is offered as an ideal with which one should identify, moving the gloss from a literalistic to a tropological register. The *Glossed Gospels*, in other words, contain a blending of literal and moral interpretations for which, as we have seen, there is ample precedent in the tradition of commentaries specific to these biblical books.

While the compilers did not favor one or another of the senses of Scripture, their selection of glosses does seem to have been guided by some overriding, if comparatively vague, hermeneutic priorities. The different *Glossed Gospel* prologues, as well as the epilogue to the long recension of Matthew, all invoke what is variously called the "opyn" or "pleyn" quality of their glosses. The prologue to short Matthew specifies that the compilers have provided only the "opyn sentensis of eld holi doctours," a phrase repeated in the short John prologue with only slight variation, "þe opyn and schorte sentencis of holy doctours."[141] Likewise, in the prologue and epilogue to long Matthew, as well as the prologue to short Luke, the writer claims to have provided "pleinly and schortly þe sentence of þes doctours."[142] In these cases, *pleinly* and *schortly* seem to refer not to the glosses themselves – as they appear, that is, in the Latin *originalia* – but rather to how the compilers have selected and translated them. Then again, it may be wrong to try to distinguish too clearly between the glosses and their handling by compilers, since in all cases the result seems to be the kind of exegesis that, in the epilogue to long Matthew, Hrabanus is said to have provided in his own compilation: "pleyn mater."[143]

In her account of these prologues, Copeland equates "the open and plain sense" with "the literal sense" of Scripture, and she suggests that these references to "pleyn mater" reflect the compilers' commitment to presenting the biblical text's "literal meaning according to the principle of *intentio auctoris*."[144] As we have seen, however, the *Glossed Gospels* do not focus solely, or even predominantly, on the literal sense of Scripture, and many of Copeland's terms (e.g., *lettre*, *entente*) appear only in the prologues and epilogue as part of the catenas surrounding long Matthew.[145] Instead, *opyn* and *pleyn* seem to refer not to the senses of Scripture, but to the same thing as they do in other examples of Wycliffite prose, namely, as Andrew Cole puts it, "the interpretive accessibility of texts and performances, words, and deeds."[146] Perhaps the clearest example of this use of *opyn* occurs in the General Prologue to the Later Version Bible, where the writer claims to have rendered the text "so þat þe sentence [is] as opene or openere in English as in Latyn," though without straying "fer fro þe lettre" of the Vulgate.[147] The prologuer seems to claim that the meaning of the biblical text is clearer in the Wycliffite translation than in the Latin which it translates, even for someone who can read Latin, and he goes on to provide an account of how this clarity has been achieved, by "resolu[inge]," for example, the ambiguities of Latin ablative absolute constructions.[148]

It may be unsurprising, then, to see the *Glossed Gospels* prologuer describing the compilers' attempt to translate glosses "pleinly," eschewing ambiguities in the phrasing of the Latin sources, but it is more startling to see the interpretive content of the glosses described as "opyn" or "pleyn." Though in some texts the Wycliffite insistence on "openness" is tied to a sense that glosses are either unnecessary or potentially misleading, here the term would seem to describe the generally unambiguous and straightforward quality of the interpretations that have been compiled.[149] And, just as it would be absurd to conclude that the compilers' preference for "schort" glosses implies a hostility toward long ones, it is far from clear that their preference for "opyn" glosses implies a rejection of "derke" ones, glosses that are challenging, complicated, ambiguously worded, or, perhaps, too speculative.[150] Without making a claim about hermeneutic content, the focus on interpretations that are "opyn and schorte" should be seen instead as reflecting the compilers' pragmatic belief that the "lewid men and sympli-lettrid prestis" for whom they wrote would be unable to wrestle with (or would simply be uninterested in) more sophisticated exegesis.[151] The *Glossed Gospels* provide an entry point into the tradition of scholastic exegesis, like the Latin commentary that was read to the Durham novices while they ate their meals, and they offer a similarly "solid diet" of uncomplicated interpretations.¹⁵² Further, and in contrast to the "general emphasis on the non-hierarchical intellectual accessibility of the Bible" that Kantik Ghosh has identified in the English Wycliffite sermon cycle, this account of "opyn" glosses holds out at least the possibility of advancing to "derker" ones, and the prologuer regularly defers to the expertise of "lerned m[e]n" who might have more experience and facility with this exegetical material.¹⁵³

This implicit notion of the value of more sophisticated exegesis, even if it is deemed unsuitable for readers of the *Glossed Gospels*, would seem to be challenged by the prologuer's continued insistence on the importance of "pleyn resoun" when interpreting the biblical text. Throughout the prologues (and epilogue), alongside his focus on "opyn and schorte" interpretations, the writer repeatedly claims that his glosses are "groundid in Goddis lawe and resoun," or that they "may lyȝtly be prouyd by Holy Writ and resoun."¹⁵⁴ At first blush, these appeals to "Holy Writ and resoun" may make the interpretations assembled by the compilers appear almost unnecessary, offering little more than could be deduced with an unglossed copy of Scripture and careful application of one's rational faculties. Though this writer clearly upholds the importance of reason in biblical interpretation, however, it is the different glosses, not Scripture itself, that he claims should be subjected to the reader's rational scrutiny, and the prologuer by no means suggests that, if one or another gloss is found wanting, the reader should come up with his or her own interpretation of the biblical text. His appeals to reason are explained most clearly in the catena on patristic authority in the long Matthew epilogue. Quoting at length from Augustine's *Contra Faustum*, the epiloguer emphasizes the difference between the authority of Scripture and of the Fathers:

> Forsoþe, in litle werkis of latter men þat ben conteyned in bokis wiþout noumbre – but in no maner euened to þe alle-holyeste excellence of canoun Scripturis or reulis of Holy Writ – ȝhe, in whiche-euer of hem þe same treuþe is foundun, neþeles þe autorite is fer vneuene treuly in þese lattere mennes bokis. If ony þingis in hap ben gessid to discorde fro treuþe, for þei ben not vndirstondun as þei ben seid, neþelis þe reder or herer haþ þere fre demynge bi whiche eþer he approue þat þat plesiþ or reproue þat þat offendeþ.¹⁵⁵

This assessment of exegetical authority appears in other basic works of scholastic interpretive theory, such as Abelard's *Sic et Non*, emphasizing that, compared with the unquestionable inerrancy of scriptural truth, the works of "latter men" like patristic commentators will be at best "vneuene" or inconsistent.¹⁵⁶ Patristic writings consequently offer a wide array of conflicting, contradictory opinions, and this interpretive disagreement (or, more positively, variety) is reflected in the strings of quotations that make up *Sic et Non* and the *Glossed Gospels* alike. Similarly, in another excerpt included in the long Matthew epilogue, this time from the *De Trinitate*, Augustine avers,

> If he þat rediþ my writyngis vndirstondiþ oþere men in þat word in whiche he vndirstondiþ not me, leye he my book asidis or cast awey if it semeþ good to him, and ȝeue he trauel and tyme to hem þat he vndirstondiþ.[157]

In part, this passage is meant to illustrate how the Fathers "chargiden neiþer constreynede ony man to take her bookis," but it also provides an explanation of the different and mutually exclusive interpretations of verses included in the *Glossed Gospels*, and it points to a way of reading the text, a basic method of scholasticism: the use of reason to judge the merit of contradictory authorities. Applying Augustine's words to the English commentary, if "he þat rediþ" one or another gloss on a particular verse disagrees with what he finds there, he should "leye [it] asidis" and consider one of the alternative explanations instead.

In light of statements like these, it would seem that the prologuer has insisted on the importance of using "Holy Writ and resoun" not because of some belief in the greater authority of the inspired reader compared with the "eld holi doctours" that served as his sources. Instead, lacking access to the larger world of Latin learning and without any more understanding of interpretive theory than the prologuer has been able to provide, the "lewid men" for whom the *Glossed Gospels* were prepared would have recourse *only* to "Holy Writ and resoun" in their assessment of these interpretations. If they are unconvinced by one gloss, then they should consider another, but the implication is that somewhere in the "pleyn mater" of these interpretations they will find one (or more) that satisfies their "resoun." In this way, as the prologuer maintains, "pore Cristen men mown sumdel knowe þe text of þe gospel wiþ comyn sentence of olde holy doctours."[158]

By addressing these theoretical issues and providing detailed accounts of how this commentary-translation should be read, the author of the *Glossed Gospels* prologues reveals his awareness of the relative novelty of biblical exegesis in English. Indeed, though we have seen similar indications of the newness of vernacular commentaries in the prologues to the *English Psalter* and Northern Matthew, the *Glossed Gospels* prologuer does considerably more to prepare his readers for this specialized and unfamiliar form of literature. This careful treatment, like the much fuller range of sources painstakingly consulted by the compilers of the *Glossed Gospels*, almost certainly reflects the commentary-translation's production in a university setting and by writers more familiar with the complex field of scholastic exegesis. While the other English commentaries discussed in these chapters were written for specific communities of readers and circulated (at least at first) locally in the North, the *Gospels* purport to have a broader aim, intended generally for "lewid men in Englische tunge" and "þe pore men of [þ]is nacioun."[159] In the nation's premier center of biblical study, the experimental form of commentary-translation received its most elaborate treatment.

Again, though, even when produced in this academic setting and as a chain of discontinuous glosses, the *Gospels* are presented as a devotional text. To return to the passage with which this chapter began, they are said to offer "counfort and sekernesse to come to þe blysse of heuene," ends which require "þinkynge, lernynge, and spekynge Cristis gloriose gospel."[160] Or, as it is put in the prologue to short Matthew, "Y desire noon oþer þing in þis werk no but þat Cristen puple knowe and kepe treuli Holi Writ."[161] This notion of both "knowing" and "keeping" the text implies not just study, but study aimed at effecting moral change in the reader, and we have seen that this focus on tropology is in keeping with the tradition of scholastic commentaries on the gospels, in their literal and spiritual senses alike. In this regard, both Northern Matthew and the Wycliffite *Glossed Gospels* continue a literary experiment initiated in Rolle's *English Psalter*, offering further attempts to adapt scholastic exegesis to meet the devotional needs of English readers.

Epilogue: John Bale's Dilemma

Nothinge wyl be hydden from him that asketh w^t mekenesse, seketh in faith, & in prayer desyreth the glory of the Lord. Euident wyll those secrete mysteryes be vnto hym whyche are preuylye hydde vnto other vndre darke ambages and parables. Though this heauenlye treasure of helth be vnder locke and keye of vnknowne similitudes, and so be shutt vp from the vntowarde and wycked generacion for theire vnbeleues sake, yet wyl it be playne inough to the faithfull beleuers instauntly callynge vpon him which hath the kaye of Dauid to open vnto them the dore of his infallyble verytees.[1]

Throughout the foregoing chapters, scholastic commentary has emerged as a form of writing that encouraged creativity and experimentation, with successive generations of exegetes attempting at once to affirm the authority of inherited interpretations and to find ways to offer new readings of their own. In fourteenth-century England, these efforts at conservation and innovation included work in both Latin and the English vernacular, and exegetes responded to trends developing outside the universities and explored the possibilities of commentary in a new language. In the eyes of John Bale (d. 1563), however, the reformer who sought to catalogue the legacy of medieval English literature, this outpouring of exegetical energy was apparently unnecessary. Claiming that the meaning of the "heauenlye treasure" of Holy Writ will be "euident" and "playne" to faithful readers who persevere with urgent ("instaunt") prayers, Bale maintains that even the most obscure portions of Scripture can be understood without recourse to commentaries, and he thus signals his commitment to the new reformist approaches to biblical interpretation championed, in English, by William Tyndale (d. 1536).[2] Like Bale, Tyndale had insisted that "whosoeuer hathe the profession of baptyme wryten in his harte cannot but vnderstond the Scripture," provided that he is willing to "exercise hymselfe therin, and compare one place to another, and marke the maner of speache, and axe here and there the meanynge of a sentence of them that be bettre exercysed."³ Indeed, Tyndale derided scholastic commentaries for their various conflicting interpretations, taking these disagreements to be a sure sign of error, and he mercilessly mocked exegetes who "wandre as in a myst" and "cannot come to the right way," finally turning biblical texts into "no thinge but very ridels, ... at the whiche they cast as a blynde man dothe at the crowe, & expounde by gesse, an hundrethe doctoures an hundrethe wayes."⁴ Confident in the clarity of Scripture for the faithful, and frustrated by the variety of readings in scholastic commentaries, Tyndale could only conclude that these "cruell ennemyes" were attempting to deceive readers, their "devilish glosses" nothing more than "cobwebbes which those poysoned spiders had spreade vpon the face of the cleare texte."⁵

Yet all of these descriptions of proper and improper biblical interpretation, including Bale's account of meaning that is "playne inough to the faithfull beleuers," come from reformist exegesis, from Tyndale's and Bale's own attempts to offer lemmatized English commentaries on different books of the Bible. It is hard to avoid the sense of contradiction here. Certainly, Tyndale's theoretical statements could be seen as leaving space, conceptually, for such works – they could be considered textual stand-ins for readers "that be bettre exercysed" in biblical interpretation – but it remains the case that these reformers have produced commentaries following many of the same conventions as their scholastic antecedents and presenting new interpretations of their own.⁶ In his *Obedience of a Christen man*, Tyndale had satirized scholastic exegetes, whose works were so numerous that "if thou haddest but of every auctor one boke thou coudest not pyle them vp in any warehouse in London, and every auctor is one contrary vnto another."⁷ Yet he does not hesitate to contribute more volumes to this imagined exegetical stockpile, and Bale is happy to follow him in this effort.

Commentary is a dangerous genre for reformist writers. If they admit that readers could benefit from texts offering biblical interpretation, they run the risk of appearing to deny the clarity of Scripture's meaning, and they raise the possibility that other exegetes (perhaps even the scholastics) might have a better claim to proper interpretation, almost inevitably leading us back to Tyndale's warehouse of contradictory commentaries. The question that follows this passage in *Obedience* – "In so grete diversite of sprites, how shall I know who lyeth and who saith trouth?" – is thus more urgent for a would-be exegete than it might otherwise appear.⁸ Tyndale's response is to insist on his own interpretive authority, to present himself as an ideal or model reader with "the profession of baptyme wryten in his harte," and persistently to reject scholastic commentary *en masse* as nothing more than a collection of "false gloses," "fylthie gloses," and "naughtye arguments."[9] For Bale, however, whose bibliographic interests led him to engage in detail with many of the texts in Tyndale's imagined warehouse, such wholesale and undifferentiated dismissal of medieval writing was simply not an option. Bale confronts this dilemma with greater care than his forerunner, and in his own commentary he is therefore able to offer a subtler account of the value of biblical exegesis, scholastic and reformist, as a literary form.

Bale's efforts to position his work in relation to medieval commentaries – or, rather, his attempts to describe medieval commentaries in such a way as to make them fitting precedents for his own undertakings – continued in his great bibliographical catalogues, some of the earliest efforts to assemble and account for the texts discussed in the foregoing chapters. Born in part from his need to address a pressing problem in reformist hermeneutics, his work with scholastic exegesis has helped to shape the reception of these texts, and especially Middle English commentary-translations, in even the most recent scholarship. It is therefore with Bale and his exegetical dilemma that this study concludes.

Bale's vernacular commentary on the Apocalypse, written in the 1540s during his exile in Antwerp and titled *The Image of Bothe Churches*, quite clearly continues Tyndale's work, drawing on the reformer's translation of the final biblical book and interspersing lengthy expository passages headed "the paraphrase," apparently under the influence of Erasmus (see Fig. 17).[10] Even here, he cannot resist the urge to catalogue. In his preface, Bale first provides, in prose, an account of patristic exegesis of the Apocalypse up to Isidore of Seville (d. 636), and he then lists seventy-five later exegetes, organized by the religious orders to which they belonged, with the most recent interpreters (beginning with Luther) collected at the end under the heading *ex neotericis* ("from the new writers").[11] Some of this material has been drawn from intermediaries, especially Trithemius and, for Carmelite exegetes, Bale's earlier *Anglorum Heliades*, both of which are cited in the margins of the preface's catalogue (e.g., sig. A8r), but other entries quite clearly reflect his direct consultation of a variety of earlier interpretive texts.[12] Bale's reading of medieval commentaries appears to have been almost wholly limited to what was available in recent printed editions, but it was nevertheless substantial, indicated by the naming of a range of medieval exegetes in the commentary's margins, where they appear amid numerous biblical cross-references (see Fig. 17).[13] Intriguingly, Bale's valuing of these works seems to have informed his

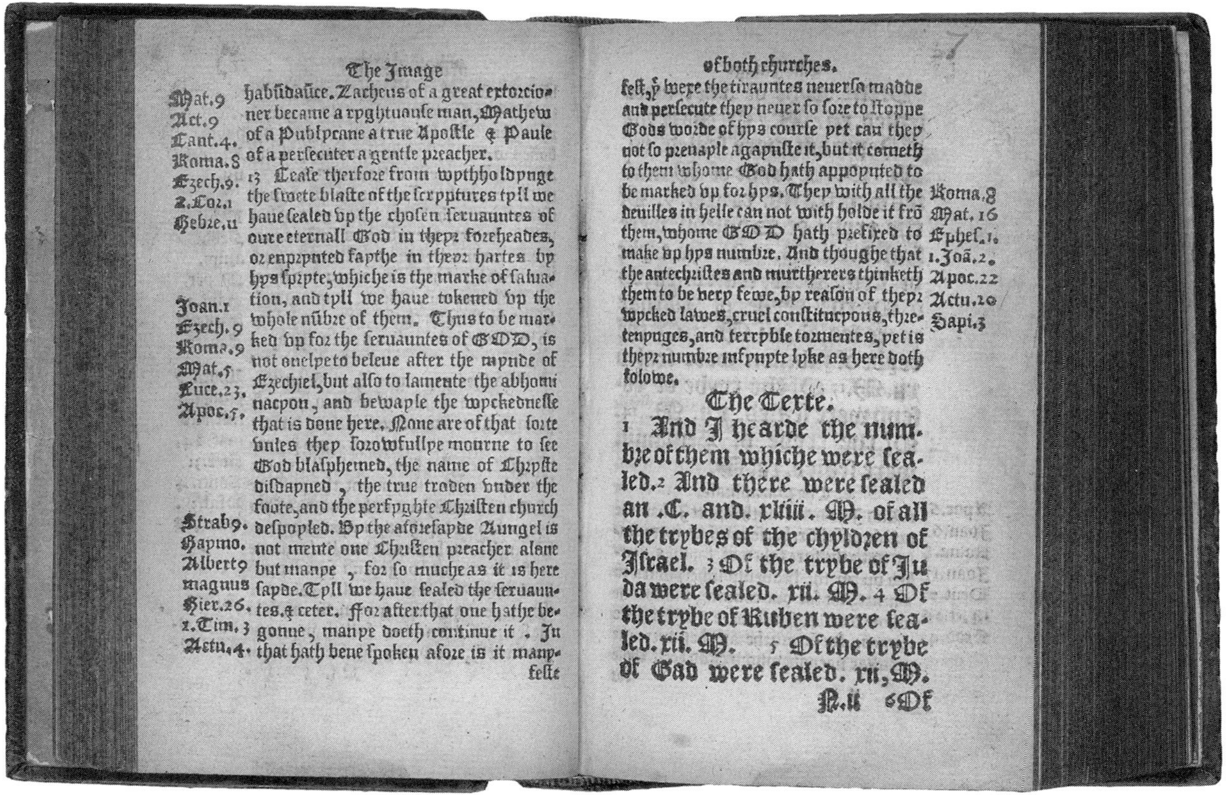

Figure 17 John Bale, *The Image of Both Churches* (London: John Day, 1550), sig. N1ᵛ–N2ʳ.

evaluation of their authors: even as he charts the continuous decline of the patristic and medieval Church, the figures the reformer singles out for praise are frequently drawn from his prefatory list of exegetes. In the perilous age begun at the sounding of the fourth trumpet (cf. Apoc. 8.12), for example, even though there were "so many heresyes abrode, yet ... there reygned some godly mynisters ... whome God had appoynted to be saued," including "Beda, Alcuinus, Strabus, and such other many," writers sometimes given to "supersticion, though they lyued in much purenesse of lyfe."[14] These three figures – Bede, Alcuin, and Walafrid Strabo – are also listed in the opening catalogue, while Bede and Strabo's names appear in the margins of the commentary.[15] Likewise, Bale's appreciation of a commentary he spuriously attributed to Albertus Magnus, cited marginally more than a dozen times throughout the *Image* (cf. Fig. 17), may explain why that Dominican does not appear in the list of scholastic authors whose "wor[l]dlye learnynge and earthlye fantasyes" the reformer condemns.[16] The notion of a faithful remnant – that "no tyme hath there bene wherin the faythfull beleuers and constaunt witnesses of the veryte in this lyfe hath not resisted the masters of lyes" – is of course a commonplace of reformist historiography, Bale's included, but it would seem that authoring biblical commentaries could help medieval writers, even scholastics, show themselves to be part of this company.[17]

Looking to explain Bale's interest in these earlier commentators, and in particular his marginal references to their interpretive works, John King points to the *Image*'s title page, where Bale is described as the work's "compyle[r]."[18] According to King, this description ties Bale to "medieval commentary traditions that presuppose incremental accumulation and assimilation of the work of predecessors."[19] That is, as the *Image*'s compiler, Bale is using the marginal space to identify and cite the sources of his glosses, the various texts from which he has cobbled together his interpretation, and he is thereby acknowledging his place as the most recent contributor to a long-standing interpretive tradition. To a limited degree, this is surely right, and at least some of the marginal references to earlier commentaries almost certainly indicate where Bale initially found the interpretations that he presents in the *Image*. Yet the reformer's continuation of medieval compilational practice should not be exaggerated, and this for at least two reasons. First, as the foregoing chapters have made clear, an important part of scholastic *compilatio* was not just the selection and repetition of earlier sources, but the assembly of an array of often contradictory exegetical options, and, like Tyndale, Bale consistently presents only a single right reading of the biblical text.[20] Second, this notion of citationality is inconsistent with Bale's interpretive-theoretical claims, concerning both Scripture's inherent clarity (which would make the compilation of earlier exegesis seemingly irrelevant) and, more specifically, the role of these commentaries in the formulation of his own interpretations. In the preface, he writes that he has "of these commentaries . . . taken both example to do thys thinge" (that is, to write the *Image*) "and also counsell to vnderstand the text," a claim that would seem to support the identification of the earlier works as sources and the marginal references as citations.[21] But he immediately goes on to insist that he has been "to none of them wholly addyct, but as I perseyued them always agreynge to the scripturs."[22] At the same time as he acknowledges having consulted these texts and considered their glosses, Bale claims to have repeated their interpretations only when they agreed with what he already knew to be the meaning of the clear biblical text. Even as he identifies some medieval exegetes as insightful interpreters, then, Bale's work with these earlier sources seems only to compound the basic problem of why any of the elect would read commentaries (his own included) rather than Scripture itself.

A tentative solution to this dilemma is suggested later in the prologue, immediately before the claims of Scripture's interpretive clarity quoted above. Bale encourages his reader to "dylygentlye examine" the materials, both biblical and non-biblical, which are "alleged in the margente. Ffor only ministre I an occasyon here vnto them of a farder serche."[23] With regard to the references to other commentaries in particular, the implication here would seem to be that Bale has scoured this exegesis to identify worthwhile passages, ones where earlier writers have interpreted the "secrete mysteryes" of the biblical text correctly and, perhaps, have offered fuller discussions than Bale chooses to provide. The marginal references to these other commentaries would, then, be citations of a sort, but ones that recommend further reading rather than seek to lend authority to Bale's interpretations, which are necessarily correct insofar as he, like Tyndale, "hathe the profession of baptyme wryten in his harte." All of this effectively turns medieval discourses of compilation and commentary on their head: rather than seeking to ground his interpretative authority in the "incremental accumulation and assimilation of the work of predecessors," the modern critic is already authoritative, and he looks back across a long exegetical tradition in order to identify isolated readings in specific earlier works as correct and worthy of consideration. Still, in contrast to Tyndale's dismissal, Bale's approach attempts to recuperate at least some medieval exegesis for Protestant reading, suggesting that, even if "faithfull beleuers" will already know the meaning of the biblical text, they will find some value, and perhaps some pleasure, in "serch[ing]" through commentaries to find that meaning carefully expounded. The *Image* provides a model for this "serche," revealing how, confident in his own access to the text's true meaning, a reformist reader can study earlier writings and assess the historical development (or decline) of biblical interpretation. Yet, at the same time, Bale's marginalia – his desire to specify that *these* are the places where earlier exegetes interpreted the text correctly – may suggest his misgivings about his readers' interpretive abilities. His need to curate the medieval commentary tradition seems to register the dangerous possibility that, confronted with so many interpretive options, one could easily be led astray.

This "farder serche" would also require the ability to read Latin. Intriguingly, Bale does not draw any attention to the difference in languages between his commentary, on the one hand, and, on the other, the Latin in which almost all of the works in his prefatory catalogue were written. Similarly, and perhaps more surprisingly, Tyndale does not offer any arguments about the need for exegesis in the vernacular in the prologues to either of his commentaries – there are no discussions of English as a vehicle for biblical interpretation to match, for example, *Obedience*'s well-known arguments for its particular suitability as a scriptural language.[24] Even Tyndale's attacks on scholastic exegesis, quoted above, do not mention the commentators' use of Latin. This reticence would seem to reflect the reformers' valuation of the differing work of commentary and translation, the latter at once clearly a higher priority, more contentious, and therefore in need of vigorous defense. In contrast, the decision to write biblical exegesis in English, though obviously related to (indeed, dependent on) the work of scriptural translation, appears to be comparatively uncontroversial, perhaps akin to writing *Obedience* or any other polemical or theological treatise in the vernacular. The language of commentary is simply a less pressing issue for the reformers, and Bale therefore encourages a further search of the Latin works of Bede or Ps.-Albertus – or, for that matter, the German of Martin Luther or Melchior Hoffman – presumably fully aware that only some of his readers will be able to undertake this task.

This implicit distinction between biblical commentary and translation can also be found in Bale's two massive works of national bio-bibliography, the *Summarium* (1548) and *Catalogus* (1557), where it informs his handling of some of the medieval Latin and English sources discussed throughout this study. Famously, Wyclif looms large in both of these catalogues, where Bale dubs him the Reformation's "morning star" (*stella matutina*) and claims that he "composed works for the utility of the Christian republic" ("Edidit nempe ad utilitatem Christiane reipublicae opuscula"), adding in the *Catalogus* that these *opuscula* were "partly in Latin and partly in the vernacular" ("partim Latine, partim in lingua uulgari").[25] Bale's listings of Wyclif's works are sprawling, with the

Catalogus adding more than fifty texts to the more than one hundred and fifty already assembled in the *Summarium*, and biblical commentaries, in Latin and English, feature prominently in both lists. The earlier catalogue, for example, includes works described as "Glossas scripturarum," "Glossam Nouellam," "Glossas uulgares," and "Glossas manuales" (sig. Qq4[r]), a sequence retained in the later *Catalogus* (ll4[r]), as is a separate entry for "Scholia scripturarum" (Qq4[v] and ll3[r]). None of these works is given an incipit, and they do not appear in Bale's notebook (BodL MS Selden supra 64): while one or more of them may record copies of Wyclif's authentic postils, they seem more likely to reflect secondhand information. Other entries, though spurious, are easier to identify with surviving texts: Bale misattributes the Later Version prologue to Wyclif, for example, rendering its incipit in Latin ("Vigintiquinque libri ueteris testa[menti]"), and an exposition "In Apocalypsin Ioannis" may be identified, again on the basis of its incipit ("Sanctus apostolus Paulus dicit"), with a Middle English commentary-translation which predated Wyclif and was, like Rolle's *English Psalter*, subject to Wycliffite interpolation.[26] While Bale's entries for Wyclif thus present him (however misleadingly) as an author of commentaries in both Latin and English, all of these works are set apart from his alleged activities as a translator. After the lists, Bale resumes his prosaic account of the author's life, and it is only here that he claims that Wyclif "translated the whole Bible into English, together with added prefaces and the arguments for each book" (ll4[v]: "Transtulit in Anglicum sermonem Biblia tota, adhibitis praefationibus atque argumentis cuique libro suis").[27] In part, this separation of translation from commentary seems to reflect the higher esteem in which Bale holds the work of rendering Scripture in English – it is *this* writing, he says, that could be done only because "the Holy Ghost was dwelling in [Wyclif's] breast" (ll4[v]: "hoc pectus Spiritus sanctus inhabitarit") – but it has the effect of cordoning the Middle English Bible off from the work of commentary.

Wyclif is not the only medieval writer to receive this treatment in Bale's bibliographies. In another prominently positioned entry in the *Catalogus*, for example, the listing of Bede's works includes many biblical commentaries (authentic and spurious), and it is only in the concluding prose that Bale describes how "he also translated the Gospel of John, the Psalter, and other books of the Bible into his native tongue" (sig. n1[r]: "Euangeliumque Ioannis, Psalterium, & alios Bibliorum libros in patriam linguam transtulit").[28] More immediately relevant to the foregoing chapters, Bale presents Richard Rolle as the author of numerous biblical commentaries, almost all in Latin, including his authentic but rare commentaries on Lamentations and the Apocalypse, as well as the more common *Latin Psalter*, identifiable from its incipit (hh4^r: "Magna spiritualis suauitatis"; cf. Chapter 3, 95).[29] And again, the *English Psalter* is mentioned only after the list: "Psalteriumque in Anglicum sermonem transtulit, & alia multa fecit" (hh4v: "He translated the Psalter into English and did many other things"). More than the treatment of the Wycliffite Bible, this presentation of the *English Psalter* clearly reflects the higher value Bale placed on biblical translation compared with commentary, since it effaces all the exegetical material Rolle supplied in the vernacular, identifying the *Psalter* as notable specifically, and only, because it translates Scripture. In Bale's hunt for coreligionists, the existence of medieval translations is more valuable than commentaries, regardless of their language.

But the *English Psalter* makes another appearance in Bale's catalogues, and in this case it is treated as any other exegetical text, described as "Commentarios in Psalterium" and identifiable by its incipit, translated into Latin: "Magnam abundantiam consolationis di[uine]."[30] This entry, however, appears in the *Catalogus* among the writings of Wyclif, and, though the earlier prosaic account gives Rolle credit for the work of translation, the greater specificity of this entry seems successfully to have encouraged the *Psalter*'s misattribution to Wyclif in the following centuries.[31] Bale's mistake is arguably unsurprising, reflecting his tendency to associate any works of Middle English biblicism with Wyclif, and in this regard it matches his treatment of the Wycliffite Bible, the Later Version prologue, and the anonymous commentary-translation of the Apocalypse, all spurious attributions. More significantly, the double presentation of the hermit's vernacular exegesis seems to foreground the major inconsistency between Bale's approach to biblical translation and commentary, inherited from Tyndale, and the approach taken in the medieval works he sought to catalogue. These medieval texts – in which the translation of Scripture emerges from a tradition of commentary and, in almost all cases, retains clear indications of that affiliation – are difficult to accommodate to what Bale appears to see as a clear (or at least clearer) division between exegesis and translation. Indeed, were he to acknowledge more fully the substantial indebtedness of Middle English translations to the then-ongoing tradition of scholastic exegesis and, as a consequence, to list these works alongside other Latin commentaries in his catalogues, Bale would lose almost all of his medieval precedents for the activities of reformist biblical translation. Further, identifying these Middle English translations as commentaries would position them in a larger field which, as we have seen, appears to be useful to a reformist reader only after careful curation, the sort of work done in the margins of the *Image*. At least by attributing them (almost *en masse*) to Wyclif, Bale is able to preserve the reformist appeal of vernacular exegesis and distance works like the *English Psalter* from their scholastic origins.[32]

In practice, of course, sixteenth-century reformers found it hard to keep the work of biblical translation distinct from that of commentary, made clear in Henry VIII's 1538 pronouncement restricting printed vernacular Scripture to only "the plain sentence and text" and forbidding "any annotations in the margin, or any prologue or additions."[33] But the simple belief that this kind of distinction was possible sets sixteenth-century English biblicism apart from its late medieval antecedents. In this regard, despite the obvious affinities and continuities between Middle English commentary-translations and the vernacular exegesis of Tyndale and Bale, it is crucial to keep in mind that the latter texts were only published beginning five years *after* Tyndale's New Testament, the earliest being his 1531 work on the First Epistle of John. Commentary supplements the work of translation for these reformers, while, for the Middle English writers discussed in the foregoing chapters, the translation of Scripture is concomitant with the creation of vernacular exegesis. The obvious exception would seem to be the Wycliffite *Glossed Gospels*, where interpretive prose is added to the already existing Early Version translation. As noted above, it would certainly be wrong to deny the possibility that the Wycliffite biblical versions were read, perhaps already in the fourteenth century, without any reference to scholastic glossing, but to focus only on this kind of reading overlooks the clear evidence that these vernacular versions were themselves part of a larger scholastic interpretive program, following the theory of translation as exposition *per aliam linguam*.[34] Considered in this light, the decision to outfit the Early Version Gospels with an apparatus of glosses is simply to continue the work of vernacular interpretation begun in the translation itself, since, in this framework, the tasks of the translator and the commentator cannot be separated. This approach to translation is utterly foreign to Tyndale and Bale, and it is seemingly impossible to reconcile with the categorical distinctions implied in Bale's bio-bibliographies.

Recent revisionist approaches to this material have fruitfully stressed, as Brian Cummings puts it, that the "literary culture" of the Reformation "can be seen not as a break but a continuity." Yet, when looking to identify specific points of continuity in England, Cummings mentions only the "concern for the . . . vernacular" that Wyclif (and, presumably, his followers) shared with the later reformers.[35] Thomas Betteridge likewise argues that Tyndale should be understood as operating "within a medieval tradition of biblical interpretation and in particular Wycliffe's insistence on the authority of unglossed Scripture," a claim that seemingly overlooks the important place of commentary in the careers of both writers.[36] Such moves are unsatisfying not simply because the continuity they propose is far from new – the idea of a "Wycliffite prelude" is set out already in Dickens's *English Reformation* (1964) – but also because, even as they would appear to gesture toward the various routes by which medieval thought continued to inform early modern undertakings, they assume an assessment of Wyclif's exceptionality that would belie any claims of the broader relevance of medieval intellectual culture, and especially scholasticism. In this view, Reformation biblicism continues in a medieval tradition insofar as it can look to the precedent of Wyclif, but Wyclif, as a purported critic of scholasticism, stands apart from larger trends in late medieval thought.

It might seem like a minor adjustment to insist that this continuity be traced not just to Wyclif – who, after all, very likely never wrote a word of vernacular Scripture – but through him and his followers to Rolle. The implications of this shift are significant, however, demanding a more rigorous and complex conception of the early history of English biblical literature. Beginning this narrative with the Hermit of Hampole foregrounds the prominence of scholastic exegesis in Middle English biblical translation, showing these works to be so many attempts to give readers of the vernacular access not just to Scripture, but also to the ways of interpreting it that were fostered in the universities. It presents the Wycliffite biblical program – which included, we should recall, not just the *Glossed Gospels* but also the revision of Rolle's *Psalter* – as the most successful of various contemporary attempts to develop the Rollean model of vernacular scholastic exegesis.[37] And as much as this success can be traced to the completeness of the resulting Bible, even if it tended to circulate in pieces, it was also importantly a result of the wider range of recent scholastic sources available to the Wycliffites and their associates in Oxford. With their extensive indebtedness to – or, rather, participation in – scholastic interpretation more clearly established, these Middle English biblical texts appear to be less perfect precedents for later reformist projects. Yet, as their positioning in Bale's catalogues makes clear, the vernacularity of these works was itself sufficient for the Tudor reformers, who, by hitching these texts collectively to Wyclif's *stella matutina*, worked to distance them from their scholastic sources. These reformers also produced vernacular commentaries, though (again) without yoking the work of exegesis to translation as had been the case for late medieval writers. At the same time as this reassessment of medieval biblical translations sets them apart from their early modern successors, then, it should also provoke a reassessment of what we have seen to be the precarious positioning of commentary in the larger program of reformist vernacular biblicism. English commentary continued to exercise its appeal in the sixteenth century, even if newer theories of interpretation had trouble accommodating this kind of literature. Of course, the continuous history of the English Bible can (and should) be extended back further still, looking beyond Rolle's work to include both the early Middle English texts with which he may have been familiar and, even more importantly, the Latin commentaries that shaped his and his successors' approach to Scripture.[38] In the second half of the fourteenth century, the work of making Scripture available in English was inseparable from the work of scholastic Latin commentary.

The persistent but mistaken view of Middle English biblical translation as a rejection of scholasticism has surely been fostered by more than a simple deference to the views of John Bale. After all, it has been comparatively easy for the last century of scholarship to review and reject the many misattributions of medieval English biblical texts to Wyclif that are canonized in his catalogues. The recognition that these texts not only originate in scholastic interpretive traditions, but also develop those traditions and work to extend them in experimental ways, must also involve a new assessment of the value and potential creativity of Latin commentary in later medieval England. Though it was always possible for exegesis to be wielded as a tool by clergy seeking, self-interestedly, to control lay understandings of the Bible, many more exegetes seem instead to have viewed the meaning of Scripture as potentially limitless, their task being to apply all the scholarly (and other) resources at their disposal to assess the received *auctoritates* and potentially offer new readings of their own. The commentary tradition was generally and pragmatically additive, robust enough to accommodate long-standing patristic glosses alongside the latest trends. In fourteenth-century England, one major trend included experimenting with the devotional utility of scholastic commentary, the possibility that the ways of interpreting Scripture promoted in the university could also be used to support the devotional reading of the clergy and spiritually ambitious laity. In addition to new forms of Latin commentary, this shift toward devotional literature encouraged the creation of exegesis in the vernacular, including substantial scholarly translations of biblical texts, and it was in this tradition that Rolle and his followers, including the Wycliffites, wrote.

APPENDIX A

Subject Matter Symbols in Wyclif's Postils

As noted in Chapter 2, 61–62, in addition to borrowing glosses from the mid-twelfth-century *Media glosatura* of Gilbert of Poitiers, John Wyclif also adapted that earlier commentary's system of subject matter symbols and cross-references, meant to facilitate easy movement between non-adjacent but related psalms. Different marginal symbols indicate the subject of the psalm currently under discussion, and, in the single extant copy of Wyclif's Psalter commentary, Oxford, St. John's College MS 171, each instance of a symbol is accompanied by two or three Arabic numerals. One, placed over the symbol, indicates the psalm's position in the relevant sequence, another to the left identifies the previous psalm in the sequence (omitted for the first psalm in the group), and another to the right points to the next psalm (omitted for the last instance). Manuscripts of the *Glosatura*, in contrast, use Roman numerals and lack the backward citations, which are apparently Wyclif's innovation. (For the likelihood that Wyclif himself was responsible for the adaptation of the cross-index in his postil, see above, 62 and esp. n. 31.) Other changes are relatively minor: Wyclif includes an additional psalm among the brief discussions of the passion and resurrection (b), and he omits one of the psalms Gilbert had identified as a prayer (d). More significantly, Wyclif dispenses with an entire category from the *Glosatura*'s cross-index, namely, perfect acrostics, identified by Gilbert as Pss. 110, 111, and 118. Wyclif describes only the last of these as being *perfecte alphabeticus* (f. 266ᵛ), and it could be that he decided not to retain a category with only a single psalm.

Though there is some variation in the scribe's execution of each symbol, the following attempts to reproduce their typical form. Wyclif's figures closely resemble those used in the *Media glosatura* (with some small changes, noted below), reproduced from MGT MS 988 by Theresa Gross-Diaz, *Psalms Commentary*, 158–59. Wyclif assigns fifty-one psalms to eleven groups, with the details of each category defined at the start of his gloss on these psalms:

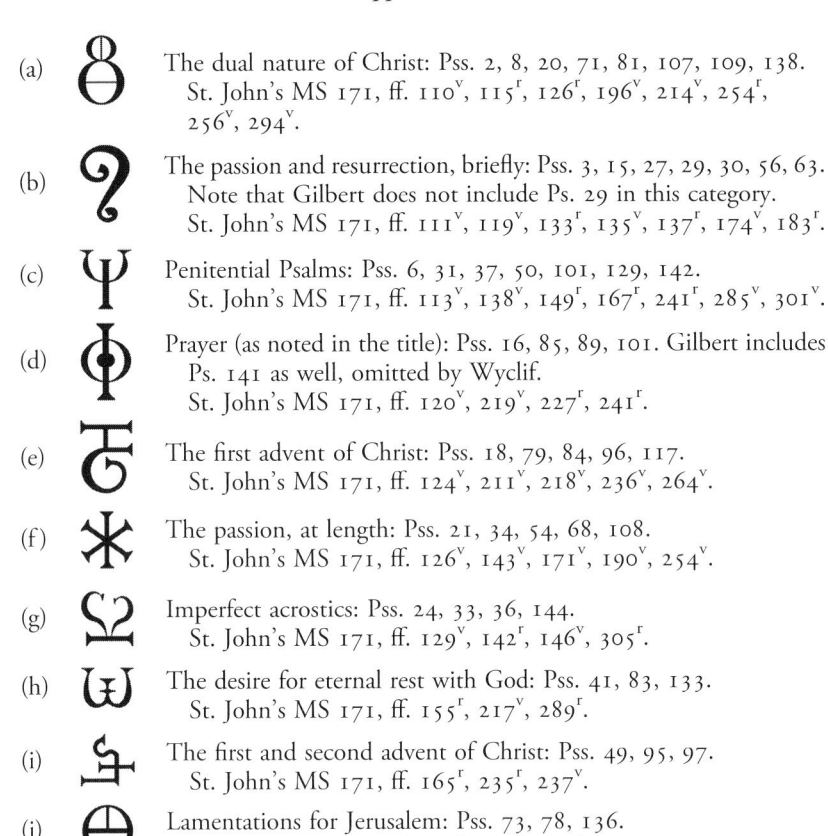

Appendix A 189

(a) ⊗ The dual nature of Christ: Pss. 2, 8, 20, 71, 81, 107, 109, 138.
St. John's MS 171, ff. 110ᵛ, 115ʳ, 126ʳ, 196ᵛ, 214ᵛ, 254ʳ, 256ᵛ, 294ᵛ.

(b) ⸮ The passion and resurrection, briefly: Pss. 3, 15, 27, 29, 30, 56, 63. Note that Gilbert does not include Ps. 29 in this category.
St. John's MS 171, ff. 111ᵛ, 119ᵛ, 133ʳ, 135ᵛ, 137ʳ, 174ᵛ, 183ʳ.

(c) Ψ Penitential Psalms: Pss. 6, 31, 37, 50, 101, 129, 142.
St. John's MS 171, ff. 113ᵛ, 138ᵛ, 149ʳ, 167ʳ, 241ʳ, 285ᵛ, 301ᵛ.

(d) Φ Prayer (as noted in the title): Pss. 16, 85, 89, 101. Gilbert includes Ps. 141 as well, omitted by Wyclif.
St. John's MS 171, ff. 120ᵛ, 219ᵛ, 227ʳ, 241ʳ.

(e) ♅ The first advent of Christ: Pss. 18, 79, 84, 96, 117.
St. John's MS 171, ff. 124ᵛ, 211ᵛ, 218ᵛ, 236ᵛ, 264ᵛ.

(f) ✳ The passion, at length: Pss. 21, 34, 54, 68, 108.
St. John's MS 171, ff. 126ᵛ, 143ᵛ, 171ᵛ, 190ᵛ, 254ᵛ.

(g) ℞ Imperfect acrostics: Pss. 24, 33, 36, 144.
St. John's MS 171, ff. 129ᵛ, 142ʳ, 146ᵛ, 305ʳ.

(h) ω The desire for eternal rest with God: Pss. 41, 83, 133.
St. John's MS 171, ff. 155ʳ, 217ᵛ, 289ʳ.

(i) ⚵ The first and second advent of Christ: Pss. 49, 95, 97.
St. John's MS 171, ff. 165ʳ, 235ʳ, 237ᵛ.

(j) ⊖ Lamentations for Jerusalem: Pss. 73, 78, 136.
St. John's MS 171, ff. 201ʳ, 210ᵛ, 292ʳ.

(k) ⊓ Atomic psalms (lacking internal divisions): Pss. 116, 132, 150.
St. John's MS 171, ff. 264ʳ, 288ʳ, 312ʳ.

Mary Rouse and Richard Rouse, *Authentic Witnesses*, 205, describe these symbols as "conventional," and Gross-Diaz, *Psalms Commentary*, 55 n. 113, identifies them as "true symbols, arbitrarily assigned to represent subject categories." Yet these designs are certainly more complex – demanding more care from a scribe – than the crosses, barbells, arrows, and clusters of dots used, for example, by Robert Grosseteste (d. 1253) in the system he devised for indexing theological texts (see Richard Hunt, "Indexing Symbols"), and used more generally in some glossed books to note the continuation of longer passages over multiple columns or to tie a marginal gloss (or a correction) to a specific point in the text (for reproductions, see De Hamel, *Glossed Books*, 30–31; Kuczynski, "Rolle among the Reformers," 193). Part of this greater complexity is surely a function of size. While these other marks were typically small, often only the height of a single line of text, Gilbert's system required more prominent figures that would stand out to someone hunting in his commentary for related psalms. At the same time, however, in selecting at least some of these symbols, their author seems almost certainly to have considered the material with which they were associated.

The most obvious connection between a symbol and its corresponding subject matter involves the psalms categorized as laments for Jerusalem (j). In manuscripts of the *Glosatura*, the marginal symbol associated with these psalms is a circle with a small cross in the middle and some of the interior filled with ink or darkened with cross-hatching (see, e.g., MGT MS 815, ff. 108^v and 121^v). In some copies, the cross has been rotated to form an *x*-shape (e.g., Oxford, Balliol Coll. MS 36, ff. 79vb and 134ra), but the resulting figure is still recognizable as a simplified world map, with the cross or *x* marking the location of Jerusalem. This symbol was certainly recognized as such by some later reader – whether Wyclif himself, the scribe of the copy of the *Glosatura* that served as his source, or perhaps the scribe of St. John's MS 171 – since the earlier design has been changed in St. John's to a more familiar *T* and *O* map, which, again, draws attention to the location of Jerusalem at the cross of the *T*. It is very likely, then, that the different versions of this symbol were preferred for this category because of the focus of these psalms (according to the exegetes) is on the city of Jerusalem and, specifically, its captivity. Likewise, if more abstractly, the figure used for psalms that treat Christ's divine and human natures (a) seems to reflect the duality of this subject matter. In St. John's the symbol for this category resembles an Arabic numeral *8*, but the shape was used among Roman numerals in manuscripts of Gilbert's commentary, and its form could vary even in a single manuscript of that earlier text. In MGT MS 815, f. 2^v, for example, when the figure first appears, its two circles do not touch but are joined by a pair convex lines, while in later instances the circles overlap and resemble links in a chain (e.g., ff. 29^r, 104^v, and 126^r). Even in St. John's, the bisecting lines set this shape apart from the scribe's typical execution of the numeral. In its various forms, this symbol thus suggests some kind of connection between its two constituent parts, making it an apt figure for the hypostatic union that the exegetes identify as the *materia* of these psalms.

Even the symbols derived from Greek letters may have been favored because of a perceived connection to the content of a group of psalms. The three psalms identified as expressing a desire for eternal rest with God (h), for example, are denoted with a stylized omega. Most obviously, Christ identifies himself with this letter as an endpoint in Apoc. 1.8, and this association is reinforced in the *Glosatura*, e.g., in his discussion of the *titulus* to Ps. 4, where Gilbert describes Christ as "finis consummationis, uel in hac uita in qua est Christus finis legis ad iusticiam uel in futuro cum consummat in beatitudine" (MGT MS 815, f. 5^r: "the end in the sense of 'consummation,' either in this life in which Christ is the end of the law in justice, or in the future when he ends in blessedness"). This identification of Christ as an apocalyptic end may have encouraged the use of this letterform for these psalms, which express not simply a desire for God but rather "desiderium ... eternorum per sanctos in hac valle miserie peregrinantes" (St. John's MS 171, f. 289^r: "the longing for eternal things felt by the saints traveling in this vale of misery"). Admittedly, this connection is much more tenuous than the earlier two, but in light of the connections between the symbol and the subject matter in those examples, it seems more likely that this figure – along, indeed, with the remaining ones – was selected with at least some consideration of its larger associations.

Further study would likely yield similarly plausible (if not definitive) interpretations of more of these symbols as they relate to the topics identified by Gilbert and Wyclif, and, more generally, more work needs to be done to advance the paleographical study of non-alphanumeric characters beyond the work of Parkes, *Pause and Effect* (1992), especially for later medieval manuscripts. The essential point here is that Wyclif engaged thoughtfully with this system of cross-references, drawing on it as part of his larger attempt to make up for the lack of a significant ordering principle in the Psalter. Wyclif may now be identified as the first medieval commentator to adopt – and improve – the *Media glosatura*'s cross-index.

APPENDIX B

The Texts and Revisions of Rolle's Latin Psalter

In his "Rolle as Biblical Commentator," John Clark observed that the *Latin Psalter* is preserved in two distinct versions (166–67). According to Clark, the extant manuscripts and the 1536 Faber printing agree, with minor variants, concerning the text of the prologue and the first thirty-five psalms, as well as the *epilogus* and ferial canticles, but the intervening commentary – that is, the commentary on the majority of psalms – presents at times considerable divergences. Clark's discovery was anticipated by Curt Bühler, who noted that a Latin quotation of Rolle's *Psalter* in *First seiþ Bois* corresponded to the reading in BL MS Royal 2 D. xxviii, but not to Faber's edition ("Lollard Tract," 182, and see Chapter 3, 123). Since he was concerned primarily with the theological content of the hermit's exegesis, Clark declined to investigate which of these two versions is earlier, which represents a revision, and whether that revision could be authorial. Likewise, further exploration of the discrepancy between Faber and Royal lay beyond the scope of Bühler's work.

By considering representative examples from my more extensive collation, this appendix offers some preliminary findings concerning the relationship between these versions. Certainly, a full critical edition of the *Latin Psalter* may complicate these conclusions. What follows is based on my work with all of the English-provenance manuscripts of the *Latin Psalter* identified in Allen's *Writings Ascribed*, as well as three copies of continental origin and the Faber printing (165–68). Additionally, one English copy unknown to Allen, now Urbana, University of Illinois MS 106 (*olim* Phillipps 4451), has been included (a copy discussed briefly in Chapter 3, 102 and nn. 38–40). Only copies produced on the Continent have been omitted, for a listing of which see Van Dussen, "Central European Manuscripts." The close affiliation of the continental copies included below, supported by Van Dussen's discussion of the group, indicates that the omission of these manuscripts is of little consequence for my purposes here. Allen also identified two partial copies, containing

Appendix B 193

only the commentary on the ferial canticles and therefore not relevant to the present study: Oxford, Magdalen College MS lat. 115 and PNK MS IV.E.1. In sum, then, the discussion that follows is based on fifteen complete or near-complete copies of the *Latin Psalter*, represented with the following sigils:

B	BodL MS Bodley 861
Cc	Cambridge, Corpus Christi College MS 365
Co	Oxford, Corpus Christi College MS 193
F	*D. Richardi Pampolitani . . . Enarratio*, ed. Faber (Cologne: Novesianus, 1536)
H	Hereford Cathedral Library MS O.viii.1
J	Oxford, St. John's College MS 195
K	Krakow, Biblioteka Jagiellońska MS 1628
L	London, Lambeth Palace Library MS 352
P	BnF MS lat. 431
Pr_1	PNK MS V.D.4 (*olim* University Library 872)
Pr_2	PNK MS X.D.3 (*olim* University Library 1882)
R	BL Royal MS 2 D. xxviii
Sh	Shrewsbury School MS 25
T	Cambridge, Trinity College MS B.1.15
U	Urbana, University of Illinois MS 106

Without considering all of the differences among these copies in the selected passages, this appendix illustrates the degree to which the two versions differ, identifies which of the versions is most likely earlier, provides some account of the relative textual priority of manuscripts of the earlier version and where in that version's history the source for the later version should be located, and interprets, provisionally, what all of this might mean for Rolle's potential involvement in the copying and revision of his text.

A typical and straightforward example of the differences between the two versions of the *Latin Psalter* appears at the opening of Ps. 47. As in all of the following passages, BodL MS Bodley 861 (here f. 17vb) has served as my copy-text, and the variants have been divided into two banks to make the differences between the two versions of the text more readily visible.

> *Magnus Dominus*, qui omnia facit potenter, *et laudabilis nimis*, et vltra quam potest concipere intellectus humanus. Non tamen vbique digne laudatur, sed *in ciuitate Dei nostri* sita *in monte sancto eius*, id est in altitudine contemplacionis Dei, super quem montem posita non potest abscondi.

Version I 1. facit] fecit *CcJKPr₁Pr₂RTU* et²] id est *CcJKPr₁Pr₂RShTU* vltra] *om*. *H* **2.** Non] Modo *CcJKPr₁Pr₂RTU* digne] *om*. *CcJKPr₁Pr₂RTU* **3.** sancto eius] Syon *Sh* **4.** montem] *om*. *CcJKPr₁Pr₂RTU* potest] possunt *KPr₁Pr₂*

Version II 1. qui—potenter] quia incomprehensibilis *CoFLP* et²] id est *CoFLP* **2.** intellectus humanus] *tr*. *CoFLP* Non—(3)sed] *om*. *CoFLP* **3.** sita] edificanda et compaginanda que est ecclesia *CoFLP* **4.** Dei] eius *CoFLP* super—(5)abscondi] *om*. *CoFLP*

Both versions contain glosses not found in the other, with Version II lacking two phrases found in the more commonly attested Version I (*Non—sed, super—abscondi*), but including a novel gloss of its own (*edificanda—ecclesia*). Both versions share a gloss on the phrase *et laudabilis nimis*, though they disagree, importantly, about how to interpret the psalm's first two words. In Version I, the Lord is great because he powerfully makes (or has made) all things (*qui omnia facit/fecit potenter*), while Version II attributes this greatness to his ineffability (*quia incomprehensibilis*).

At this point it will be useful to consider Rolle's major source, the mid-twelfth-century *Magna glosatura* of Peter Lombard. The importance of the Lombard's work for the opening sections of the *Latin Psalter* – portions that, according to Clark, do not vary significantly across the two versions – has been established above (see esp. 96–97), and it is therefore clear that Rolle was working with the *Glosatura* from the outset of his commentary. (That is, it cannot be the case that one or the other version of the *Psalter* records his interpretations *before* he became familiar with this source.) The Lombard's treatment of this psalm includes a gloss on *magnus*, reading "quia omnia potenter fecit" (*PL* 191, 458c: "because he made everything powerfully"), apparently borrowed in Version I manuscripts of the *Latin Psalter*. Since this use of the Lombard seems to indicate the priority of Version I, the reading in Version II could then be understood as a later attempt to give greater coherence to the interpretation of the verse as a whole: the notion that the Lord is "incomprehensible" is of a piece with the interpretation (in both versions) of "greatly to be praised" as meaning "beyond what the human intellect can conceive."

The priority of Version I, as well as the likelihood that Version II represents an attempt to unify the interpretation of a whole verse, can also be seen at the opening of the commentary on Ps. 37. Here, again, comparison with the Lombard can help to determine the relationship between the two versions (Bodley 861, f. 15[rb]):

Domine ne in furore tuo arguas me, quando dices, *Ite maledicti, neque in ira tua corripias me*, id est inter eos me emendes qui per ignem saluabuntur, sed sic hic me corripe vt ibi non indigeam igne. Augustinus hunc psalmum de recordacione peccatorum vult intelligi. Christus enim transfigurat in se animum penitentis, per gemitum instruens nos qualiter ob recordacionem 5
amisse beatitudinis in Adam nobis sit gemendum.

 Ver. I 1. in¹] in in *K* **2.** id est] *add*. neque *CcJKPr₁Pr₂RShTU* inter eos me] me inter eos *CcKPr₁Pr₂RTU* me me inter eos *J* qui] quia *Sh* **3.** hic me] *tr. CcJKPr₁Pr₂RShTU* **5.** animum penitentis] anime penitentis *KPr₁Pr₂R* animi penitentis *ShTU* per] *om. CcJKPr₁Pr₂RShTU* **6.** gemendum] gerendum *Sh*

 Ver. II 1. quando—maledicti] id est ne duplici contricione conteras me *CoFLP* **2.** corripias] corripies *Co* id est—saluabuntur] id est neque in purgaturio igne commendes (emendes *F*) et purges animam meam *FLP om. Co* **3.** hic me] *tr. CoFLP* indigeam] exeam *P* egeam *CoF* **5.** animum penitentis] penitentis anime *CoFLP* per] *om. CoFLP*

Both versions note the Psalmist's desire to suffer chastisement in the present life (*sed sic—igne*), though they vary in their close parsing of the verse, in which this desire is explained. In Version I, the first half-verse presents the Psalmist's fear of damnation at the Last Judgment, while in the second portion of the verse he expresses his wish to avoid fiery punishment immediately after death, even if such punishment would ultimately save him, and he therefore wants to suffer now. Again, Version II appears to present a more coherent gloss across the verse as a whole, with the Psalmist's hope of avoiding purgatorial fires (*neque in purgatorio igne commendes/emendes et purges animam meam*) and his willingness to suffer before death apparently anticipated by the reference to a "double sorrow" (*duplex contritio*) in the gloss on the first half-verse. That is, the reading in these copies suggests that the Psalmist is already suffering in the present, and that he therefore hopes that he will not have to suffer after death as well. Version II thus seems to lack reference to the threat of damnation at the Last Judgment. As in the previous example, Version I reflects Rolle's reading of the Lombard, who glosses the opening of the verse with a fuller quotation of the apocalyptic Matthean commonplace (*Ite maledicti in ignem aeternum*), and who similarly paraphrases the Psalmist: "Neither let me be among those who, corrected by fire, will be saved, but correct me here" (*PL* 191, 381ab: "Ne inter eos sim qui per ignem emendati salvabuntur, sed hic emenda"). Again, Version I appears to represent an initial interpretation, remaining closer to Rolle's immediate source, while Version II is a reworking, adding details that move the commentary away from the

196 Appendix B

Glosatura and create a more consistent interpretation of the verse. (Note also that, though he names Augustine as the source of his general interpretation of Ps. 37, Rolle appears to have drawn this material, too, from the Lombard, most likely repeating a spurious marginal attribution in his copy of the *Glosatura* – no such gloss appears in Augustine's *Enarrationes*. Cf. CCSL 38, pp. 383–84 and *PL* 191, 380c, and see Chapter 3, 112–13, and esp. nn. 17 and 74.)

In these passages, variants among the Version 1 manuscripts are all relatively minor, with most examples representing small errors introduced by the scribe of Bodley 861 and taken up by the scribes of Hereford, Cathedral Library MS O.viii.1 (*H*), who used Bodley as their exemplar for several other of the hermit's works as well (see Kraebel, "Rolle Reassembled"). More significantly, Shrewsbury School MS 25 (*Sh*) agrees with Bodley (and Hereford) against all of the other Version 1 copies in five instances, and it is not entirely clear, at least in these passages, whether these shared readings represent an earlier or later form of the Version 1 text. In the opening of Ps. 83, however, at least one significant variant does indicate the direction of change (Bodley 861, f. 29rb):

> *Quam dilecta tabernacula tua*, vel ecclesia in qua hic militamus, vel eterna in quibus recipiemur, vbi nulla pressura. Quasi dicat: Quantum sint dilecta non potest dici, O *Domine virtutum* celestium, id est angelorum, quos nobis meritis in auxilium. Et vere dilecta, nam *anima mea concupiscit et* pre magnitudine desiderii *deficit* a se et ab omni concupiscencie terrene fortitudine tendens et ardens, ardentique desiderio transit *in atria Domini*, id est in celestis curie beatitudinem, que multitudine gaudet ciuium sanctorum. Hec sunt contemplatiue et amore Christi ardentis anime, que solum Christum sapiens et pre nimio amoris feruore pene moriens ac deficiens ait: *Nunciate dilecto quia amore langueo*. Languens autem gaudet in spe, nam *cor meum* . . . .   5 . . . 10

    Ver. I 2. pressura] *add.* fuit *Pr₁ add.* erit *KPr₂* sint] fuit *CcCoJKPr₁Pr₂RTU* **3.** quos] *om. Sh* **4.** meritis] mittis *CoJKPr₁Pr₂RShTU om. Cc* et pre] id est pre *CcJRTU* scilicet pre *KPr₁Pr₂* **5.** desiderii] *add.* et *KPr₁Pr₂* concupiscencie terrene] *tr. CcJKPr₁Pr₂RTU* **6.** et ardens ardentique] et ardens quia *TU* ardens quia *R* quia *Cc* ardensque *JKPr₁Pr₂* **8.** sunt] est *KPr₁Pr₂ add.* verba *CoSh* contemplatiue] contemplanti *Pr₁Pr₂* contemplatiui *K* anime] anima *KPr₁* **9.** pre nimio] pre nimii *CcJKPr₂RTU* premium *Pr₁* **10.** dilecto] dilecte *Sh* autem] tamen *CcCoJKPr₁Pr₂RShTU* nam] *om. K*

    Ver. II 1. vel ecclesia—(3)dici] Domine uirtutum id est *FLP* **3.** id est—(4)mea] quam incomparabiliter (incorporabiliter *F*) diligende sunt mansiones superne quas (que *L*) preparasti electis tuis quam (contra *P*) omnia gaudia pro quibus frustra laborant mundani et eciam tribulaciones magis amande sunt que paciencium operantur in quibus nunc militas in membris (tenebris *L*) tuis et per quas perduces (perducis *F* educes *L*) eos ad eterna tabernacula, ad que *FLP* **4.** et pre—(5)desiderii] animus meus et *FLP* **5.** deficit] deficit anima mea *P* defecit anima mea *L* defecit anima mea id est *F* concupiscencie terrene] cupidine terrenorum *FLP* fortitudine] *om. FLP* **6.** et ardens ardentique] ardenti *FLP* transit] *om. FLP* **7.** beatitudinem] latitudinem *FL* latitudine *P* **8.** sunt] *add.* verba *FLP* contemplatiue] contemplantis *FLP* Christi] *om. FLP* **9.** pre nimio] *om. P* feruore] ardore *FLP* **10.** dilecto] *add.* meo *LP* Languens—nam] Nam in languore meo *FLP*

More will be said about this passage below, but note the range of variants that other Version I manuscripts offer in place of *et ardens ardentique* (6), the reading in Bodley, Hereford, Shrewsbury, and Oxford, Corpus Christi College MS 193 (*Co*, which apparently had a split exemplar, since it is a witness to Version II on earlier psalms). In these four copies, the soul "yearns and burns, and with burning desire passes into the courts of the Lord." In addition to being almost stereotypically Rollean, the overwrought repetition of burning in these four copies seems unnecessarily complicated and perhaps therefore more likely authorial than scribal. Indeed, the differing variants in other Version I witnesses make sense as scribal responses to a perceived erroneous dittography, with the causal *quia* (an obvious easier reading) introduced as an erroneous attempt to expand an abbreviated enclitic *–que*. Other Version I variants in this passage then appear to create a pattern: *sint* (2) in the same manuscripts (except *Co*) has the plural *tabernacula* as its implied subject, while *fuit* in other copies treats *quantum* as an adjective rather than an adverb parallel to *quam*, and the preference for *nimii* in the phrase *pre nimio amoris feruore* (9) seems to represent a similar simplification.

Though they frequently disagree with the great majority of Version I manuscripts, then, Bodley (along with its derivative, Hereford), Shrewsbury, and (for later psalms) Corpus 193 appear to be the best witnesses to the earliest form of the *Latin Psalter*. In a marginal note on f. 10^r, discussed further below, the Bodley scribe indicates that he traveled throughout Yorkshire in search of copies of Rolle's texts, naming Hampole and Richmondshire as, at least in part, the geographical range of his scribal pilgrimage. Corpus 193 is also a Yorkshire production, bearing an early mark of ownership from Pontefract (see Thomson, *Manuscripts of Corpus*, 97). Shrewsbury seems likely to have originated in the West Midlands, if not further to the north, and it is thus another witness to the general interest in Yorkshire religious texts, especially those of Rolle, in this region in the second half of the fourteenth century, an interest discussed in detail by Ralph Hanna (see his "Yorkshire Writers" and "Lichfield"). The copying of Version I manuscripts therefore fits with the larger trends in the dissemination of Rolle's Latin works, as Hanna describes them (see esp. "Transmission"). Very few copies of the *Psalter* seem to have circulated in the north in the hermit's lifetime or immediately after his death, and as his writings grew in popularity in the second half of the century, the resulting exemplar poverty meant that any witness available to scribes in the south could consequently account for a disproportionately large number of the surviving copies.

Determining that Bodley, Hereford, and Shrewsbury (and, for later psalms, Corpus) preserve an earlier form of Version I can help to account for the process of revision that resulted in Version II. We have already seen that this process involved a thoughtful and sustained engagement with the Version I text, seizing on some of its *Glosatura*-derived content and crafting more consistent and focused interpretations. The example from Ps. 83 presents, in contrast, a more substantial rewriting of what had been, in Version I, a straightforward gloss (though only in part taken from the Lombard; cf. *PL* 191, 788cd). In place of the pithy parsing of the *tabernacula* as the Church militant and triumphant, and of the *virtutes* as "the angels which he sends to our aid," Version II reads:

> *Quam dilecta tabernacula tua, Domine virtutum*, id est O *Domine virtutum celestium, quam incomparabiliter diligende sunt mansiones superne, qu[as] parasti electis tuis, quam omnia gaudia pro quibus frustra laborant mundani, et eciam tribulaciones magis amande sunt que pacienciam operantur, in quibus nunc militas in [mem]bris tuis et per quas educes eos ad eterna tabernacula.* (Lambeth, f. 150ʳ)

> *How lovely are your tabernacles, Lord of hosts*, i.e., Oh *Lord of* the heavenly *hosts*, how incomparably more ought we to love the heavenly mansions which you have prepared for your elect than all the joys for which the earthly toil in vain. And we should even love tribulations more, which instill patience, in which you now soldier in your members and through which you lead them to the eternal tabernacles.

This passage's emphasis on the joys promised for the elect, its sharp distinction between the elect and the *mundani*, and the purgative or preparatory nature of tribulation for the elect – all of these find ready parallels in *Incendium Amoris* and *Melos Amoris* (see, e.g., *Melos*, ed. Arnould, 38, 80, 186–87, etc.), and these glosses also include some restrained instances of alliteration (e.g., *magis amande, pacienciam operantur, militas in membris, eos ad eterna tabernacula*). All of which point to the intriguing possibility that the hermit himself was responsible for the revision from Version I to II.

The evidence of the *Latin Psalter*'s transmission supports this possibility, as a final example will help to make clear. Glossing Ps. 2.8, Bodley reads (f. 1vb):

> *Postula a me*. In cruce orauit et se pro nobis sacrificium optulit, et orat vt nobis det exemplum orandi. *Et dabo tibi gentes*, et per conuersionem tue erunt que per auer[s]ionem diaboli fuerunt, *hereditatem tuam*, id est que sunt hereditas tua quam excolas, *et possessionem tuam* faciam *terminos terre*, id est omnium creaturarum integritatem possidebis. Termini enim terre sunt qui tellurem cingunt et concludunt. Et vere homines termini sunt, quia simul sunt in eis incipere et desinere.

> **Ver. I 1.** cruce] *add.* qui KPr_1Pr_2 optulit] obtulit $CcHKPPr_1Pr_2T$ et orat] *om. KPr_1Pr_2* **2.** et^2] id est Sh *om. CcR* tue (3)erunt] *om. R* **3.** per auersionem] per auercionem B *om. R* **4.** faciam] faciant $CcKPr_2TU$ faciat RJ sicient Pr_1 **5.** possidebis] possidebitis K enim terre] *tr. R* **6.** termini] *add.* terre KPr_1Pr_2 **7.** quia] qui $CcJKPr_1Pr_2RTU$ sunt in eis] cum in eis $CcJKPr_2RT$ cum eis U *om. Pr_1* desinere] *add.* dicuntur $CcJKPr_1Pr_2RTU$

> **Ver. II 1.** In] id est CoL et F cruce—(2)orandi] esto obediens mihi in assumpta humanitate F **2.** nobis det] *tr. Co* et per—(3)fuerunt] *om. F* et per] id est per CoP **3.** fuerunt] fuerant Co erant P id est] *om. F* **4.** sunt] erunt F quam excolas] cum excolueris illas F faciam] *om. F* **5.** possidebis] *add.* quia F enim] *om. PF* **6.** qui] quia $CoPL$ Et—(7)desinere] Postulat Christus non pro se sed pro nobis, et vt det nobis exemplum orandi. Oratio autem est ascensus intellectus in Deum. F

Ps. 2 appears in the portion of the commentary that, Clark notes, does not vary significantly between the two versions, and, apart from Faber (discussed below), the variants recorded here support his observation. Important variation does appear, however, among the Version I copies. The superior witnesses to Version I, Bodley (with Hereford) and Shrewsbury, conclude this passage with a relatively obscure and abstract explanation of why the "ends of the earth" are interpreted as a figurative way of referring to "human beings," with the two infinitives *incipere et desinere* providing the subject of *sunt*: "because beginning and ending are within them." Unsurprisingly, the textually belated copies of Version I seek to improve upon this enigmatic phrase: *quia sunt* becomes *qui cum*, eliminating the finite verb, and so a rather innocuous *dicuntur* is tacked on at the end of the sentence. Urbana, University of Illinois MS 106 (*U*) drops the now apparently redundant *in* from *cum in eis*, and one of the Bohemian copies (Pr_1) omits all three of these words. Some muddle thus seems to have been introduced in the ancestor common to all Version I copies except Bodley (with Hereford) and Shrewsbury, and, significantly, the Version II manuscripts Lambeth and (at this point) Corpus 193 agree with the superior readings of Bodley, Hereford, and Shrewsbury. To be sure, the superiority of the copy from which the Version II revision derived is by no means a sure sign that the Rolle was himself responsible for the revision, just as, conversely, it is certainly possible for an author to base a revision on an inferior copy of their text. But this evidence *does* indicate that the revision took place early in the textual history of the *Latin Psalter*, and it seems to localize the revision to Yorkshire.

This example from Ps. 2 introduces yet one more complication in the commentary's textual history, since, as the last entry in the bank of variants indicates, the Faber printing (*F*) in this case disagrees with the other Version II witnesses. It is tempting to attribute this substantial variation to Johannes Faber himself, especially in light of his claim that the hermit's texts are "non sine ingenti labore a me repurgatos atque recognitos" (sig. $\pi 2^v$: "not without considerable labor re-cleansed and reclaimed by me"). The definition of prayer with which the Faber gloss ends is a commonplace, deriving from John of Damascus, *De fide orthodoxa*, 3.24 (*PG* 94, 1090), and repeated in, for example, Thomas's *Summa*, 2a2ae.83.2, the sort of thing that Faber could easily have supplied himself. Yet other evidence indicates that, even if Faber modified the text to some degree, he began with a manuscript that did not follow other Version II witnesses as closely as the foregoing examples have suggested.

This evidence appears in the margins of Bodley 861, among the annotations that indicate the scribe's travels through Yorkshire and his consideration of a variety of *Latin Psalter* manuscripts. At f. 11va, as he was copying the commentary on Ps. 27.4, the Bodley scribe appears to have noticed that his exemplar lacked any discussion of a portion of the verse, and so he left some blank space at the bottom of the column and resumed copying the gloss on Ps. 27.5 at the top of f. 11vb. He later found another copy of the commentary, one which included some treatment of the text omitted in his earlier exemplar, and he added the missing material, in a darker ink, in the space he had previously left blank. The added material reads:

> *Secundum opera manuum eorum tribue illis*, quia colaphis ceciderunt, flagellis flagellauerunt et crucifixerunt. *Redde retribucionem eorum ipsis*, id est sicut pro veritate falsitatem reddebant, ita fallacia eorum fallat eos. Et \vere/ sic fiet cum illis. *Quoniam* et cetera.

Give to them according to the works of their hands, for they have struck with their fists and whipped with their whips and crucified. *Render to them their reward*, i.e., just as they returned falseness for truth, thus their deceit deceives them. And it will indeed be so with them, *for*, etc.

In the margin to the left of this addition, the scribe writes, "Iste est secundus versus quem non inueni in glosa Richardi Heremite, nisi in nouo libro uno" ("This is the second verse which I have not found in the gloss of Richard Hermit, except in a single new book"). The specification of this as the "second" such missing verse refers to a similar note in the margins of f. 10^r, where the scribe remarks that, despite searching throughout Yorkshire, he has not found a gloss on Ps. 21.29 "in aliquo antiquo libro, sed in vno nouo scripto" ("in any old book, but in one newly written"). These missing glosses do not appear in any other surviving manuscripts of the *Latin Psalter* in either version (apart from Hereford, where only the second of Bodley's additions is incorporated, f. 14va). But they are both included in the Faber printing, which, for example, at Ps. 27.5 reads: "*Secundum opera manuum eorum tribue illis*, quia colaphis ceciderunt, flagellis flagellauerunt et crucifixerunt. *Redde retributionem eorum ipsis*, id est sicut pro veritate falsitatem reddebant, ita fallacia eorum fallat eos. Et vere sic fiet cum illis, *quoniam* . . ." (sig. C3^r; for the added gloss on Ps. 21.29, see B6^v and my "Rolle Reassembled"). The material for both glosses matches verbatim, indicating either that the Bodley scribe's *liber novus scriptus* would later be taken to the Continent where it served as Faber's exemplar, or at least that this *liber* was more closely related to Faber's exemplar than any other surviving copy. In other words, a further revision of the *Latin Psalter*, one based on Version II, existed in at least one manuscript when Bodley was copied early in the fifteenth century.

At the same time, however, the quality of the material in the Faber version of Pss. 2.8 and 27.4 is markedly different from the revised material with which Ps. 83 opens in Version II copies. The commonplace quality of the Faber variants, which could plausibly have been generated by nearly any intelligent reader of the *Latin Psalter*, should serve to reinforce the possibility that the comparatively sophisticated revision from Version I to II could have been an authorial undertaking. At the very least, that revision was based on a relatively good copy of Version I, and it seems likely to be localizable to Yorkshire. In light of the strong possibility of substantial authorial revision, any critical edition of the *Latin Psalter* should not bury Version II among the variants but rather present both versions as separate texts. As the passages presented above indicate, Shrewsbury appears to be the best candidate to serve as copy-text for an edition of Version 1, though, simply because Bodley 861 – the other independent surviving witness to the early form of Version 1 – was more readily accessible, my quotations of the *Latin Psalter* in Chapter 3 have made use of that manuscript, emended in light of other copies.

APPENDIX C

The Durham Matthew Prologue

The prologue edited below appears at the beginning of a Latin commentary on Matthew in Durham Cathedral Library MS A.1.10, here ff. 1va–4va (*D*). This manuscript, my copy-text, was prepared at Durham Priory, c. 1115–30. Most of the prologue was excerpted in an apparent priestly miscellany from the early thirteenth century, BodL MS Laud. misc. 5, ff. 109^v–113^v (*L*). The text as a whole served as the basis for a Middle English commentary-translation of Matthew prepared toward the end of the fourteenth century, perhaps at Durham (see Chapter 4, 136–47), and the present edition is meant to help illustrate this indebtedness. To that end, it should be consulted alongside the edition of the Middle English prologue published in my "Gospel Glosses," 109–20.

The Durham commentary is a complexly compiled text, drawing material from two recent and closely related sources (see above, 143). The earlier of the two is a commentary attributed in one copy to Anselm of Laon. This work was revised and expanded to create a second commentary, circulating more widely than the "Anselm" text and attributed to (and cited as the work of) Geoffrey Babion. In his prologue, the Durham compiler draws on both of these sources, sometimes favoring one and sometimes the other, sometimes interpolating a phrase from one into a sentence he has otherwise copied faithfully from the other, while also adding some material of his own. To recover some of this compilational process, the notes included below record the Durham writer's indebtedness to these sources, but since neither has been edited or printed in full, the form of my citations requires some explanation. Each note indicates whether material has been drawn from "Anselm" or "Babion" (or both), with further explanation offered when the compiler has done more than simply quote or closely adapt the source. Parentheticals then specify where the text in question may be found. Most of the relevant "Anselm" text appears in Glunz, *History of the Vulgate*, 316–22, cited here by line number, and, after Glunz's text breaks off, I cite the work from Alençon

BM MS 26, here f. 92^{rv}. Though the "Babion" commentary was reprinted from Maternus Cholinus's 1573 edition of the works of Anselm of Canterbury in *PL* 162, Migne (like Cholinus) does not include the prologue. Consequently, most of my citations of "Babion" refer to MGT MS 227, here ff. 1ra–2rb.

I have retained the copy-text's orthography, silently expanding all abbreviations, writing out Roman numerals, and standardizing punctuation and capitalization. The scribe's habit of presenting the names of Jesus and Mary in capitals has been retained, and I have extended this practice to include instances of the Holy Name that are written in abbreviated form. Italics indicate direct quotations of biblical texts, with citations supplied in square brackets. Though the scribe marks the beginning of major sections of the text with larger initials, it has seemed more convenient for the paragraphing to match my edition of the Middle English translation.

The textual notes record substantive variants from *L* and, in a small number of cases, obvious errors in *D* and *L* which have required editorial intervention and emendation. These notes also include references to the Middle English translation, preserved uniquely in CUL MS Ii.2.12, ff. 4rb–8ra (*C*). In these cases, I have either recorded a reading in the Middle English that could be useful in adjudicating between the variants in *DL*, or I have noted corrections to my edition of the Middle English (cited by line number) suggested by the identification of this source.

[Introitus ad Litteram Libri]

Cum[1] post ascensionem Domini Spiritus sanctus corda discipulorvm illustrasset et illos ad predicanda que Christus fecit et docuit promouisset, quattuor ex omnibus specialiter segregati sunt, qui et predicauerunt et dominicam conuersationem in terris simul et predicationem suam (que proprie euangelium uocatur) propriis uoluminibus conscripserunt, 5 hac uidelicet intentione, ut uita Domini IESU et in terris | conuersatio, que morum nostrorum perfecta fuit instructio, in memoria et pre oculis nostris haberetur, et ne eiusdem doctrina et predicatio heretica prauitate distorqueretur.

---

[1] Cum—et cetera(39)] The opening follows Anselm (Glunz, 1–35), with a few phrases added from Babion (see nn. 2, 3, and 5).

Illorum uero quattuor primus fuit Matheus, qui cum primum in Iudea 10
cum aliis apostolis euangelium Christi[2] predicasset, ad gentes uolens
transire sicut et alii apostoli euangelium scripsit Hebraico sermone, ut
fratribus quos corporaliter deserebat per hoc memoriale quod eis reliquit
quasi presens esset, et maxime primitiuorum fratrum fidem confirmaret,
ne ulterius euangelice ueritati legis umbra succederet neue falsi predica- 15
tores et ecclesie peruersores in euangelio Christi aliquos superseminarent
errores.[3] Dilatata autem deinceps ecclesia, sancti patres curauerunt ut idem
euangelium in Grecum et Latinum transferretur eloquium.

Secundus fuit Marcus, qui discipulus apostoli Petri IESUM quidem in
carne non uidit, sed que magistrum predicantem audierat.[4] Cum secun- 20
dum carnem sacerdotio in Israel fungeretur, factus Dei et Petri in baptis-
mate filius, scripsit euangelium in Italia sub Claudio Cesare.

Cunque iam floreret fides euangelica per Matheum quidem in Iudea,
per Marcum in Italia, sancto instigante Spiritu Lucas discipulus Pauli
successit tercius in ordine, qui quedam altius repetens euangelium scripsit 25
Theophilo in partibus Achaie et Boetie. Hic dicitur unus fuisse de duobus
discipulis qui iuerunt in Emaus, et postea fuit socius Pauli in predicatione
gentium.[5] Cui etiam hec necessitas laboris fuit, ut fidelibus Grecis huma-
nitas Christi manifestaretur, ne Iudaicis fabulis legis desiderio adhererent
uel heretica persuasione seducti a ueritate recederent.[6] 30

Quartus sequitur Iohannes apostolus et euangelista. Is cum in Asia, ubi
Cherinthi et Hebionis aliorumque humanitatem Christi impugnantium
heretica semina pullulauerant, postquam reuocatus est ab exilio Pathmos,
coactus est ab omnibus episcopis ceterisque fidelibus Asiane ecclesie, ut
aliquid de diuinitate scriberet unde heretica rebellio conuinci posset. Quia 35
igitur precibus fratrum ita coarctabatur, respondit se illud facturum, si
2ra omnes | indicto ieiunio IESU implorarent auxilium. Quo expleto, diuina
saturatus reuelatione quasi de celo ueniens eructauit in illud prohemium
dicens: *In principio erat uerbum*, et cetera [Ioh. 1.1].[7] Preterea cum alii

---

[2] cum aliis—Christi] Not in Anselm; Babion (MGT 227, f. 1rb/9) includes a similar phrase, "euangelium Christi cum aliis Apostolis," in the middle of a different but apparently related sentence.

[3] neue(15)—errores] Not in Anselm; Babion (MGT 227, f. 1rb/12–14), contains a similar phrase, though the context is different: "Ne falsi predicatores et ecclesiarum peruersores aliquos errores in euangelio Christi superseminarent."

[4] audierat] Anselm (Glunz, 18–19) adds *predicauit et*, but the Middle English (l. 54) follows the present text.

[5] Hic(26)—gentium] Not in Anselm, though a similar phrase appears in Babion (MGT 227, f. 1rb/19–21).

[6] uel—recederent] Not in Anselm or Babion.

[7] At this point, the Durham prologue ceases its close following of Anselm.

euangeliste multa de humanitate Christi dixissent, pauca tamen de diuini- 40
tate eius scripserant, et ideo incepit euangelium ut altius de diuinitate
Christi scriberet et quedam que ab aliis pretermissa fuerant suppleret.

Sed cum diuersi scribant euangelium, tamen diuersis modis et diuersis
intentionibus, scilicet secundum quattuor figuras Christi, id est secundum
quod homo, uitulus, leo, aquila uocatur.[8] Cum enim due rationales 45
creature peccauissent, homo scilicet et angelus, quia angelus ex sola
superbia non ex infirmitate substantie neque ex alterius persuasione cor-
ruerat, homo uero et ex infirmitate et ex diabolica persuasione peccauerat,
ideo Deus hominem tantum redemptione dignum iudicans, sola tamen
pietate sua humanam non angelicam assumpsit naturam. Dignum enim 50
erat ut sicut homo a diabolo deuictus fuerat, sic homo homines liberaturus
diabolum superaret. Sed quia purus homo facile peccaret, conueniens fuit
deitatem que non poterat peccare humanitati quam sustentaret couniri.[9]
Cum ergo luceret lux uera in tenebris et tenebre eam non possent com-
prehendere, quia inuisibilis erat, ut homo panem angelorum comederet, 55
Deus factus est homo, ut per uisibilem formam eum cognoscerent saltem
sic, qui per inuisibilem nullo modo eum intelligebant.

Et quia cum homo esset non sufficeret nisi sacerdos fieret, qui pro nobis
interpellaret Patrem et sufficientem hostiam ad abolitionem peccatorum
nostrorum offerret, factus est et sacerdos et hostia. Sacerdos in hoc quod se 60
obtulit, hostia in hoc quod oblatus est, quod designatur per uitulum.[10]

Sed quia non sufficiebat homo fieri et pro nobis mori nisi et nos liberaret
et nos insuper regeret, factus est leo frangens infernum, suos liberans,
tercio die resurgens, per hoc ostendens regnum suum et potentiam suam.
Leo enim et rex animalium est, et quando nascitur dormiens et quasi 65
mortuus per duos dies permanet. Tercio | autem die dicitur rugitu patris
excitari et moueri.[11] Similiter Christus tercio die imperio Patris resuscita-
tus est, qui priori uita (que per duos dies significatur) dormisse quandiu
passibilis et corruptibilis erat uidebatur. Deinde ascendens in altum,
captiuam duxit captiuitatem, ubi aquila effectus est. In qua uidelicet 70
ascensione ostendit manifeste diuinitatem suam, que non ita aperte per
cetera poterat comprobari. Si enim miracula fecit, hoc et prophete

---

[8] Sed(43)—uocatur] Babion (MGT 227, f. 1rb/35–38).
[9] Cum(45)—couniri] Babion (MGT 227, f. 1rb/40–f. 1va/2).
[10] Et quia(58)—uitulum] cf. Babion (MGT 227, f. 1va/3–8).
[11] Sed quia(62)—moueri] Adapted loosely from Babion (MGT 227, f. 1va/8–15), though with some common language; cf. Anselm (Glunz, 74–76).

fecerunt. Si resurrexit, hoc et quidam mortui. Sed ascendere in celum diuine potentie erat, et ideo per aquilam diuinitas designatur.[12]

Secundum has quattuor diuersitates agunt de Christo quattuor euange- 75
liste. Matheus autem principaliter circa hominem ostendendum uersatur, quanuis et alia secundario dicat. Vnde incipit a generatione humanitatis[13] dicens: *Liber generationis* [Matth. 1.1]. Qui merito primus ponitur, non naturali ordine sed artific\\i/ali. Naturali quidem ordine Iohannes (qui ultimus est et excellentius tractat de diuinitate) primus deberet esse. 80
Diuinitas enim prior est et dignior humanitate. Sed consilio Spiritus sancti factum esse credimus ut qui de Christi humanitate agit primus ponatur. Conueniens enim erat ut sensus noster a minori paulatim ad maius ascenderet et per fidem et sacramentum humanitatis assumpte promoueretur ad agnitionem eternitatis diuine.[14] Quidam tamen dicunt quod 85
Matheus intelligitur suscepisse incarnationem Domini secundum stirpem regiam, et narrat quod magi uenerunt ab oriente ad regem querendum, qui et per stellam ut rex apparuit, et quod rex Herodes timuit natum regem.

Lucas uero principaliter de sacerdotio Christi agit, quanuis et cetera secundario non sileat. Vnde incipit a sacerdotio Zacharie patris Iohannis[15] 90
sic: *Fuit in diebus Herodis regis sacerdos quidam nomine Zacharias* [Luc. 1.5]. Qui uidelicet Lucas merito uitulo comparatur, quia quasi animal hostiis deputatum cura templum maxime et Ierosolimam uersatur sue narrationis incessu. In principio sacerdotem collocat ad aram orantem populo foris stante, MARIAM concepto | Domino Ierosolimam mittit ad 95
domum pontificis, ibi cognationem MARIE et Elisabeth commemorat, que fuit de tribu Aaron,[16] ibi Baptistam natum refert, illuc Dominum natum cum hostia transfert, ibi officium Simeonis sacerdotis circa Christum dicit,[17] illuc Christum cum parentibus singulis annis ducit, duodennem in templo choris doctorum interserit, et post cetera talia discipulos Deum 100
in templo laudantes in euangelii sui fine concludit. Iste in computatione generationis per Nathan exit, cum Matheus per Salomonem regem.

Marcus uero circa regnum Christi immoratur,[18] quanuis similiter alia non taceat. Sed principaliter uult Christum regem comprobare et leonem esset. Vnde a uoce clamantis in deserto incipit, quasi diceret: Iohannes fuit 105

---

[12] In qua(70)—designatur] cf. Babion (MGT 227, f. 1va/20–25).
[13] Matheus(76)—humanitatis] cf. Babion (MGT 227, f. 1va/27–31).
[14] Qui(78)—diuine] Anselm (Glunz, 61–68).
[15] Lucas(89)—Iohannis] Babion (MGT 227, f. 1va/31–33).
[16] ibi(96)—Aaron] cf. Babion (MGT 227, f. 1va/33–35).
[17] ibi officium(98)—dicit] cf. Babion (MGT 227, f. 1va/36–37).
[18] Marcus—immoratur] cf. Babion (MGT 227, f. 1va/39).

uox leonis, id est Christi, regis scilicet omnium, in deserto clamantis per ipsum Iohannis preconium, quasi quodam leonino rugitu perterrefacientis bestialiter uiuentes. Exponit etiam Marcus euidentius ordinem resurrectionis que in leone notatur,[19] qui (ut predictum est) tercio die uoce patris dicitur excitari. Vnde in die resurrectionis dominice euangelium illius in omnibus ecclesiis recitatur.[20]

Iohannes uero expressius de diuinitate Christi, id est de uerbo Dei, agit, quanuis et alia non pretermittat, et ideo circa aquilam plus immoratur, per quam diuinitas significatur que apertius in ascensione ostensa est.

Et quia de Christo agunt secundum has figuras, ideo ipsi in eisdem figuris representati sunt et premonstrati Ezechieli in Ueteri Testamento et Iohanni in Nouo, sed alio et alio ordine. Ezechiel enim prius uidit hominem, deinde uitulum, postea leonem, deinde aquilam. Sed Iohannes prius leonem et postea hominem, deinde uitulum, ad ultimum aquilam uidit. Nam Ezechiel loquens rudibus et carnalibus uidit ordinata illa animalia secundum infirmitatis nostre cognitionis ordinem. Rudi enim homini facilius potest insinuari homo natus, deinde passus, deinde altiora, scilicet resurrectio et postea ascensio. Iohannes uero loquens de re completa iam agit secundum ordinem competentem hominibus | nostri temporis. Cum enim uelimus ostendere conuertendis quod in Christo possunt habere confidentiam, si premitteremus infirmitatem humanitatis et passionis potius in eis generaremus diffidentiam, et ideo prius predicandus est esse leo, hoc est potens iuuare suos et a mortuis resurrexisse,[21] et postea cetera. Quod autem Ezechiel uidit quattuor facies uni esse et quattuor alii easdem quidem, Iohannes uero uidit illa animalia sub singulis specibus, significat quod singuli euangeliste de quattuor figuris Christi agunt, uel principaliter uel secundario, et quod singuli de una figura principaliter.

Quod autem quattuor sunt non uacat a misterio. Quanuis enim multi alii scripser[u]nt euangelia, sicut Thomas, Bartholomeus, et alii, tamen deciderunt aliorum euangelia nec recepta sunt, ita quidem diuino iudicio prouidente, non quia falsa essent sed quia nolebat Deus numerum prefinitum in prouidentia quassari, propter uirtutem sacramenti.[22] Sicut enim certum numerum in apostoli posuit de multis discipulis eos eligens et per Iudam diminutum in Mathia restituens, sic et certum numerum uoluit

---

[19] quasi diceret(105)—notatur] cf. Babion (MGT 227, f. 1va/44–49).
[20] Vnde(110)—recitatur] Babion (MGT 227, f. 1va/49–50).
[21] Ezechiel(117)—resurrexisse] This closely matches Babion (MGT 227, f. 1vb/13–29).
[22] Quanuis(134)—sacramenti] cf. Babion (MGT 227, f. 1rb/30–35).

esse in euangelistis. Duodenarius enim numerus fit ex ternario et quaternario. Ternarius enim significat fidem sancte Trinitatis, quaternarius quattuor partes mundi.[23] Sacramentum uero Trinitatis non predicatum fuerat in Ueteri Testamento aperte, nisi per quedam obscura signa, ut in Abraham, qui uidit tres pueros (scilicet angelos), et Moyses refert Deum dixisse: *Faciamus hominem ad imaginem nostram* [Gen. 1.26], et Dauid: *Dixit Dominus Domino meo* [Ps. 109.1], et iterum: *Verbo Domini celi firmati sunt* [Ps. 32.6], et cetera.[24] Sed in Nouo Testamento aperte reuelatum est mundo, et certos elegit Deus quibus sacramentum committeret. Quattuor ergo euangeliste significant qui euangelium Christi, in quo illud sacramentum continetur, per quattuor mundi partes essent delaturi.

Hi sunt quattuor rote in quadriga et curru quo Deus uehitur, id est in predicatione euangelii. Cuius quadrige mentionem, id est predicationis euangelice, facit Spiritus sanctus per Salomonem dicens ex uoce Sinagoge: *Anima mea conturbauit me propter quadrigas Aminadab* [Cant. 6.11],[25] id est Christi, pro salute populi sponte sacrificati. Significatur etiam aliud in hoc quaternario, quod | ex unitate et ternario conficitur, quod scilicet genus humanum quadrifida morte corruptum per fidem sancte Trinitatis et unitatis, quam intimat, erat uiuificandum. (Mors dicitur quadrifida quia sicut sunt quattuor principales uirtutes per quas anima uiuificatur, sic et quattuor sunt principalia uitia eisdem uirtutibus contraria, per que anima mortificatur.)[26] Et quia eadem doctrina per omnia sibi consonans equalibus lateribus more quadratorum firma subsistit, merito tali numero predicatores eius continentur.

Ipse uero predictorum animalium figure, in quibus ostenduntur Ezechieli et Iohanni, non sunt uane et illusorie sed potius certi et iocundi misterii sunt conscie. Qui enim huiusmodi figuris figurantur illum predicant et intimant, qui ad restituendum eterne beatitudinis statum nasci uoluit ut homo, immolari ut uitulus, surgere ut leo, ascendere ut aquila.[27] Quanuis etiam uniuersaliter omnes fideles hec predicta animalia significent. Omnis nanque fidelis dum ratione uiget, homo est. Quando uero in se uoluptatem carnis mortificat, uitulus est. Cum autem mortificata carne fortitudinem securitatis habet ut nil preter Deum timeat, leo est. Si sullimiter et subtiliter celestia contemplatur, aquila est.

---

[23] Sicut(138)—mundi] cf. Babion (MGT 227, f. 1ra/37–43).
[24] Sacramentum(143)—cetera] cf. Babion (MGT 227, f. 1ra/18–25).
[25] Hi(152)—Aminadab] cf. Anselm (Glunz, 47–49) and Babion (MGT 227, f. 1ra/43–48).
[26] Significatur(156)—mortificatur] Almost verbatim from Babion (MGT 227, f. 1ra/48–f. 1rb/4).
[27] Ipse(165)—aquila] Almost verbatim from Anselm (Glunz, 54–59).

Notandum quoque quia cum Matheus primum locum Iohannes obtineat ultimum, qui uterque apostolus fuit, reliqui duo, qui non erant ex duodecim sed tamen Christum in illis loquentem audierant, tanquam filii amplectendi in medio loco constituuntur, ut quasi utroque latere ab eis muniantur.[28]

[N]ota quod ille quattuor Christi figure in Ueteri Testamento designate fuerunt. In Genesi enim in ipso principio describitur creatio siue generatio primi hominis, in qua generatio secundi figuratur. Primus enim Adam, ut ait Apostolus, est forma secundi. Sicut enim ille fuit primus carnalium ita iste primus spiritualium, et sicut de costa Ade dormientis creata est Eua, ita et de latere Christi dormientis in cruce nata est ecclesia. Fluxerunt enim inde duo principalia redemptionis nostre sacramenta:[29] sanguis et aqua. Postea scribitur casus primi hominis et pena, | scilicet expulsio de paradiso, precipitatio humani generis in peiora uitia sicut Cain in fratricidium, deinde adbreuiatio uite et commune diluuium, exilium Abrahe in terram alienam in qua fuerunt et Ysaac et Iacob, postea captiuatio Israelitici populi in Egipto. Que omnia, etsi non fuerunt figurata in Christo, saltem fuerunt causa quare factus est homo. Tandem ostensa est figura nostre reductionis de inferno, quando filii Israel educti sunt de Egypto, in qua eductione per desertum constitutum est sacerdotium in Aaron in figura sacerdotii Christi. In Melchisedech etiam sacerdotium Christi prefiguratum est. In Moyse et Naason (qui fuit primus dux in tribu Iuda) et Dauid figuratum est regnum Christi. Introitus uero in terram promissionis per Iosue significauit ascensionem Christi, in qua captiuam duxit captiuitatem et eam in terram uiuentium collocauit.[30] Ecce generatio Christi, sacerdotium, regnum, ascensio in celum in Ueteri Testamento prefigurata sunt.

Numerus etiam iste quaternarius in figuris Christi usque in septem extenditur. Septem enim bona in euangelio notantur. Primum scilicet quod Christus factus est homo. Secundum quod contulit mundo maximum sacramentum baptismatis a Iohanne Baptista prenuntiatum, qui solum consuescebat homines lauare, ne quando baptismus Christi ueniret homines baptizari abhorrerent. Que duo ad primam figuram pertinent. Tercium bonum est quod pro nobis immolatus est, quod scilicet ad uitulum tendit. Quartum quod spoliauit infernum, quintum quod resurrexit, que duo leoni attribuuntur. Sextum quod ascendit in celum ut

---

[28] uniuersaliter(170)—muniatur] Almost verbatim from Anselm (Glunz, 93–102).
[29] Nota(180)—sacramenta] Babion (MGT 227, f. 1vb/29–38).
[30] In(195)—collocauit] cf. Babion (MGT 227, f. 1va/38–44).

Appendix C 211

Spiritum sanctum daret. Septimum futurum est, scilicet secundus aduentus, qui promissus est in euangelio. Que duo aquile ascribuntur.[31]

Sciendum uero est quod sancti euangeliste uno quidem Spiritu repleti ad officium scribendi accesserunt, sed diuersum sue narrationis exordium diuersumque finem statuerunt. Matheus enim ab humana Domini natiuitate exordium sumpsit et usque ad tempus dominice resurrectionis seriem sue narrationis perduxit. Marcus incipiens ab initio euangelice predicationis prosequitur usque ad tempus ascen|sionis et predicationem discipulorum cunctis gentibus predicandam per mundum.[32] Ubi notandum quod Matheus ab humanitate Christi incipiens filium Dauid et Abrahe Christum appellauit. Marcus uero paulo altiorem gradum conscendens, filium Dei Dominum nostrum IESUM Christum appellare uoluit dicens: *Initium euangelii IESU Christi filii Dei* [Marc. 1.1]. Quia nimirum et humane nature erat de progenie patriarcharum siue regum carnem suscipere, quod prosequitur Matheus, et diuine fuit potentie euangelium mundo predicare, quod intendit Marcus.[33] Lucas quidem a natiuitate Iohannis precursoris inchoans terminat in ascensione dominica. Iohannes ab eternitate uerbi Dei principium sumpsit et usque ad tempus dominice resurrectionis euangelizando pertingit.

Sed licet, ut supra diximus, quodammodo tractandi ratione disconueniant, a predicatione tamen Christi nullatenus discordant. Que enim Christus predicauit predicant, et septem (unde supra diximus) bona que Deus Pater humano generi contulit annuntiant. Vnde eorum predicatio euangelium, id est bonum nuntium, uocatur, quanuis ipsa principaliter Christi annuntiatio sibi hoc nomen sortiatur. Quid enim melius potuit nuntiari quam quod cum Christo sumus glorificandi et deificandi, si ueterem hominem exuentes sibi festinemus conformari?

Euangelium igitur septem modis principaliter dicitur, quia septem principalia bona nuntiat.[34] Hec autem septem bona per septem dona Spiritus sancti designata sunt, que predixit Ysaias altiora premittens sic: *Et requiescet super eum*, Christum uidelicet, *spiritus sapientie et intellectus, spiritus consilii et fortitudinis, spiritus scientie et pietatis, et spiritus timoris Domini* [Is. 11.2–3].[35] Que alio ordine recipiuntur ab hominibus: timor enim Domini initium est sapientie.

---

[31] Septem(203)—ascribuntur] cf. Babion (MGT 227, f. 1vb/45–f. 2ra/1).
[32] Sciendum(213)—mundum] cf. Anselm (Glunz, 103–109), adapted more freely at the beginning of the borrowing.
[33] Ubi(219)—Marcus] cf. Anselm (Glunz, 76–82).
[34] Lucas(226)—nuntiat] Adapted closely from Anselm (Glunz, 110–23).
[35] Hec(239)—Domini] cf. Babion (Troyes 227, f. 2ra/7–10).

Sed iam uideamus quod bonum cui dono possit aptari. Primum 245
igitur bonum est, ut diximus, Christi incarnatio, mirabile quidem et
necessarium.[36] Nisi enim homo taliter repararetur, omnia que propter
hominem facta sunt frustra esse uiderentur. Ordo etiam angelicus non
restituto sociali numero remaneret imperfectus. In isto ergo tanto bono
nobis celitus collato, spiritum sapientie non incompetenter | possumus 250
notare. Que enim est maior sapientia quam diabolum superare et hominem perditum reuocare et deificare?[37] Quod ut fieret sapientia Patris, que
prius erat inuisibilis, sub uisibili forma hominibus apparuit, et sicut
panis quo mater utitur ad opus pueri in lac commutatur, sic sapientia
Patris, qu[e] est panis et solidus cibus angelorum, assumpta humana natura 255
quasi in lac uersa est.[38] Sed hic est nobis lac, quia per fidem tantvm eum
hic habemus: ibi uero nobis erit panis, ubi per speciem facie ad faciem eum
contemplabimur.

Secundum bonum nobis nuntiatum baptismus Christi est. Christus
nempe, licet a peccato immunis esset, baptizari tamen uoluit ut nostrum 260
baptisma sanctificaret et consecraret.[39] Cui bono spiritus intelligentie
potest aptari. In baptismo enim intelligentia ualde necessaria est, ubi tot
mistica continentur. Ibi enim intelligere debemus quid olim fuimus,
scilicet diaboli, quid modo per gratiam facti sumus, scilicet filii Dei. Ibi
etiam reuelata est [tota] Trinitas: Pater in uoce, Spiritus in columbe specie, 265
Filius in homine cui dictum est: *Hic est Filius meus dilectus, in quo mihi
complacui* [Matth. 3.17]. In quo nos intelligere uoluit quod dum baptizamur Spiritum sanctum recipimus et in filios Dei adoptamur et celestis
regni ianua nobis aperitur.[40] In hoc differunt intelligentia et sapientia, quia
intelligentia est inuestigatio et consideratio singularum rervm, sapientia 270
uero est quasi perfectio et summa omnium que comprehenduntur.

Tercium bonum est passio Christi, in qua tande[m] patuit diuinum
consilium de reparatione humani generis, quod et angelis ante absconditum fuit et etiam ipsi diabolo. (Si enim cognouisset nunquam Iude
intimaret ut eum traderet; tunc uero tandem cognouit et doluit, quare 275
per uxorem Pilati ne crucifigeretur disturbare uoluit.) Ex illo itaque tanto
Dei consilio nostrum debet informari consilium, ut prospera mundi contempnamus et aduersa pati non subterfugiamus, ut prospera infelicia

---

[36] Primum(245)—necessarium] cf. Anselm (Glunz, 123–24).
[37] Nisi(247)—deificare] Anselm (Glunz, 130–35).
[38] sapientia(252)—uersa est] cf. Babion (MGT 227, f. 2ra/12–18).
[39] Secundum(259)—consecraret] Anselm (Glunz, 136–38).
[40] In baptismo(262)—aperitur] cf. Babion (MGT 227, f. 2ra/18–25) and Anselm (Glunz, 138–46).

et aduersa putemus felicia, ut pro nobis passo compatiamur et mortui mundo uiuamus Deo.⁴¹ Ecce spiritus consilii ascribitur passioni.

Quartum bonum est quod sepultus infernum adiit et confregit, diabolum superauit, [et] suos liberauit, | quod sine spiritu fortitudinis facere non potuit. In quo et nobis fortitudinem dedit, qua omnia aduersa et prospera conculcando diabolum impugnemus⁴² et nos a laqueis eius liberemus.

Quintum bonum est quod uictor surgens a mortuis fidem apostolum confirmauit,⁴³ Scripturas illis aperuit, et in terra cum eis per quadraginta dies conuersatus fuit. In quo nos spiritum scientie habere docuit. Maxima enim scientia est a uitiis remoueri et in mundo licite conuersari. In hoc igitur quod resurrexit, remoueri nos a morte docuit. In hoc quod conuersatus est in mundo docens apostolos recte conuersari, docuit et nos rectam habere conuersationem in mundo.⁴⁴ Ecce qualiter spiritus scientie coniungitur resurrectioni, ut scilicet pro certo sciamus quod si a uitiis in presenti surgimus et bona que possumus facimus, tandem resurgentes uita interminabili donabimur.

Sextum bonum est quod celum ascendens Spiritum sanctum apostolis misit, in quo spiritus pietatis manifestissime claruit. Pietas nanque fuit quod celum ascendens uiam nobis ascendendi initiauit et terrenum hominem posse fieri celestem designauit. Quod etiam Spiritum Paraclitum misit pietas fuit, cum illos quos deserebat corporaliter consolari uoluit spiritualiter. Unde et a nobis pietatem exigit,⁴⁵ ut scilicet sobrie et iuste et pie uiuamus, quo similiter ascendamus.⁴⁶

[S]eptimum bonum est quod uenturus est iudicare et unicuique prout gessit reddere, in quo patenter spiritum timoris possumus notare. Dies enim illa dies ire, calamitatis, et miserie.

Hec igitur septem bona spiritualia⁴⁷ sunt multis figuris significata,⁴⁸ ut in septem mulieribus que apprehenderunt uirum unum, id est Christum, qui ea compleuit, ut in septem columpnis quas excidit sapientia, quibus

---

⁴¹ Tercium(272)—Deo] Almost all of this passage is taken from Anselm (Glunz, 147–54), except the phrase *ut prospera—felicia* (279–80), the first portion of which (*ut prospera—subterfugiamus*) is from Babion (MGT 227, f. 2ra/28–29). The rest appears to be the compiler's own addition.
⁴² Quartum(281)—impugnemus] Anselm (Glunz, 154–57).
⁴³ Quintum(285)—confirmauit] Anselm (Glunz, 157–58).
⁴⁴ Scripturas(286)—mundo] Babion (MGT 227, f. 2ra/36–40).
⁴⁵ ut scilicet(292)—exigit] Anselm (Glunz, ll. 160–68).
⁴⁶ pie—ascendamus] cf. Babion (MGT 227, f. 2ra/46–47).
⁴⁷ Septimum(302)—spiritualia] Anselm (Glunz, 169–72).
⁴⁸ sunt—significata] Babion (MGT 227, f. 2ra/50–f. 2rb/1).

sustenatur ecclesia.⁴⁹ Hec sunt septem sigilla quibus signatus erat liber quem nemo poterat aperire preter agnum, quem Iohannes uidit in Apocalipsi. Nullus enim illa poterat complere nisi solus Christus. Libri autem impletio, in quo omnia sunt scripta quecunque in Christo sunt completa, est libri apertio.⁵⁰ Hec sunt septem filii ueri Iob, qui pro nobis passus doluit, qui uocant tres sorores ad conuiuia, quia fides, spes, caritas in nullo recte epulantur nisi in quo septem illa morantur.⁵¹ Hec sunt septem sacrificia | que Iob noster obtulit pro amicis, qui eum prius iniuriauerant. Redigitur iterum quaternarius numerus in ternarium. Docet enim habere fidem, iustitiam, premii expletionem.

Premissis igitur omnibus que utiliter premittenda esse cognouimus, quid quattuor euangeliste communiter intendant uideamus. Omnium communis intentio est unam commendare ueri Dei et hominis personam simulque nos instruere per ea que gessit uel passus est in homine, que omnis sunt eorum materia, ut deposita imagine ueteris hominis de cetero portemus imaginem celestis quatinus in eum credendo, promissa sua certa spe expectando, et illum salutis nostre auctorem corde, uoce, et opere diligendo, conregnare possimus in eterno solio.⁵² Interpositio uero miraculorum est comprobatio diuinitatis. Quanuis enim quidam euangeliste agant de homine, non tamen ut de puro homine sed affirmant Deum factum hominem. Modus uero omnium est commendare persona Christi, tum per humanitatem a peccatis immunem, tum per sacerdotium, tum per regnum, tum per eius diuinitatem.⁵³

Dicitur tamen Matheus iste ob eorum causam qui ex circuncisione crediderant euangelium scripsisse. Nolebant enim quanuis in Christo renati a carnalibus obseruantiis ex toto reuelli. Intendit ergo specialiter eos a carnali legis et prophetarum sensu ad spiritualem qui de Christo est erigere, quatinus sacramenta fidei Christiane tanto securius perciperent et firmius retinerent, quanto non alia quam que prophete predixerant impleta esse uiderent. Cuius tale principium est:⁵⁴

---

⁴⁹ ut(305)—ecclesia] Adapted from Anselm (Glunz, 176–78) and Babion (MGT 227, f. 2ʳᵇ/1–5).
⁵⁰ Hec(308)—apertio] cf. Anselm (Glunz, 173–75) and (closer in its wording) Babion (MGT 227, f. 2ʳᵇ/6–11).
⁵¹ Hec(312)—morantur] Anselm (Glunz, 178–81).
⁵² Premissis(318)—solio] Anselm (Glunz, 182–89), with two phrases (*que omnis—materia, corde—opere*) interpolated.
⁵³ Modus(328)—diuinitatem] Babion (MGT 227, f. 2ʳᵇ/14–16).
⁵⁴ Dicitur(331)—est] Anselm (Glunz, 190–96).

Liber Generationis Iesu Christi: Capitulum Secundum

In ipso exordio satis ostendit Matheus quod de generatione Christi acturus sit, sed de carnali, non de alia que eterna est, quia *generationem eius quis enarrabit* [Is. 53.8; Act. 8.33]?[55] Patet etiam quia merito humana figura depingitur, cum ab humana generatione principium libri sui exordiatur.[56]

Et notandum quod secundum materiam exordii libro suo nomen imposuit. Morem Hebreorum secutus est, quorum libri ex primordiis intitulantur, sicut liber Genesis uocatur, quia in exordio de genitura mundi agit, etsi | permodicus inde tractatus habeatur, et sicut Exodus in cuius exordio de exitu filiorum Israel de Egipto tractatur.[57] Notandum quoque quia generationem noui hominis opponit corrupte generationi ueteris, ut sciamus per istam posse reparari quicquid per illam potuit corrumpi.[58] Bene ergo conuenit Nouum Testamentum Ueteri, quia illud incipit a generatione primi hominis et creatione mundi, istud uero similiter a generatione secundi hominis et restauratione mundi. Illud uocatur Genesis, istud Liber Generationis. Illud agit de initialibus institutionibus sed imperfectis, quia neminem ad perfectum ducebat lex, istud uero de institutionibus sed perfectis, quia ducunt hominem ad perfectionem. Illud agit de sacerdotio et hostiis, sed figuratiuis, istud uero de quodam sacerdote sed uero et quadam hostia sed perfecta, ceteras complente. Illud agit de liberationie ꞌEgiptiꞌ, istud de liberatione inferni. Illud agit de introductione in terram promissionis, istud de ascensione in celum nostre captiuitatis.[59] Itaque quecunque in illo prefigurantur, in isto completa ostenduntur. Sed hec generatio, ut dictum est, opposita est priori, quia illa quidem duxit nos ad dampnationem, ista ad reparationem. Illa de paradiso expulit, ista reduxit.[60]

---

[55] In ipso(338)—enarrabit] Here material is being adapted from both Anselm (Alençon 26, f. 92rb/34–37) and Babion (*PL* 162, 1227c).
[56] Patet(340)—exordiatur] Anselm (Alençon 26, f. 2rb/37–39).
[57] Et notandum(343)—tractatur] Taken primary from Babion (*PL* 162, 1227c), though with at least one phrase (*permodicus—habeatur*) lifted verbatim from the corresponding material in Anselm (Alençon 26, f. 92va/1–2).
[58] Notandum(347)—corrumpi] Anselm (Alençon 26, f. 92va/19–22).
[59] Bene(349)—captiuitatis] Babion (*PL* 162, 1227cd), with the compiler interpolating the allusion to Hebr. 7.19.
[60] Sed hec(360)—reduxit] Babion (*PL* 162, 1227d).

Textual Notes

Title   *Suppl. from the chapter list on f. 1ra of D; om. L*
19   apostoli Petri] beati Petri apostoli *L*
48   homo—persuasione] *The Middle English (l. 89) drops this phrase, likely a result of eyeskip by the scribe of C.*
64   tercio] tertia *L*
86   stirpem] strirpem *L*
112   Christi] *om. L*
115   quia] *Translated* for *in C; erroneously emended to* [þer]for *in my edition (l. 172)*
115   ideo—(116)sunt] *The Middle English (l. 172) does not include this phrase, and the resulting awkwardness suggests that the omission is the fault of C's scribe rather than the translator.*
118   Sed—(120)uidit] *This sentence also does not find an equivalent in the Middle English (l. 175), and the repeated words for the different creatures suggest the possibility of scribal error.*
128   iuvare] iurare *before corr. D*, iuuare *L*
135   scripserunt] scripserint *D, though perhaps with some effort at correction;* scripserunt *L*
143   uero] *om. L*
159   Mors] *thus in DL*, God *C, the latter being an easier reading that could be the fault of either the scribe or the translator.*
174   sullimiter] sublimiter *L*
180   Nota] ota *with space left for an initial in D*
196   et²] *add. in L*
226   intendit] intulit *L*
230   disconueniant—(231)Christi] *The Middle English in C (ll. 301–2) has dropped some text equivalent to this phrase; in my edition, I conjectured* þei discorde, *but in light of this Latin,* þei ben disconuenient *also seems possible, and a phrase like* fro þe prechyng of Crist *must also be added.*
248   uiderentur] uide|derentur *in L, with the dittography occurring over the break from f. 112^v–f. 113^r (also a quire break).*
255   que] qui *DL*
264   quid] qui *after eras. in L*
265   tota] *Thus in L*, sancta \uel tota/ *D*, holy *C*. Sancta *is clearly an easier reading, and the superior reading in L could suggest that it was not copied directly from D. Alternatively, the scribe of L could have treated the interlinear insertion in D as a correction.* Holy *then seems likely to be a mistaken, easier reading for* hole, *requiring an emendation in my edition (l. 339).*
267   dum] *The Middle English (l. 342) does not include a translation of this word, which seems necessary for the sense of the passage.*
272   tandem] tande *D*, tandem *L*
274   nunquam—(275)intimaret] *The Middle English (l. 351) presents this as a question,* wolde not he, *which could represent a transpositional error on the part of C's scribe; perhaps it should be emended to read* he wolde not.

282 et] *om. DL,* and *C*
302 Septimum] eptimum *with space left for an initial in D*
310 Libri—(311)impletio] *This Latin seems to support my conjectural Middle English (l. 396), supplying material dropped in C.*
313 sorores] *add.* suas *L*
317 expletionem] *The text ends at this point in L.*
Title *No such division occurs in C, which instead renders all of this material as a single, unified prologue (cf. ll. 422–24).*
363 reduxit] *The prologue of the Middle English translation ends at this point in C, f. 8ra, though the second chapter of the Latin commentary continues to the bottom of f. 16rb in D, with the third chapter beginning at Matth. 1.18b.*

Notes

Introduction

1 BodL MS Bodley 861, f. 11[rb]. Here, as throughout the following study, biblical lemmata quoted in the commentary are in italics. On the use of Bodley 861 for quotations of Rolle's *Latin Psalter*, see Appendix B.
2 For this quotation, see Chapter 3, 101.
3 This retrospective reading is supported by Rolle's habit of beginning his commentary with a gloss on the opening verse, then pausing to offer general remarks on the psalm of the type that would more usually be found in a commentator's preface; see Chapter 3, 97–98, and n. 23
4 Rolle's notion of his privileged position at the Last Judgment and his attacks on those who criticize his way of life are discussed by Watson, *Invention of Authority*, 56–60 and 43–53, respectively; see too Sargent, "Contemporary Criticism of Richard Rolle." On the question of his divine inspiration, see Kraebel, "Inspired Commentator."
5 *PL* 191, 268ad.
6 *PL* 191, 265d–267d.
7 On Rolle's time at Oxford, see Chapter 3, 93; for glosses describing his mystical experiences, see Chapter 3, 98–100.
8 Renevey, *Language, Self, and Love*, usefully reads Rolle as building on earlier monastic traditions of exegesis, especially on the Song of Songs. Yet, as we will see, Rolle's work on the Psalter is indebted to developments in scholastic exegesis on that book, and his commentaries were recognized as scholastic authorities.
9 For university writers, this provisionality seems to have been enabled by their status as *magistri* and the license to teach that came with it: see Chenu, *Introduction*, 113–16, and his *La théologie*, 358–60. On the apparently inexhaustible meaning of Scripture, see Dahan, *L'exégèse chrétienne*, 55–56 and 71–73, and his *Lire la Bible*, 10–19 and 27–33, usefully extending the arguments of Bori, *L'interpretazione infinita*, into the scholastic period; cf. Chapter 1, 49–51.
10 On this point, see especially Rouse and Rouse, *Authentic Witnesses*.
11 To be sure, the phenomenon of writing scholastic texts for a wider readership was by no means limited to England in this period. See, e.g., Hobbins, *Authorship and Publicity*.

12 Smalley, *English Friars and Antiquity*, 1, notes that this narrower study, focused on the neoclassicizing interests of a group of English friars, developed out of an effort "to write a continuation" of the *Study of the Bible in the Middle Ages*.

13 Dinshaw, *Sexual Poetics*, 122–23. Dinshaw's account describes the interpretive habits of Robertsonian critics better than it does medieval biblical exegesis: see further Kraebel, "Chaucer's Bibles." And see too Simpson, "Interrogation Over," whose account of the priorities of earlier "interrogationist" criticism matches nicely with the suspicious posture adopted in these approaches to medieval exegesis.

14 Geary, "What Happened to Latin?" 871. Likewise, Geary's argument that such glosses cordoned Scripture off from the interpretive insights of "other linguistic traditions" is not supported by the vernacular glosses discussed below.

15 For examples, see Kraebel, "Inspired Commentator."

16 Conte, *Poetry of Pathos*, 189.

17 Fowler, "Criticism as Commentary," 434 and 442.

18 Kraus and Stray, "Form and Content," 8–9. See too Kraus, "Reading Commentaries," 16.

19 For recent assessments of medieval biblical commentary as an intellectually diverse and compelling discursive field, see the work of Gilbert Dahan, esp. his magisterial survey, *L'exégèse chrétienne*, and his collection of essays on medieval interpretive theory and practice, *Lire la Bible*. Relevant to the issue of interpretive multiplicity is Dahan's notion of "un 'mitraillage herméneutique' … qui n'est autre que l'accumulation des interprétations" (*Lire*, 223).

20 See Chapter 1, 37–38.

21 Ingham, *Medieval New*, 15 and 3.

22 With regard to the voicing of commentaries, Lawton, "Psalms as Public Interiorities," is exemplary.

23 Von Nolcken, "Lay Literacy," 181.

24 Ghosh, *Wycliffite Heresy*, 1, emphasis in original.

25 Marsden, "Bible in English," 230; a similar view is offered by Morey, *Book and Verse*, 11 and 26.

26 Wyclif's postils and the *Glossed Gospels* are discussed in Chapters 2 and 4, respectively. On marginal glosses in Lollard Bibles, see Dove, *English Bible*, 152–72, while her "Biblical Agenda" helpfully traces trends in Wycliffite commentary.

27 Norton, *Bible as Literature*, I, 77–84, rightly describes these translators as "commentators on the Latin, reproducing, revising and adding to older glosses" (80), noting that their work was meant to "be studied minutely rather than flow as an open piece of literature" (83) – yet he presents these characteristics as failings, reflecting a lack of "literary awareness" (78). See Lawton, "The Bible," and "Englishing the Bible."

28 See, for example, the Later Version Wycliffite New Testament preserved in Dallas, Bridwell Library MS 7 (Protho B-01), which contains a reader's Latin annotations on the verso of the front flyleaf and in the margins of ff. 1^r–3^v.

29 Most substantially, see Dove, *English Bible*, and Kelly, *English Bible* (though see Kathleen Kennedy's review of the latter in *Journal of Medieval Religious Cultures* 43 (2017): 254–57). *Wycliffite Bible*, ed. Solopova, presents essays on various topics related to the translation, while studies of the manuscripts are offered by Kennedy, *Courtly and Commercial Art*, and Solopova, *Manuscripts*. Different paratexts meant to support the reading of these Bible versions have been studied by Peikola, "Tables of Lections," with references to his earlier studies. Moessner, "Translation Strategies," provides a detailed comparison of the two (major) versions of the translation. More useful work will come from the "Towards a New Edition of the Wycliffite Bible" project now being run at Oxford by Solopova and Hudson.

30 The phrase is used by Minnis, *Magister Amoris*, 266–72, to describe scholastic French translations of secular material; more recently, in *Valuing the Vernacular*, 2–4, 20, 28, 33, he has adopted A. D. Menut's description of these works as "commentated translations" (cited on 173 n. 16; cf. *traductions commentées*), a phrase which could be seen as foregrounding their status as translations.

31 Lawton, *Faith, Text, and History*, 1.

32 Minnis, *Valuing the Vernacular*, 9.

33 See Chapter 3, 122–128.

34 As Minnis, *Valuing the Vernacular*, 23–25, observes, one force lacking in this English setting is royal patronage of translation, which accounts for much of the comparable activity in France in the period. The closest English analogue to the support French translators found in Charles V seems to be Thomas Berkeley (d. 1417), under whose auspices John Trevisa prepared his translations. See further Hanna, "Berkeley and His Patronage."

35 On the *cura pastoralis* and vernacular religious literature, see Gillespie, *Holy Books*, esp. 3–47.

36 Waters, *Translating Clergie*, 2. Though the present book focuses on Latin commentaries and English works with Latin sources, Waters's study should remind us that Anglo-French exegesis contributed to the growing multilingual body of English scholasticism. Sutherland, *English Psalms*, 120–35, presents a useful account of an English translation of the Psalter (*Middle English Glossed Prose Psalter*, ed. Black and St.-Jacques) that borrows brief glosses from a French source, and two versions of an English commentary on the Apocalypse develop an even more robust tradition of insular exegesis in French (see *English Apocalypse Version*, ed. Fridner, and *Mittelenglische Übersetzung*, ed. Sauer).

37 Wei, *Intellectual Culture*, 410.

38 On the *Pety Job*, see Appleford, *Learning to Die*, 107–117, attributed to Rolle in BodL MS Douce 332, f. 10ra, Cambridge, Trinity Coll. MS R.3.21, f. 38^r, BL MS Harley 1706, f. 11^r. Maidstone's poem is attributed to Rolle in BodL MS Digby 18, f. 38^r.

39 Copeland, *Rhetoric, Hermeneutics, and Translation*, 107. Copeland's arguments are compelling for the secular literature that is her focus, but these

writings have a smaller commentary tradition and different sources of authority than Scripture.
40 The pragmatic primacy of Latin – as opposed to the kind of absolute authority that would identify the biblical text with (and only with) the Vulgate – is common in scholastic commentary, seen, for example, in Trevet's account of the Hebraicum translation of the Psalter (discussed in Chapter 1), in the recourse to Jerome's writing on Hebrew names, and in various discussions of the Vulgate as itself a translation. See Watson, "Idea of Latinity."
41 Smalley, "Problems of Exegesis"; Courtenay, "Bible in the Fourteenth Century." Cf. Chapter 2, 90.
42 See especially Courtenay, *Schools and Scholars*, and Ghosh, *Wycliffite Heresy*, as well as several of his more recent essays: "Probabilism and Hermeneutics," "Logic, Scepticism, and 'Heresy,'" and "University Learning, Theological Method, and Heresy."
43 *Book*, ed. Windeatt, 280.
44 *Book*, ed. Staley, 141.
45 Rolle's *Incendium Amoris* was translated by Richard Misyn in 1435, according to the colophon in Oxford, Corpus Christi Coll. MS 236, f. 44^r.
46 In his edition, 280 n., Windeatt suggests that this is "presumably a Latin Bible with glosses."
47 *Mirror*, ed. Sargent, 75.
48 Ghosh, *Wycliffite Heresy*, 147, but see the critique of this view advanced by Karnes, "Nicholas Love," 402–407. See too Johnson, *Life of Christ*, whose discussion of the relevance of academic culture to late medieval devotional reading is consistent with the argument advanced in this particular example, as in the present study more generally.
49 *Mirror*, ed. Sargent, 247; cf. *Chastising*, ed. Bazire and Colledge, 180 (with notes on 291–92), quoting the *Opus* on Matth. 7.15 (cf. *PG* 56, 742), concerning "men and wymmen þat bien clepid dyuinours or soothseiers. Suche men sein sooþ bi her spirites, and sumtyme fals, but þe Hooli Goost seiþ alwei sooþ."
50 See *Biblia sacra*, V, sig. c4^{vab} (Lyre); Aquinas, *Catena Aurea*, ed. Guarienti, I, 57–59; BL MS Add. 41175, ff. 9vb–10ra (Wycliffite *Glossed Gospels*); CUL MS Ii.2.12, f. 29^{rb-vb} (non-Wycliffite commentary-translation).
51 Citing this passage, Bradley, "Censorship and Continuity," 124–25, argues that Love "expects his audience to have access to other books," and that this intertextuality was not just directed at "clerical or educated readers."
52 *Book*, ed. Windeatt, 280.
53 Parkes, *Scribes, Scripts, and Readers*, 35. On monastic *lectio*, see Leclercq, *Love of Learning*, 72–77 and (more generally) 191–228, as well as his "Commentary," 29–32 (there called "prayerful reading"); more recently, see Stock, *After Augustine*, 101–114. On scholastic *lectio*, see Hamesse, "Scholastic Reading," and, especially, Chenu, *Introduction*, 67–71. Different reading practices are usefully discussed by Taylor, "Readers and Manuscripts."
54 See, e.g., Alford, "Biblical *Imitatio*," and his "Rolle's *English Psalter* and *Lectio Divina*," classifying Rolle as reflecting this monastic tradition. Also relevant to

this division is the attempt by Colish, *Peter Lombard*, I, 158–88, to distinguish between monastic and scholastic Psalter commentaries on the basis of their style and content. Colish is an excellent reader of these texts, but her sorting has been made problematic by subsequent work with these commentaries, re-dating some and identifying more complicated lines of influence among others. See Kraebel, "Prophecy and Poetry," with further bibliography.

55 Hamesse, "Scholastic Reading," 107.
56 Quotations from the *English Psalter* throughout the following chapters are based on HEHL MS HM 148, which is serving as the copy-text for the edition currently in preparation by Jill Havens and Kevin Gustafson. I have corrected these quotations against the other surviving manuscripts, and I provide references to the relevant pages in Bramley's edition (based on Oxford, University Coll. MS 64), here 13. Note that two quires in HM 148 have been bound out of order: see Hanna, *English Manuscripts*, 196–98, for a description.
57 Hudson, *Premature Reformation*, 260.
58 De Hamel, *Glossed Books*, is the most sustained study of the relationship between exegetical literature and developments in *mise-en-page*. Glossed bibles and related twelfth-century commentaries are also discussed in, e.g., Ker, *Books, Collectors, and Libraries*, 71–74; Parkes, *Scribes, Scripts, and Readers*, 35–37, and his "Layout and Presentation," 60–61; Rouse and Rouse, *Authentic Witnesses*, 192–201. Subsequent studies of exegesis building on this work are numerous, but for prominent examples, see Gibson, "Place of the *Glossa*," and her "Twelfth-Century Glossed Bible"; Matter, "Legacy of the School of Auxerre"; Smith, *Glossa ordinaria*, 91–139; Gross-Diaz, *Psalms Commentary*, 35–65.
59 Rouse and Rouse, "*Ordinatio* Revisited," 123. As Hanna, "Transmission of Rolle's Latin," 328, notes, one of the authors studied here, Richard Rolle, likely served as his own scribe, producing "autographs directed to specific known audiences."
60 See Chapter 1, 46–49 and Chapter 2, 67–72 and 83–84. On authorial working copies, see Beadle, "English Autograph Writings"; Fisher, "Authors as Scribes," esp. 216–22; Hamesse, "Les autographes"; Wakelin, *Scribal Correction*, 279–81. The difficulties of confidently discerning the impact of an author's scribal habits on texts are explored further in Kraebel, "Modes of Authorship."
61 See Chapter 4, 150–54. In this case, it seems likely that instructions for the resulting volume's preparation were supplied either in person by some director or in the form of short written notes. For the rare survival of such notes, see Kraebel, "Rolle Reassembled."
62 Cf. Courtenay, "Franciscan Learning," 59–64, who argues that most "published commentaries" by medieval schoolmen are the result of "several years of study, reflection, and writing," rather than being directly tied to the lecture courses required of biblical bachelors and regent masters.
63 Logan, *University Education*, has drawn attention to the large number of priests who were able to spend short stints at Oxford thanks to the

implementation of different papal and episcopal policies. This previously unappreciated class of priests with limited university training could help to account for the wide copying of para-scholastic Latin texts like Rolle's commentaries in the fourteenth and, especially, fifteenth centuries.
64 *PL* 191, 57b.
65 On these possible connections, see especially Cummings, "Justifying God."

1 Interpretive Theories and Traditions

1 *Catalogus*, ed. Rouse and Rouse, 529–39; see further *ibid.*, xci, cxxiv–cxxv. As Rouse and Rouse note, much of Henry's information is drawn directly from the Franciscan *Registrum Anglie*, but the index of commentaries appears to be his own creation.
2 For examples of each, see *Catalogus*, cxxv nn. 114 and 115. In all likelihood, then, Henry prepared his *Catalogus* in unbound booklets, and he therefore need not always have had the catalogue and the index to hand at the same time.
3 For one study using the *Catalogus* in this way, see Mynors, "Latin Classics."
4 See esp. Smalley, *Study of the Bible*, and de Lubac, *Exégèse médiévale*. Smalley addresses her differences with de Lubac in the preface to *Study*, esp. xii–xvii, discussed further by Minnis, "Figuring the Letter." For the intellectual context in which de Lubac wrote, see Holsinger, *Premodern Condition*, 152–94.
5 Dahan describes this tendency as "un mitraillage herméneutique," essentially the accretion of differing interpretations, in many cases without any attempt being made to adjudicate between them or to parcel them out one or another of the senses of Scripture. See *Lire la Bible*, 17–18 and 223, and his *L'exégèse chrétienne*, 140–41.
6 Hunt, "Introductions to the *Artes*"; Minnis, *Theory of Authorship*.
7 See the related discussion in the Introduction, 4–5.
8 Cf. Dahan's call to attend to "l'effort de conceptualisation ou de théorisation ... que l'on peut tirer sur ce plan de la pratique des commentateurs" (*Lire la Bible*, 8).
9 To be sure, there are limits to the utility of Henry's lists. Beyond issues of attribution, Henry sometimes identifies commentaries based on quite dubious grounds. For example, among the Psalter commentaries, he includes "Anselmus," "Menegaldus," "Yvo," and "Serlo." In the *Catalogus* proper, Henry has simply taken his accounts of the commentaries by Anselm (of Laon?) and Ivo (of Chartres?) from the *Registrum*. A Psalms commentary is also attributed to Manegold (of Lautenbach?) in the catalogue, without identifying Henry's source for this information. There is no Psalms commentary attributed to anyone named Serlo in the catalogue, and there is little evidence for the circulation of Psalter commentaries by any of these figures. But these four entries in the index could be explained, collectively, if Henry were familiar with BL MS Royal 3 B. xi, a late twelfth-century gloss on the Psalter from Ramsey Abbey, the books of which Henry seems to have known

well (*Catalogus*, lix and cxviii–cxx). The preface to the gloss in Royal names sources that include "nobilium glosulas magistrorum Yvonis et Anselmi, Monogoldi atque Serlonis" (f. 1ᵛ).

10 On the developing tradition of Latin Psalter commentaries, see Kraebel, "Prophecy and Poetry"; in what follows, citations are limited to works that supplement the references given there.

11 On Cassiodorus and the influence of his *Expositio*, see Grondeux, *À l'école de Cassiodore*.

12 As Rouse and Rouse indicate (*Catalogus*, 240), Henry does not appear to have known a copy of Hilary's commentary, with his entries for the text taken from bibliographical intermediaries.

13 See further Kraebel, "Poetry and Commentary."

14 On the Lombard's influence, see Doyle, *The Lombard*. Grosseteste appears on Henry's list as *Robertus Lincolniensis*. See Ball, "Grosseteste on the Psalms," with further references. In *Catalogus*, 227 and 533–34, Rouse and Rouse identify both instances of "Gilbertus" in the index with Gilbert of Hoyland, to whom a Psalter commentary is attributed in the catalogue, an entry taken from the *Registrum*. The cataloguers of the *Registrum* conflate the works of the Englishman Gilbert of Hoyland and the Frenchman Gilbert of Poitiers, and it seems more likely that Henry intended to refer to the commentary of the French Gilbert, a copy of which was in Bury's library (B13. 133; see *Catalogus*, 229).

15 For one particularly colorful example, see the prologue edited in Kraebel, "John of Rheims," 282: "Totum istud opus ... lyrico carmine est compositum. Hymnus enim dicitur laus Dei lyrico carmine composita. Sed tamen apud nos lyrico carmine non distinguitur, et hoc propter translationes."

16 As noted by Szerwiniack, "L'*Interpretatio nominum*," 254–55, Hrabanus appears to have adapted his system of marginal citations from the works of Bede; see, e.g., BnF MS lat. 11683 (s. ix). On parabolic language, see Chapter 2, 74.

17 For an important precedent to the scholastic theorists discussed here, see the collection of Victorine writings assembled in *Interpretation of Scripture*, ed. Harkins and van Liere.

18 Minnis, *Theory of Authorship*, 21.

19 Alexander of Hales, *Summa theologica*, I, 10; a similar list of modes appears earlier in the *Summa*, I, 8.

20 *Doctoris Seraphici S. Bonaventurae opera omnia*, V, 206.

21 On the distinction between these two general modes, see Minnis, *Theory of Authorship*, 119–30. Scholastic accounts of Scripture, theology, and poetry in relation to "sciential" language are considered further by Dahan, "Poetics and Hermeneutics."

22 *Sancti Thomae ... opera omnia* (Parma edn.), XIV, 148.

23 *Summa theologiae* (Blackfriars edn.), I, 36–38/37–39.

24 *Sancti Thomae ... opera omnia* (New Leonine edn.), XXV.1, 31: "Inter omnia autem que in sacra Scriptura narrantur, prima sunt illa que ad Vetus

Testamentum pertinet, et ideo ea que secundum litteralem sensum ad facta Veteris Testamenti spectant, possunt quatuor sensibus exponi."
25 *Ibid.* Cp. Bonaventure's comments in the *Breviloquium: Opera*, V, 207.
26 Cf. Minnis, "*Quadruplex sensus.*"
27 Thomas was by no means the first writer to attempt such a totalizing interpretive theory, and two of his most important antecedents, Augustine and Hugh of St. Victor, are cited at this point in the *Summa*.
28 On Lyre, see especially *Nicholas of Lyra*, ed. Krey and Smith, and *Nicolas de Lyre*, ed. Dahan. Turner, "Allegory in Christian Late Antiquity," describes the tensions in the understanding of the senses of Scripture that Lyre inherited from Thomas. Krey and Smith, "Introduction," 3–4 and 7–8, give the dating of the postils.
29 *Biblia sacra*, I, sig. †6va.
30 *Ibid.* Lyre's Hebraism has recently been discussed by Klepper, *Insight of Unbelievers*, and Geiger, "Student and Opponent." His exegetical priorities are described by Dahan, "Herméneutique et méthodes."
31 See Ryan, *Aquinas as Reader*, 17–20.
32 Lyre's work on the Psalms can be dated *c*. 1326: see Krey and Smith, "Introduction," 3.
33 Cf. Smalley, "Les commentaires bibliques." For the manuscripts of Trevet, see Stegmüller 6038; for Waleys, Smalley, "Thomas Waleys," 67–69; Cossey's survives only in Cambridge, Christ's Coll. MS 11. Krey and Smith, "Introduction," 8, estimate that "an astonishing eight hundred manuscripts or more" preserve Lyre's literal postils.
34 See Smalley, "Waleys," 51–52 and 70. This origin explains why the commentary was frequently attributed to "Frater Thomas Anglicus," accounting for its common misattribution to another Englishman, Thomas of Jorz (d. 1310).
35 The English manuscripts are Cambridge, Pembroke Coll. MS 262, BL MS Royal 2 E. vi, Manchester, John Rylands MS 32826 (frag.), and Oxford, Pembroke Coll. MS 39.
36 *Commentarius super Psalmos F. Tho. Iorgii Anglici*, sig. A2^{rb}; all subsequent citations refer to this edition. Cf. Stegmüller 8245.
37 Otter, "Entrances and Exits," 302.
38 Lawton, *Voice*, 63–64.
39 *PL* 191, 55a. The following discussion draws on Kraebel, "Poetry and Commentary."
40 Kraebel, "John of Rheims," 282.
41 FitzGerald, *Inspiration and Authority*, esp. 50–72, stresses the continuities in scholastic theories of prophecy, including specifically the Lombard, Aquinas, and Trevet. While he is right to contrast these commentators' ideas of Davidic prophecy with the theories of Hugh of St. Victor (to which he devotes the first chapter of his useful and engaging study), his approach runs the risk of effacing the disagreements in their treatment of the Psalms and their author.
42 Parma edn., XIV, 149.

43 On the manuscripts of Thomas's commentary, see Morard, "Commentaire des Psaumes," 655–56 n. 7. *Catalogus*, 471, records one English copy, likely known to Kirkestede in the library of St. Albans.

44 This threefold schema is derived Augustine's *De Genesi ad litteram*, adapted in the prefaces to earlier commentaries on other prophetic books. Typically, the third mode of sight was reserved for the ascent of Paul in II Cor. 12.2–4 and Moses in Ex. 24.15–18, though some exegetes maintained that John, as author of the Apocalypse, also saw in this mode. See my introduction to Richard of St. Victor, *On the Apocalypse*, 330–36. Accounts of the *genera prophetiae* are common in the prologues to Psalter commentaries following Cassiodorus, but the attempt to synthesize them with the Augustinian modes of sight is a later development, with Aquinas being one of the earlier exegetes to bring the two paradigms together (see Parma edn., XIV, 149). It could be that the middle section of the quotation from Waley's prologue (*Ad cuius euidentiam—prophetandi tertio*), which is not based on the Lombard, was inspired by Aquinas. With this section, contrast the two passages of near verbatim quotation from the *Magna glosatura*, PL 191, 55a and 59b.

45 This move is also drawn from the *Magna glosatura*, PL 191, 57cd; cf. Minnis, *Theory of Authorship*, 103–112.

46 For the liturgical use of the first two nocturns (Pss. 1–25 and 26–37), see *Breviarium*, ed. Procter and Wordsworth, II, 5–28, 37–42, 69–84. Rather than this text being unfinished, then, it seems likely that the end of the nocturn provided Waleys with a convenient stopping point. Cf. Smalley, "Waleys," 66.

47 Cf. *PL* 191, 111cd (Lombard) and CCSL 38, ed. Dekkers and Fraipont, 36 (Augustine).

48 Cf. *PL* 191, 159c (Lombard); CCSL 97, ed. Adriaen, 123 (Cassiodorus); Rheims BM MS 132, f. 16[rb–va] (Remigius).

49 Parma edn., XIV, 182. Cf. *ibid.*: "Allegorice dicitur de patribus Veteris Testamenti, qui continue expectabant Christum, et Deus quasi oblitus eorum, differebat remedium adhibere."

50 In this regard, Waleys's commentary develops a habit seen in his earlier *Moralitates* on other Old Testament books, on which see Smalley, *English Friars*, 79–88, and "Thomas Waleys," 58–66.

51 Smalley, *English Friars*, 1. The need to extend Smalley's work is stressed by Clark, "Friars and Classics," and Hanna, "Beyond Smalley's Assessment." See too Courtenay, "The Bible in the Fourteenth Century."

52 Dean, "Earliest Known Commentary on Livy," 92.

53 Smalley, *English Friars*, 86–88.

54 Though Waleys cites both Valerius Maximus and Livy, he quotes verbatim from the latter (II.xl.2): ". . . quoniam armis uiri defendere urbem non possent, mulieres precibus lacrimisque defenderent."

55 Sig. Aa3[vb]: "Sic et Christus, qui multos in ecclesia persecutores sentit, se confert saepe quasi in exilium, sed cum populo suo bellum indicit, multas tribulationes immittens, et grauiora praedicens, nec credit nos sufficere ad

defensionem populi Christiani nisi mulieres istae, scilicet mater suis precibus et speciosa Magdalena suis lachrymis, id est merito lachrymarum suarum et exemplo, pacem miseris impetraret."

56 Smalley, in contrast, generally tended to see the classicizing interests of these exegetes as a distraction from the work of biblical interpretation, or as an excuse to indulge in antiquarian interests: e.g., on Waleys, *English Friars*, 88. For a further critique of the shortcomings of her approach on this point, see Hanna, "Beyond Smalley's Assessment."

57 *PL* 191, 251b (Lombard); CCSL 38, ed. Dekkers and Fraipont, 136–37 (Augustine).

58 In *Friars*, 58–65, Smalley focuses on Trevet's work with classical texts, and in *Study*, 346–47, she identifies his Hebrew sources. Kleinhans, "Nicolaus Trivet," supplements these briefer discussions. Most recently, FitzGerald, *Inspiration and Authority*, 152–92, provides a valuable account of Trevet's thought, focusing on his commentary on *De consolatione*.

59 BodL MS Bodley 738, f. 1rb. All subsequent citations refer to this copy of the text, but note that its early folios have been damaged by damp and repaired, and my transcription of this material is necessarily provisional. Shields, "Commentarius," provides a convenient though error-prone edition of selections. On the dating of the commission, see *BRUO* 1902.

60 Though he almost certainly did not know this text, Trevet's positioning of himself here is reminiscent of another avowed interpreter of the Psalms' literal sense, Herbert of Bosham (d. after 1189), who in the preface to his commentary writes, "Velud cum animalibus gressibilibus super terram terre hereo, solum littere psalmorum sensum infimum prosequens." Quoted in Smalley, "Herbert of Bosham," 32.

61 Cf. Thomas's justification of his literalistic Job commentary, much more widely attested than his work on the Psalter, including the assertion that his major antecedent, Gregory's *Moralia*, had addressed its "mysteria tam subtiliter et diserte ... ut his nihil ultra addendum videatur" (Parma edn., XIV, 2).

62 Trevet may have been familiar with the commentary (cf. n. 43 in this chapter), but Shields, "Commentarius," 17–22, did not find Aquinas among his named sources, and I have not identified substantial borrowings.

63 Bodley 738, f. 1rb. On his Hebrew sources, see Shields, "Commentarius," 23–33, and Stadler, "Textual and Literary Criticism."

64 Cf. the comparison of the Psalms' lyric meter to Horace in Isidore, *Etymologies*, VI.ii.17, ed. Lindsay (unpaginated).

65 *PL* 191, 59d–60a. See further Chapter 2, 57–60 and Chapter 3, 101–102. As FitzGerald, *Inspiration and Authority*, 70–71, notes, Trevet later raises the possibility that Ezra served as a compiler, but here he is simply explaining Jerome's position, not offering his own (Bodley 738, f. 3ra). Likewise, discussing the book's *causa efficiens*, Trevet notes first the Augustinian identification of David as the author of all the Psalms, and then provides the opinion of the Hebrews (*secundum Hebraeos*) that he wrote the greater part of them, the latter

66 Parma edn., XIV, 163.
67 See n. 33 in this chapter.
68 See Little, *Franciscan Papers*, 139–41. Smalley refers to Cossey in passing in *Study*, 347–48, refining her earlier *Hebrew Scholarship*, 4–6. Kleinhans offers a useful if limited supplement: see his "Heinrich v. Cossey." My "English Hebraism" provides a fuller study of the text, along with an edition and translation of the prologues.
69 All quotations are drawn from the only surviving copy of the commentary (Stegmüller 3155), Cambridge, Christ's Coll. MS 11. On f. 6^v, for example, Cossey quotes Trevet and Lyre as agreeing on the translation history of the Psalms: "Et dicit Triuet, et Lira, quod Psalterium prime translacionis est in vsu ecclesie Romane vsque in presens . . . ." On the localization of his text to Oxford, see "English Hebraism."
70 The note on Hebrew prepositions occurs on f. 252^r; for examples of transliterated Hebrew, see Kleinhans, "Cossey," 250; James, *Descriptive Catalogue*, 28–36.
71 See n. 44 in this chapter.
72 For Lyre's discussion, see *Biblia sacra*, III, sig. o3^{rb-va}.
73 Cf. *PL* 191, 55a.
74 Cf. Bodley 738, f. 53vb, where Trevet maintains that this psalm "continet gratiarum accionem pro reditu de captiuitate babilonica, et cantabatur in templi dedicacione."
75 *PL* 191, 291c.
76 This second manuscript contained a Latin translation interlineated in the Hebrew, and Cossey refers to this version as the *superscriptio Lincolniensis*. See my "English Hebraism" for further discussion and some correction of earlier misunderstandings surrounding this *superscriptio*. The identity of the owner of the other Hebrew psalter is suggested by a series of references, where the manuscript is referred to as, for example, "psalteri[um] Hebraic[um] illius iam conuersi magistri" (f. 14^r), "psalteri[um] Hebraic[um] magistri Iohannis" (f. 155^r), and "psalteri[um] magistri I. dudum conuersi" (f. 168^r).
77 The late medieval appreciation of correction has recently been explored by Wakelin, *Scribal Correction*, esp. 116–27, whose comments make me suspect that Cossey is describing a manuscript with an extensive series of corrections.
78 On authorial working copies, see the discussion in the Introduction, 15–16 and n. 60.
79 For the relevant passage in Trevet, see Bodley 738, f. 13^r.
80 Further examples are offered in "English Hebraism."
81 *Opera Omnia*, VI, 98.
82 *Summae*, I, sig. i4^v–5^r. The entire *quaestio* is translated into French by Dahan, *Interpréter la Bible*, 123–42.
83 *Lire la Bible*, 32: "La fin des temps . . . rendra inutile le travail exégétique. Mais nous n'en sommes pas encore là et avons pour mission de continuer à

(being Jerome's opinion as well – and Trevet immediately affirms David's title as the *egregius Psalmista* (Bodley 738, f. 2rb).

construire le bâtiment herméneutique, génération après génération, pierre après pierre."
84 Dahan treats this notion of progress at greater length in *Lire la Bible*, 27–33 and 409–25, with further examples.
85 Cf. *PL* 191, 104c: "In persona ergo poenitentis in iudicio puniri metuentis orat."
86 Klepper, *Insight of Unbelievers*, 5. On the postils' reception, see further Reinhardt, "Les controverses."

2 Eclectic Hermeneutics: Biblical Commentary in Wyclif's Oxford

1 Here I single out the topics in *De veritate* addressed in admirable detail by Ghosh, *Wycliffite Heresy*, 25–61.
2 Cf. Gellrich, *Discourse and Dominion*, 90, who refers to Wyclif's "idealism of almost mystical proportions." In contrast, Catto, "Culture and History," 119, claims that Wyclif was uninterested in the "devotional practice by which the art of contemplation was nurtured."
3 Minnis, *Valuing the Vernacular*, 107.
4 Wyclif, *Trialogus*, ed. Lechler, 238–39; cf. Stephen Lahey's full translation of *Trialogus* (Cambridge, 2013), here 191.
5 *Select English Works*, ed. Arnold, III, 186–87, here 187; cf. Minnis, "'Authorial Intention,'" 15–16. The English text survives in only a single copy, Dublin, Trinity Coll., MS 244, ff. 210^v–211^r; cf. Hanna, *Pursuing History*, 48–59.
6 Ghosh, *Wycliffite Heresy*, 56; see too Minnis, *Valuing the Vernacular*, 108, and Catto, "Wyclif and Wycliffism," 209.
7 Smalley, "John Wyclif's *Postilla*," 191, records the extant and lost portions of the commentary. Of the two parts identified by Smalley as "not yet found," the *pars ethica* may have been preserved (anonymously) in the library of the Syon brethren: see *Syon Abbey*, ed. Gillespie, 135. On the division of the text, see the discussion later in this chapter, 60.
8 Smalley, "*Postilla* and *Principium*," 256.
9 *Ibid.*, 282–83. Courtenay, "Bible in the Fourteenth Century," 184, likewise notes that "scriptural studies at the universities" were "almost a silent topic" between 1335 and 1375. See further Courtenay, *Schools and Scholars*, 373; Smalley, "Bible in the Schools," 208; Smalley, "Problems of Exegesis," 274.
10 Smalley, "John Wyclif's *Postilla*," 258 and 283; Smalley, "*Postilla* and *Principium*," 197.
11 Dove, "Wyclif and the English Bible," 370. Cf. Catto, "Wycliffite Bible," 19, and Kelly, *English Bible*, 34.
12 Dove, *English Bible*, 31; repeated in Dove, "Wyclif and the English Bible," 376.
13 Levy, *Quest for Authority*, 59.
14 See, e.g., *De veritate*, I.vi, ed. Buddensieg, I, 114: "De Scriptura vero quarto vel quinto modo dictis Scriptura sacra facit nullam aut modicam mencionem."

15 Ghosh, *Wycliffite Heresy*, 42 and 64.
16 *Ibid.*, 28.
17 Benrath, *Wyclifs Bibelkommentar*. For examples of studies that appear to draw exclusively on these intermediaries, see Dove, "Wyclif and the English Bible," 370–72; Ghosh, *Wycliffite Heresy*, 41–42; Krey, "Many Readers," 195–97; Lahey, *John Wyclif*, 149–53; Levy, *Quest for Authority*, 56–57 and 69–70; McDermott, *Tropologies*, 59–61.
18 Smalley, "John Wyclif's *Postilla*," 198–99.
19 All quotations from Wyclif's Psalter postil (Stegmüller 5070,2) are taken from Oxford, St. John's Coll. MS 171, here f. 109^{rv}.
20 *Biblia sacra*, III, sig. o2^v–3^v and o7^r; for translations see *Medieval Literary Theory*, ed. Minnis and Scott, 271–74.
21 Later in this prologue, Wyclif refers to what he has said "in prefacione Prouerbiorum de propheta Dauid," apparently a fuller discussion of David's abilities as a prophet (St. John's MS 171, f. 109^v). Unfortunately, his postils on Proverbs are lost; see Smalley, "John Wyclif's *Postilla*," 191.
22 See Chapter 1, 39–40 and n. 65.
23 Reading *nunc* for the manuscript's *non*.
24 Lyre raises the idea of this division in his prologue to Ps. 1, though there he indicates that the final part begins with Ps. 145, since "huius enim libri intentio est diuina laudatio" (*Biblia sacra*, III, sig. o7^{rb}; cf. *Medieval Literary Theory*, ed. Minnis and Scott, 275). At the beginning of his gloss on Ps. 2, however, he locates the break at the start of Ps. 109 and identifies the two major parts with the subject matter repeated by Wyclif (sig. p1^{ra}). This arrangement is invoked again at the start of Lyre's commentary on Ps. 109 (sig. S2^{rab}), and he is followed at this point by Wyclif, who writes, "Hic incipit pars tercia huius libri, tractans de sacerdocio Christi" (St. John's MS 171, f. 256^v). Benrath, *Bibelkommentar*, 23–24, does not notice that this division comes from Lyre, and he confusingly states that Wyclif brings up the division in his prologue only to ignore it in his commentary.
25 Smalley, "John Wyclif's *Postilla*," 187–91 and 197; Smalley, "*Postilla* and *Principium*," 253–54 and 256. Little scholarly attention has been paid to Auriol's *Compendium*, but see Ocker, *Biblical Poetics*, 49–51; likewise, Krey, "Many Readers," who compares later exegetes' use of Lyre's literal postils and the *Compendium*, specifically on the Apocalypse. Similarly, Krey, "Problems in History," reads Lyre's Apocalypse commentary with some reference to his use of Auriol.
26 St. John's MS 171, f. 108^v, quoting and adapting *Compendium*, ed. Seeboeck, 51–52. For discussion of Auriol's classifications of the "hymnidic" books, see Minnis, *Theory of Authorship*, 135–36 and 141–42.
27 St. John's MS 171, ff. 108^v–109^r: "Quedam vero dicuntur cantica a labio exteriori, quia ore [*MS:* hore] a Leuitis et sacerdotibus canebantur. ... Quedam vero dicta sunt intellectus a radio profundiori vt vbi Propheta in finem, hoc est in futurum, de Christo profundius speculabatur." Cf. *Compendium*, ed. Seeboeck, 52–53.

28 Gross-Diaz, *Psalms Commentary*, 51–65 and 158–59, discusses Gilbert's marginal symbols in detail, and her handlist of manuscripts identifies copies with the symbols (160–80). Gilbert's system is also discussed by Rouse and Rouse, *Authentic Witnesses*, 195–96. On the complex interrelation of these Psalms commentaries, see Kraebel, "Prophecy and Poetry."

29 The symbols are not mentioned by Smalley in her "John Wyclif's *Postilla*" or "*Postilla* and *Principium*," by Benrath, *Bibelkommentar*, or by Hanna, *Descriptive Catalogue of St. John's*, 235–37.

30 Rouse and Rouse describe the lack of backward references as the "principal drawback" of Gilbert's system (*Authentic Witnesses*, 195). Cf. Gross-Diaz, *Psalms Commentary*, 56.

31 St. John's MS 171, f. 241^r: "Iste est quintus penitencialium et quartus psalmorum oracionis titulo prenotatus"; cp. Gilbert in MGT MS 815, f. 147^r: "Psalmus iste penitencialium quintus est, quartus eorum qui dicuntur oratio." Benrath, *Bibelkommentar*, 24, notes that these references in the body of the commentary are sometimes attributed to a *glosa*, which he believes to be the Lombard's *Magna glosatura*. Further examples of Wyclif's indebtedness to Gilbert are therefore in order, confirming that similarities between Wyclif and the Lombard should be attributed to their shared reliance on Gilbert rather than Wyclif's use of the Lombard. Emphasis has been added throughout the following to highlight Wyclif's borrowings from Gilbert; these passages are taken from the beginnings of the commentaries on Pss. 41, 73, and 132, respectively:

Wyclif St. John's MS 171, f. 155^r	Gilbert MGT MS 815, f. 61^v	Peter Lombard *PL* 191, 415b
Vnde secundum glosam iste est *primus psalmus agens de desiderio Dei*.	*Primus psalmus de desiderio Dei*, qui non solum chatecuminis fontem baptismi desiderantibus conuenit sed etiam baptizatis adhuc in hac uita a Deo peregrinantibus.	Convenit enim hic psalmus omni Christiano qui flamma divinae charitatis accenditur, de qua re, id est de charitate Dei, hic psalmus primus est.

Wyclif St. John's MS 171, f. 201^r	Gilbert MGT MS 815, f. 109^r	Peter Lombard *PL* 191, 683a
Est primus psalmus lamentacionis *de vltima captiuitate facta per Titum*, de qua sequuntur alii duo.	Primus psalmus lamentationis *sed de ultima captiuitate facta per Titum*. Sequuntur alii duo de lamentatione.	Et est iste psalmus primus lamentationis Jerusalem, de qua re sequuntur alii scilicet duo, 78 et 136.

Wyclif St. John's MS 171, f. 288^{rv}	Gilbert MGT MS 815, f. 193^r	Peter Lombard *PL* 191, 1182cd
Et quia psalmus iste non *causam* materie *mutat nec personam* nec modum loquendi, que solent *generare diuisionem psalmorum*, ideo iste est secundus psalmus athomus.	Vnde psalmus iste simplex nec *causam mutat nec personam*, nec locutionem conuertit, que tamquam athomi *diuisionem* uidentur *generare psalmorum*.	Et est hic psalmus atomus, id est sine divisione, ubi charitas proximi commendatur, quae nullam admittit alienationem mentis seu divisionem.

32 Rouse and Rouse, *Authentic Witnesses*, 196, citing Oxford, Oriel Coll. MS 77 as the single early thirteenth-century copy they have found with the indexing symbols. Based on Gross-Diaz, *Psalms Commentary*, 160–80, several other examples could be added to Oriel, though the sources of Gross-Diaz's dating are uncertain, and in several later manuscripts she notes that the marginal system is "incomplete."

33 Smalley, "*Postilla* and *Principium*," 256. Smalley's "recipe" has been frequently quoted: see Benrath, *Bibelkommentar*, 11 n. 26; Dove, "Wyclif and the English Bible," 370 n. 32; Krey, "Many Readers," 185; Lahey, *John Wyclif*, 150.

34 Cf. *Biblia sacra*, III, sig. R7^{ra}: "... gratiarum actio de r[e]stituione regni Israel ... tempore Dauid."

35 In this case, Wyclif must be identifying the subject matter of the psalm on the basis of the indexing symbol, which appears, e.g., in the margin of MGT MS 815, f. 161^r at this point, and Gilbert identifies the subject matter of Ps. 107 more specifically as "humilitas Christi secundum carnem et altitudo secundum diuinitatem." The language used by Wyclif here appears, e.g., in Gilbert's introduction to Ps. 81 (MGT MS 815, f. 126^r: "Iste psalmus quintus est de duabus naturis in Christo") and Ps. 109 (MGT MS 815, f. 164^r: "Psalmus iste septimus de duabus naturis in Christo").

36 E.g., Wyclif repeats Gilbert's claim that the two hemistiches of Ps. 107.3, divided by the repeated *exurge*/*exurgam*, should be read as a dialogue between, first, "vox Patris ad Filium vel Verbi ad corpus sibi personaliter coniunctum" and, second, the Son speaking in response (St. John's MS 171, f. 254^v). Cf. Gilbert in MGT MS 815, f. 161^v: "*Exurge* uox est Patris ad Filium uel Uerbi ad corpus personaliter sibi unitum, quasi: 'Cantabo et psallam, ergo tu qui es psalterium quantum ad morum probitatem et cythara quantum ad passionem, *exurge*.' Et ta[m]quam Filius responderet supponit, '*Exurgam diluculo* diei Dominico.'" Wyclif's commentary on Pss. 3 and 4 follows a similar format as Ps. 107, with a mystical "postscript" coming after a historicist interpretation, but in these cases the "mystical" readings seem to be original to Wyclif: St. John's MS 171, ff. 111^v and 112^v.

37 St. John's MS 171, f. 171^v: "Lira dicit cum Hebreis quod Dauid fecit psalmum pro graciis agendis Deo, quando fugiens de Ceila saluatus est de

manibus Saul, qui eum in Ceila voluerat obsidisse ([I] Reg. 23). Sed glosa exponit mistice de Christo, cum sit tercius psalmus agens late de Christi Passione." Cf. *Biblia sacra*, III, sig. C6[rb]: "Dauid fecit hunc psalmum gratias agens Deo, quando fugiens de Ceila saluatus fuit de manibus Saulis, qui volebat eum in Ceila obsidere," and Gilbert, MGT MS 815, f. 78[v]: "... tendens *in finem* [id est] Christum, de cuius passione et resurrectione iste psalmus tercius latius tractat." For an example of a specific gloss taken from Gilbert, cp. Wyclif's reading of Ps. 54.3, "*Contristatus sum in exercitacione mea*. Christus autem exercitatus est quia nullo ocio ab incepto remissus, qui imminente passione ex humana infirmitate tristatur" (St. John's MS 171, f. 171[v]), to Gilbert's, "Christus exercitatus est, id est nullo ocio ab incepto remissus, qui ex humana infirmitate tristatur" (MGT MS 815, f. 78[v]). Wyclif immediately goes on to offer a Davidic reading of Ps. 54.4, "*Et a tribulacione peccator[is]* mala pro bonis michi reddentis. Sic Dauid sensit ingratitudinem Ceilitarum volencium eum tradere in manus Saul" (f. 171[v]), taken from Lyre, "... id est a tribulatione mihi praeparata, et per dolum populi Ceilae, qui in hoc pecauit grauissime. ... Illi enim qui volebant eum tradere in manus Saulis ..." (*Biblia sacra*, III, sig. C6[va]).

38 See Chapter 1, 28 and 37–38.
39 Cf. *Biblia sacra*, III, sig. L3[va]: "De materia vero huius psalmi dicunt expositores Hebraei et catholici quod Asaph fecit hunc psalmum contra peruersos iudices."
40 Cf. MGT MS 815, f. 126[r]: "Iste psalmus quintus est de duabus naturis in Christo, in quo exprobrat Propheta Sinagoge quia Christum presentem uidit non tamen agnouit."
41 *Biblia sacra*, III, sig. s7[ra]: "Dicunt autem Hebraei quod iste psalmus factus est a Dauid pro gratiarum actione de datione legis. ... Primo Dauid ostendit magnitudinem diuinae sapientiae generaliter ex excellentibus creaturis," and MGT MS 815, f. 26[v]: "Hic enim agit Propheta de incarnatione Domini, que nouissimis temporibus facta est, per quam diabolus destruitur et homo primum a peccato deinde a morte liberatur."
42 Though, for example, the material taken from the *Postilla litteralis* in the passage quoted above, 63–64, gestures toward Lyre's general two-part division of the psalm (*ostendens primo* ...), Wyclif draws on Gilbert's *divisio* rather than Lyre's to identify the start of the *pars secunda* at Ps. 18.8. Cp. St. John's MS 171, f. 125[r]: "*Lex Domini* etc. In secunda parte ostenditur quod dictus sponsus dedit sponse dotem," to Lyre, "Secundo specialiter ex datione legis, ibi: *Lex Domini*. ... Hic consequenter ostenditur ordo diuinae sapientiae specialiter ex legis datione" (*Biblia sacra*, III, sig. s7[ra] and s7[va]), and to Gilbert, "*Lex Domini*. Pars secunda, in qua legem sponsi commendat" (MGT MS 815, f. 27[r]).
43 Wyclif is not the only exegete to treat Pauline allusions as a justification for identifying Christological readings as the literal sense of certain psalms: cf. De Visscher, *Reading the Rabbis*, 137–59.
44 Ghosh, *Wycliffite Heresy*, 42.

45 *Ibid.*, 28, 42, 54, 65.
46 Smalley, *Thought and Learning*, 415.
47 *Biblia sacra*, III, sig. 07rb; tr. *Medieval Literary Theory*, ed. Minnis and Scott, 275.
48 MGT MS 815 omits Gilbert's prologue, and this last quotation has therefore been taken from MGT MS 488. See further Kraebel, "Prophecy and Poetry," and Gross-Diaz, *Psalms Commentary*, 78–81.
49 Ghosh, *Wycliffite Heresy*, 37.
50 The examples from Wyclif's Psalter postil should also contradict the bizarre suggestion, in Kelly, *English Bible*, 33, that "Wyclif had never learned to speak or write Latin properly." On the contrary, though his style is often compressed, I have never found his Latin writings to be anything but clear and in keeping with the norms of scholastic prose.
51 *Opus Evangelicum*, ed. Loserth, I–II, 1.
52 *Ibid.*, 336 n.; cf. Cambridge, Trinity Coll. MS B.16.2, p. 816 and Dublin, Trinity Coll. MS 242, p. 332.
53 *Ibid.*, 108/9; the whole passage is 108/9–109/28.
54 *Ibid.*, 73/21 (the passage being 73/21–74/11); cf. BodL MS Bodley 716, f. 5ra. Though it is not similarly flagged as being drawn from this *glossa*, *Opus Evangelicum*, ed. Loserth, I–II, 71/33–72/15, also corresponds verbatim to the postils in Bodley 716, ff. 4vb–5ra. The same correspondences are noted by Benrath, *Bibelkommentar*, 122 n. 133. Smalley, "John Wyclif's *Postilla*," 200, provides another quotation from the postils occurring later in the *Opus*. Thorough comparison would almost certainly yield further borrowings.
55 Gradon, "Wyclif's *Postilla*," 76–77. Gradon draws attention to the correspondence between the postils and *Opus* following the reference to the *glossa privata*, but she does not mention the other parallels noted above.
56 Note that the readings attributed to this *glossa* do not match Lyre on these verses (*Biblia sacra*, V, sigs. d1^v and D4^v).
57 Stegmüller 5088/5091. An additional manuscript, PNK III.F.20, is misidentified by Williell Thomson, *Latin Writings*, 204–205, as containing the same postils, compounding the error of S. H. Thomson, "Unnoticed MSS," 35. The misidentification may be based on an annotation added by a later reader on f. 1^r: "Doctor ewangelicus super omnes ewangelistas." This misattribution is repeated by Smalley, "John Wyclif's *Postilla*," 186–87, and Gradon, "Wyclif's *Postilla*," 69.
58 Smalley, "John Wyclif's *Postilla*," 202.
59 Benrath, *Bibelkommentar*, does not address these textual issues, and he seems to have completed most of his work on the gospel postils without reference to the Oxford manuscripts. Early in his study, Benrath notes that the English copies are superior to Vienna (4 n. 8), though he still quotes from Vienna throughout. Later, citing Smalley, he raises the possibility that the Vienna scribe "hat … den Text Wyclifs gekürzt" (97).
60 Cp. *Compendium*, ed. Seeboeck, 191.
61 Smalley, "John Wyclif's *Postilla*," 202.

62 Bodley 716, f. 1va: "Huius ergo euangelii talis est diuisio. Primo stabilit suum subiectum ostendo quater Christum verum Deum et verum hominem: testimonio angelico et prophetico, secundo ex veneracione regia cum illustracione celesti, tercio ex predicacione Iohannis et testimonio Dei Patris, et quarto ex demonis temptacione et angelorum obsequio. Et illud declaratur per ordinem vsque ad medium capituli quarti. Et ab hinc declarat redempcionem factam per Christum." To this point Wyclif follows the *divisio* provided at the opening of Lyre on Matth. 1 (*Biblia sacra*, V, sig. 8va). Lyre divides the remainder of the gospel after Matth. 4.12 into three major sections: first "de Christi legislatione" (subdivided into "populi adunationem ad Christum per eius praedicationem" in the remainder of Matth. 4 and "Christi legislationem" in Matth. 5–25), then "de ipsius passione" in Matth. 26–27, and finally "de ipsius resurrectione" in Matth. 28 (*Biblia sacra*, V, sig. c6^{rab}). In contrast, without specifying in his prologue where these breaks occur, Wyclif divides this material thus (Bodley 716, f. 1va): "Primo vocando populum per predicacionem et internam inspiracionem, secundo dando legem, tercio confirmando et auctorando per miraculorum faccionem et legis declaracionem, et quarto declarat Christi passionem et resurreccionem." For the same passages in Magdalen MS lat. 55, see f. 77^{vab}.

63 Lyre, in contrast, simply notes that Matth. 1.1 is "quendam prologum seu prefationem" (*Biblia sacra*, V, sig. a8^{va}).

64 The *Glossa* provides marginal comments on the first preface, and Lyre glosses both of them: see *Biblia sacra*, V, sigs. a7^r–a8^r. See further De Bruyne, *Préfaces*, 171–72 and 183–84. On the practice of commenting on these prefaces, see Smalley, *Study*, 217, and *Gospels in the Schools*, 64, 91, 149, and 249.

65 ÖNB MS 1342, f. 1^r: "*Matheus ex Iudea sicut in ordine* etc. Iste prologus est beati Ieronimi, qui diuiditur principaliter in quattuor partes. In prima tractatur de vocacione miraculosa ipsius Mathei, secundus tanguntur duo principia generacionis ipsius Christi, et tercio tangitur sufficiencia conscripcionis ewangelii per ipsum Matheum, et quattuor ter capitularis tangit sue ipsius Ieronimus conscripcionis intencionem.... *Cuius vocacio ad Deum* etc. Pro quo sciendum Romani habentes Iudeos sibi tributarios ordinauerunt in ciuitatibus publicanos, hoc est monetarios, curum habentes de tributis publicam, de quorum numero fuit Matheus. *Hec Io. Wi....Et numero satisfaciens et tempori* etc. In quattuordecim namque numero sunt quattuor, iste numerus significans...." The second *Glossa* prologue is quoted briefly on f. 1vb ("*Et sunt quasi quattuor rote in* etc. Item sciendum quod lex ewangelorum est cunctis aliis prestancior..."), acknowledged by the scribe, who wrote "Sequitur in secundo prologo" in red ink over the column. This note led Thomson, *Latin Writings*, 204, to mistakenly describe Wyclif's Matthew postil as having two prologues in this manuscript.

66 On the other hand, it should be noted that Wyclif's *divisio* of the Monarchian preface shows some signs of his interpretive interest: though he divides the preface at the same points as Lyre, his account of the content of each *pars* is distinct. With the material quoted in n. 65, cp. Lyre in *Biblia sacra*, V, sig.

a7[ra]. Note that John Bacanthorpe also divided the Monarchian preface at the same points, and he too offered his own interpretation of each part's significance: see Cambridge, Trinity Coll. MS B.15.12, f. 99ra.

67 ÖNB MS 1342, f. 1ra: "Pro intellectu istius textus moueo istam questiunculam: Quare inter ewangelistas Matheus primum ewangelium dicitur scripsisse." This topic is conventional in Matthew prologues: it appears in Lyra's general prologue to the four gospels (*Biblia sacra*, V, sig. a2[r]) and in the twelfth-century prologue edited in Appendix C.

68 Bodley 716, f. 1[ra] (cf. Magdalen 55, f. 77[ra]): "Matheus, qui interpretatur datus, primo inter quattuor ewangelistas scripsit. Vnde animal habens quattuor facies, de quo Ezechiel, primo habuit faciem hominis directe oppositam prophete, faciem leonis ad dexteram, faciem bouis ad sinistram, et faciem aquile retro ex opposito faciei hominis – et talis fuit ordo istorum quattuor euangelistarum scribendo ewangelium. Sicut ergo vnum animal habuit istas quattuor facies, sic de vno Christo sunt quattuor noticie quattuor conclusionum quas principaliter intendunt quattuor euangeliste. Per *faciem* enim designatur noticia secundum Gregorium, quia inter omnes partes hominis facies maxime docet noscere intrinsecas passiones. Sicud ergo Matheus principaliter intendit quod Christus fuit Messias in lege promissus, et sic ostendit eius generacionem et humanitatem, sic designatur per faciem hominis proximam prophete. Et sicut Marcus intendit quod fuit vere rex et sic incistit eius resurrec[c]ioni, sic secundo scribendo euangelium figuratur per faciem leonis." At this point, moving on to discuss Luke's intention and position, the Oxford manuscripts begin to correspond verbatim to the text in ÖNB MS 1342. The discussion is conventional, and some glosses are borrowed from Lyre – e.g., the etymology of Matthew's name as *datus* appears in his commentary on the Monarchian preface (*Biblia sacra*, V, sig. a7[ra]), and the Gregorian gloss on *facies* as *noticia* (though not the explanation that follows) is in his prologue on the four gospels (sig. a2[ra]) – but in many of its details it appears to be original to Wyclif. Exceptionally, it should be noted that one instance of a lemma drawn from the Monarchian prologue (*Et sic satisfecit numero et tempori*) is preserved in Magdalen MS lat. 55, f. 77[ra], though omitted in Bodley 716, f. 1[ra].

69 Smalley, "John Wyclif's *Postilla*," 202.

70 To provide just a few examples: (1) above Bodley 716, f. 1[va] [prol. to Matth.]: "Augustinus in epistola ad Vincencium de scriptis sanctorum doctorum dicit: Hoc genus scripturarum a canonicis Scripturis distinguendum est. Non enim ex eis sic testimonia proferuntur vt contrarium sentire non liceat etc." [cf. CSEL 34.2, ed. A. Goldbacher, 480]; (2) below Bodley 716, f. 2[ra] and below Magdalen MS lat. 55, f. 78[rab] [prol. to Matth.; see Fig. 5]: "Nota de hoc nomine Iesu Bernardus super Cantica cap. 15: Hoc nomen lucet predicatum, pascit meditatum, lenit inuocatum, quid eque mentem cogitantis inpinguat, virtutes roborat, castas affecciones fouet. Aridus est omnis cibus si non isto olio infundatur, si scribere voluero non sapit vbi non legero Iesum, si confero vel disputo, non sapit michi vbi non sonuerit nomen Iesu. Iesus (inquit) est

mel in ore, melos in aure, iubilus in corde. Nichil ita ire impetum cohibet, superbie tumorem cedat, liuorum uulnus sanat, libidinis flammas extinguit, sitim temporat auaricie, et tocius malicie fugat pruriginem. Hec Bernardus" [*Opera*, ed. Leclercq et al., I, 85–86]; (3) above Bodley 716, f. 13rb [on Matth. 16–17]: "Nota quod Ecclesia non consistit in hominibus racione potestatis vel dignitatis ecclesiastice vel secularis, quia multi principes et summi pontifices et alii inferiores inuenti sunt apostatasse a fide, propter quod Ecclesia consistit in illis personis in quibus est noticia et vera confessio fidei et veritatis. Hec Lyra super illo Matth. 16: *Porte inferi non preualebunt* etc." [*Biblia sacra*, V, sig. i6^{vb}].

71 My collation of the Matth. prologue and the beginning of the commentary on Matth. 1 supports the conclusion that Bodley and Magdalen shared a common exemplar for at least these texts. Note, further, that the lower margin of f. 78^r in Magdalen contains ruling in hardpoint to accommodate one of these glosses. Discussing Bodley 716, Robson, *Wyclif and the Schools*, 241, seems not to realize that these marginal notes are by the main scribe.

72 On authorial working copies, see the Introduction, n. 60. For a comparable use of *schedulae*, see Hunt, "Library of Grosseteste," 127.

73 Hudson, "Books and Survival," 230–31. The possibility that this shared exemplar was copied from Wyclif's working papers may also help to explain the various blanks in both copies, typically involving biblical citations apparently meant to indicate parallel examples: e.g., Bodley 716, f. 1vb l. 52 and Magdalen MS lat. 55, f. 78ra l. 51 (a passage from the prologue not in the ÖNB version). Such blanks could reflect (among other things) illegible text, unclear revision, or blank space in Wyclif's working copy.

74 Smalley, "John Wyclif's *Postilla*," 200–201, cites four passages in the *Opus* on John 13.1–15 that refer to "quidam postillans," with only the first corresponding to a passage in the postils, Bodley 716, f. 142vb. In part, Smalley anticipates the possibility suggested here, indicating that Wyclif may have been "quoting from a version of his postill which he had expanded after its publication, making it reflect his extreme, later views" (*ibid.*, 201).

75 For the postils as perfunctory and propaedeutic, see Evans, *Wyclif*, 115–17; Ghosh, *Wycliffite Heresy*, 23; Hudson, "Wyclif's *Summa*," 70.

76 Similarly, in the preface to the sermons he composed or compiled at Lutterworth, Wyclif favors spiritual exposition, writing, "Supposito sensu literali intendo breviter sensum misticum explanare" (*Sermones*, ed. Loserth, I, pref., n.p.).

77 *Doctoris Seraphici S. Bonaventurae Opera*, VII, 12b. For Docking, see Balliol Coll. MS 80, f. 161va.

78 Following Smalley, this kind of literal-historicist approach has been discussed especially in studies of Victorine exegesis: see, e.g., Coulter, "*Historia* and *Sensus*," Harkins, *Reading and Restoration*, 171–96, and Van Liere, *Introduction*, 125–27. See also the remarks on "la critique narrative" by Dahan, "La méthode critique," 118–19. Likewise, Hazard, *Literal Sense*, 17–83, focuses on discussions of biblical narrative in his account of Lyre's literal postil on John.

238 *Notes on pages 73–74*

79 See Franklin-Brown, *Reading the World*, esp. 95–128, Harris, "Bible and History," and, more broadly, Steiner, "Compendious Genres."
80 See Clark, *Making of the Historia*, as well as his essays, "Commentaries on Comestor's *Historia*," "Stephen Langton and Hugh of St. Cher," and "Commentaries of Stephen Langton"; cf. Delmas, "La réception."
81 Bodley 716, f. 3va (the citation of the *Historia* occurs at l. 39, oddly in the middle of a paraphrase from the biblical text, Matth. 2.19, and the burning of the ships at ll. 20–22). See *Historia Scholastica*, PL 198, 1543bc. Lyre mentions Herod's summons to Rome just a few verses later, discussing the Massacre of the Innocents (*Biblia sacra*, V, sig. c1^{rb}).
82 *Biblia sacra*, V, sig. b7^{rb}: "Et sequentes stellam venerunt ad Iudaeam die tertia decima, quia illa terra vbi habitabat Balaam non multum distabat a Iudea."
83 Bodley 716, f. 3rb: "Quidam dicunt quod stella in aere per annum ante apparuit ducens eos, quidam quod tantum die natiuitatis et quod anno reuoluto primo venerunt, et quidam quod eodem anno die 13." Comestor, citing Chrysostom, raises the possibility that the star appears to the Magi "multo ante tempore quam Christus nasceretur" and that they traveled "multo tempore de longinquo" (*PL* 198, 1541cd).
84 In the sermons prepared at Lutterworth, Wyclif favors the third option presented here, but he still notes the length of the Magi's journey in a way that conflicts with Lyre's reading: "Et (ut opinatur) venerunt a die nativitatis, quando primo apparuit stella, super dromedarios die decimo tercio in Jerusalem. Nec oportet quod per annum fuerant in viando, quia poterant per ita paucos dies multiplici miraculo pergere tantum iter" (*Sermones*, ed. Loserth, I, 43).
85 The status of parables in scholastic theory has received considerable attention: see, e.g., Wailes, "Why Parables?"; Bain, "Le commentaire des paraboles." Madigan, "Lyra on Matthew," 214–19, discusses Lyre's glossing of specific parables, and the status of parables in Wyclif's *De veritate* is taken up by Ghosh, *Wycliffite Heresy*, 32–35.
86 Glossing Ps. 77.1 ("Aperiam in parabolis os meum"), for example, the Lombard explained *parabolae* as "similitudines rerum" (*PL* 191, 724d), and in his *De schematibus et tropis*, 13, Bede wrote, "Parabole est rerum genere dissimilium comparatio," citing Matth. 13.31 and John 3.14 as examples (CCSL 123a, ed. C. B. Kendall, 170). See further Bain, "*Parabola, similitudo*, et *exemplum*."
87 For an example of Wyclif considering Christ's historical audience, see Bodley 716, f. 11rb: "Locutus est autem Christus in parabolis quia secreta que debuerunt latere turbas et sciri a discipulis et alia inmiscuit que turba potuit capere, vt sic alliceret accendentes. Semper enim disponit sermonem secundum dignitatem auditorii." These hermeneutic distinctions within the gospels have not figured prominently in earlier scholarship on medieval commentary: see, e.g., Madigan, "Lyra on Matthew," and *Interpretation of Matthew*, esp. 13–28, as well as Hazard, *Literal Sense*, 17–83, where emphasis is placed on approaching the Gospels *qua* narratives.
88 Bodley 716, f. 7rb: "Duplex tamen est fructus huiusmodi qualitatum, scilicet vie and patrie. Fructus vie est finalis operacio comparata intencioni et qualitati

a qua procedit, sed fructus patrie est perpetua fruicio bonorum vel dampnacio perpetua malorum. Vnde quicumque defecerit a fructu bono vie damnabitur vt arbor infructuosa ad ignem perpetuum. Sic ergo ex duplici fructu cognoscentur caritative vel venenose operantes coniunctura probabili hic in via secundum fines in quibus quiescunt et medio infallibili. Inde dies Domini ostendet opus vniuscuisque, I Cor. 4[.5]: *Manifestabitur* etc."

89 Without mentioning the fruit, Lyre simply notes, "Arbor bona dicitur hic homo habens voluntatem bonam, et talis vt sic semper facit opus bonum" (*Biblia sacra*, V, sig. e6^{va}).

90 Bodley 716, f. 7ra; cf. *Biblia sacra*, V, sig. e5^{rab}.

91 Benrath, *Bibelkommentar*, 110 n. 87, says that simply Wyclif is "in enger Anlehnung an Lyra."

92 *Biblia sacra*, V, sig. c8^{ra}: "*Ascendit in montem*, quia in tali loco multi possunt audire, ex hoc etiam designatur excellentia legis euangelicae propter eminentiam montis in quo data est lex euangelica."

93 *Biblia sacra*, V, sig. c8^{ra}: "Quia Mosaica lex a Deo data est mediantibus angelis."

94 For the citation of the *Metaphysics*, I.i, see *Metaphysica*, ed. Vuillemin-Diem, II, 12–13; issues of *artifices* and *forma* are foregrounded in, for example, Thomas's commentary on this passage: *In duodecim libros Metaphysicorum*, ed. Cathala and Spiazzi, 9–10.

95 Bodley 716, f. 4vb. Though I have preferred to continue quoting from Bodley, note that this passage, as well as the discussion of salt that follows, is edited (with some errors) from ÖNB MS 1342 in Benrath, *Bibelkommentare*, 352–54. The marginal note on Christ's penchant for parables occurs in Bodley 716, f. 11^{r}, below col. b, as Wyclif glosses Matth. 13: "Nota quod multis de causis Christus parabolice loquebatur. Primo vt morem Palestine vrbis vbi predicabat obseruaret. Secundo vt studiosis occasionem se exercendi daret. Tercio vt melius memorie infigeretur, quam causam Crisostomus ponit. Quarto ne veritatem indignis panderet." Unlike other marginal notes in Bodley, discussed later in this chapter, 78–79, this one is unattributed, and, in light of the echo of the commentary on Matth. 5.13, it seems likely to be original to Wyclif. This historicized and rhetorical account of parables contrasts with the realist theories discussed by Ghosh, *Wycliffite Heresy*, 32–35.

96 Note that, though much more briefly and without overlapping with Wyclif's account, Lyre also reads these comparisons as describing "virtutes prelatorum." This reading comes after his account of the Beatitudes as the virtues of the contemplative life, and it is followed by his account of Matth. 5.21 ff. as giving the virtues of the active life, with prelates apparently positioned between the two (*Biblia sacra*, V, sigs. c8^{rab}, d1^{va}–2ra, and d3^{rab}). Wyclif, in contrast, treats the Beatitudes with the same generalizing tropological approach found elsewhere in his (and Lyre's) postils.

97 E.g., Bodley 716, below f. 6ra (on Matth. 5.42): "*Qui petit a te, da ei.* Semper enim dandum est vel res vel verbum secundum quod dixit Augustinus, quia si

iuste petit non debet sibi denegari quod petit. Si autem irracionaliter petit dandum est ei verbum docendo eum de irracionabilitate sue peticionis. Doctrina enim est quoddam donum bonum. Vnde Augustinus exponens hoc verbum dixit: Tunc enim melius aliquid dabis cum iniuste petentem correxeris. Hec Lyra."

98 Similar arguments have been made about source glosses included in manuscripts of the *Canterbury Tales* and *House of Fame:* see Partridge, "Glosses in the *Canterbury Tales*," 2.1–2.24, and Griffiths, *Diverting Authorities*, 56–63. The utility of such marginalia in the postils (as a reference text) is much clearer than it is in these other cases.

99 Respectively, Bodley 716, above f. 17rb: "Augustinus ad inquisiciones Ianuarii loquens de religione Christiana: Ipsam religionem nostram quam Dominus noster Iesus Christus in paucissimis sacramentorum celebracionibus voluit esse liberam, quidam seruilibus premunt honeribus adeo vt tollerabilior sit condicio Iudeorum qui non humanis presumpcionibus sed diuinis subiciuntur institutis"; above f. 11rb: "Augustinus epistola 77 [*recte* 21] ad Valerium: Cogitet religiosa prudencia nichil esse in hac vita, maxime hoc tempore, difficilius, laborosius, periculosius episcopi aut presbiteri aut diaconi officio, sed apud Deum nichil beacius si eo modo militetur quo imperator noster iubet. Hec ille"; above f. 1va: "Augustinus in epistola ad Vincencium de scripturis sanctorum doctorum dicit: Hoc genus scripturarum canonicis Scripturis distinguendum est. Non enim ex eis sic testimonia proferuntur vt contrarium sentire non liceat etc." For the *originalia*, see CSEL 34, ed. A. Goldbacher, II.210, I.49–50, and II.480.

100 The inclusion of this general point about the authority of exegetical sources at the start of the Matthew postils, rather than any of the earlier biblical books, may indicate that Wyclif considered this volume to have a sort of primacy of place among his commentaries – a point reinforced by his decision not to include – uniquely at the start of the gospel postils – any discussion of these books' place in the eight-part division he borrowed from Auriol. The idea that this omission is deliberate is reinforced by his extensive quotation, in his prologue to Matthew, of Auriol's listing of the prophetic *conditiones* fulfilled in this gospel: cf. Bodley 716, f. 1^{vab}; *Compendium*, ed. Seeboeck, 194 and 195–210.

101 Similarly, in his postil on Luke 8.16 (the *lucerna* not hidden under a bushel), Wyclif writes that the lantern "signat *mistice* quamlibet creaturam in qua lucet lux sapiencie vel quelibet lux spiritualis . . ." (Bodley 716, f. 43ra, emphasis added).

102 *Opus Evangelicum*, ed. Loserth, I–II, 72.

103 Positioned awkwardly between two unrelated discussions adapted from Lyre, this passage may have been added to his working copy on a separate *schedula*, and either marked for insertion at a particular point in the prologue or positioned by the scribe of Bodley and Magdalen's exemplar, who made his best guess at where to include it. Cf. *Biblia sacra*, V, sigs. a7^{rb} and a2^{ra}, the latter noted by Benrath, *Bibelkommentar*, 98–99.

104 Bodley 716, f. 1^(rab). Some glossing of the terms used toward the end of this passage will be useful. Wyclif provides some of the only examples in *DMLBS* of the two adverbs used in the complex final sentence, *communicative* and *participative*. The first (translated here simply as "by communication") is used in *De veritate*, ed. Buddensieg, to describe how knowledge of scriptural law allows one to assess the utility of something foreign (II, 141: ". . . est medium quod communicative respicit utile alienum"), and the means of scriptural signification (III, 141: "Scriptura significat comunicative et composite sensus suos"), the latter citing I Cor. 12.17 ("If the whole body were an eye, where would be the hearing?") as an analogue. In both cases, *DMLBS* s.v. "communicatio" 2a ("participation of individual in species") seems to be the relevant meaning, as it does here. The second adverb (translated "by participation") is sometimes used in contradistinction to *per se* in Wyclif's Latin writing, as in *De Composicione Hominis*, ed. Beer, 73, 74, and 82; more directly related are the uses in *De Benedicta Incarnacione*, ed. Harris, where *participative* qualifies the deification of humanity described in, e.g., Ps. 81.6: e.g., "Verbi participacione sit multitudo hominum in Christum directe credencium deificanda participative, sicut carbo ex ignis participacione est ignitus" (16; cf. also pp. 45, 74, 90).

105 Julian of Norwich, *Revelations*, ed. Windeatt, 164. For the discussion of Matthew's intentions and focus on Christ's birth and humanity, see Bodley 716, f. 1^(ra), and *Compendium*, ed. Seeboeck, 191, 193–94, and 211.

106 Hudson, *Premature Reformation*, 46.

107 Catto, "Woodford," 42–164. For other studies focusing on Woodford's later writings (especially his *Quattuor determinaciones*) and either omitting any reference to the *postilla* or only noting its existence, see Doyle, "Woodford on Scripture," 481–504 (cf. 483 n. 12); Ghosh, *Wycliffite Heresy*, 67–85 (cf. 235 n. 52); Levy, *Quest for Authority*, 92–117; Minnis, "Tobit's Dog," 41–52. Smalley, "Quotation," notes Woodford's citation of Ridevall's commentary on *De civitate*, while Catto, "New Light," uses Woodford's citations to identify Docking's lost commentary on Luke (building on Catto, "Woodford," 89–90). The commentary was first identified by Walmsley, "Two Lost Works," 460–62; it is not listed by Stegmüller.

108 Catto, "Woodford," 56–67 (description of the manuscript), 71–85 (summary of topics), and 86–132 (sources).

109 The first three quires of the commentary (ff. 69–92) are in a current anglicana, and most of the remainder of the work is in a textualis also used for most of the manuscript's first text, Woodford's *Quaestiones de sacramento altaris*. A blockier and more angular textualis is used for some material in ff. 199^r–200^r: Catto, "Woodford," 58, identifies this as a third hand, though it may simply represent variations in the hand used in the surrounding pages.

110 E.g., "Intendo inferius super alio passu euuangelii in ista materia facere plures conclusiones" (f. 97^(vb)). For further examples, see Catto, "Woodford," 64–65. Catto concludes that "the pressure of other work and controversy prevented the completion of so enormous a commentary" (64), and Smalley,

more fancifully, suggests that Woodford "brok[e] off" his work "in order to dispute with Wyclif" ("Quotation," 25). On the text's dating and composition at Oxford, see Smalley, "Quotation," 21–22, summarized by Catto, "Woodford," 66–67.

111 Such features are typical in other commentaries: see, e.g., Baconthorpe on Matthew (Stegmüller 4200) in Cambridge, Trinity Coll. MS B.15.12. In CUL MS Add. 3571, I was able to find only one isolated example of underlined lemmata, on f. 171ra.

112 Catto, "Woodford," 63.

113 No commentary by a Grimestone is listed by Stegmüller, and no obvious candidates appear in *BRUO* or *BRUC*. It could be that Woodford is referring to a lost work by John Grimestone OFM, the scribe of Edinburgh, National Library of Scotland MS Advocates 18.7.21, though, as Wenzel, *Preachers*, 102 n. 5, observes, "we know next to nothing about him," and the Norfolk dialect of his book may make it more likely that he attended Cambridge.

114 The text before the blank lines reads, "Ad hoc respondet Holcote super 13° capitulo Sapiencie dicens quod homo viuus habet in se magnam nobilitatem . . . ." Cf. Catto, "Woodford," 63–64.

115 Cambridge, Trinity Coll. MS B.15.12, f. 99^{rv}. On the dating, see Smalley, *Thought and Learning*, 295–306.

116 BnF MS lat. 15588, ff. 15ra–16ra, summarized by Madigan, *Interpretation of Matthew*, 74. Cf. Stegmüller 6709. On extrinsic prologues, see Minnis, *Theory of Authorship*, 30–32 and 63–71. Catto, "Woodford," 93–95, discusses Woodford's use of Olivi.

117 The first question in this series asks, "Qualis fuit iste euuangelista Matheus, qui fuit autor illius euuangelii?" (f. 72rb), answered with material drawn from William of Nottingham's commentary on *Unum ex quattuor*. See Smalley, *Thought and Learning*, 249–87; Catto, "Woodford," 90–92.

118 Respectively, BnF MS lat. 15588, ff. 16ra–18ra, Cambridge, Trinity Coll. MS B.15.12, ff. 102vb–103ra, and Oxford, Balliol Coll. MS 80, ff. 159vb–161vb. For Woodford's use of Docking, see Catto, "Woodford," 88–90, and "New Light," and on Docking more generally, see Smalley, *Study*, 278–80 and 323–25, and Little, *Franciscan Papers*, 98–121.

119 Woodford's treatment of Matth. 1 is complicated by the discussion of the genealogy in his introductory *quaestiones*. On f. 74vb he again quotes Matth. 1.1, explains how the preceding text fulfilled the first prophetic *conditio* and the rest of Matth. 1 fulfills the second, and then gives a *divisio* for Matth. 1.18–25. His list of *dubia* for this section begins on f. 75rb.

120 *Compendium*, ed. Seeboeck, 194–210; Wyclif: Bodley 716, f. 1^{vab} and ÖNB MS 1342, ff. 2ra–4ra; Baconthorpe: Cambridge, Trinity Coll. MS B.15.12, f. 99^{vab} (on which, see Smalley, *Thought and Learning*, 294–95 and 302).

121 E.g., Woodford's *divisio* of Matth. 2.1–12 begins, "Hanc ergo condicionem declarat Matheus de homine Iesu in euuangelio isto pro cuius declaracione. Primo narrat modum inquisicionis solicite, ibi: *Cum natus esset Iesus in Bet[leh]em Iude* etc. Secundo narrat modum inuencionis certe, ibi: *Qui*

cum audissent regem abierunt. Tercio modum veneracionis exibite, ibi: *Et procedentes adorauerunt eum*. Quarto narrat modum redicionis congrue, ibi: *Responso accepto in sompnis per aliam viam reuersi sunt in regionem suam*. Narrat ergo euuangelista modum inquisicionis solicite, et primo modum inquisicionis Gencium ex d[euo]cione, secundo modum inquisicionis Herodis et Iudeorum ex malignacione. Narrando igitur modum inquisicionis Gencium ex deuocione premittit requisiti pueri originem, nomen, originis locum et temporis termen. Tangit eius originem dicens, *Cum natus esset*, nomen cum dicit, *Iesus*, originis locum, *In Bethelem Iude*, termen temporis, *Quia in diebus Herodis regis*" (Add. 3571, f. 86rb ll. 31–53; this *divisio* continues through f. 86vb l. 30).

122 Catto, "Woodford," 68; cf. Smalley, *Study*, 276–81.
123 Smalley, *Study*, 276; see further Smalley, *Wisdom Literature*, 39–46.
124 Cambridge, Trinity Coll. MS B.15.12, f. 116rb: "*Defuncti sunt enim*, vbi ponitur admoniti assecuracio, quasi dicat angelus: Vade et non timeas, *quia defuncti sunt qui querebant animam*, id est uitam corporalem pueri. Sed quare dicit *defuncti* in plurali cum superius isto eodem capitulo scriptum sit, *Futurum est ut Herodes querat . . .* , et hic statim immediate, *Defuncto Herode*, ergo debuit consequenter dixisse *defunctus* uel *mortuus est* etc., precipue cum vnus tantum queret animam Iesu Christi et ille vnus tantum dicatur fuisse defunctus. Ad hoc dicendum est secundum Ieronimum . . . ." Woodford raises the same question, CUL MS Add. 3571, f. 82^{rb-va}.
125 Woodford, *Defensorum Fratrum Mendicancium*, ch. 44, ed. in Doyle, "Bibliographical List," 103.
126 Add. 3571, ff. 90vb–91rb and 150^{vb-ra}, respectively; cf. *Biblia sacra*, V, sigs b7^{rb} and c8^{ra}. Of course, in the first case, Lyre says that the star fulfills the prophecy of Num. 24.17, but Woodford is asking why it was chosen (and therefore prophesied) in the first place. After giving five arguments against Gregory's claim that Gentiles would only believe *signa* rather than *verba*, he argues that the choice of a star had to do with the training of the Magi, who "quamuis in diuersis scienciis erant pariti, maxime tamen astronomie erant dediti et in spectacionibus stellarum" (f. 91rb).
127 Add. 3571, f. 72ra; cf. *Biblia sacra*, V, sig. a8^{va}. Of Woodford's three additional explanations, the last is especially noteworthy as a development of the appeal to conventions: "Quarta est quia accepi potest aliquociens in scriptura forma pro subiecto, abstractum pro concreto, et sic potest accepi in loco isto generacio pro genito vt sic sensus huius tituli: *Liber generacionis*, id est liber geniti, et sic hiis nominis et viis congrue dicitur liber iste *Liber generacionis*."
128 Though very rare, Woodford does on occasion draw on Lyre to provide the only answer to a given question, and, in these cases, it could be that he felt Lyre provided especially noteworthy information that was not shared by his other major sources. See, e.g., his account of why Matthew began his work with a genealogy, Add. 3571, f. 72^{vab}.
129 Catto, "Wyclif and Wycliffism," 197, and "Woodford," 85; cf. Ghosh, *Wycliffite Heresy*, 235 n. 52. In "Wycliffite Bible," 20, however, Catto

describes the postil as offering Woodford's "exhaustive treatment of the literal sense."
130 CUL MS Add. 3571, ff. 87^{vab} and 93vb–94ra. Considering the abundance of these literalistic and historicist details, it is hard to accept Catto's description of the text as "mainly an aid for confessors," an assessment that seems to be based primarily on the tropological focus of the material on Matth. 5, supported by a single passage in which Woodford insists that, though a topic may be unsavory – specifically, the question whether a man sins mortally by having intercourse with his wife only for reasons of carnal pleasure – it is still necessary for those who have to hear confession (Catto, "Woodford," 82, citing Add. 3571, f. 213ra; the same passage is cited to advance this claim in Catto, "Culture and History," 115, and "Wyclif and Wycliffism," 197). Of course, the acknowledgment that his audience would be hearing confession, and that some of his text would be useful for that task, does not at all imply that the postil as a whole was aimed at supporting that particular activity.
131 CUL MS Add. 3571, ff. 174^{ra-va} and 175rb.
132 For the former, see his discussion of the equivocal word *legem* in Matth. 5.17 (CUL MS Add. 3571, f. 175^{vab}).
133 CUL MS Add. 3571, f. 93vb.
134 *Compendium*, ed. Seeboeck, 197–98; for Woodford's reassessment, see CUL MS Add. 3571, f. 99^{vab}, from which the following quotations have been drawn.
135 Lyre interprets Ps. 17.30–31 as describing "liberatio Dauid per modum insecutionis aduersariorum," citing I Reg. 25. See *Biblia sacra*, III, sig. s5^{va} and (for his discussion of Ps. 90) sigs N7^{v}–O1^{r}. Cf. Woodford's discussion of Matth. 4.14–16, where he asks whether Is. 9.1–2 "primo ad litteram de Christo fuerat predicta" (Add. 3571, ff. 124va–125ra). He answers in the affirmative, but apparently because he has found that to be the consensus among his sources, rather than because of any hermeneutic commitments on his part. In light of his correction of Auriol here, and his use of the *conditiones* throughout, it is unfortunate for Catto, "Woodford," 93, to have claimed that he "made little use of the other great stand-by of late medieval commentators, the *Compendium* ... of Peter Aureol."
136 Minnis, "Tobit's Dog"; cf. the studies cited in n. 107 of this chapter.
137 Smalley, "Problems of Exegesis," 274, and "The Bible in the Schools," 208; Courtenay, "Bible in the Fourteenth Century," 186, and cf. his *Schools and Scholars*, 373, and "Bible in the Universities," 558.
138 Woodford's postil is similarly positioned at the head of a "revival of interest in the Bible at Oxford" by Catto, "Woodford," 156; see too Kelly, *English Bible*, 31–32.

3 Richard Rolle's Scholarly Devotion

1 On Add. 37049, see Doyle, "Origins and Circulation," I, 85, and II, 191–93; Hanna, *English Manuscripts*, 78–80; and esp. Brantley, *Reading in the Wilderness*, passim, but 138–43 on this portrait.

2 E.g., *Incendium*, ed. Deanesly, 234, 237, 238, 245, 247; *Melos*, ed. Arnould, 135, 138, 147, 155, 179.
3 For the full lyric, see *Prose and Verse*, ed. Ogilvie-Thomson, 45.
4 Watson, *Invention of Authority*, xi and 18.
5 Zieman, "Perils of *Canor*," 137 and 144; cf. McGinn, *Vernacular Mysticism*, 340–47.
6 *Officium*, ed. Woolley, 23. It is important to note, however, that this criticism is directed at "phisicis aut secularis sciencie disciplinis," an intramural critique also made, e.g., by Richard Fitzralph: "Cum ranis et buffonibus in paludibus crocitabam" (in Hammerich, *Beginning*, 20–21).
7 Watson, *Invention of Authority*, 242.
8 The phrase is Hanna's, "Transmission of Rolle's Latin," 313.
9 Of the manuscripts listed in Appendix B, *BCcCoHT* present the *Latin Psalter* as the first text in an anthology of Rolle's Latin writings, as does the 1536 print (*F*), while in *JSh* it stands at the head of what was originally a distinct manuscript with multiple works by the hermit, now a fascicle within a larger collection. Despite its prominence in Rolle's corpus, the *Latin Psalter* has been especially neglected in scholarship. It is the only work undiscussed in Watson's magisterial study, with Watson citing its prohibitively complex textual history (*Invention of Authority*, xii). Horstman, *Yorkshire Writers*, II, xli, justifies his neglect by describing the *English Psalter* as "substantially a translation" of the Latin commentary. Allen, *Writings Ascribed*, 165–69 and 177–92, remains the fullest published treatment.
10 See, e.g., the otherwise useful discussion in Moyes, *Introduction*, I, esp. 7 and 18. For subtler views, see Renevey, "Richard Rolle," and Sutherland, "Biblical Text," 695–96.
11 Here I quibble with Alford, who brilliantly treats Rolle's "constant meditation on Scripture" as an important part of his formation as a writer ("Biblical *Imitatio*," 3). Alford persistently distinguishes between, on the one hand, Rolle's "meditating upon and memorizing" of the unglossed text of the Bible and, on the other, his consultation of exegesis, which is said to "reinforce" this apparently primary mode of scriptural reading (*ibid.*, 7 and 10; cf. 16). Based on the evidence of his *Psalters*, it seems unlikely that Rolle would have recognized this distinction, and he apparently understood commentary, like Scripture itself, as ripe for rumination.
12 Hanna, "Rolle and Related Works," 19.
13 Quotations of the *Latin Psalter* (Stegmüller 7298) are taken from BodL MS Bodley 861 (here f. 1ra), emended in light of other copies. For rationale, see Appendix B. Kraebel, "Rolle Reassembled," offers a detailed discussion of this manuscript.
14 Allen, *Writings Ascribed*, 185; cf. *English Writings*, ed. Allen, 2.
15 *Prose and Verse*, ed. Ogilvie-Thomson, 28, 29, 31; cf. too his recommendation to read Ps. 50 in *Form of Living* and *Meditation A* (*ibid.*, 16–17 and 66).
16 That Rolle believed these experiences to represent the full range of the contemplative life is reinforced in the final chapter of *Emendatio*, ed. Spahl,

232, where he writes, "Flere et gemere est iam noviter conversorum, incipiencium, et proficiencium, sed iubilare et in contemplacione exire non est nisi perfectorum."

17 *PL* 191, 59b–60d. Further examples of Rolle's adaptation of the Lombard are provided throughout this chapter, and see too Clark, "Rolle as Commentator." Rolle evidently drew on other sources in the *Latin Psalter*, but, compared with the Lombard, these remain ancillary. In glossing Ps. 1.1's *beatus* (f. 1[ra]), e.g., he offers a fivefold distinction concerning what makes someone blessed (or happy), and the same list appears in a commentary misattributed to Albertus Magnus (ed. Borgnet, XV, 9–10), suggesting a lost source shared by the two. Note, however, that an apparent citation of a source in the *Latin Psalter* can be misleading. Though Rolle cites Augustine's understanding of Ps. 37 as being "de recordacione peccatorum" (f. 15[rb]), for example, it is unlikely that he consulted the *Enarrationes* directly. In fact, Augustine interprets Ps. 37 in different terms, and Rolle is instead drawing on the Lombard (379d), a gloss attributed in some manuscripts to Cassiodorus.

18 The Lombard notes that some psalms *de corpore* discuss that body "secundum malos qui sunt in ecclesia corpore non mente, nomine non numine" (*PL* 191, 59d), but he does not apply this concept in his preface to Ps. 1.

19 The Lombard writes that "primo versu ostendit eum [i.e., Christum] immunem ab omni malo, secundo plenum omni bono in se" (*PL* 191, 60c), without this structural observation being extended to a general moral point.

20 Cf. *PL* 191, 64ab: "*Non sic impii.* Hic est secunda pars, ubi agit de ultionibus iniquorum et terret adversis."

21 Apart from his treatment of Ps. 9, discussed below, 98–99, the one exception I have found comes in another departure from the Lombard, at the beginning of Ps. 14, where Rolle writes, "Intendit hic Propheta nobis viam regiam monstrare, quomodo per Christianam miliciam peruenire possimus ad patriam" (f. 5[rb]; cf. *PL* 191, 167c).

22 See Chapter 1, 31.

23 Rolle may have favored this format, beginning with the first verse of a psalm before giving a prefatory account, because it allows each of the psalms to be found with relative ease, with their familiar incipits prominent on the page. It may be seen in other late medieval commentaries, either apparently part of the text as the commentator wrote it (as in Henry Cossey's work, discussed in Chapter 1) or the result of scribal adaptation (as in, e.g., the copy of the *Magna glosatura* that is now BL MS Add. 18299).

24 Cp. *PL* 191, 261a and 625d.

25 For Rolle on Ps. 42, see Bodley 861, f. 16[vb]; for the Lombard on Pss. 42 and 142, see *PL* 191, 423d and 1247bd.

26 *PL* 191, 787b–88b.

27 The opening of Rolle's commentary on this psalm has a particularly complicated textual history, discussed in Appendix B; the essential identification of the psalm's voice, however, remains consistent across the different copies.

28 Cf. *PL* 191, 130c–31a.

29 Cf. Rolle's discussion of the apparently unjust suffering of the righteous in *Incendium*, ed. Deanesly, 165–67.

30 On Rolle's place among the *perfecti*, see Watson, *Invention of Authority*, esp. 7–18 and 132. Alford, "Biblical *Imitatio*," 10, notes Rolle's habit of adopting the voice of biblical figures. For another example of Rolle's attribution of a psalm to the voice of the perfect, see his commentary on Ps. 60: "Iste psalmus est cuiuslibet perfecti, perseuerantis in laudibus Christi vsque ad finem vite" (f. 21[rb]).

31 Though he does not discuss the *vox* of Ps. 35, Rolle associates its words with the figures he elsewhere describes as the *iusti* and *perfecti*: "*Dixi*, id est in corde meo firmiter proposui, vt deliberant iusti antequam loquantur, *custodiam vias meas*, id est locuciones et acciones, *vt non delinquam in lingua mea*. Qui enim non peccat in lingua perfectus est" (f. 15[va]).

32 Rolle's desire to be seen as performing a pastoral function is expressed in various writings, perhaps most directly in his commentary on the Lessons of the Dead: see Moyes, *Introduction*, II, 196. The *Latin Psalter*'s presence in what appear to be priestly miscellanies, including London, Lambeth Palace MS 352 and Oxford, St. John's Coll. MS 195, indicate that the text did, at least in some cases, find such an audience: see James and Jenkins, *Descriptive Catalogue of Lambeth*, part 3, 466–70; Hanna, *Descriptive Catalogue of St. John's*, 281–84. Moyes, "Manuscripts," 84–86 and 92–95, argues for the popularity of Rolle's Latin among the secular clergy.

33 *Incendium*, ed. Deanesly, 145, and cf. 185, the latter with a reference *de eterno amore* as well. I have corrected Deanesly's text against other witnesses of the long version; see Hanna, "Prospectus."

34 His treatment of Ps. 38.2b, for example, "*Proposui ori meo custodiam, vt non exeant nisi congrua, cum consisteret peccator aduersum me* querens calumpniam, vt me caperet in sermone" (f. 15[va]), abbreviates the *Magna glosatura* (*PL* 191, 389d–390a), with the last phrase (*ut me* ...) glossing the Lombard's gloss. Likewise, Rolle's discussion of the sparrow of Ps. 83.4 interpolates a phrase (*virtutum—ubi*) in a sentence otherwise borrowed almost verbatim: "Sicut passer siluas deserit et inuenta domo letatur, sic anima virtutum pennis vtens et seculi sterilitatem relinquens cogitacione volat ad Deum vbi scit sibi sedem paratam" (f. 29[rb]; cf. *PL* 191, 789c, with the image of *pennae virtutum* drawn from earlier in the Lombard's gloss, 789a). Though examples may be found throughout his writings, praise of the contemplative potential of solitaries takes up the whole of Rolle's *De vita activa et contemplativa* (aka *Super mulierem fortem*), discussed in Kraebel, "Modes of Authorship," 102–106. See, generally, Watson, *Invention of Authority*, 7–18.

35 For the various portions of the Lombard's prologue on which Rolle draws, see *PL* 191, 55c–60a.

36 Though the inclusion of such material at the end of a later medieval biblical commentary is extremely unusual, one significant exception is, in fact, the *Glosatura* (cf. *PL* 191, 1293d–96b, and preserved in medieval copies of the text, e.g., BodL MS Auct. E. inf. 6, f. 139[ra–va]). It is therefore all the more important

to note that the material included by Rolle after his commentary from Ps. 150 comes from the Lombard's prologue, not from this postscript.

37 De Bruyne, *Préfaces*, 77–78. The various collocations of this tract in the *Patrologia Latina* (e.g., *PL* 131, 142b–44c and *PL* 142, 46ac) more likely reflect the work of early modern printers than medieval scribes. The text appears to be a translation of Basil of Caesarea (*PG* 31, 1725–26). Most copies begin, "Canticum psalmorum animas decorat," the incipit recorded in Hamesse, *Repertorium*, I, 306. The incipit shared by *Latin Psalter* manuscripts (adding *corpus sanctificat* before *animas decorat*) is comparatively rare, especially among insular copies, but see, e.g., Edinburgh, Univ. Lib. MS 331, ff. 133^r–134^v.

38 Those three manuscripts being Cambridge, Trinity Coll. B.1.15, f. 106^{vab}, BnF lat. 431, f. 116^{vab}, and Urbana, Univ. of Illinois 106, pp. 200^b–201^a. The Bohemian copies are discussed by Van Dussen, "Central European Manuscripts"; as noted in Kraebel, "Rolle at Illinois," all of these copies appear to derive from Urbana's exemplar.

39 The same incipit and attribution appear in all three insular copies: "Augustinus de laude Psalmorum sic prorumpit in loquelam." See Appendix B for discussion of these affiliations: though the Trinity and Urbana copies are closely related, Paris presents a distinct recension of the work. On Trinity and Urbana, see further Kraebel, "Rolle at Illinois"; on the priorities of some of the major compilations, see Hanna, "Transmission," and Kraebel, "Rolle Reassembled."

40 Quoting from Urbana, p. 201^a: "Psalmi enim totum de superioribus, id est de celestibus, locuntur. Psalmus est enim ymnus vel laus Dei." Cf. *PL* 191, 55b and 58a. Similar glosses are common in scholastic Psalter commentaries: for an early example, see *PL* 152, 637b–638b.

41 The dedication of *Form* to Kirkeby is found commonly in the surviving manuscripts: see *Prose and Verse*, ed. Ogilvie-Thomson, 25 and 134. The suggestion that *Ego Dormio* was "scriptus cuidam moniali de ʒedyngham" and the *Commandment* "cuidam sorori de Hampole" is found only in CUL Dd.5.64: see *Prose and Verse*, lxvi and lxxix.

42 Watson, *Invention of Authority*, 329 n. 11, claims that "there is no reason to doubt" the details in the metrical prologue, yet, as Gustafson, "Lollard Text," 296–301, persuasively argues, the prologuer's attempt to tie the *English Psalter* to a specific reader should be seen as part of his larger concern with the commentary's reception. On what can be known of Rolle's relationship to the Hampole nuns, see Freeman, "Priory of Hampole."

43 E.g., "the less educated reader of the vernacular could not be expected to deal with the fourfold senses of Scripture, so the more complicated exegesis was reserved for the Latin work," i.e., for the *Latin Psalter* (*Tractatus super Psalmum XX*, ed. Dolan, xiii). Dolan builds on Allen, *Writings Ascribed*, 178. Cf. Lagorio and Sargent, "English Mystical Writings," 3056; Hanna, "Transmission," 320.

44 All quotations from the *English Psalter* (Stegmüller 7303) are taken from HEHL MS HM 148 (here f. 23ra), with reference to Bramley's edition (here 3); for rationale, see the Introduction, n. 56.

45 Cf. Urbana MS 106, p. 201^a: "Canticum psalmorum ... inuitat angelos in adiutorium, fugat demones, ... omnem furorem deprimit, iracundiam frangit, ... carmen electum est apud Deum, omne peccatum expellit, ... perfeccionem construit, ... desiderium regni celestis dat, pacem inter corpus et animam facit."

46 HM 148, f. 23^{rab}; Bramley, 3. CCSL 97, ed. Adriaen, 4–5: "Hortus conclusus et fons signatus, paradisus plenus omnium pomorum [Cant. 4.12–13]. ... Cum angelis Dei, quos audire non possumus, laudum uerba miscemus." Since extended quotations from Cassiodorus's commentary are not forthcoming in the rest of the *English Psalter*, Watson, *Invention of Authority*, 329 n. 14, suggests that Rolle may only have had access to Cassidorus's prologue.

47 Deanesly, *Lollard Bible*, 144; cf. Lawton, "Englishing," 469. In contrast, Alford, "*Lectio Divina*," esp. 49–50, goes too far when he opposes this devotional orientation to the priorities of scholastic reading, and Gayk, "Vernacular Exegesis," 169, citing the opening of the *English Psalter*'s prologue, misleadingly describes "Rolle's direct and devotional translation," which "maintains a safe distance from contemporary scholastic exegesis."

48 HM 148, f. 23rb; Bramley, 4; cf. *PL* 191, 57a; Bodley 861, f. 46rb.

49 HM 148, f. 23va; Bramley, 4; cf. *PL* 191, 59c.

50 Hanna, "Rolle and Related Works," 20; elsewhere, however, Hanna describes the *English Psalter* as "Rolle's scholarly and explanatory prose Psalter" ("Yorkshire Writers," 101 n. 23). Rolle also specifies the *entent*, e.g., of Pss 1.1, 6.2, and 10.7, none of which finds a source in the Lombard's *Glosatura* (HM 148, ff. 24rb, 29vb, 37ra; Bramley, 6, 22, 42).

51 Deanesly, *Lollard Bible*, 145; Lagorio and Sargent, "Mystical Writings," 3055. For a useful reading of this passage of Rolle's prologue, see Sutherland, *English Psalms*, 74–75.

52 *Ep.* 57, CSEL 54, ed. Hilberg, 508. Copeland, *Rhetoric*, 42–55, offers a valuable discussion of Jerome's theories of translation and their influence on Middle English writers.

53 Burnett, "Arabic into Latin," 59, and his "Legend of Constantine," esp. 290–92.

54 Classen, *Burgundio von Pisa*, 87. My translations are indebted to Burnett, "Arabic into Latin," 56–57.

55 Burnett, "Legend of Constantine," 291–92; "Arabic into Latin," 68.

56 See, for example, the definition of "blisfull" that Rolle adds to the *English Psalter* (HM 148, f. 24ra; Bramley, 5), supplementing his discussion in the *Latin Psalter* (cf. Bodley 861, f. 1ra): "He is blisfull ... [þat] has alle þat he w[i]ll and wille nothing þat is ille." Cp. Huguccio, *Derivationes*, ed. Cecchini et al., II, 132: "Et est beatus ... qui habet que vult et non ea que non vult et nichil mali vult." This definition is not to be found in Hugh of Strasbourg's *Compendium Theologicae Veritatis* (see Albertus, *Opera*, ed. Borgnet, XXXIV, 1–306), noted by Watson, *Invention of Authority*, 55 and 63, as another "general guide" consulted by Rolle. Evidence of his consultation of another scholastic reference text is found in his English commentary on Ps. 90.13

(HM 148, f. 138rb; Bramley, 333), where his discussion of the basilisk is more detailed than the Lombard's (cp. *PL* 191, 853cd). When the hermit writes that the basilisk "is cald kynge of serpentis, for a white spott is in his heued, þat makys hym to seme as he had a diadem on," he is repeating a description, ultimately from Pliny, also found in Bartholomaeus Anglicus, *De proprietatibus rerum*, XVIII.xv (sig. D2^{ra}): "Candida in capite macula velut diademata insignitur." (But note that Rolle's description of the animal also contains details not found in the *De proprietatibus*.) Likewise, his citation of "Strabȝ" (i.e., Walafrid Strabo) on Ps. 148.4 suggests an encyclopedic source: to this authority he attributes the view that "thare is foure bodyly heuens are men cume til heuen þat aungels are in" (HM 148, f. 190va; Bramley, 488). No relevant glosses appear at this point in the Lombard (*PL* 191, 1285b) or the *Latin Psalter* (Bodley 861, f. 45vb), and I have been unable to trace Rolle's source.

57 Huguccio, *Derivationes*, II, 536; see further Hanna et al., "Latin Commentary," 363–64.
58 ÖNB MS 4133, f. 196va. See the brief but clarifying discussions of this passage in Copeland, *Rhetoric*, 90–91, and Gillespie, "Vernacular Theology," 412–13, on whose translations I have drawn. A full critical edition and translation are currently being prepared by Anne Hudson, Elizabeth Solopova, and Jeremy Catto.
59 ÖNB 4133, f. 198va (Latin); *EAEB*, 146 (English).
60 These visual affinities are noted by Hanna, "Yorkshire Writers," 101–102, and in his *English Manuscripts*, xxx–xxxi.
61 The classic account of the development of this *mise-en-page* is De Hamel, *Glossed Books*, 14–27, with this particular format reflected in his pl. 9. Other examples of copies of the Lombard with this *mise-en-page* include Durham, Cath. Lib. MSS A.II.9 and A.III.7, both now digitized: www.durhampriory.ac.uk (accessed Jan. 25, 2019).
62 For exceptions to this trend, see Cambridge, Corpus Christi Coll. MS 387, BL MS Harley 1806, BodL MS Laud. misc. 448, Oxford, Magdalen Coll. MS lat. 52, and BAV MS Reg. Lat. 320.
63 This format, treated as the standard form of the *Psalter* in many earlier accounts, is preserved in only five uninterpolated copies: BL MS Arundel 158, BodL MS Bodley 953, BodL MS Tanner 1, Worcester Cath. Lib. MS F.158, and MS 148 in the Green collection (formerly the Rosebery Rolle). Arundel 158 is the only copy consistently to underline the translation in the text ink rather than red.
64 Aberdeen Univ. Lib. MS 243, Eton Coll. MS 10, and BodL MS Laud. misc. 286, ff. 3ra–8rb only (this last containing Wycliffite interpolations up to Ps. 17.53).
65 On the ways visual presentation could signal the discursive registers of texts, see Parkes, *Their Hands*, 127–45.
66 HM 148, f. 129ra; Bramley, 305–306; cf. *PL* 191, 788bd.
67 On backbiters, see his gloss on Ps. 3.7: "No man may be excusede þat harmes a gude man in worde or dede, for all are haldyn to helpe him in his myster and

to luf his gudenes. Þe *tethe of synfull* are þe malycyous gnaghinges of bakbyters and þe desayuabill wordes of flaterers, þe whilk Crist sall all-to breke" (HM 148, f. 27^(rb); Bramley, 14; cf. *PL* 191, 80ab). For a comparable complaint in his Latin works, see Moyes, *Introduction*, II, 150, and see too the reference to an "enuyouse man" in the *English Psalter*'s prologue, quoted above. On lovers of the world, see, e.g., his gloss on Ps. 145.2: "Trowes þaim not þat amonestys and egges ȝow to luffe erthli gudis, for in þo men is not ȝoure hele bot more dampnacioun, if ȝe folow þaim" (HM 148, f. 188^(rb); Bramley, 482; cf. *PL* 191, 1270cd). This is, of course, the major theme of Rolle's *Contra Amatores*, ed. Theiner.

68 For examples, see Rolle's treatment of Pss. 11, 22, and 60 (HM 148, ff. 37^(rb), 51^(vb), and 97^(rb); Bramley, 43, 83, and 213).

69 HM 148, f. 38^(rb) and 38^(vb); Bramley, 47; cf. *PL* 191, 159bc (where Rolle is following one of two interpretive options given by the Lombard) and 162bc. In contrast, though Rolle does refer to his experiences of *canor* in his gloss on this verse in the *Latin Psalter*, his treatment there is much more restrained: "... *cantabo Domino* id est laudes ei in spirituali canore iubilans immolabo" (Bodley 861, f. 5^(ra)).

70 HM 148, f. 132^(ra); Bramley, 314; cf. *PL* 191, 805d. Sutherland's assertion that Rolle is not "overtly preoccupied by David as *auctor* of the psalms" is based on her observation that "David's name ... features in his English gloss on only four occasions" (*English Psalms*, 193). Unfortunately, this neglects to consider the many more instances in which David is invoked by his common antonomastic title.

71 HM 148, f. 38^(vb); Bramley, 47; cf. *PL* 191, 161d–162d. In the *Latin Psalter*, Rolle reads this psalm as directed against lovers of the world, but without the opening identification of the Psalmist as speaker (cf. Bodley 861, f. 5^(ra)).

72 HM 148, f. 92^(rb); Bramley, 163; cf. *PL* 191, 437d.

73 See, e.g., his treatment of Ps. 2, where Rolle first glosses the opening of the psalm with material from the Lombard, then writes, "Gastely to speke," and offers his own spiritual readings of the same text. He thereafter continues to juggle these two interpretive options (the former eventually described as "þe l[e]tter") throughout the remainder of his treatment of the psalm. See HM 148, ff. 25^(va)–26^(vb); Bramley, 8–9.

74 The other instance occurs in his gloss on Ps. 51.5: for discussion, see Kraebel, "Inspired Commentator." Rolle appears to depend on this apparatus, for example, when he writes, "Raban and Cassiodire sayes þat by þeis thre foules" (i.e., the three birds named in Ps. 101.7–8) "ere vndirestandyn thre maner of men" (HM 148, f. 145^(rb); Bramley, 353). He is evidently drawing on the Lombard (cf. *PL* 191, 908cd), though copies I have consulted only contain a citation of Augustine at this point (e.g., Durham Cath. Lib. MS A.11.9, f. 249^(rb)).

75 In Durham Cath. Lib. MS A.11.9, f. 64^(vb), only the gloss "in ecclesia toto orbe diffusa" has a citation, indicating Augustine as the Lombard's source.

76 See the discussions of Waleys and Cossey in Chapter 1, 32–34 and 41–49.

77 The novelty of the *English Psalter*'s form must remain qualified, for, though Rolle does not seem to have had any direct knowledge of them, there are some French antecedents with similar *mises-en-page;* see Hasenohr, "Bibles et psautiers."
78 Earlier discussions by Hudson, esp. *Premature Reformation*, 259–64, and "Variable Text," 55–58, are now superseded by the magisterial introduction to her critical edition, *Two Revisions*. The Wycliffite revisions were identified by Everett, "Prose Psalter," esp. vol. 18, 381–93, whose comparisons of the unrevised and revised texts remain useful.
79 *Two Revisions*, III, 1153–76 and 1180–94. The inclusion of all of these canticles in liturgical Psalters is noted by Pfaff, *Liturgy*, 8, and their appearance in glossed Psalters is described by Gibson, "Glossed Psalters," 83–84. The impulse to supplement Rolle's *English Psalter* was not limited to Wycliffite writers. It may also be seen in the non-Wycliffite commentary-translation of the *Benedictus* added to an unrevised copy of the *English Psalter* in Newcastle upon Tyne, Public Lib. MS Th. 1687. For this text, see *Commentary on the Benedictus*, ed. Wallner.
80 *Two Revisions*, I, cvi–cix and cxlvi–cxlvii. On a third partial (and considerably more expansive) revision, not edited by Hudson and not discussed here, see Somerset, *Feeling Like Saints*, 150–52 and 159–65.
81 Somerset, *Feeling Like Saints*, esp. ch. 1 and 2.
82 Similarly, Ps. 72 is presented as spoken by the Psalmist in his own voice in both the *Latin* and *English Psalters*, suggesting that the account of burning love quoted above is meant to reflect David's own ecstatic experiences. Bodley 861, f. 24vb: "Querens ergo Propheta eterna et redarguens se ... ait ..."; HM 148, f. 112ra (cf. Bramley, 256): "Þe Prophett, sekend endles ioy and reprehendand himself ... sayes ... ."
83 Notes on the shifting *persona* in a single verse (or series of verses) within a psalm are less common, but they do appear in Rolle's *English Psalter* and its Wycliffite revisions. See, e.g., Rolle's treatment of Pss. 4.6 and 11.6 (HM 148, ff. 28ra and 37vb; Bramley 17 and 44; cf. *Two Revisions*, I, 34–35 and 122).
84 For accounts of *perfectus amor*, see *Incendium*, ed. Deanesly, 200, 208, 217, and 274, and *Contra Amatores*, ed. Theiner, 108. On Rolle and the Holy Name, see Renevey, "Name above Names," and Depold, "Preaching the Name," with further studies cited at 195 n. 1.
85 Clark, "Psalm Commentary," and cf. his "Problem of Authorship." No surviving manuscript attributes *Qui Habitat* to Hilton, though such an attribution is preserved in the medieval catalogue of Syon Abbey (*Syon Abbey*, ed. Gillespie, 469–70). For the text, see *Exposition of Qui Habitat*, ed. Wallner, to which subsequent citations refer. Sutherland, *English Psalms*, 179–81, discusses the similarities between Rolle's and Hilton's approaches.
86 Clark, "Psalm Commentary," notes similarities between the ideas of the religious life in *Qui Habitat* and Hilton's *Scale*. The idea of expanding commentary on a single psalm into a fuller treatise is already anticipated by Rolle, who in his *Latin Psalter* departed from the *Magna glosatura* in

identifying the *rex* of Ps. 20.2 not as a prophetic reference to Christ (cf. *PL* 191, 220c), but instead as "quilibet sanctus super mundanas concupiscencias constitutus" (Bodley 861, f. 9va), and he later returned to this reading, developing it at greater length to create his *Tractatus super Psalmum XX*, ed. Dolan.

87 Maidstone, *Penitential Psalms*, ed. Edden, hereafter cited by line. For details of Maidstone's life and career, see *BRUO* 1204; for valuable readings of the *Psalms*, see Edden, "Maidstone's *Psalms*," Staley, "Limits of Lordship," and Sutherland, *English Psalms*, 168–74. Driscoll, "Penitential Psalms," discusses the history of this grouping.

88 The similarity between the arrangement of Maidstone's and Rolle's texts is noted by Kuczynski, *Prophetic Song*, 130.

89 Sutherland, "Performing the Psalms," 25.

90 The resulting dialogic form is noted by Lawton, *Voice*, 95, and Edden, "Maidstone's *Psalms*," 79.

91 See *Psalms*, ed. Edden, 47 and 109. This attribution appears at the end of the first stanza of the verse preface in BodL MS Rawl. A. 389 (reproduced in Fig. 9) and Manchester, Rylands MS Eng. 5. Rawl. served as Edden's copy-text, and her rationale for emending this line and suppressing the entirety of the preface's second stanza is unclear: see *Psalms*, ed. Edden, 22 and 39–42.

92 The phrase appears most frequently in the Wycliffites' added commentary on the *Benedicite*, ed. Hudson, III, 1153–65, but it is also interpolated in their treatment of various psalms (e.g. I, 271 and II, 879, added to glosses otherwise preserved from Rolle's original: see HM 148, ff. 50vb and 138^{rab}; Bramley, 80–81 and 333).

93 *Qui Habitat*, ed. Wallner, 27–28; cf. a similar disavowal at 37.

94 Gillespie, "Nearly Man"; see too his "Fatherless Books."

95 On the *English Psalter*, see *Two Revisions*, ed. Hudson, I, cxc–cxci. Hanna, "Miscellaneous Manuscripts," identifies a series of exemplars for *Emendatio*, *Incendium*, *Contra Amatores*, and the commentary on the Lessons of the Dead apparently available in Oxford in this period. My own work editing the last of those texts associates two further manuscripts with this group, Urbana, Univ. of Illinois MS 144 and Oxford, St. John's Coll. MS 195, the last of which also contains the *Latin Psalter* in a discrete fascicle; see Kraebel, "Rolle at Illinois."

96 For a summary of Ullerston's career, with further bibliography, see Kraebel, "Manuscript Tradition," 50–51.

97 See the discussion earlier in this chapter, 106–107.

98 ÖNB MS 4133, f. 199ra (Latin); *EAEB*, 147 (English). On Ullerston's *determinatio*, see Hudson, *Lollards and Their Books*, 67–84; Watson, "Censorship and Change," 840–51; Somerset, "Professionalizing Translation"; Ghosh, *Wycliffite Heresy*, 87–93 and 102–111; Gillespie, "Vernacular Theology," 412–15; *EAEB*, xlix–liv; Kelly, *English Bible*, 53–58.

99 Bodley 861, f. 40ra: "Nonnulli qui pro Deo volunt sustinere verbum falsitatis, sciencioribus et melioribus credere nolentes, similes amicis Iob, qui dum

Deum defendere nitebantur, offenderunt. Tales, si occidantur quam[uis] miracula faciant, tamen sunt (vt vulgo dicitur) fetentes martires."
100 On the *Defensorium*, see Harvey, "English Views," esp. 21–34.
101 BL MS Lansdowne 409, f. 66^r; cf. *Emendatio*, ed. Spahl, 174/3–5.
102 The texts are dated in their explicits: see BL MS Lansdowne 409, f. 69^v and Cambridge, Gonville and Caius Coll. MS 803/807 frag. 36 verso.
103 See Kraebel, "Manuscript Tradition," 58, and "Use of Rolle," 143 n. 10, for the explicit's two versions.
104 All quotations from Ullerston's commentary (Stegmüller 7353) are taken from BodL MS Lyell 20, here f. 206ra, corrected against other manuscripts. See Kraebel, "Manuscript Tradition," esp. 63–73, for rationale.
105 Though it remains unstudied, Herentals's gloss (Stegmüller 6616) seems to have enjoyed some popularity in the fifteenth century, including in England. Multiple copies are preserved in Oxford college libraries, as well as one in Cambridge, Trinity Coll. MS B.2.12, and Herentals's "ful noble" work on the Psalms is praised in Capgrave's *Life of St. Norbert*. See Kraebel, "Manuscript Tradition," 59–60.
106 See Courtenay, *Schools and Scholars*, 364; I argue this point at greater length in "Manuscript Tradition," 57–60.
107 Lyell 20, f. 209va; see Kraebel, "Use of Rolle," 139–40.
108 Catto, "Wyclif and Wycliffism," 257.
109 Cf. *Biblia sacra*, I, sig. Gg1^v: "*Haeccine reddis*, scilicet malum pro bono, *popule stulte*, credens vtile quod non est, *et insipiens*, non cognoscens vtilitatem vbi est"; Bodley 861, f. 48ra: "O *popule stulte*, qui non attendis in quantis malis es, *et insipiens*, qui non precaues in futurum."
110 Cf. Bodley 861, f. 48vb: "*Venenum aspidum insanabile*, id est maliciam incorrigibil[e]m intra se retinent, ne salutis medicinam recipiant, et si quandoque corripiuntur deteriores fiunt."
111 See Chapter 1, 26–27.
112 At the start of his gloss of Deut. 32 in the *Latin Psalter*, Rolle suggests the general (and historically non-specific) applicability of his reading, glossing the opening things said by Moses (*quae loquar*) as "vestre salute pertinencia, non inanes fabulas quales poete protulerunt" (Bodley 861, f. 48ra). Ullerston, in contrast, foregrounds his historicist interests throughout his gloss, describing, for example, the idolatrous Israelites addressed by Moses as those who "sacrificabant soli et lune vniuerseque milicie celi, quod tamen crebro Moyses prohibuit, et precipue Deut. 4[.3]" (Lyell 20, f. 212vb). Further examples of Ullerston's dependence on the *Latin Psalter* are offered in Kraebel, "Use of Rolle."
113 Bodley 861, f. 47ra: "... *preparantur*, id est prepari deberent cogitaciones, qui vere nouit quid intus cog[it]amus, quem omnino nulla latet cogitacio."
114 HM 148, 194vb; Bramley, 500. It is unlikely that Ullerston consulted the revised Wycliffite *Psalter*, which expands the account of thought as "holy" to "deuoute and holi" (*Two Revisions*, III, 1121). Note that, in the examples from Deut. 32 discussed above, Ullerston reproduces material from the *Latin*

Psalter verbatim, making it clear that he is not translating from the *English Psalter* in these cases.
115 See, e.g., the discussion of Waleys in Chapter 1.
116 Here quoting from the translation of *Emendatio* preserved uniquely in Worcester, Cath. Lib. MS F.172, ed. Hulme, 47; cf. Spahl's edition of the Latin, 208. For further discussion of Rolle's presentation of himself as an exegete, and especially a comparison of his views to contemporary scholastic theory, see Kraebel, "Inspired Commentator."
117 On Holcot (Stegmüller 7416 and 7422) and Ringstead (8172), see Smalley, *English Friars*, 137–48 and 214–20. Holcot is discussed by Hanna, "Beyond Smalley's Assessment." On Bradwardine, see Minnis, *Valuing the Vernacular*, 41–44, and cf. 190 n. 87.
118 See Doyle, "Origins and Circulation," I, 5–7, where the term is used to describe religious material written in the vernacular by the Latinate clergy. For recent developments, see Gillespie, "Vernacular Theology."
119 For a fuller account of this image-text, and the complex process of reading it demands, see Brantley, *Reading*, 79–119, and on the scribe as artist in the manuscript, *ibid.*, 10. The entirety of Add. 37049 is available in color facsimile online: www.bl.uk/manuscripts (accessed Feb. 13, 2019).
120 Scase, "Patronage Symbolism," pp. 236–38 and pl. 35; color reproductions of Vernon are available online: digital.bodleian.ox.ac.uk (accessed Feb. 13, 2019).
121 For one clear example, see the initial that begins the entry on "Doctrina sive doctor" in BL MS Royal 6 E. vi, f. 541ra, reproduced in Sandler, *Omne Bonum*, II, 161. See too Lerer's discussion of the depictions of Boccaccio in HEHL MS HM 268, in *Chaucer and His Readers*, 40–44.
122 See Brantley, *Reading*, 138–41, with further bibliography at 364 n. 61. Scott, *Later Gothic Manuscripts*, II, 194, suggests that Stowe was not prepared on the basis of a complete exemplar, but rather depended upon an oral or written description of the images and their layout.
123 We can be fairly certain that these details represent the Additional artist's departure from his exemplar, since on f. 37^r he includes a second Rolle portrait that more closely resembles the image in Faustina, this accompanying a unique verse translation of a brief passage from *Incendium*, including Rolle's account of sitting "in a chapel in my prayere," framing a version of "I syt and synge"; see Brantley, *Reading*, 143–46, and Zieman, "Compiling the Lyric."
124 Add. 37049 features several further examples of clerks in scholarly headgear: see ff. 85^r, 85^v, 87^v, 89^v, and 96^r, some of which are reproduced in Brantley, *Reading*, 236–38.

4 Moral Experiments: Middle English Matthew Commentaries

1 *EAEB*, 125/23–31.
2 Hudson, *Premature Reformation*, 424; *EAEB*, 103 and 108. *Middle English Mirror*, ed. Duncan and Connolly, xix–xx, and esp. Hunt, "Tracts," I, 80–85, offer fuller descriptions of Ii.6.26 than *EAEB*, xxxiv. The *Cambridge Tracts*

have yet to attract much critical attention, but see Havens, "Imagined Community," Dove, "Biblical Agenda," 216–17 and 220, and Somerset, *Feeling like Saints*, 210–15.
3 *EAEB*, xxxiii.
4 *EAEB*, 155.
5 See *EAEB*, xxiii–xlix, and Hudson, *Lollards and Their Books*, 106–7 and n. 105; *Tracts* ii, vi, vii, ix, x and xi are either preserved apart from the rest of the collection, or they adapt or share material with texts found in other sources, and it seems likely that at least some of the remaining *Tracts* were similarly quarried from sources that no longer survive or have not yet been identified.
6 The material in *Tract* x is preserved as the *Glossed Gospel* epilogue in BL MS Add. 28026, ff. 185^v–187^r, and BodL MS Laud. misc. 235, ff. 263^r–264^v. Cambridge, Fitzwilliam Museum MS McClean 133, which also preserves the epilogue, is a sixteenth-century copy of Laud. misc. 235. The epilogue is printed in *EAEB*, 180–83.
7 *EAEB*, 155–56.
8 Hudson, *Doctors in English*, cxlviii–cliv. This valuable study builds on Professor Hudson's earlier essays on the *Glossed Gospels*, but it has still been useful to cite some of the opinions and arguments advanced in her earlier works.
9 Hudson, "Variable Text." Though the *Glossed Gospels* are not discussed, several of the essays in *Probable Truth*, ed. Gillespie and Hudson, are germane to this question of variable and experimental textual form. See too Catto's account of fourteenth-century English prose as "an experiment, . . . a series of essays in a new and difficult medium, a form of English which had to be created" ("Written English," 54).
10 Hudson, "Five Problems," discusses this possibility; on the Wycliffite redactions of the *Psalter*, see Chapter 3, 114–17.
11 Hudson, *Premature Reformation*, 248; Copeland, *Pedagogy*, 130. Copeland's classification is part of a larger argument about the complexity of the literal sense as both a hermeneutic and a pedagogic category, but that she here has in mind the hermeneutic literal sense is reinforced by her comments elsewhere: see Copeland, "Lollard Instruction," 30.
12 On scholastic theories of literal tropology, see Chapter 1, 26–27.
13 Somerset, *Feeling like Saints*, 230 and 209.
14 See above, Chapter 3, 104.
15 By this last caveat, I hope to distinguish the work of this chapter from Annie Sutherland's recent exploration of the "chain of translation" of Middle English Psalms versions. See Sutherland, *English Psalms*, esp. 86–87 and (more generally) 88–135. Though it is possible that the writer of the non-Wycliffite Matthew commentary knew Rolle's *Psalter*, by no means do I want to suggest that his work was known, in turn, by the *Glossed Gospels* team.
16 For an edition of the prologue, see Kraebel, "Gospel Glosses," 109–120 (here 110). The dating of the commentary depends on the dating of its two manuscripts. Doyle, "Origins and Circulation," I, 128, dates Egerton

17 842 to the end of the fourteenth or beginning of the fifteenth century, and there is little reason to think Ii.2.12 was copied much later.
17 See Chapter 3, 105. The Matthew prologue, however, lacks Rolle's suggestion that the close translation can help a reader learn Latin.
18 Additionally, like many early manuscripts of the *English Psalter*, the translated verses from Matthew are sometimes underlined in red in Ii.2.12: see, for example, the reproduction of f. 96^r, in Kraebel, "Gospel Glosses," 108, Fig. 2.
19 For examples, see De Hamel, *Glossed Books*, plates 9 and 10. See Chapter 3, nn. 17 and 74–75, as well as Appendix B, 196–97, for examples suggesting the likelihood that Rolle's copy of the Lombard included the marginal apparatus.
20 Identifying the Durham text as the major source for this commentary requires the revision of some claims advanced in "Gospel Glosses," 95–98, where I wrongly concluded that the *Catena Aurea* was the most likely source of many of the English text's glosses. Note that the more prominent medieval foliation in A.1.10 fails to account for the first folio; my citations follow the modern pencil foliation, always one integer higher.
21 Color reproductions of the manuscript are now available at www.durhampriory.ac.uk (accessed March 2, 2019). As I note in "Gospel Glosses," 93–94, this marginal apparatus is particularly unstable: some citations present in one copy are omitted in the other, and it seems likely that scribes were able to generate new marginalia of their own, repeating citations of authorities made within the prose of the commentary. Nevertheless, examples like the one described here indicate that a core body of glosses was an intrinsic part of the English commentary, carried over from its Latin source.
22 Throughout the following, the Latin source of quotations from the English commentary is provided in the notes, confirming the identification of the text in A.1.10 as the source for the vernacular work.
23 Egerton 842, f. 209^v. Egerton suffers from two inconsistencies in foliation: the first numbering scheme failed to account for a leaf inserted after f. 117 to supply material dropped due to eyeskip (the inserted leaf is copied in the same hand as the rest of the manuscript), and the earlier foliator also labeled two consecutive leaves as 206. Throughout, I prefer the higher numbering. For the Latin, see Durham A.1.10, f. 146^v: "Inter pascha uero et azima hoc distat, quod pascha proprie solus dies dicitur quo agnus ad uespera occidebatur, id est quartadecima luna primi mensis. Quartadecima uero luna quando filii Israel egressi sunt de Egipto erant azima, septima diebus, id est usque ad uigesimam primam diem eiusdem mensis ad uesperam." The translator has apparently attempted to correct the source by changing the second fourteen to fifteen.
24 Egerton 842, f. 209^v; cf. Durham A.1.10, f. 146^v: "Ideo autem indifferenter alterum pro altero ponitur, quia et pasche dies in azimis celebratur."
25 Egerton 842, f. 209^v; cf. Durham A.1.10, f. 146^v: "Uno quippe die agno immolato ad uespera, septima ordine dies sequuntur azimorum, quia Christo pro nobis semel in fine temporum passo, per totum huius seculi tempus quod septima diebus agitur in azimis sinceritatis et ueritatis uiuere iubemur et omni

nisu desideria terrena quasi Egipti fugere retinacula. Et uelut a mundana conuersatione secretam solitudinem, iter scilicet uirtutvm, subire monemur."

26 Egerton 842, f. 212^r; cf. Durham A.I.10, f. 147^v: "Significat autem unguentum fidei deuotionem, que non solum Christi incarnationem sed et diuinitatem complectitur."
27 Egerton 842, f. 212^r; cf. Durham A.I.10, f. 147^v: "Quanuis ignorans passionem eius annuntiat."
28 Smalley, *Gospels*, 37–41 (here 37).
29 *Ibid.*, 278.
30 Egerton 842, f. 210^v; cf. Durham A.I.10, f. 147^r: "Iccirco Dominus Bethaniam uenit, ut resuscitatio Lazari recenter facta memorie omnium arctius traderetur."
31 Egerton 842, f. 210^v; cf. Durham A.I.10, f. 147^r: "... mistice significat illam partem populi que Domino per fidem obediuit et per obedientiam curata est."
32 Egerton 842, f. 160^r. In this case, the gloss embedded in the close translation is not matched in the Latin text's presentation of the lemma; cf. Durham A.I.10, f. 124^v.
33 Egerton 842, f. 160^v; cp. Durham A.I.10, f. 125^r: "Caueamus impendio ne qua inter nos de prelatione possit esse contentio. Si enim ambiebant uel inuidebant apostoli, non excusationi obtenditur, sed cautioni proponitur. Omnibus una datur forma sentente, ut non de prelatione sit contentio, sed de humilitate."
34 Egerton 842, f. 212^v; cf. Durham A.I.10, f. 148^r: "... prescit euangelium suum toto orbe predicandum."
35 "Gospel Glosses," 113; for the Latin source of this line, see Appendix C, ll. 124–25. Cf. Smalley, *Gospels*, 38.
36 Egerton 842, f. 213^v; cf. Durham A.I.10, f. 148^v: "Non ad quemlibet mittuntur sed ad aliquem certvm, quem ex persona sua loquens euangelista recte posuisset. Modo autem cum uerba Domini posuit *Ite in ciuitatem* interposuit *ad quendam*, non quia hoc Dominus dixerit, sed ut ipse nobis insinuaret tacito nomine ibi fuisse quendam ad quem mittebantur. Quod ergo ait *ad quendam* tanquam ex persona sua et non Domini studio reuitatis illum compendio insinuauit, eundem significans quem Marcus *Dominum domus* et Lucas *patremfamilias* nominat. Vel ideo hominem non exprimit, quia nondum fuerat credentibus honor Christiani nominis prestitus."
37 Egerton 842, ff. 213^v–214^r; cf. Durham A.I.10, f. 148^v: "Consulte quoque et aque baiuli et domini domus tacentur nomina, ut omnibus uerum pascha celebrare, id est Christi sacramentis imbui, uolentibus, eumque sue meritis hospitio suscipere querentibus facultas danda signetur."
38 Further supporting this idea is the observation that, in the last example, the "berers of þo watyr" are not mentioned in Matthew, taken instead from Mark 14.13 and Luke 22.10 apparently to strengthen the tropological point. For a similar case of the commentator turning to another gospel to develop his moral interpretation, see Egerton 842, f. 73^r, following Durham A.I.10, f. 72^r.
39 Gillespie, "Authorship," 138.

40 "Gospel Glosses," 119. The English exegete is inconsistent on the question of Matthew's earliest audience, since he had earlier maintained that, though he wrote "in Hebrew tung," Matthew sought "to passe to techyng of oþir nacyons þat wer callid gentyls" (110). This inconsistency is present in the Durham text, reinforcing the idea (advanced later in this section) that this Latin commentary has been compiled from at least two major sources. See Appendix C, ll. 11–12 and 331–32.

41 Though he does not consider the Durham commentary in detail, much of what follows is indebted to Andrée, "Le *Pater* dans l'école de Laon." My thanks to Professor Andrée for sharing his work with me before its publication, and for a wonderful afternoon spent working through some of these questions of borrowing and textual history.

42 That copy being Alençon BM 26, at f. 91^r. Smalley, *Gospels*, 15, rejects this attribution, though, more recently, Andrée, "Le *Pater*," critiques the grounds for her dismissal. See too Giraud, *Per verba magistri*, 92–95. Perhaps because of their shared incipit, the Durham text has been misidentified as another example of the "Anselm" commentary by Piper, "Monks of Durham," 95, and by Gameson, *Early Norman England*, 78 (no. 208), and *Manuscript Treasures*, 64–67 (no. 14).

43 See Smalley, *Gospels*, 20–29, esp. 27–29 for the possible identification of Babion with an archbishop of Bordeaux who died in 1158.

44 See Appendix C. Noting the similarities between these texts, Ballentyne, "Reassessment of Alençon 26," posits an additional, lost commentary serving as a common source for all three of the surviving works, a hypothesis that is at once untestable and, more importantly, a poor explanation for the sorts of borrowings evident in the Durham text.

45 Gullick, "Hand of Symeon," 16–17 and 28–29.

46 Smalley, *Gospels*, 19, noticed that the prologue in Laud. misc. 5 alternately "elaborates and abbreviates" the "Anselm" prologue, but she did not realize that Laud. misc. 5 had been excerpted from the larger Durham revision, of which she was apparently unaware, nor that the material used to supplement "Anselm" was taken from the "Babion" text. Note that a significant number of Laud. misc. manuscripts can be tied to Durham: see Ker, *Medieval Libraries*, 74–75.

47 Gameson, *Manuscript Treasures*, 67. For this entry, see *Catalogi veteres*, 76 and 81. Owing to the inclusion of a second folio ("indicto ieiunio"), this volume can be identified with A.I.10 (see Appendix C, l. 37). My thanks to Professor Sharpe for supplying me with this material from the forthcoming CBMLC volume, and for alerting me to the point, in the previous note, about Durham manuscripts in the Laudian misc. collection.

48 See, e.g., Appendix C, nn. on titles. Another sign of later medieval interest, the list of contents on f. 1^{rv} has been annotated, with folio numbers added to specify where each chapter is to be found, corresponding to the foliation of the manuscript likely undertaken as the same time.

49 These are ch. 14–21 in the list of contents in A.I.10, f. 1ra. Ch. 21 appears on ff. 52va–55ra; Matth. 6.1 is glossed on f. 54ra, and there is nothing to signal the beginning of the new biblical chapter.

50 See Egerton 842, f. 204^r, for the rubric beginning "Omelia lxxxii." The system was by and large dropped in Ii.2.12, though see ff. 95^r, 102^r, 104^r, 105^v, 106^r, 107^v, 109^r, and 110^r. These *homelia* divisions do not correspond to the (usually) 54 homilies of the *Opus Imperfectum*, for discussion of which, see CCSL 87b, ed. J. van Banning, xix–xx.

51 As noted above, n. 21, marginal citations were particularly prone to scribal tampering; by invoking them as evidence here, I simply mean to indicate that I have not found any marginal citations in Egerton 842 or Ii.2.12 that cannot be explained as either scribal additions based on a reference in the text of the commentary or borrowings from A.i.10.

52 Egerton 842 is acephalous, making it impossible to determine whether such a note is based on something present in their antecedent copies.

53 Hanna, "Yorkshire Writers," 109 and n. 43, echoing Doyle, "Origins and Circulation," I, 128 n. 3. McIntosh et al., *Linguistic Atlas*, places Ii.2.12 in Notts. (LP 164) and Egerton 842 in NW Notts. (I, 109).

54 Kraebel, "Gospel Glosses," 109–110.

55 For Trevisa's dialogue, see Waldron, "Original Prefaces," 289–94. The opening of the *Fourteenth-Century Biblical Version*, ed. Paues, 4–18, has been read as a trialogue, though I suspect that the initial petitioning brother and the later petitioning sister are meant to be one and the same figure, with the gender split resulting from the compiler's imperfect emendation of his source material. See Lawton, *Voice*, 83–102.

56 Piper, "Monks of Durham," 95, building on observations made by Dobson, *Durham Priory*, 64. For the refectory reading of A.i.10, see *Catalogi veteres*, 80–81 (item D, with the "D" still visible on f. 1^r of the commentary).

57 Harvey, *Lay Religious Life*, 125–28. See further Horner, "Benedictines and Preaching." Horner focuses on one Durham Benedictine preacher of this period, Robert Rypon, for whom see Wenzel, *Sermon Collections*, 66–73. Rypon's sermons are preserved in BL MS Harley 4894.

58 Dobson, *Durham Priory*, 342–43. Parkes, "Provision," 447–49, notes the movement of at least some books between Durham Priory and the college. See further Coates, "Library of Durham College," and Foster, "Durham Monks."

59 Constable, "Twelfth-Century Spirituality," and "Popularity of Spiritual Writers"; cf. Gillespie, *Holy Books*, 113–44.

60 On the different Wycliffite versions, see now Hudson, "Origin and Textual Tradition," which provides a useful and rigorous supplement (and in some cases corrective) to Dove, *English Bible*.

61 *EAEB*, 81.

62 The preference for the Early Version on the part of the compilers of the *Glossed Gospels* would seem to contradict the dubious claim of Dove, *First English Bible*, 3, that this version was a draft, "never intended to be copied as a translation in its own right." Further doubt is cast on Dove's view by Hudson, *Doctors in English*, xlviii–lii, who observes that the compilers used portions of the Later Version when translating the biblical quotations that were part of

their glosses – this, again, makes the use of the Early Version in the lemmata even more clearly a considered choice on the part of the compilers. The appropriateness of the Early Version's style for supporting a vernacular gloss was suggested by Deanesly, *Lollard Bible*, 145–46, who compares it in this respect with the *English Psalter*.

63 The three copies preserved in this form are BodL MS Bodley 143 (pictured in Fig. 14), BodL MS Laud. misc. 235, and York, Minster Library MS XVI.D.2. Even here there are some differences: in both Laud. misc. and York, for example, the marginal citations are written in text ink, and in York, after f. 38va, the spacing of the blocks of lemmata changes, now written on every line but underlined in red (see the descriptions in Hudson, *Doctors*, xxxv, and *MMBL*, IV, 695). That is, after this point York more closely resembles the format of BL MS Add. 28026 and CUL MS Kk.2.9. My count of "medieval copies" includes the fragmentary Edinburgh, National Library of Scotland MS 6124, but excludes McClean 133 (on which see n. 6).

64 Unfortunately, the commentaries on Mark and John are preserved only in their shorter versions, though there is some evidence that longer versions did once exist. Most straightforwardly, at the start of the short commentary on John, the prologuer claims to have cited his sources by name only, "remyttinge to þe grettir gloos writun on Ioon where and in what bokis þes doctours seyen þes sentences" (*EAEB*, 186). See further Hudson, *Doctors*, xix–xxviii, and "Two Notes," 379–84.

65 For reproductions of Add. 28026 and Kk.2.9, see Hudson, *Doctors*, pl. 1 and 3, and Fig. 15 below.

66 At Add. 28026, f. 122ra, for example, on Matth. 21.12–13, the exegete writes, "God seiþ by Ma[la]chie þe profete: Y schal curse to ȝoure blessynge, þat is, what-euere schal be blessid by ȝou schal be cursid by me. Ierom on Malachie and in þe comyn lawe." This is met in the margin with a more specific citation (rubrication given here in bold), "**Ierom** i q maledicam," referring to Gratian's *Decretum*, C. 1 q. 1 c. 76 (ed. Friedberg, col. 385), "Maledicam benedictionibus uestris, hoc est, quicquid a uobis benedicetur per me erit maledictum," a gloss drawn from Jerome's commentary on Mal. 2.2 (cf. *PL* 25, 1553b).

67 Cf. the discussion of the apparatus in Egerton 842 earlier in this chapter, 137–39, and esp. n. 21. All of the apparent marginal citations that I have found in Kk.2.9 seem to be corrections, marked for insertion or correction in the text block. For a sampling, see ff. 70^v, 73^v, 99^r, and 110^v; cf. the dropped text (including a citation of "Cirille") added in the outer margin of f. 45^v.

68 My work with Kk.2.9 supports Hudson's identification of four scribal stints, each beginning at the start of a quire: see *Doctors*, xxxiii n. 16.

69 For an unusual instance of rubrication in the manuscript, see Trinity Coll. MS B.1.38, f. 103^r, where some red ink has been added in a way that contributes little to (and may interfere with) the parsing of the text.

70 This error, noted by Hudson, *Doctors*, xxxix, would seem to explain why glossed John begins in B.1.38 with a quire of twelve folios, while the rest of the text is copied in eights. The pages bearing the scribe's mistake (ff. 99–102)

have been marked "vacat" in their upper margin, and if these folios were indeed trimmed away, the result would be another quire of eight. For the collation of B.1.38, see Hudson, *Doctors*, xxxviii.

71 Hudson, *Doctors*, xxxix, raises this possibility, but maintains that it is "unclear."

72 The notion that the short commentaries on Matthew and John in B.1.38 were once distinct units is supported by the quire structure of both texts. As noted above, John begins with a quire of twelve folios (meant to be trimmed to a quire of eight) and then concludes with seven uniform quires of eight. Matthew begins awkwardly (a quire of two bifolia with a shorter bifolium, ff. 3–4, nested in the middle and a singleton, f. 7, added after) but then runs uniformly through ten quires of eight folios. The final quire began with ten folios, presumably in anticipation of fitting the end of the text, but that proved insufficient, and the scribe had to add a final singleton (now f. 98) on the recto of which the Matthew commentary ends. See Hudson, *Doctors*, xxxviii.

73 The quire structure of both manuscripts suggests that they were originally prepared as four booklets. In Add. 41175, glossed Matthew occupies the singleton noted above plus twelve quires of eight folios and a quire of six, while glossed Mark begins a new quire of eight, followed by six more quires of eight and a final quire of four. In BodL MS Bodley 243, glossed Luke runs through fourteen quires of eight plus one quire of four (with the fourth leaf trimmed away and the third leaf blank apart from the prologue to John on its verso), and glossed John occupies seven quires of eight plus a final quire of four. This structural evidence is supported by the discontinuous series of signatures discernible in Bodley 243, a–g visible in quires 1–7, and a–h in quires 16–23. See Hudson, *Doctors*, xxxi–xxxii, who also supports the identification of a single scribe working across both volumes.

74 Since Add. 41175 is the only surviving copy of glossed Mark in either recension, it is impossible to determine whether such a prologue ever existed.

75 Neither Hudson, *Doctors*, xxxvii–xxxviii, nor Dove, *EAEB*, lxvi, note the differences in the scripts, which certainly may be the work of a single scribe.

76 Such notes of scribal direction rarely survive today, but for one elaborate example see Kraebel, "Rolle Reassembled."

77 Hudson, *Doctors*, cxxxiv. Ghosh, "The Prologues," while not directly addressing the prologues to the *Glossed Gospels*, describes a number of similar issues in the General Prologue and the Hieronymian prologues included in Early Version and Later Version copies.

78 *EAEB*, 186/1–6 (at 5). For the corresponding sections in the other short prologues, see *EAEB*, 172/1–18 (Matth.) and 184/1–17 (Luke).

79 *EAEB*, 184/18–22; cf. *EAEB*, 172/19–21 (Matth.) and 186/7–9 (John), as well as the similar move in the General Prologue to the Later Version, *EAEB*, 80.

80 E.g., Deanesly, *Lollard Bible*, 275–76.

81 Copeland, *Pedagogy*, 132.

82 *EAEB*, 184–85/22–43 (at 22–25); cf. *EAEB* 172–73/21–47 (Matth.) and 186/9–16 (John).

83 Cf. *MED* s.v. *knouen* 6d.
84 See Chapter 3, 105. As noted above, Hudson, *Doctors*, xlviii–lii, shows that the *Glossed Gospels* draw on the Later Version translation within their glosses, making the preference for the Early Version in the longer lemmata more clearly a motivated choice.
85 *EAEB*, 173; cf. *EAEB*, 184–85.
86 *EAEB*, 186.
87 Most obviously, while the longer recension of Luke and all of the short recensions draw on the *Catena Aurea* of Aquinas, that compilation was evidently not used in the long recension of Matthew (see below). Hudson, *Premature Reformation*, 250–52, suggests the likelihood of long Matthew's priority on those grounds, supported more recently in *Doctors*, xxiv–xxv, where she draws attention to references to "þe firste glos/exposicioun on Matheu" in the shorter recensions of Matthew and Mark in BL Add. 41175, which apparently refer to the longer recension. Hudson therefore concludes that the longer recension was "an initiatory exercise, known as such at least to the compilers of short Matthew and short Mark" (xxvi).
88 See Chapter 3, 105, and the discussion earlier in this chapter, 136–37.
89 *EAEB*, 182/89–118. Cf. *EAEB*, xlvi–xlvii, lxiv, and 124–25.
90 *EAEB*, 180.
91 Likewise, in the Matthew prologue in Laud. misc. 235 (discussed below), the writer insists that he "takiþ pleinly and shortly þe sentence of þes doctours, wiþ groundis of Holy Scripturs, wiþouten any settyng-to of oþer men, for þe sekenesse of oure peple is so gret þat þei nylen suffre pore men lyuynge now to reproue her synnes" (*EAEB*, 178).
92 *EAEB*, 180.
93 *Ibid.*
94 *Ibid.*
95 Though earlier scholarship has treated Laud. misc. 235 as representing an "intermediate" version of Matthew, Hudson, *Doctors*, liv–lv, has shown it to be a witness to the long text, with some of the commentary omitted in the final third of the work, making for a shorter and imperfect copy. Cf. Hudson, *Premature Reformation*, 249–59, and *EAEB*, lx–lxv and 173–83.
96 *EAEB*, 177.
97 *Ibid.*
98 *Ibid.*, 177–78.
99 *Ibid.*, 174–77.
100 See *EAEB*, 211–22. On *De doctrina* in the General Prologue, see Copeland, "Wycliffite Ciceronianism."
101 E.g., an excerpt from Augustine's *De doctrina*: "Autours of Holy Writ speken derkely, þat (prudently) misteris be hid fro vnpitouse men and goode men be excercisid and, in expownynge it, haue grace vnlik fro þe first autours of Holy Writ" (*EAEB*, 177).
102 *EAEB*, 177. For the Latin text of the *Moralia*, see CCSL 143b, ed. Adriaen, 1447.

103 For these conjunctions in the prologue, apparently Englishing *item* in the same specialized lexicon as *here* for *hic*, see *EAEB*, 174–77/8, 15, 27, 95. Cp. *MED* s.v. *also* 5a(c) and *DMLBS* s.v. *item* 3b.

104 For the texts of these pieces, see *EAEB*, 103–105 and 187. In addition to BL MS Arundel 254, these three texts appear in this order before *Oon of Foure* in Glasgow Univ. Lib. MS Gen. 223, ff. 7^r–13^r and Peterborough Cath. Lib. MS 8, ff. 9^r–12^v. Additionally, the Laud. misc. 235 catena and *Cambridge Tract* ii appear together before *Oon of Foure* in BL MS Harley 6333, ff. 18^r–21^v, while the catena appears without the other tracts before *Oon of Foure* in Oxford, Christ Church Coll. MS Allestree L.4.1, ff. 9^r–10^v. Finally, and importantly indicating the circulation of the texts as a set apart from *Oon of Foure*, they appear together in Dublin, Trinity Coll. MS 76, with *In þe Begynnynge of Holy Chirche* and the Laud. misc. catena prefacing an (unglossed) Early Version copy of Matthew (ff. 6^r–8^r) and *Cambridge Tract* ii appearing before an incomplete copy of the (also unglossed) Early Version of John (ff. 99^r–100^r). These are the only extant copies of *In þe Begynnynge of Holy Chirche*. See *EAEB*, xxxviii–xxxix, lxiii–lxiv, and lxvii.

105 In Arundel 254, the two bifolia of ff. 9^r–12^v are copied in anglicana, while the main text of the *Oon of Foure* is in a gothic textualis; the anglicana appears to match the hand that copied Catholic Epistles (in the Early Version) on ff. 86^v–103^v. Indeed, all of the "front matter" of Arundel 254 is in the form of discrete booklets (including ff. 1^r–8^v and 13^r–18^v) before the start of *Oon of Foure* on f. 19^r.

106 These being Manchester, John Rylands MS Eng. 77, ff. 13^r–15^r and Dresden, Sächsische Landesbibliothek MS Od. 83, ff. 15^r–19^v, in both cases followed by the LV translation of Jerome's preface ("Mathew þat was of Iudee ..."; cf. *Holy Bible*, ed. Forshall and Madden, IV, 2). See *EAEB*, xxxix and lxiv. On Rylands, see Hanna, "English Biblical Texts," 150–51.

107 Hanna, *Pursuing History*, 26.

108 In University Coll. MS 96, the Prologue occupies ff. 1^r–94^r, followed by a brief catena of materials drawn from the Wycliffite Bible (94^v–95^r), and the Holy Week and Easter Gospel lections taken from the Later Version (97^r–109^v). *EAEB*, xxvii, provides a summary description. Of course, the Prologue was presented as a stand-alone text in its early modern printings, by Gough (London, 1540) and Crowley (London, 1550); on these printings, see Aston, *Lollards and Reformers*, 229–31 and 250–54, and Hudson, *Lollards and Their Books*, 227–48. For further discussion of the different scribal treatments of the General Prologue, see Ghosh, "The Prologues."

109 See the summary descriptions in *EAEB*, xxvii–xxviii.

110 Hudson, *Doctors*, cxxxi–cxxxii.

111 This presumes that the prologues and the epilogue are by a single author, which seems to be the most likely of the scenarios proposed by Hudson, *Doctors*, cxxxiv. It is certainly possible that the self-styled "symple creature," "synful caytif," "scribeler," and "pore caityf" are not the same person, and indeed composite authorship of any one of these works cannot be ruled out.

Yet their stylistic and polemical consistency, as well as their consistent presentation of their texts as humble attempts to fulfill pastoral responsibilities, suggests a single writer. Further support is offered by Kelly, *English Bible*, 27–30, though see the review of his book by Kathleen Kennedy, cited in the Introduction, n. 29.
112 *EAEB*, 180.
113 Cf. the claim in the General Prologue that the translator had first attempted "to make o Latyn Bible sumdeel trewe" (*EAEB*, 80). While Deanesly, *Lollard Bible*, 258–60, and Dove, *English Bible*, 172–88, take these claims at face value, it seems hard to believe that, in the case of the General Prologue, this more accurate Vulgate did not receive any contemporary attention. It could be that these cases present a kind of trope of diligence.
114 *EAEB*, 173.
115 *Catena Aurea*, ed. Guarienti, I, 4.
116 Holmes's description of the *Catena* as "arranged in such a way as to permit continuous reading, as though the entire gloss were written by one author" is therefore misleading. See Holmes, "Aquinas' *Lectura in Matthaeum*," 86. Perhaps because of its derivative nature, little scholarly attention has been paid to the *Catena*, but see Bataillon, "Thomas et les Pères," and his "Les sermons de saint Thomas," as well as Conticello, "San Tommaso."
117 For a representative English example, see BodL MS Bodley 377, containing the *Catena Aurea* on Matthew and Mark; f. 242^r is reproduced on digital.bodleian.ox.ac.uk (accessed March 2, 2019). Aquinas discusses his citation practices in *Catena*, ed. Guarienti, I, 4, an account referenced in the prologue to the short recension of Matthew in the *Glossed Gospel*, in *EAEB*, 173/44–45. Hudson, *Doctors*, 103–105, offers an important account of the differences in the formatting of manuscripts of the *Catena* and Guarienti's modern edition.
118 Hudson, *Doctors*, lxi. Hargreaves, "Biblical Scholarship," 182, observes the tendency in earlier scholarship to focus on the importance of Aquinas for the *Glossed Gospels* and "overlook or ignore" the compilers' other sources.
119 Throughout the following, for the sake of convenience, I have drawn my quotations of long glossed Matthew from Laud. misc. 235, and I therefore focus on the portions of the text before the abridgments beginning in Matth. 19; see Hudson, *Doctors*, liv–lv. Though I consistently refer to the text's *compilers* in the plural, it seems at least possible that this work could have been carried out by a single writer.
120 For further discussion of these sources, see Hudson, *Doctors*, lvi–lix.
121 Cf., n. 50 in this chapter.
122 CCSL 141, ed. R. Étaix, 69–70.
123 *PG* 56, 642; *PL* 26, 26bc.
124 *PG* 56, 642.
125 *PL* 26, 27c–28a; *PG* 56, 645.
126 For the whole passage, see Laud. misc. 235, ff. 8va–9ra, with the "gostly" portion beginning at the bottom of f. 8vb. These two passages of spiritual exegesis purportedly present "Rabanus here aleggyn[g] Ambrose" and

"rehersynge Illarie," translating material found in CCCM 174, ed. B. Löfstedt, 69–70. As noted in Chapter 1, 25, Hrabanus's commentary made use of a system of marginal citations, from which the compilers almost certainly drew these references. See further Hudson, *Doctors*, 101–103.

127 On the short recension compilers' familiarity with the long recension, see Hudson, *Doctors*, lxiii–lxx.
128 *Catena Aurea*, ed. Guarienti, I, 42a.
129 *Ibid.*, 39a. Most telling with regard to Gregory's gloss is the long recension's inclusion of the phrase "if we brennen þou3tis of fleisch bi holy studies of preieris in þe autter of oure herte" (Laud. misc. 235, f. 7vb; cf. Gregory, CCSL 141, ed. Étaix, 70: "si cogitationes carnis per sancta orationum studia in ara cordis incendimus"), which is simplified in the short recension to "if we smellen swote to God bi studies of preieris" (BL Add. 41175, f. 6va), following Aquinas, "si per orationum studia Deo redolere valeamus."
130 PG 56, 642: "Si quis ergo praebet se Christo fidei sapientia plenum, obtulit ei aurum.... Si quis ergo Christo mundam offert orationem, obtulit ei thus.... Myrrham aestimo esse bona opera, quoniam sicut myrrha corpus defunctorum insolubile servat, sic bona opera Christum crucifixum in memoria hominis perpetuam servant et hominem servant in Christo. Primum ergo oportet Christo offerre fidem rationabilem, deinde orationem mundam, et tertio opera sancta."
131 Hudson, *Doctors*, cxxxix, describes how the compilers have put "the ball firmly into the receiver's court for deciding which patristic interpretation to be accepted," but she suggests that this approach is equally possible in all of the versions of the *Glossed Gospels*.
132 See, for example, Smith's discussion of the attributions or citations provided in some manuscripts of the *Glossa ordinaria*, in *Making of a Commentary*, 56–72. For the prologuer's emphasis on the inaccessibility of Latin for the imagined readers of the *Glossed Gospels*, see EAEB, esp. 184/20–21 (quoted earlier in this chapter, 155), and cf. 172/19–20 and 177/108.
133 See Waldron, "Original Prefaces," 290. On the possibility of readers using Wycliffite translations to help access Latin material, see Solopova, "Introduction," 2–3.
134 See Chapter 2, 61–62.
135 Gillespie, *Holy Books*, 114.
136 Bryan, *Looking Inward*, 15. See further Stock, *After Augustine*, as well as the essays in *Late Medieval Devotional Compilations*, ed. Cré et al.
137 EAEB, 173.
138 BL Add. 41175, f. 2ra; cf. BodL Laud. misc. 235, f. 2vb: "þe bok. As in a riche mannes shoppe eche man may fynde þat þing þat he desireþ, so in þis book eche soule fyndiþ þat þing þat is necessarie. *Crisostom here.*" Cf. PG 56, 612; the gloss does not appear in the *Catena*, ed. Guarienti, I, 10.
139 *Orchard*, ed. Hodgson and Liegey, 1; see Bryan, *Looking Inward*, 14, and Brown, *Fruit of the Orchard*, esp. ch. 4.
140 Hudson, *Premature Reformation*, 248; see too Copeland, *Pedagogy*, 130.
141 EAEB, 172 and 186.

142 *Ibid.*, 178/128–29; cf. 180/2–3 and 185/47–48.
143 *Ibid.*, 180/14.
144 Copeland, *Pedagogy*, 134 and 132.
145 E.g., when *De doctrina Christiana* is quoted in the Laud. misc. 235 prologue (*EAEB*, 174/8–9).
146 Cole, "English Lesson," 1147; see too Lawton, "The Bible," 200.
147 *EAEB*, 81; see Cole, "English Lesson," 1151, and Dove, *English Bible*, 173–74.
148 Kelly, *English Bible*, 45–46, argues that this desire to make the translation "better than the original" has led the Later Version adapters to "destroy what might be considered a divinely inspired uncertainty." Yet he offers no evidence for the translators' belief in the "divinely inspired uncertainty" of ablative absolute constructions.
149 One clear example of this purported Wycliffite disdain for glosses appears in the General Prologue to the Later Version Bible, *EAEB*, 73: "God boþe can and mai, if if likiþ him, spede symple men out of þe vnyuersite as myche to kunne Holy Writte as maistres in þe vniuersite." See Hudson, *Premature Reformation*, 228–31; Levy, *Quest for Authority*, 93–94, and his *Wyclif's Theology*, 83–126.
150 For "derke" as the opposite of "opene," see the Laud. misc. 235 prologue (*EAEB*, 177/100), as well as various examples in the General Prologue (*EAEB*, 59/2036 and 2049, and, most extensively, 5/72–82). Cf. too *MED* s.v. *derk* (adj.) 4, and Hanna, "Difficulty," 336–37.
151 *EAEB*, 172/17.
152 See the discussion earlier in this chapter, 145–46.
153 Ghosh, *Wycliffite Heresy*, 132; *EAEB*, 180/8, and cf. 173/50–51 and 185/44.
154 *EAEB*, 172/24, 178/132–33, 180/14; cf. 180/22, 23–24, and 26, 185/49, and 186/14.
155 *EAEB*, 181/53–60.
156 See *Medieval Literary Theory*, ed. Minnis and Scott, 97–98, and cf. Kraebel, "Inspired Commentator."
157 *EAEB*, 181/37–40.
158 *Ibid.*, 185/53–54.
159 *Ibid.*, 172/19–20 and 184/20. The national audience articulated here echoes the nationalist rhetoric seen, for example, in Trevisa's dialogue (Waldron, "Original Prefaces," 291–92); cf. Havens, "Imagined Communities," esp. 100–111. These examples are thus very specific illustrations of Turville-Petre's general claim, in *England the Nation*, 27, that "the clerical writer was able to appeal to the laity through a sense of nationhood."
160 *EAEB*, 125/23–31; cf. *ibid.*, 182–83/112–14.
161 *Ibid.*, 173/55–56.

Epilogue: John Bale's Dilemma

1 Bale, *Image*, sig. B3[rv]; ed. Minton, 45–46.
2 King, *Reformation Literature*, 72, describes Bale striving to present himself "as the apostolic successor to ... Tyndale."

3 Tyndale, *Exposition of the fyrst epistle*, sig. A3^v; ed. Walter, 138–39. Cf. his better-known comments in *Obedience*, sig. R3^r; ed. Daniell, 158, that the meaning of a biblical phrase can readily be determined on the basis of "the processe of the texte" (i.e., the context of the larger passage) or, for more difficult verses, "by a lyke texte of another place."

4 *Exposition of the fyrst epistle*, sig. A4^v; ed. Walter, 139–40.

5 Tyndale, *Exposicion vppon Mathew*, sig. d7^v–8^r and l6^v; ed. Walter, 39 and 100. On Tyndale's hermeneutic commitments, see Cummings, *Grammar and Grace*, esp. 190–206, and for a general overview of these controversies, Cummings, "Reformed Literature."

6 Snare, "Tyndale's Bibles," esp. 307–308 and 313, thus aptly describes these reformist commentaries as offering "a demonstration of what [right reading practice] is and what it will discover." His assertion that they present "a radical alternative" to scholastic glossing, however, or to what he calls the "system of commentary in the procedures of the schools," simply begs the question.

7 *Obedience*, sigs. B7^v–C1^r; ed. Daniell, 19–20.

8 *Ibid.*

9 *Exposicion vppon Mathew*, sig. g1^v and a5^r; ed. Walter, 58 and 7. In the preface to his *Exposicion vppon Mathew*, for example, Tyndale crafts an authoritative *persona* deriving chiefly from his comparison of his task with the Sermon on the Mount, in which Christ "diggeth agayne the welles of Abraham, whiche welles the Scribes and Pharases, those wicked and spitefull Philistines, had stopped and filled vp with the erth of their false exposicions." (*Exposicion vppon Mathew*, sig. a2^r; ed. Walter, 3.) By presenting himself as an ideal reader, Tyndale thus offers his interpretations as a standard against which others can judge their own baptismal profession and, with it, their salvation or damnation: see Simpson, *Burning to Read*, 99. Cf. Cummings, "Problem of Protestant Culture," esp. 183–85.

10 In Part III of the *Image*, these sections are titled "the commentarye." The first two parts, covering Apoc. 1–17, were published together, in Antwerp, c. 1545, and the first complete edition was published in London by Richard Jugge, c. 1548. Quotations are drawn from this printing, with reference to Minton's recent edition. On Erasmus's paraphrases and their exegetical style, see Rabil, "Erasmus's *Paraphrases*," and Vessey, "Tongue and Book"; their English versions are discussed by Devereux, "English *Paraphrases*," and their influence on Bale by Minton, "English Paraphrase." John Day's 1550 edition of the *Image*, included in Fig. 17, is a line-by-line resetting of the 1548 Jugge text.

11 *Image*, sig. A6^r–B1^r; ed. Minton, 39–43.

12 On Trithemius and his *De scriptoribus ecclesiasticis*, see Eisenstein, *Printing Press*, I, 94–99. Bale's use of Trithemius in his later catalogues is discussed by Warner, "Bale: Bibliographer." The unedited *Anglorum Heliades* is preserved in BL MSS Harley 3838 and 7031; on this text, see Hamilton, "Bale and His *Anglorum Heliades*." Compared with the medieval sources discussed here, much more attention has been devoted to Bale's use of two reformist exegetes, Francis Lambert and Sebastian Meyer: see Bauckham, *Tudor Apocalypse*, esp. 23–29; Fairfield, *John Bale*, 72–80; Firth, *Apocalyptic Tradition*, 39–42.

13 *Image*, ed. Minton, 493–500, provides a listing of these marginal citations. Firth, *Apocalyptic Tradition*, 40, identifies these sources as "standard medieval commentators" (as does Bauckham, *Tudor Apocalypse*, 23 and 29), but it would be more accurate to say that their exegetical writings had recently been made standard by being disseminated in print. In addition to the works discussed here, for example, Rupert of Deutz's commentary on the Apocalypse (Stegmüller 7581, listing nine MSS) was printed by Franz Birckman in Cologne in 1526, while the commentary attributed to Haymo of Halberstadt (Stegmüller 3122 and 7247, actually by Haimo of Auxerre and indeed a widely copied text) was printed by Eucharius Cervicorn in Cologne in 1531. Likewise, the Apocalypse commentary attributed to Gilbert of Poitiers in the catalogue (and cited three times in Bale's preface) is a bibliographical ghost, likely reflecting Bale's use of the *Glossa ordinaria*, first printed by Adolph Rusch in Strasbourg c. 1480, IV, sig. a1^{vab}, where the prologue to the glossed Apocalypse is attributed to Gilbert. (This prologue matches the incipit provided in Bale's preface, sig. A7^v; ed. Minton, 41). On the printing of early medieval commentaries, see Edwards, "Revival of Exegesis."
14 *Image*, sig. P3^v; ed. Minton, 140.
15 Bede's Apocalypse commentary survives in more than one hundred manuscripts (see CCSL 121a, ed. R. Gryson, 13–130), and it was first printed among Bede's New Testament glosses by Josse Bade (Paris, 1521); see Gorman, "Canon of Works." Bale's prefatory attribution of an Apocalypse commentary to Alcuin does not include an incipit, and the reformer was likely depending on Trithemius, *De scriptoribus*, sig. f5^v. Note that the Ps.-Alcuinian commentary listed at Stegmüller 1102 was not printed until 1837. The listing of Strabo in the preface almost certainly refers to the *Glossa ordinaria*, since the incipit he provides ("Sicut in secularibus literis [*rectior* libris?]") matches a preface to the glossed Apocalypse in the 1480 Rusch printing, IV, sig. a1^{vb}. Here, again, Bale may be following Trithemius, *De scriptoribus*, sig. f8^r, who attributed the *Glossa* to Strabo (see Froehlich, "Strabo and the *Glossa*"), but note that he does apparently refer marginally to Strabo on the Apocalypse (see Fig. 17), likely indicating direct consultation of this work as well.
16 *Image*, sig. M3^v; ed. Minton, 119–20. In her edition, 494, Minton notes sixteen marginal references to Ps.-Albertus's commentary in Part I of the *Image*. This commentary, printed by Jakob Wolff aus Pforzheim (Basel, 1506), provides the postil on Apoc. 1–18 by Albertus's younger contemporary, Bernard of Trilia OP, with the remaining chapters filled in from the postil of Peter of Tarantasia OFM, later Innocent V. Bernard's commentary survives in only two manuscripts (see Stegmüller 1040 and 1745), both supplying Peter's text for the chapters Bernard omits.
17 *Image*, sig. K7^r; ed. Minton, 108. Minton, "Exilic Imagination," esp. 91–92, develops Bale's notion of the "remnant," though without reference to medieval authors. See too Fairfield, *John Bale*, 82–85; Bauckham, *Tudor Apocalypse*, 54–90.
18 *Image*, sig. A1^r; ed. Minton, 35.

19 King, *Reformation Literature*, 69.
20 In many cases, this preference for a single interpretive option seems to be a function of Bale's Erasmian paraphrasal style. E.g., glossing Apoc. 1.7b ("And all eyes shall se hym"), he retains several details of the biblical phrase, but rearranges them and sews them into his own more elaborate construction: "And vpon hym shall all eyes loke, both man and angel shal behold him, & stande before hys terryble iudgement seate, no creature good nor bad exempt" (sig. C2^{rv}; ed. Minton, 54). But he still provides only a single reading when writing in a more traditional lemmatized style, as on Apoc. 1.4: "Grace (which is the mercy, fauer, and acceptacion of God) be with you, and also peace (which is the tranquilite of conscience in them that beleue in Chryste)" (sig. B8^v–C1^r; ed. Minton, 53).
21 Cf. the claim, in the preface to Part II, that he included the marginal notes in Part I "to sygnifye … that I dyd nothinge therin without autoryte," a claim which would seem to support the notion that the marginal references to other commentaries are citations of Bale's sources. Yet here he is describing marginal "alegacions both of the scryptures and doctors," and it could be that Bale was locating this "autoryte" specifically in the scriptural cross-references, which (as Fig. 17 illustrates) vastly outnumber the references to other commentators (*Image*, sig. a3^{rv}; ed. Minton, 174).
22 *Image*, sig. B1^r; ed. Minton, 43–44.
23 *Image*, sig. B3^r; ed. Minton, 45.
24 See Cummings, *Grammar and Grace*, 198.
25 *Summarium*, sig. Qq2^v–3^r; *Catalogus*, sig. ll1^v–2^r. On Bale's handling of Wyclif, see Aston, *Lollards and Reformers*, 244–48.
26 *Catalogus*, sig. ll2^r and ll3^r, respectively. Identifying the English commentary is made easier by the fuller description in Bale's notebook (*Index*, ed. Poole and Bateson, 265), "In Apocalipsim Anglice, li. 1. 'Sanctus Paulus Apostolus dicit quod omnes qui.'" This would seem to match the work listed in the *Summarium*, sig. Rr1^r, as "In Apocalypsim quoque, li. 1. 'Omnes qui pie uolunt uiuere.'" *English Apocalypse*, ed. Fridner, 1, begins, "Seint Poul þapostle seiþ þat alle þoo þat willen pytiuosli leuen …"; cf. the start of the interpolated version, *Mittelenglische Übersetzung*, ed. Sauer, 1.
27 This account in the *Catalogus* appears to clarify the earlier *Summarium*, which reads, "… Biblia tota, cum quibusdam ueterum doctorum tractatibus" (sig. Rr1^v).
28 The notion that Bede was translating John at the time of his death derives from the letter of Cuthbert to Cuthwin (see *Ecclesiastical History*, ed. Colgrave and Mynors, 582–83), repeated influentially in William of Malmesbury's *Gesta regum*, ed. Mynors et al., I, 90–91, whose account was in turn repeated in Higden's *Polychronicon*, ed. Lumby and Babington, VI, 222–25, with this last intermediary cited in Ullerston's *determinatio* on biblical translation (cf. *EAEB* 145 and nn.). Bale seems to introduce the claim that Bede also translated the Psalter.
29 The rare commentaries on Lamentations and the Apocalypse are carried over from Leland (*De uiris illustribus*, ed. Carley and Brett, 582–83), who lists

them among the works he found in the library of St. Mary's, York, apparently describing the book now divided between Oxford, Corpus Christi Coll. MS 193 and BL MS Cotton Tib. A. xv, ff. 181–94. (The overlap in contents and ordering, though not perfect, is substantial enough to be convincing.) Rolle is largely overlooked by Hudson, "*Visio Baleii*," who offers an otherwise useful account of Bale's cataloguing of major Middle English writers; see further Allen, *Writings Ascribed*, 422–25.

30 *Catalogus*, sig. ll2ʳ; for the English incipit, see above, 104.
31 In his *Apologie for John Wickliffe* (1608), for example, Bodleian librarian Thomas James identifies Wyclif, the "worthie instrument and chosen vessel of Gods glorie," as being moved not only "to translate the whole Bible," but also "to comment vpon some parts therof, & chiefly those parts of Holy Scripture which are most in vse, as the Psalmes of David, the *Te Deum*, *Nunc dimittis*, *the Magnificat*, and other Hymnes now read and retained to this day in the vsage and Liturgie of the Church of England" (sig. b3ᵛ). Tied to this statement is a marginal citation, identifying these Psalms as "extant in the publike librarie, verie fairely bound, of the guift of M. Doct. Bond," i.e., Nicholas Bonde, president of Magdalen from 1589 to 1608, whose private library seems to have been considerable. (See Ker, "Provision of Books," 473.) James does not specify that this commentary is in English, but that seems to be implied by the preceding discussion of translation, and the account of an apparently vernacular gloss on the Psalter together with the liturgical canticles almost certainly describes the *English Psalter*. And if "the publike librarie" refers to the Bodleian, then James could be citing the book that is now BodL MS Bodley 877, acquired, according to Madan et al., *Summary Catalogue*, II.1, 587, "between 1605 and 1611." For a second example, see BL MS Arundel 158, an incomplete copy of the *English Psalter*, in which a seventeenth-century hand has identified the text as "John Wicklyfe vppon the Psalmes" (f. 8ʳ). See Kraebel, "Further Book," 459.
32 This treatment of Middle English biblical material contradicts the claims to objectivity and accuracy made, for example, by King, *Reformation Literature*, 68, who insists that "correct attribution, biography, and chronology enable Bale to assign writers to a specific place in the conflict between the two churches." Cf. Fairfield, *John Bale*, 115.
33 *Tudor Royal Proclamations*, ed. Hughes and Larkin, I, no. 186; see further Cummings, "Reformed Literature," 841. On early modern censorship, with reference to this proclamation, see Kastan, "Naughty Printed Books."
34 See Chapter 3, 106–107.
35 Cummings, *Grammar and Grace*, 19.
36 Betteridge, "Tyndale and Religious Debate," 452.
37 In addition to the Northern commentary-translation of Matthew discussed in Chapter 4, see too the Northern translation of the *Pauline Epistles*, ed. Powell, which includes interpretive material drawn from the *Glossa ordinaria*, the commentary–translations of Mark and Luke preserved in Cambridge, Corpus

Christi Coll. MS 32 (discussed in Kraebel, "Gospel Glosses"), and the glossed Catholic Epistles compiled as part of the Paues biblical version.

38 Everett, "Prose Psalter," vol. 17, 337–50, proposes the influence of Old English interlinear Psalter glosses and the Surtees Psalter on Rolle's *English Psalter*, a possibility discussed by Sutherland, *English Psalms*, 103–106.

Bibliography

Note: The following lists omit texts printed in the *Patrologia Latina* and *Graeca*, as well as materials edited in the Corpus Christianorum and Corpus Scriptorum Ecclesiasticorum Latinorum series, which are cited by volume number in the notes. Full citations of book reviews, and of some referenced but unquoted translations, are provided in the notes and are not duplicated here. For unprinted sources, see the index of manuscripts below.

Printed Sources

Albertus Magnus. *B. Alberti Magni Ratisbonensis episcopi, ordinis Praedicatorum, Opera omnia*. Edited by Auguste Borgnet. 38 vols. Paris: Vivès, 1890–95.

Alexander of Hales. *Doctoris irrefragabilis Alexandri de Hales Ordinis Minorum Summa theologica*. 4 vols. in 5. Quaracchi: Collegio di San Bonaventura, 1924–48.

Aquinas, Thomas. *Catena Aurea in Quatuor Evangelia*. Edited by Angelico Guarienti. Rev. edn. 2 vols. Turin: Marietti, 1953.

In duodecim libros Metaphysicorum Aristotelis Expositio. Edited by M. R. Cathala and Raymond Spiazzi. 2nd edn. Turin: Marietti, 1971.

Sancti Thomae Aquinatis doctoris angelici opera omnia iussu Leonis XIII P. M. edita. Leonine edn. 50 vols as of 2000. Rome: Vatican Polyglot Press, 1882–. Since 1987, various revised volumes have appeared as the New Leonine edn. (*editio altera retractata*).

Sancti Thomae Aquinatis doctoris angelici, ordinis Praedicatorum, opera omnia. 25 vols. Parma: Fiaccadori, 1852–73.

Summa theologiae. Blackfriars edn. 61 vols. London: Eyre and Spottiswoode, 1964–80.

Aristotle. *Metaphysica, lib. I–IV.4: Translatio Iacobi sive "Vetustissima" cum Scholiis et Translatio Composita sive "Vetus."* Edited by Gudrun Vuillemin-Diem. 2 vols. Aristoteles Latinus, 25.1–1a. Brussels: Desclée de Brouwer, 1970.

Auriol, Peter. *Compendium sensus litteralis totius divinae Scripturae*. Edited by Philibert Seeboeck. Quaracchi: Collegio di San Bonaventura, 1896.

Bale, John. *Illustrium Maioris Britanniae scriptorum, hoc est Angliae, Cambriae, ac Scotiae, summarium*. Wesel: Dirik van der Straten, 1548.

The Image of Both Churches. Edited by Gretchen Minton. New York: Springer, 2013.

The image of bothe churches after the moste wonderfull and heuenly Reuelacion of Sainct Iohn the Euangelist. London: Richard Jugge, (?)1548.

Index Britanniae scriptorum quos ex variis bibliothecis non parvo labore collegit Ioannes Baleus, cum aliis: John Bale's Index of British and Other Writers. Edited by Reginald Lane Poole with Mary Bateson. Oxford: Clarendon, 1902.

Scriptorum illustrium maioris Brytannie quam nunc Angliam & Scotiam uocant catalogus. Basel: Johannes Oporinus, 1557.

Bartholomaeus Anglicus. *De proprietatibus rerum*. Nürnberg: Anton Koberger, 1492.

Bede. *Bede's Ecclesiastical History of the English People*. Edited by Bertram Colgrave and R. A. B. Mynors. Oxford: Clarendon, 1969.

Bernard of Clairvaux. *Sancti Bernardi Opera*. Edited by Jean Lerclercq, Charles Talbot, and Henri-Marie Rochais. 8 vols. Rome: Editiones Cistercienses, 1957–77.

Biblia sacra cum Glossa ordinaria nouisque additionibus. Edited by François Feruardent. 6 vols. Venice: Giuntas, 1603.

Bonaventure. *Doctoris Seraphici S. Bonaventurae opera omnia*. 11 vols in 10. Quaracchi: Collegio di San Bonaventura, 1882–1902.

Breviarium ad usum insignis ecclesiae Sarum. Edited by Francis Procter and Christopher Wordsworth. 3 vols. Cambridge: Cambridge University Press, 1879–86.

Catalogi veteres librorum ecclesiae cathedralis Dunelm: Catalogues of the Library of Durham Cathedral, at Various Periods, from the Conquest to the Dissolution. London, J. B. Nichols, 1838.

The Chastising of God's Children, and the Treatise of Perfection of the Sons of God. Edited by Joyce Bazire and Eric Colledge. Oxford: Blackwell, 1957.

A Commentary on the Benedictus. Edited by Björn Wallner. Lund: Gleerup, 1957.

The Earliest Advocates of the English Bible: The Texts of the Medieval Debate. Edited by Mary Dove. Exeter: University of Exeter Press, 2010.

An English Fourteenth-Century Apocalypse Version with a Prose Commentary. Edited by Elis Fridner. Lund: Gleerup, 1961.

An Exposition of Qui Habitat and Bonum Est. Edited by Björn Wallner. Lund: Gleerup, 1954.

A Fourteenth-Century English Biblical Version. Edited by Anna C. Paues. Cambridge: Cambridge University Press, 1904.

Henry of Ghent. *Summae quaestionum ordinarium theologi recepto preconio Solennis Henrici a Gandauo*. Paris: Josse Bade, 1520.

Henry of Kirkstede. *Catalogus de Libris Autenticis et Apocrifis*. Edited by Richard Rouse and Mary Rouse. CBMLC 1. London: British Library, 2004.

Higden, Ranulf. *Polychronicon Ranulphi Higden monachi Cestrensis, together with the English Translations of John Trevisa and of an Unknown Writer of the Fifteenth Century*. Edited by Joseph Rawson Lumby and Churchill Babington. 9 vols. London: Longman, 1865–86.

The Holy Bible … in the Earliest English Versions. Edited by Josiah Forshall and Frederic Madden. 4 vols. Oxford: Oxford University Press, 1850.

Huguccio of Pisa. *Derivationes*. Edited by Enzo Cecchini et al. 2 vols. Florence: SISMEL, 2004.

Interpretation of Scripture: A Selection of Works of Hugh, Andrew, Richard, and Godfrey of St. Victor, and of Robert of Melun. Edited by Franklin Harkins and Frans van Liere. Turnhout: Brepols, 2012.

Isidore of Seville. *Etymologiarum sive originum libri XX*. Edited by W. M. Lindsay. 2 vols. Oxford: Clarendon, 1911.

James, Thomas. *An apologie for John Wickliffe, shewing his conformitie with the now Church of England*. Oxford: Joseph Barnes, 1608.

Julian of Norwich. *Revelations of Divine Love*. Edited by Barry Windeatt. Oxford: Oxford University Press, 2016.

Kempe, Margery. *The Book of Margery Kempe*. Edited by Barry Windeatt. Woodbridge: D. S. Brewer, 2004.

The Book of Margery Kempe. Edited by Lynn Staley. Kalamazoo, MI: Medieval Institute, 1996.

Leland, John. *De uiris illustribus: On Famous Men*. Edited by James Carley with Caroline Brett. Toronto: PIMS, 2010.

Love, Nicholas. *Mirror of the Blessed Life of Jesus Christ*. Edited by Michael Sargent. Exeter: University of Exeter Press, 2005.

Maidstone, Richard. *Penitential Psalms*. Edited by Valerie Edden. Heidelberg: Winter, 1990.

Medieval Literary Theory and Criticism, c. 1100–c. 1375: The Commentary-Tradition. Edited by Alastair Minnis and A. B. Scott with the assistance of David Wallace. Rev. edn. Oxford: Oxford University Press, 1991.

Middle English Glossed Prose Psalter. Edited by Robert Black and Raymond St.-Jacques. Heidelberg: Winter, 2012.

The Middle English Mirror: Sermons from Advent to Sexagesima. Edited by Thomas Duncan and Margaret Connolly. Heidelberg: Winter, 2003.

Die mittelenglische Übersetzung der Apokalypse mit Kommentar (Version B). Edited by Walter Sauer. [Heidelberg], 1971.

Nicholas of Lyre. See *Biblia sacra*.

The Officium and Miracula of Richard Rolle. Edited by Reginald Maxwell Woolley. London: SPCK, 1919.

The Orcherd of Syon. Edited by Phyllis Hodgson and Gabriel Liegey. EETS os 258. London: Oxford University Press, 1966.

The Pauline Epistles Contained in MS Parker 32, Corpus Christi College, Cambridge. Edited by Margaret Joyce Powell. EETS es 116. London: Paul, Trench, Trübner, 1916.

Peter of Herentals. *Collectarius super librum Psalmorum*. Cologne: Conrad Winters, 1480.

Registrum Anglie de Libris Doctorum et Auctorum Veterum. Edited by Richard Rouse and Mary Rouse with R. A. B. Mynors. CBMLC 2. London: British Library, 1991.

Richard of St. Victor. *On the Apocalypse of John.* Selections translated by A. B. Kraebel. In *Interpretation of Scripture,* ed. Franklin Harkins and Frans van Liere, 327–70. Turnhout: Brepols, 2012.

Rolle, Richard. *The Contra Amatores Mundi of Richard Rolle of Hampole.* Edited by Paul Theiner. Berkeley: University of California Press, 1968.

De emendatione vitae: eine kritische Ausgabe des lateinischen Textes von Richard Rolle. Edited by Rüdiger Spahl. Göttingen: V&R Unipress, 2009.

The English Writings of Richard Rolle, Hermit of Hampole. Edited by Hope Emily Allen. Oxford: Clarendon, 1931.

The Incendium Amoris of Richard Rolle of Hampole. Edited by Margaret Deanesly. Manchester: Manchester University Press, 1915.

The Melos Amoris. Edited by E. J. F. Arnould. Oxford: Blackwell, 1957.

Mending of Life from the Fifteenth-Century Worcester Cathedral Manuscript F. 172. Edited by William Henry Hulme. Cleveland: Western Reserve University Press, 1918.

Prose and Verse. Edited by S. J. Ogilvie-Thomson. EETS os 293. Oxford: Oxford University Press, 1988.

The Psalter, or Psalms of David and Certain Canticles, with a Translation and Exposition in English by Richard Rolle. Edited by Henry Ramsden Bramley. Oxford: Clarendon, 1884.

The Tractatus super Psalmum XX of Richard Rolle of Hampole. Edited by James Dolan. Lewiston: Mellen, 1991.

Select English Works of John Wyclif. Edited by Thomas Arnold. 3 vols. Oxford: Clarendon, 1869–71.

Syon Abbey. Edited by Vincent Gillespie. Printed with *The Libraries of the Carthusians.* Edited by A. I. Doyle. CBMLC 9. London: British Library/British Academy, 2001.

Trithemius, Johannes. *De scriptoribus ecclesiasticis.* Basel: Johann Amerbach, 1494.

Tudor Royal Proclamations. Edited by Paul Hughes and James Larkin. 3 vols. New Haven: Yale University Press, 1964–69.

Two Revisions of Rolle's English Psalter Commentary and the Related Canticles. Edited by Anne Hudson. EETS os 340–41 and 343. Oxford: Oxford University Press, 2012–14.

Tyndale, William. *An exposicion vppon the v. vi. vii. chapters of Mathew, which thre chaptres are the keye and the dore of the Scripture.* Antwerp: (?)Johannes Grapheus, (?)1533.

The exposition of the fyrst epistle of seynt Ihon with a prologge before it by W. T. Antwerp: Merten de Keyser, 1531.

Expositions and Notes on Sundry Portions of the Holy Scriptures, together with the Practice of Prelates. Edited by Henry Walter. Cambridge: Cambridge University Press, 1849.

The Obedience of a Christian Man. Edited by David Daniell. London: Penguin, 2000.

The obedience of a Christen man and how Christen rulers ought to governe. Antwerp: Jan Hillen van Hoochstraten, 1528.

Waleys, Thomas. *Commentarius super Psalmos F. Tho. Iorgii Anglici.* Venice: Evangelista Deuchino, 1611.
William of Malmesbury. *Gesta regum Anglorum: The History of the English Kings.* Edited by R. A. B. Mynors, and completed by Rodney Thomson and Michael Winterbottom. 2 vols. Oxford: Clarendon, 1998–99.
Wyclif, John. *De Compositione Hominis.* Edited by Rudolf Beer. London: Wyclif Society, 1884.
   De Veritate Sacrae Scripturae. Edited by Rudolf Buddensieg. 3 vols. London: Wyclif Society, 1905–1907.
   Opus Evangelicum. Edited by Johann Loserth. 4 vols. in 2. London: Wyclif Society, 1895–96.
   Sermones. Edited by Johann Loserth. 4 vols. London: Wyclif Society, 1886–89.
   Tractatus de Benedicta Incarnacione. Edited by Edward Harris. London: Wyclif Society, 1886.
   Trialogus, cum supplemento Trialogi. Edited by Gotthard Lechler. Oxford: Clarendon, 1869.

Secondary Studies

Alford, John. "Biblical *Imitatio* in the Writings of Richard Rolle." *ELH* 40 (1973): 1–23.
   "Rolle's *English Psalter* and *Lectio Divina*." *Bulletin of the John Rylands Library* 77 (1995): 47–59.
Allen, Hope Emily. *Writings Ascribed to Richard Rolle, Hermit of Hampole, and Materials for His Biography.* New York: Heath, 1927.
Andrée, Alexander. "Le *Pater* (Matth. 6, 9–13 et Luc. 11, 2–4) dans l'exégèse de l'école de Laon: la *Glossa ordinaria* et autres commentaires." In *Le Pater noster au XIIe siècle: Lectures et usages*, ed. Francesco Siri, 29–74. Turnhout: Brepols, 2015.
Appleford, Amy. *Learning to Die in London, 1380–1540.* Philadelphia: University of Pennsylvania Press, 2015.
Aston, Margaret. *Lollards and Reformers: Images and Literacy in Late Medieval Religion.* London: Hambledon, 1984.
Bain, Emmanuel. "Nicolas de Lyre universitaire? Le commentaire des paraboles évangéliques." In *Nicolas de Lyre*, ed. Gilbert Dahan, 125–52. Paris: Institut d'Études Augustiniennes, 2011.
   "*Parabola*, *similitudo*, et *exemplum*: Bonaventure et le rhétorique des paraboles dans son Commentaire sur Luc." In *Etudes d'exégèse médiévale offertes à Gilbert Dahan par ses élèves*, ed. Annie Noblesse-Rocher, 141–59. Turnhout: Brepols, 2012.
Ball, R. M. "Robert Grosseteste on the Psalms." In *Robert Grosseteste: His Thought and Its Impact*, ed. Jack Cunningham, 79–108. Toronto: PIMS, 2012.
Ballentyne, Adrian. "A Reassessment of the Exposition on the Gospel according to St. Matthew in Manuscript Alençon 26." *Recherches de Théologie ancienne et médiévale* 56 (1989): 19–57.

Bataillon, "Saint Thomas et les Pères: de la *Catena* à la *tertia pars*." In *Ordo sapientiae et amoris: image et message de saint Thomas d'Aquin à travers les récentes études historiques, hérméneutiques et doctrinales*, ed. Carlos-Josaphat Pinto de Oliveira, 15–36. Fribourg: Editions Universitaires, 1993.

"Les sermons de saint Thomas et la *Catena Aurea*." In *St. Thomas Aquinas 1274–1974: Commemorative Studies*, I, 67–75. Toronto: PIMS, 1974.

Bauckham, Richard. *Tudor Apocalypse: Sixteenth-Century Apocalypticism, Millennarianism, and the English Reformation*. Oxford: Sutton Courtenay, 1978.

Beadle, Richard. "English Autograph Writings of the Later Middle Ages: Some Preliminaries." In *Gli autografi medievali: problemi paleografici e filologici*, ed. Paolo Chiesa and Lucia Pinelli, 249–68. Spoleto: CISAM, 1994.

Benrath, Gustav. *Wyclifs Bibelkommentar*. Berlin: de Gruyter, 1966.

Betteridge, Thomas. "William Tyndale and Religious Debate." *JMEMS* 40 (2010): 439–61.

Bori, Pier Cesare. *L'interpretazione infinita: l'ermeneutica cristiana antica e le sue transformazione*. Bologna: Il Mulino, 1987.

Bradley, Christopher G. "Censorship and Cultural Continuity: Love's *Mirror*, the *Pore Caitif*, and Religious Experience before and after Arundel." In *After Arundel: Religious Writing in Fifteenth-Century England*, ed. Vincent Gillespie and Kantik Ghosh, 115–32. Turnhout: Brepols, 2011.

Brantley, Jessica. *Reading in the Wilderness: Private Devotion and Public Performance in Late Medieval England*. Chicago: University of Chicago Press, 2007.

Brown, Jennifer. *Fruit of the Orchard: Reading Catherine of Siena in Late Medieval and Early Modern England*. Toronto: University of Toronto Press, 2019.

Bryan, Jennifer. *Looking Inward: Devotional Reading and the Private Self in Late Medieval England*. Philadelphia: University of Pennsylvania Press, 2008.

Bühler, Curt. "A Lollard Tract: On Translating the Bible into English." *MÆ* 7 (1938): 167–83.

Burnett, Charles. "The Legend of Constantine the African." *Micrologus* 21 (2013): 277–94.

"Translating from Arabic into Latin in the Middle Ages: Theory, Practice, and Criticism." In *Éditer, traduire, interpreter: essais de methodologie philosophique*, ed. Steve Lofts and Philipp Rosemann, 55–78. Louvain-la-Neuve: Editions de l'Institut supérieur de philosophie, 1997.

Catto, Jeremy. "1349–1412: Culture and History." In *The Cambridge Companion to Medieval English Mysticism*, ed. Samuel Fanous and Vincent Gillespie, 113–32. Cambridge: Cambridge University Press, 2011.

"New Light on Thomas Docking OFM." *Mediaeval and Renaissance Studies* 6 (1968): 135–49.

"William Woodford OFM (c. 1330–c. 1397)." D.Phil. diss., University of Oxford, 1969.

"Written English: The Making of the Language, 1370–1400." *Past and Present* 179 (2003): 24–59.

"Wyclif and Wycliffism at Oxford, 1356–1430." In *The History of the University of Oxford,* II, *Late Medieval Oxford,* ed. Jeremy Catto and Ralph Evans, 175–261. Oxford: Clarendon, 1992.

"The Wycliffite Bible: The Historical Context." In *The Wycliffite Bible,* ed. Elizabeth Solopova, 11–26. Leiden: Brill, 2017.

Chenu, Marie-Dominique. *Introduction à l'étude de saint Thomas d'Aquin.* Paris: Vrin, 1993.

La théologie au douzième siècle. Paris: Vrin, 1957.

Clark, James. "The Friars and the Classics in Late Medieval England." In *The Friars in Medieval Britain: Proceedings of the 2007 Harlaxton Symposium,* ed. Nicholas Rogers, 142–51. Donington: Shaun Tyas, 2010.

Clark, John P. H. "The Problem of Walter Hilton's Authorship: *Bonum Est, Benedictus,* and *Of Angels' Song.*" *Downside Review* 101 (1983): 15–29.

"Richard Rolle as a Biblical Commentator." *Downside Review* 104 (1986): 165–213.

"Walter Hilton and the Psalm Commentary *Qui Habitat.*" *Downside Review* 100 (1982): 235–62.

Clark, Mark. "The Commentaries of Stephen Langton on the *Historia scholastica* of Peter Comestor." In *Etienne Langton, prédicateur, bibliste, théologien,* ed. Louis-Jean Bataillon, 373–93. Turnhout: Brepols, 2010.

"The Commentaries on Comestor's *Historia scholastica* of Stephen Langton, Pseudo-Langton, and Hugh of St. Cher." *Sacris Erudiri* 44 (2005): 301–446.

The Making of the Historia scholastica, 1150–1200. Toronto: PIMS, 2015.

"Stephen Langton and Hugh of St. Cher on Peter Comestor's *Historia scholastia:* The Lombard's *Sentences* and the Problem of Sources used by Comestor and His Commentators." *Recherches de Théologie et Philosophie médiévales* 74 (2007): 63–117.

Classen, Peter. *Burgundio von Pisa: Richter, Gesandter, Übersetzer.* Heidelberg: Winter, 1974.

Coates, Alan. "The Library of Durham College, Oxford." *Library History* 8 (1990): 125–31.

Cole, Andrew. "Chaucer's English Lesson." *Speculum* 77 (2002): 1128–67.

Colish, Marcia. *Peter Lombard.* 2 vols. Leiden: Brill, 1994.

Constable, Giles. "The Popularity of Twelfth-Century Spiritual Writers in the Late Middle Ages." In *Renaissance: Studies in Honour of Hans Baron,* ed. Anthony Molho and John Tedeschi, 3–28. Florence: Sansoni, 1971.

"Twelfth-Century Spirituality and the Late Middle Ages." *Medieval and Renaissance Studies* 5 (1971): 27–60.

Conte, Gian Biagio. *The Poetry of Pathos: Studies in Virgilian Epic.* Translated by S. J. Harrison. Oxford: Oxford University Press, 2007.

Conticello, Carmello Giuseppe. "San Tommaso ed i Padri: la *Catena aurea super Ioannem.*" *Archives d'histoire doctrinale et littéraire du moyen âge* 57 (1990): 31–92.

Copeland, Rita. "Lollard Instruction." In *Medieval Christianity in Practice,* ed. Miri Rubin, 27–32. Princeton: Princeton University Press, 2009.

    Pedagogy, Intellectuals, and Dissent in the Later Middle Ages: Lollardy and Ideas of Learning. Cambridge: Cambridge University Press, 2001.

    Rhetoric, Hermeneutics, and Translation in the Middle Ages: Academic Traditions and Vernacular Texts. Cambridge: Cambridge University Press, 1991.

    "Wycliffite Ciceronianism? The General Prologue to the Wycliffite Bible and Augustine's *De doctrina Christiana*." In *Rhetoric and Renewal in the Latin West, 1140–1540: Essays in Honour of John O. Ward*, ed. Constant Mews et al., 185–200. Turnhout: Brepols, 2003.

Coulter, Dale. "*Historia* and *Sensus litteralis:* An Investigation into the Approach to Literal Interpretation at the Twelfth-Century School of St. Victor." In *Transforming Relations: Essays on Jews and Christians throughout History in Honor of Michael A. Signer*, ed. Franklin Harkins, 101–24. Notre Dame: University of Notre Dame Press, 2010.

Courtenay, William. "The Bible in the Fourteenth Century: Some Observations." *Church History* 54 (1985): 176–87.

    "The Bible in Medieval Universities." In *The New Cambridge History of the Bible, II, From 600 to 1450*, ed. Richard Marsden and E. Ann Matter, 555–78. Cambridge: Cambridge University Press, 2012.

    "Franciscan Learning: University Education and Biblical Exegesis." In *Defenders and Critics of Franciscan Life: Essays in Honor of John V. Fleming*, ed. Michael Cusato and G. Geltner, 55–64. Leiden: Brill, 2009.

    Schools and Scholars in Fourteenth-Century England. Princeton: Princeton University Press, 1987.

Cummings, Brian. "Justifying God in Tyndale's English." *Reformation* 2 (1997): 143–71.

    The Literary Culture of the Reformation: Grammar and Grace. Oxford: Oxford University Press, 2002.

    "The Problem of Protestant Culture: Biblical Literalism and Literary Biblicism." *Reformation* 17 (2012): 177–98.

    "Reformed Literature and Literature Reformed." In *The Cambridge History of Medieval English Literature*, ed. David Wallace, 821–51. Cambridge: Cambridge University Press, 1999.

Dahan, Gilbert. *L'exégèse chrétienne de la Bible en Occident médiévale: XIIe–XIVe siècle*. Paris: Éditions du Cerf, 2008.

    Interpréter la Bible au moyen âge: cinq écrits du XIIIe siècle sur l'exégèse de la Bible traduits en français. Paris: Paroles et silence, 2009.

    Lire la Bible au moyen âge: essais d'herméneutique médiévale. Geneva: Droz, 2010.

    "La méthode critique dans l'étude de la Bible (XIIe–XIIIe siècles)." In *La méthode critique au moyen âge*, ed. Mireille Chazan and Gilbert Dahan, 103–28. Turnhout: Brepols, 2006.

    "Nicolas de Lyre: Herméneutique et méthodes d'exégèse." In *Nicolas de Lyre*, ed. Gilbert Dahan, 99–124. Paris: Institut d'Études Augustiniennes, 2011.

    "Poetics and Biblical Hermeneutics in the Thirteenth Century." In *Medieval Literary Theory and Criticism: Beyond Scholasticism*, ed. Ardis Butterfield, Ian

Johnson, and Andrew Kraebel. Cambridge: Cambridge University Press, forthcoming.
De Bruyne, Donatien. *Préfaces de la Bible*. Repr. with introductions by Pierre-Maurice Bogaert and Thomas O'Loughlin. Turnhout: Brepols, 2015.
De Hamel, Christopher. *Glossed Books of the Bible and the Origins of the Paris Booktrade*. Woodbridge: D. S. Brewer, 1987.
De Lubac, Henri. *Exégèse médiévale: les quatre sens de l'Écriture*. 2 vols. in 4. Paris: Aubier, 1959–62.
De Visscher, Eva. *Reading the Rabbis: Christian Hebraism in the Works of Herbert of Bosham*. Leiden: Brill, 2014.
Dean, Ruth J. "The Earliest Known Commentary on Livy is by Nicholas Trevet." *Medievalia et Humanistica* os 3 (1945): 86–98 and 4 (1946): 110.
Deanesly, Margaret. *The Lollard Bible and Other Medieval Biblical Versions*. Cambridge: Cambridge University Press, 1920.
Delmas, Sophie. "La réception de l'*Historia scholastica* chez quelques maîtres en théologie du XIIIe siècle." In *Pierre le Mangeur ou Pierre de Troyes, maître du XIIe siècle*, ed. Gilbert Dahan, 267–87. Turnhout: Brepols, 2013.
Depold, Jennifer. "Preaching the Name: The Influence of a Sermon on the Holy Name of Christ." *Journal of Medieval History* 40 (2014): 195–208.
Devereux, E. J. "The Publication of the English *Paraphrases* of Erasmus." *Bulletin of the John Rylands Library* 51 (1969): 348–67.
Dickens, A. G. *The English Reformation*. New York: Schocken, 1964.
Dinshaw, Carolyn. *Chaucer's Sexual Poetics*. Madison: University of Wisconsin Press, 1989.
Dobson, R. B. *Durham Priory, 1400–1450*. Cambridge: Cambridge University Press, 1973.
Dove, Mary. *The First English Bible: The Text and Context of the Wycliffite Versions*. Cambridge: Cambridge University Press, 2007.
——— "The Lollard's Threefold Biblical Agenda." In *Wycliffite Controversies*, ed. Mishtooni Bose and J. Patrick Hornbeck, 211–26. Turnhout: Brepols, 2011.
——— "Wyclif and the English Bible." In *A Companion to John Wyclif, Late Medieval Theologian*, ed. Ian Christopher Levy, 365–406. Leiden: Brill, 2006.
Doyle, A. I. "A Survey of the Origins and Circulation of Theological Writings in English in the 14th, 15th, and Early 16th Centuries, with Special Consideration of the Part of the Clergy Therein." Ph.D. diss., University of Cambridge, 1953.
Doyle, Eric. "A Bibliographical List by William Woodford OFM." *Franciscan Studies* 35 (1975): 93–106.
——— "William Woodford on Scripture and Tradition." In *Studia Historico-Ecclesiastica: Festgabe für Prof. Luchesius G. Spätling OFM*, ed. Isaac Vázquez, 481–504. Rome: Pontificum Athenaeum Antonianum, 1977.
Doyle, Matthew. *The Lombard and His Students*. Toronto: PIMS, 2016.
Driscoll, Michael. "The Seven Penitential Psalms: Their Designation and Usages from the Middle Ages Onwards." *Ecclesia Orans* 17 (2000): 153–201.

Edden, Valerie. "Richard Maidstone's *Penitential Psalms.*" *Leeds Studies in English* ns 17 (1986): 77–94.
Edwards, Burton Van Name. "The Revival of Medieval Biblical Exegesis in the Early Modern World: The Example of Carolingian Biblical Commentaries." In *Bridging the Medieval-Modern Divide: Medieval Themes in the World of the Reformation*, ed. James Muldoon, 107–42. Farnham: Ashgate, 2013.
Eisenstein, Elizabeth. *The Printing Press as an Agent of Change: Communication and Cultural Transformations in Early Modern Europe.* 2 vols. Cambridge: Cambridge University Press, 1979.
Emden, A. B. *A Biographical Register of the University of Cambridge to 1500.* Cambridge: Cambridge University Press, 1963.
  A Biographical Register of the University of Oxford to A. D. 1500. 3 vols, paginated continuously. Oxford: Clarendon, 1957–59.
Evans, G. R. *John Wyclif: Myth and Reality.* Oxford: Lion, 2005.
Everett, Dorothy. "The Middle English Prose Psalter of Richard Rolle of Hampole." *Modern Language Review* 17 (1922): 337–50, and 18 (1923), 381–93.
Fairfield, Leslie. *John Bale, Mythmaker of the English Reformation.* West Lafayette: Purdue University Press, 1976.
Firth, Katharine. *The Apocalyptic Tradition in Reformation Britain, 1530–1645.* Oxford: Oxford University Press, 1979.
Fisher, Matthew. "When Variants Aren't: Authors as Scribes in Some English Manuscripts." In *Probable Truth: Editing Medieval Texts from Britain in the Twenty-First Century*, ed. Vincent Gillespie and Anne Hudson, 207–222. Turnhout: Brepols, 2013.
FitzGerald, Brian. *Inspiration and Authority in the Middle Ages: Prophets and their Critics from Scholasticism to Humanism.* Oxford: Oxford University Press, 2017.
Foster, Meryl. "Durham Monks at Oxford *c.* 1286-1381: A House of Studies and its Inmates." *Oxoniensia* 55 (1991): 99–114.
Fowler, Don. "Criticism as Commentary and Commentary as Criticism in the Age of Electronic Media." In *Commentaries–Kommentare*, ed. Glenn Most, 426–42. Göttingen, 1999.
Franklin-Brown, Mary. *Reading the World: Encyclopedic Writing in the Scholastic Age.* Chicago: University of Chicago Press, 2012.
Freeman, Elizabeth. "The Priory of Hampole and its Literary Culture: English Religious Women and Books in the Age of Richard Rolle." *Parergon* 29 (2012): 1–25.
Froehlich, Karlfried. "Walafrid Strabo and the Glossa ordinaria: The Making of a Myth." In *Studia Patristica, XXVIII: Papers Presented at the Eleventh International Conference of Patristic Studies*, ed. Elizabeth Livingstone, 192–96. Leuven: Peeters, 1993.
Gameson, Richard. *Manuscripts of Early Norman England (c. 1066–1130).* Oxford: Oxford University Press, 1999.
  Manuscript Treasures of Durham Cathedral. London: Third Millennium, 2010.

Gayk, Shannon. "'Among psalms to fynde a cleer sentence': John Lydgate, Eleanor Hull, and the Art of Vernacular Exegesis." *New Medieval Literatures* 10 (2008): 161–89.
Geary, Patrick. "What Happened to Latin?" *Speculum* 84 (2009): 859–73.
Geiger, Ari. "A Student and an Opponent: Nicholas of Lyra and His Jewish Sources." In *Nicolas de Lyre*, ed. Gilbert Dahan, 167–203. Paris: Institut d'Études Augustiniennes, 2011.
Gellrich, Jesse. *Discourse and Dominion in the Fourteenth Century: Oral Contexts of Writing in Philosophy, Politics, and Poetry*. Princeton: Princeton University Press, 1995.
Ghosh, Kantik. "'And so it is licly to men': Probabilism and Hermeneutics in Wycliffite Discourse." *Review of English Studies*, forthcoming.
 "Logic, Scepticism, and 'Heresy' in Early Fifteenth-Century Europe: Oxford, Vienna, Constance." In *Uncertain Knowledge: Scepticism, Relativism, and Doubt in the Middle Ages*, ed. Dallas Denery et al., 261–83. Turnhout: Brepols, 2014.
 "The Prologues." In *The Wycliffite Bible*, ed. Elizabeth Solopova, 162–82. Leiden: Brill, 2017.
 "University Learning, Theological Method, and Heresy in Fifteenth-Century England." In *Religious Controversy in Europe, 1378–1536: Textual Transmission and Networks of Readership*, ed. Michael Van Dussen and Pavel Soukup, 289–313. Turnhout: Brepols, 2013.
 The Wycliffite Heresy: Authority and the Interpretation of Texts. Cambridge: Cambridge University Press, 2002.
Gibson, Margaret T. "Carolingian Glossed Psalters." In *The Early Medieval Bible: Its Production, Decoration, and Use*, ed. Richard Gameson, 78–100. Cambridge: Cambridge University Press, 1994.
 "The Place of the *Glossa ordinaria* in Medieval Exegesis." In *Ad Litteram: Authoritative Texts and their Medieval Readers*, ed. Mark D. Jordan and Kent Emery, 5–27. Notre Dame: University of Notre Dame Press, 1992.
 "The Twelfth-Century Glossed Bible." *Studia Patristica* 23 (1989): 232–44.
Gillespie, Vincent. "Authorship." In *A Handbook of Middle English Studies*, ed. Marion Turner, 137–54. Chichester: Wiley-Blackwell, 2013.
 "Fatherless Books: Authorship, Attribution, and Orthodoxy in Later Medieval England." In *The Pseudo-Bonaventuran Lives of Christ: Exploring the Middle English Tradition*, ed. Ian Johnson and Allan Westphall, 151–96. Turnhout: Brepols, 2013.
 Looking in Holy Books: Essays on Late Medieval Religious Writing in England. Turnhout: Brepols, 2011.
 "The Nearly Man: 'Saint' Richard Rolle and His Textual Cult." In *Saints and Cults in Medieval England: Proceedings of the 2015 Harlaxton Symposium*, ed. Susan Powell, 156–71. Donington: Shaun Tyas, 2017.
 "Vernacular Theology." In *Middle English*, ed. Paul Strohm, 401–420. Oxford: Oxford University Press, 2007.
Giraud, Cédric. *Per Verba Magistri: Anselme de Laon et son école au XIIe siècle*. Turnhout: Brepols, 2010.

Glunz, Hans Herman. *The History of the Vulgate in England from Alcuin to Roger Bacon, Being an Inquiry into the Text of Some English Manuscripts of the Vulgate Gospels.* Cambridge: Cambridge University Press, 1933.

Gorman, Michael. "The Canon of Bede's Works and the World of Ps.-Bede." *Revue bénédictine* 111 (2001): 399–445.

Gradon, Pamela. "Wyclif's *Postilla* and His Sermons." In *Text and Controversy from Wyclif to Bale: Essays in Honour of Anne Hudson*, ed. Helen Barr and Ann Hutchison, 67–77. Turnhout: Brepols, 2005.

Griffiths, Jane. *Diverting Authorities: Experimental Glossing Practices in Manuscript and Print.* Oxford: Oxford University Press, 2014.

Grondeux, Anne. *À l'école de Cassiodore: Les figures "Extravagantes" dans la tradition occidentale.* Turnhout: Brepols, 2013.

Gross-Diaz, Theresa. *The Psalms Commentary of Gilbert of Poitiers: From Lectio Divina to the Lecture Room.* Leiden: Brill, 1996.

Gullick, Michael. "The Hand of Symeon of Durham: Further Observations on the Durham Martyrology Scribe." In *Symeon of Durham: Historian of Durham and the North*, ed. David Rollason, 14–31. Stamford: Shaun Tyas, 1998.

Gustafson, Kevin. "Richard Rolle's *English Psalter* and the Making of a Lollard Text." *Viator* 33 (2002): 294–309.

Hamesse, Jacqueline. "Les autographes à l'époque scolastique: Approche terminologique et méthodologique." In *Gli autografi medievali: problemi paleografici e filologici*, ed. Paolo Chiesa and Lucia Pinelli, 179–205. Spoleto: CISAM, 1994.

——— "The Scholastic Model of Reading." In *A History of Reading in the West*, ed. Guglielmo Cavallo and Roger Chartier, tr. Lydia Cochrane, 103–119. Amherst: University of Massachusetts Press, 1999.

Hamesse, Jacqueline, ed., with Slawomir Szyller. *Repertorium Initiorum Manuscriptorum Latinorum Medii Aevi.* 4 vols. Louvain-la-Neuve: Fédération internationale des instituts d'études médiévales, 2007–2010.

Hamilton, Mary Grace. "John Bale and His *Anglorum Heliades*." Ph.D. diss., University of California, Berkeley, 1931.

Hammerich, Louis. *The Beginning of the Strife between Richard Fitzralph and the Mendicants: With an Edition of His Autobiographical Prayer and His Proposition "Unusquisque."* Copenhagen: Levin and Munksgaard, 1938.

Hanna, Ralph. *A Descriptive Catalogue of the Western Medieval Manuscripts of St. John's College, Oxford.* Oxford: Oxford University Press, 2002.

——— "The Difficulty of Ricardian Prose Translation: The Case of the Lollards." *Modern Language Quarterly* 51 (1992): 319–40.

——— "English Biblical Texts before Lollardy and Their Fate." In *Lollards and Their Influence in Late Medieval England*, ed. Fiona Somerset et al., 141–53. Woodbridge: Boydell and Brewer, 2003.

——— *The English Manuscripts of Richard Rolle: A Descriptive Catalogue.* Exeter: University of Exeter Press, 2010.

——— "Lichfield." In *Europe: A Literary History, 1348–1418*, ed. David Wallace, I, 279–84. 2 vols. Oxford: Oxford University Press, 2016.

"Making Miscellaneous Manuscripts in Fifteenth-Century England: The Case of Sloane 2275." *Journal of the Early Book Society* 18 (2015): 1–28.

Pursuing History: Middle English Manuscripts and Their Texts. Stanford: Stanford University Press, 1996.

"Richard Rolle's *Incendium Amoris:* A Prospectus for a Future Editor." *Journal of Medieval Latin* 26 (2016): 227–61.

"Robert Holcot and *De vetula:* Beyond Smalley's Assessment." In *Medieval Literary Theory and Criticism: Beyond Scholasticism*, ed. Ardis Butterfield, Ian Johnson, and Andrew Kraebel. Cambridge: Cambridge University Press, forthcoming.

"Rolle and Related Works." In *A Companion to Middle English Prose*, ed. A. S. G. Edwards, 19–31. Cambridge: D. S. Brewer, 1994.

"Sir Thomas Berkeley and His Patronage." *Speculum* 64 (1989): 878–916.

"The Transmission of Richard Rolle's Latin Works." *The Library* 7th series 14 (2013): 313–33.

"Yorkshire Writers." *Proceedings of the British Academy* 121 (2003): 91–109.

Hanna, Ralph, Tony Hunt, R. G. Keightley, Alastair Minnis, and Nigel Palmer. "Latin Commentary Tradition and Vernacular Literature." In *The Cambridge History of Literary Criticism,* II, *The Middle Ages*, ed. Alastair Minnis and Ian Johnson, 363–421. Cambridge: Cambridge University Press, 2005.

Hargreaves, Henry. "Popularising Biblical Scholarship: The Role of the Wycliffite Glossed Gospels." In *The Bible and Medieval Culture*, ed. W. Lourdaux and D. Verhelst, 171–89. Leuven: Leuven University Press, 1979.

Harkins, Franklin. *Reading and the Work of Restoration: History and Scripture in the Theology of Hugh of St. Victor.* Toronto: PIMS, 2009.

Harris, Jennifer. "The Bible and the Meaning of History in the Middle Ages." In *The Practice of the Bible in the Middle Ages: Production, Reception, and Performance in Western Christianity*, ed. Susan Boynton and Diane Reilly, 84–104. New York: Columbia University Press, 2011.

Harvey, Margaret. "English Views on the Reforms to be Undertaken in the General Councils (1400–1418), with Special Reference to the Proposals made by Richard Ullerston." D.Phil. diss., University of Oxford, 1964.

Lay Religious Life in Late Medieval Durham. Woodbridge: Boydell, 2006.

Hasenohr, Geneviève. "Bibles et psautiers." In *Mise en page et mise en texte du livre manuscrit*, ed. Henri-Jean Martin and Jean Vezin, 317–22. Paris: Éditions du Cercle de la Librairie – Promodis, 1990.

Havens, Jill. "'As Englishe is comoun langage to oure puple': Lollards and Their Imagined 'English' Community." In *Imagining a Medieval English Nation*, ed. Kathy Lavezzo, 96–128. Minneapolis: University of Minnesota Press, 2004.

Hazard, Mark. *The Literal Sense and the Gospel of John in Late Medieval Commentary and Literature.* New York: Routledge, 2002.

Hobbins, Daniel. *Authorship and Publicity before Print: Jean Gerson and the Transformation of Late Medieval Learning.* Philadelphia: University of Pennsylvania Press, 2009.

Holmes, Jeremy. "Aquinas' *Lectura in Matthaeum*." In *Aquinas on Scripture: An Introduction to His Biblical Commentaries*, ed. Thomas Weinandy et al., 73–97. London: Clark, 2005.

Holsinger, Bruce. *The Premodern Condition: Medievalism and the Making of Theory*. Chicago: Chicago University Press, 2005.

Horner, Patrick. "Benedictines and Preaching the *Pastoralia* in Late Medieval England: A Preliminary Inquiry." In *Medieval Monastic Preaching*, ed. Carolyn Muessig, 279–92. Leiden: Brill, 1998.

Horstman, Carl. *Yorkshire Writers: Richard Rolle of Hampole, an English Father of the Church, and His Followers*. 2 vols. New York: Macmillan, 1895–96.

Hudson, Anne. "Books and Their Survival: The Case of English Manuscripts of Wyclif's Latin Works." In *Medieval Manuscripts, Their Makers and Users: A Special Issue of Viator in Honor of Richard and Mary Rouse*, ed. Henry Ansgar Kelly, 225–44. Turnhout: Brepols, 2011.

———. "The Development of Wyclif's *Summa theologie*." In *John Wyclif: Logica, politica, teologia*, ed. Mariateresa Fumagalli et al., 57–70. Florence: SISMEL, 2003.

———. *Doctors in English: A Study of the Wycliffite Gospel Commentaries*. Liverpool: Liverpool University Press, 2015.

———. "Five Problems in Wycliffite Texts and a Suggestion." *MÆ* 80 (2011): 301–324.

———. *Lollards and Their Books*. London: Hambledon, 1985.

———. "The Origin and Textual Tradition of the Wycliffite Bible." In *The Wycliffite Bible*, ed. Elizabeth Solopova, 133–61. Leiden: Brill, 2017.

———. *The Premature Reformation: Wycliffite Texts and Lollard History*. Oxford: Clarendon, 1988.

———. "Two Notes on the Wycliffite *Glossed Gospels*." In *Philologia Anglica: Essays Presented to Professor Yoshio Terasawa on the Occasion of His Sixtieth Birthday*, ed. Kinshiro Oshitari et al., 379–84. Tokyo: Kenkyusha, 1988.

———. "The Variable Text." In *Crux and Controversy in Middle English Textual Criticism*, ed. Alastair Minnis, 49–60. Cambridge: D. S. Brewer, 1992.

———. "*Visio Baleii*: An Early Literary Historian." In *The Long Fifteenth Century: Essays for Douglas Gray*, ed. Helen Cooper and Sally Mapstone, 313–29. Oxford: Clarendon, 1997.

Hunt, R. W. "The Introductions to the *Artes* in the Twelfth Century." In *Studia Mediaevalia in honorem admodum Reverendi Patris Raymundi Josephi Martin*, 85–112. Bruges: De Tempel, [1948].

———. "The Library of Robert Grosseteste." In *Oxford Studies Presented to Daniel Callus*, 121–45. Oxford: Clarendon, 1964.

———. "Manuscripts Containing the Indexing Symbols of Robert Grosseteste." *Bodleian Library Record* 4 (1952–53): 241–54.

Hunt, Simon. "An Edition of Tracts in Favour of Scriptural Translation and of Some Texts Connected with Lollard Vernacular Biblical Scholarship." D.Phil. diss., University of Oxford, 1994.

Ingham, Patricia Clare. *The Medieval New: Ethical Ambivalence in an Age of Innovation*. Philadelphia: University of Pennsylvania Press, 2015.
James, Montague Rhodes. *A Descriptive Catalogue of the Western Manuscripts in the Library of Christ's College, Cambridge*. Cambridge: Cambridge University Press, 1905.
James, Montague Rhodes, and Claude Jenkins. *A Descriptive Catalogue of the Manuscripts in the Library of Lambeth Palace*. 5 parts in 2 vols. Cambridge: Cambridge University Press, 2011.
Johnson, Ian. *The Middle English Life of Christ: Academic Discourse, Translation, and Vernacular Theology*. Turnhout: Brepols, 2013.
Karnes, Michelle. "Nicholas Love and Medieval Meditations on Christ." *Speculum* 82 (2007): 380–408.
Kastan, David Scott. "Naughty Printed Books." In *Cultural Reformations: Medieval and Renaissance in Literary History*, ed. Brian Cummings and James Simpson, 287–302. Oxford: Oxford University Press, 2010.
Kelly, Henry Ansgar. *The Middle English Bible: A Reassessment*. Philadelphia: University of Pennsylvania Press, 2016.
Kennedy, Kathleen. *The Courtly and Commercial Art of the Wycliffite Bible*. Turnhout: Brepols, 2014.
Ker, Neil R. *Books, Collectors, and Libraries: Studies in the Medieval Heritage*. Edited by Andrew G. Watson. London: Hambledon, 1985.
  Medieval Libraries of Great Britain: A List of Surviving Books. 2nd edn. London: Offices of the Royal Historical Society, 1964.
  "The Provision of Books." In *The History of the University of Oxford*, III, *The Collegiate University*, ed. James McConica, 441–519. Oxford: Oxford University Press, 1986.
Ker, N. R., with I. C. Cunningham and A. G. Watson. *Medieval Manuscripts in British Libraries*. 5 vols. Oxford: Clarendon, 1969–2002.
King, John. *English Reformation Literature: The Tudor Origins of the Protestant Tradition*. Princeton: Princeton University Press, 1982.
Kleinhans, Arduin. "Heinrich v. Cossey OFM: ein Psalmen-Erklärer des 14. Jahrhunderts." In *Miscellanea biblica et orientalia R. P. Athanasio Miller . . . oblata*, ed. Adalbertus Metzinger, 239–53. Rome: Herder, 1951.
  "Nicolaus Trivet OP Psalmorum Interpres." *Angelicum* 20 (1943): 219–36.
Klepper, Deeana Copeland. *The Insight of Unbelievers: Nicholas of Lyra and Christian Reading of Jewish Text in the Later Middle Ages*. Philadelphia: University of Pennsylvania Press, 2007.
Kraebel, Andrew. "Chaucer's Bibles: Late Medieval Biblicism and Compilational Form." *JMEMS* 47 (2017): 437–60.
  "English Hebraism and Hermeneutic History: The Psalter Prologues and Epilogues of Henry Cossey OFM." *Journal of Medieval Latin* 30 (2020): forthcoming.
  "A Further Book Annotated by Stephan Batman, with New Material for His Biography." *The Library* 7th series 16 (2015): 458–66.
  "The Inspired Commentator: Theories of Interpretive Authority in the Writings of Richard Rolle." In *Medieval Literary Theory and Criticism:*

Beyond Scholasticism, ed. Ardis Butterfield, Ian Johnson, and Andrew Kraebel. Cambridge: Cambridge University Press, forthcoming.

"John of Rheims and the Psalter Commentary Attributed to Ivo II of Chartres." *Revue bénédictine* 122 (2012): 252–93.

"Latin Manuscripts of Richard Rolle at the University of Illinois." *JEGP* 119 (2020): forthcoming.

"The Manuscript Tradition of Richard Ullerston's *Expositio canticorum Scripturae*." *The Mediaeval Journal* 3.1 (2013): 49–82.

"Middle English Gospel Glosses and the Translation of Exegetical Authority." *Traditio* 69 (2013): 49–82.

"Modes of Authorship and the Making of Medieval English Literature." In *The Cambridge Handbook of Literary Authorship*, ed. Ingo Berensmeyer et al., 98–114. Cambridge: Cambridge University Press, 2019.

"Poetry and Commentary in the Medieval School of Rheims: Reading Virgil, Reading David." In *Interpreting Scripture in Judaism, Christianity, and Islam: Overlapping Inquiries*, ed. Mordechai Cohen and Adele Berlin, 227–48. Cambridge: Cambridge University Press, 2016.

"Prophecy and Poetry in the Psalms Commentaries of St. Bruno and the Pre-Scholastics." *Sacris Erudiri* 50 (2011): 413–59.

"Rolle Reassembled: Booklet Production, Single-Author Anthologies, and the Making of Bodley 861." *Speculum* 94 (2019): 959–1005.

"The Use of Richard Rolle's *Latin Psalter* in Richard Ullerston's *Expositio canticorum Scripturae*." *MÆ* 81 (2012): 139–44.

Kraus, Christina Shuttleworth. "Introduction: Reading Commentaries/Commentaries as Reading." In *The Classical Commentary: Histories, Practices, Theory*, ed. Roy Gibson and Christina Shuttleworth Kraus, 1–27. Leiden: Brill, 2002.

Kraus, Christina Shuttleworth, and Christopher Stray. "Form and Content." In *Classical Commentaries: Explorations in a Scholarly Genre*, ed. Christina Kraus and Christopher Stray, 1–18. Oxford: Oxford University Press, 2016.

Krey, Philip. "The Apocalypse Commentary of 1329: Problems in Church History." In *Nicholas of Lyra: The Senses of Scripture*, ed. Philip Krey and Lesley Smith, 267–88. Leiden: Brill, 2000.

"Many Readers but Few Followers: The Fate of Nicholas of Lyra's 'Apocalypse Commentary' in the Hands of His Late-Medieval Admirers." *Church History* 64 (1995): 185–201.

Krey, Philip, and Lesley Smith. "Introduction." In *Nicholas of Lyra: The Senses of Scripture*, ed. Philip Krey and Lesley Smith, 1–18. Leiden: Brill, 2000.

Kuczynski, Michael. *Prophetic Song: The Psalms as Moral Discourse in Late Medieval England*. Philadelphia: University of Pennsylvania Press, 1995.

"Rolle among the Reformers: Orthodoxy and Heterodoxy in Wycliffite Copies of Richard Rolle's *English Psalter*." In *Mysticism and Spirituality in Medieval England*, ed. William Pollard and Robert Boenig, 177–202. Woodbridge: D. S. Brewer, 1997.

Lagorio, Valerie, and Michael Sargent. "English Mystical Writings." In *A Manual of the Writings in Middle English, 1050–1500*, ed. Jonathan Severs et al., IX, 3049–3137 and 3405–3471. New Haven: Connecticut Academy of Arts and Sciences, 1967–2005.

Lahey, Stephen. *John Wyclif*. Oxford: Oxford University Press, 2009.

Late Medieval Devotional Compilations in England. Edited by Marleen Cré et al. Turnhout: Brepols, forthcoming.

Lawton, David. "The Bible." In *The Oxford History of Literary Translation in English*, I, *To 1550*, ed. Roger Ellis, 193–233. Oxford: Oxford University Press, 2008.

——— "Englishing the Bible, 1066–1549." In *The Cambridge History of Medieval English Literature*, ed. David Wallace, 454–82. Cambridge: Cambridge University Press, 1999.

——— *Faith, Text, and History: The Bible in English*. Charlottesville: University Press of Virginia, 1990.

——— "The Psalms as Public Interiorities: Eleanor Hull's Voices." In *The Psalms and Medieval English Literature: From Conversion to the Reformation*, ed. Tamara Atkin and Francis Leneghan, 298–317. Woodbridge: Boydell, 2017.

——— *Voice in Later Medieval English Literature: Public Interiorities*. Oxford: Oxford University Press, 2017.

Leclercq, Jean. "Commentary on Biblical and Ecclesiastical Literature from Antiquity to the Twelfth Century." Translated by A. B. Kraebel. *The Mediaeval Journal* 2.2 (2012): 27–53.

——— *The Love of Learning and the Desire for God: A Study of Monastic Culture*. Translated by Catherine Misrahi. New York: Fordham University Press, 1982.

Lerer, Seth. *Chaucer and His Readers: Imagining the Author in Late Medieval England*. Princeton: Princeton University Press, 1993.

Levy, Ian Christopher. *Holy Scripture and the Quest for Authority at the End of the Middle Ages*. Notre Dame: University of Notre Dame Press, 2012.

——— *John Wyclif's Theology of the Eucharist: Revised and Expanded Edition of Scriptural Logic, Real Presence, and the Parameters of Orthodoxy*. Milwaukee: Marquette University Press, 2014.

Little, A. G. *Franciscan Papers, Lists, and Documents*. Manchester: Manchester University Press, 1943.

Logan, F. Donald. *University Education of the Parochial Clergy in Medieval England: The Lincoln Diocese, c. 1300–c. 1350*. Toronto: PIMS, 2014.

Madan, Falconer, H. H. E. Craster, Richard Hunt, and P. D. Record. *A Summary Catalogue of Western Manuscripts in the Bodleian Library at Oxford*. 7 vols. Oxford: Clarendon, 1895–1953.

Madigan, Kevin. "Lyra on the Gospel of Matthew." In *Nicholas of Lyra: The Senses of Scripture*, ed. Philip Krey and Lesley Smith, 195–222. Leiden: Brill, 2000.

——— *Olivi and the Interpretation of Matthew in the High Middle Ages*. Notre Dame: University of Notre Dame Press, 2003.

Marsden, Richard. "The Bible in English." In *The New Cambridge History of the Bible*, II, *From 600 to 1450*, ed. Richard Marsden and E. Ann Matter, 217–38. Cambridge: Cambridge University Press, 2012.

Matter, E. Ann. "The Legacy of the School of Auxerre: Glossed Bibles, School Rhetoric, and the Universal Gilbert." *Temas Medievales* 14 (2006): 85–98.

McDermott, Ryan. *Tropologies: Ethics and Invention in England, c. 1350–1600*. Notre Dame: University of Notre Dame Press, 2016.

McGinn, Bernard. *The Varieties of Vernacular Mysticism, 1350–1550*. New York: Crossroad, 2012.

McIntosh, Angus, M. L. Samuels, and Michael Benskin. *A Linguistic Atlas of Late Mediaeval English*. 4 vols. Aberdeen: Aberdeen University Press, 1986.

Minnis, Alastair. "'Authorial Intention' and 'Literal Sense' in the Exegetical Theories of Richard Fitzralph and John Wyclif: An Essay in the Medieval History of Biblical Hermeneutics." *Proceedings of the Royal Irish Academy* 75c (1975): 1–31.

"Figuring the Letter: Making Sense of *Sensus Litteralis* in Late-Medieval Christian Exegesis." In *Interpreting Scripture in Judaism, Christianity, and Islam: Overlapping Inquiries*, ed. Mordechai Cohen and Adele Berlin, 159–82. Cambridge: Cambridge University Press, 2016.

Magister Amoris: The Roman de la Rose and Vernacular Hermeneutics. Oxford: Oxford University Press, 2001.

Medieval Theory of Authorship: Scholastic Literary Attitudes in the Later Middle Ages. Reissued 2nd edn. Philadelphia: University of Pennsylvania Press, 2009.

"*Quadruplex sensus, multiplex modus*: Scriptural Sense and Mode in Medieval Scholastic Exegesis." In *Interpretation and Allegory: Antiquity to the Modern Period*, ed. Jon Whitman, 231–56. Leiden: Brill, 2000.

"Tobit's Dog and the Dangers of Literalism: William Woodford OFM as Critic of Wycliffite Exegesis." In *Defenders and Critics of Franciscan Life: Essays in Honor of John V. Fleming*, ed. Michael Cusato and G. Geltner, 41–52. Leiden: Brill, 2009.

Translations of Authority in Medieval English Literature: Valuing the Vernacular. Cambridge: Cambridge University Press, 2009.

Minton, Gretchen. "John Bale's *Image of Both Churches* and the English Paraphrase on Revelation." In *Holy Scripture Speaks: The Production and Reception of Erasmus' Paraphrases on the New Testament*, ed. Hilmar Pabel and Mark Vessey, 291–312. Toronto: University of Toronto Press, 2002.

"'Suffer me not to be separated / And let my cry come unto thee': John Bale's Apocalypse and the Exilic Imagination." *Reformation* 15 (2010): 83–97.

Moessner, Lilo. "Translation Strategies in Middle English: The Case of the Wycliffite Bible." *Poetica* 55 (2001): 123–54.

Morard, Martin. "À propos du *Commentaire des Psaumes* de saint Thomas d'Aquin." *Revue Thomiste* 96 (1996): 653–70.

Morey, James. *Book and Verse: A Guide to Middle English Biblical Literature*. Urbana: University of Illinois Press, 2000.

Moyes, Malcolm. "The Manuscripts and Early Printed Editions of Richard Rolle's *Expositio super novem lectiones mortuorum*." In *The Medieval Mystical Tradition in England: Papers Read at Dartington Hall*, ed. Marion Glasscoe, 81–103. Cambridge: D. S. Brewer, 1984.

Richard Rolle's Expositio super novem lectiones mortuorum: An Introduction and Contribution towards a Critical Edition. 2 vols. Salzburg: Institut für Anglistik und Amerikanistik, Universität Salzburg, 1988.

Mynors, R. A. B. "The Latin Classics Known to Boston of Bury." In *Fritz Saxl, 1890–1948: A Volume of Memorial Essays from His Friends in England*, ed. D. J. Gordon, 199–217. London: Nelson, 1957.

Nicolas de Lyre, Franciscain du XIVe siècle, exégète et théologien. Edited by Gilbert Dahan. Paris: Institut d'Études Augustiniennes, 2011.

Nicholas of Lyra: The Senses of Scripture. Edited by Philip Krey and Lesley Smith. Leiden: Brill, 2000.

Norton, David. *A History of the Bible as Literature.* 2 vols. Cambridge: Cambridge University Press, 1993.

Ocker, Christopher. *Biblical Poetics before Humanism and Reformation.* Cambridge: Cambridge University Press, 2002.

Otter, Monika. "Entrances and Exits: Performing the Psalms in Goscelin's *Liber confortatorius*." *Speculum* 83 (2008): 283–302.

Parkes, Malcolm B. "Layout and Presentation of the Text." In *The Cambridge History of the Book in Britain,* II, *1100–1400,* ed. Nigel Morgan and Rodney Thomson, 55–74. Cambridge: Cambridge University Press, 2008.

Pause and Effect: An Introduction to the History of Punctuation in the West. Berkeley: University of California Press, 1993.

"The Provision of Books." In *The History of the University of Oxford,* II, *Late Medieval Oxford,* ed. Jeremy Catto and Ralph Evans, 407–83. Oxford: Clarendon, 1992.

Scribes, Scripts, and Readers: Studies in the Communication, Presentation, and Dissemination of Medieval Texts. London: Hambledon, 1991.

Their Hands before Our Eyes: A Closer Look at Scribes. Aldershot: Ashgate, 2008.

Partridge, Stephen. "Glosses in the Manuscripts of Chaucer's *Canterbury Tales*: An Edition and Commentary." Ph.D. diss., Harvard University, 1992.

Peikola, Matti. "Tables of Lections in Manuscripts of the Wycliffite Bible." In *Form and Function in the Late Medieval Bible,* ed. Eyal Poleg and Laura Light, 351–78. Leiden: Brill, 2013.

Pfaff, Richard. *The Liturgy in Medieval England: A History.* Cambridge: Cambridge University Press, 2009.

Piper, A. J. "The Monks of Durham and the Study of Scripture." In *The Culture of Medieval English Monasticism,* ed. James Clark, 86–103. Woodbridge: Boydell, 2007.

Probable Truth: Editing Medieval Texts from Britain in the Twenty-First Century. Edited by Vincent Gillespie and Anne Hudson. Turnhout: Brepols, 2013.

Rabil, Albert. "Erasmus's *Paraphrases of the New Testament*." In *Essays on the Works of Erasmus,* ed. Richard DeMolen, 145–61. New Haven: Yale University Press, 1978.

Reinhardt, Klaus. "Les controverses autour de la *Postille* au XVe siècle." In *Nicolas de Lyre*, ed. Gilbert Dahan, 269-79. Paris: Institut d'Études Augustiniennes, 2011.

Renevey, Denis. *Language, Self, and Love: Hermeneutics in the Writings of Richard Rolle and the Commentaries on the Song of Songs*. Cardiff: University of Wales Press, 2001.

——— "The Name above Names: The Devotion to the Name of Jesus from Richard Rolle to Walter Hilton's *Scale of Perfection I*." In *The Medieval Mystical Tradition: England, Ireland, and Wales*, ed. Marion Glasscoe, 103–21. Cambridge: D. S. Brewer, 1999.

——— "Richard Rolle." In *Approaching Medieval English Anchoritic and Mystical Texts*, ed. Dee Dyas et al., 63–74. Cambridge: D. S. Brewer, 2005.

Robson, J. A. *Wyclif and the Oxford Schools: The Relation of the Summa de Ente to Scholastic Debates at Oxford in the Later Fourteenth Century*. Cambridge: Cambridge University Press, 1961.

Rouse, Mary, and Richard Rouse. *Authentic Witnesses: Approaches to Medieval Texts and Manuscripts*. Notre Dame: University of Notre Dame Press, 1991.

——— "*Ordinatio* and *Compilatio* Revisited." In *Ad Litteram: Authoritative Texts and their Medieval Readers*, ed. Mark D. Jordan and Kent Emery, 113–34. Notre Dame: University of Notre Dame Press, 1992.

Ryan, Thomas. *Thomas Aquinas as Reader of the Psalms*. Notre Dame: University of Notre Dame Press, 2000.

Sandler, Lucy Freeman. *Omne Bonum: A Fourteenth-Century Encyclopedia of Universal Knowledge*. London: Harvey Miller, 1996.

Sargent, Michael. "Contemporary Criticism of Richard Rolle." In *Kartäusermystik und -mystiker: dritter internationaler Kongress über die Kartäusergeschichte und -spiritualität*, ed. James Hogg, I, 160–205. Analecta Cartusiana, 55.1. Salzburg: Institut für Anglistik und Amerikanistik, Universität Salzburg, 1981.

Scase, Wendy. "Patronage Symbolism and 'Sowlehele.'" In *The Making of the Vernon Manuscript: The Production and Contexts of Oxford, Bodleian Library MS Eng. Poet. a. 1*, ed. Wendy Scase, 231–45. Turnhout: Brepols, 2013.

Scott, Kathleen. *Later Gothic Manuscripts, 1390–1490*. 2 vols. London: Harvey Miller, 1996.

Shields, Bruce Philbrook. "A Critical Edition of Selections from Nicholas Trevet's *Commentarius literalis in Psalterium iuxta Hebreos sancti Hieronymi*." Ph.D. diss., Rutgers University, 1970.

Simpson, James. *Burning to Read: English Fundamentalism and its Reformation Opponents*. Cambridge, MA: Belknap, 2007.

——— "Interrogation Over." *PMLA* 132 (2017): 377–83.

Smalley, Beryl. "The Bible in the Medieval Schools." In *The Cambridge History of the Bible*, II, *The West from the Fathers to the Reformation*, ed. G. W. H. Lampe, 197–220. Cambridge: Cambridge University Press, 1969.

——— "Les commentaires bibliques de l'époque romane: glose ordinaire et gloses périmées." *Cahiers de Civilisation Médiévale* 4 (1961): 15–22.

"A Commentary on the *Hebraica* by Herbert of Bosham." *Recherches de Théologie ancienne et médiévale* 18 (1951): 29–65.

English Friars and Antiquity in the Early Fourteenth Century. Oxford: Blackwell, 1960.

The Gospels in the Schools, c. 1100–c. 1280. London: Hambledon, 1985.

Hebrew Scholarship among Christians in XIIIth–Century England, as Illustrated by Some Hebrew-Latin Psalters. London: Shapiro, Vallentine and Co., 1939.

"John Wyclif's *Postilla super totam Bibliam*." *Bodleian Library Record* 4 (1952–53): 186–205.

Medieval Exegesis of Wisdom Literature: Essays. Edited by Roland Murphy. Atlanta: Scholars Press, 1986.

"Problems of Exegesis in the Fourteenth Century." In *Antike und Orient im Mittelalter: Vorträge der kölner Mediaevistentagungen, 1956–1959*, ed. Paul Wilpert with Willehad Eckert, 266–74. Berlin: de Gruyter, 1962.

"A Quotation from John Ridevall on *De civitate Dei* by William Woodford." *MÆ* 33 (1964): 21–25.

Studies in Medieval Thought and Learning from Abelard to Wyclif. London: Hambledon, 1981.

The Study of the Bible in the Middle Ages. 3rd rev. edn. Oxford: Blackwell, 1983.

"Thomas Waleys OP." *Archivum Fratrum Praedicatorum* 24 (1954): 50–107.

"Wyclif's *Postilla* on the Old Testament and His *Principium*." In *Oxford Studies Presented to Daniel Callus*, 253–96. Oxford: Clarendon, 1964.

Smith, Lesley. *The Glossa ordinaria: The Making of a Medieval Bible Commentary*. Leiden: Brill, 2009.

Snare, Gerald. "Reading Tyndale's Bibles." *JMEMS* 35 (2005): 290–325.

Solopova, Elizabeth. "Introduction: New Directions in Research on the First English Bible." In *The Wycliffite Bible*, ed. Elizabeth Solopova, 1–8. Leiden: Brill, 2017.

Manuscripts of the Wycliffite Bible in the Bodleian and Oxford College Libraries. Liverpool: Liverpool University Press, 2016.

Somerset, Fiona. *Feeling like Saints: Lollard Writings after Wyclif*. Ithaca: Cornell University Press, 2014.

"Professionalizing Translation at the Turn of the Fifteenth Century: Ullerston's *Determinacio*, Arundel's *Constitutiones*." In *The Vulgar Tongue: Medieval and Postmedieval Vernacularity*, ed. Fiona Somerset and Nicholas Watson, 145–57. University Park: Pennsylvania State University Press, 2003.

Stadler, H. M. "Textual and Literary Criticism and Hebrew Learning in English Old Testament Scholarship, as exhibited by Nicholas Trevet's *Expositio litteralis Psalterii* and by MS CCC (Oxf.) 11." M.Litt. thesis, University of Oxford, 1989.

Staley, Lynn. "The Penitential Psalms: Conversion and the Limits of Lordship." *JMEMS* 37 (2007): 221–69.

Stegmüller, Friedrich. *Repertorium Biblicum Medii Aevi*. 11 vols. Madrid: Instituto Francisco Suárez, 1940 [*recte* 1950]–80.

Steiner, Emily. "Compendious Genres: Higden, Trevisa, and the Medieval Encyclopedia." *Exemplaria* 27 (2015): 73–92.

Stock, Brian. *After Augustine: The Meditative Reader and the Text*. Philadelphia: University of Pennsylvania Press, 2001.

Sutherland, Annie. "Biblical Text and Spiritual Experience in the English Epistles of Richard Rolle." *Review of English Studies* ns 56 (2005): 695–711.

——— *English Psalms in the Middle Ages, 1300–1450*. Oxford: Oxford University Press, 2015.

——— "Performing the Penitential Psalms in the Middle Ages." In *Aspects of the Performative in Medieval Culture*, ed. Manuele Gragnolati and Almut Suerbaum, 15–37. Berlin: de Gruyter, 2010.

Szerwiniack, Olivier. "L'*Interpretatio nominum* d'Alcuin: Une source intermédiaire du début de l'*Expositio in Matthaeum* de Raban Maur." In *Raban Maur et son temps*, ed. Philippe Depreux et al., 251–58. Turnhout: Brepols, 2010.

Taylor, Andrew. "Readers and Manuscripts." In *The Oxford Handbook of Medieval Latin Literature*, ed. Ralph Hexter and David Townsend, 151–70. Oxford: Oxford University Press, 2012.

Thomson, Rodney. *A Descriptive Catalogue of the Medieval Manuscripts of Corpus Christi College, Oxford*. Cambridge: D. S. Brewer, 2011.

Thomson, S. Harrison. "Unnoticed MSS and Works of Wyclif." *Journal of Theological Studies* os 38 (1937): 139–48.

Thomson, Williell. *The Latin Writings of John Wyclyf: An Anotated Catalog*. Toronto: PIMS, 1983.

Turner, Denys. "Allegory in Christian Late Antiquity." In *The Cambridge Companion to Allegory*, ed. Rita Copeland and Peter Struck, 71–82. Cambridge: Cambridge University Press, 2010.

Turville-Petre, Thorlac. *England the Nation: Language, Literature, and National Identity, 1290–1340*. Oxford: Clarendon, 1995.

Van Dussen, Michael. "Richard Rolle's *Latin Psalter* in Central European Manuscripts." *MÆ* 87 (2018): 41–71.

Van Liere, Frans. *An Introduction to the Medieval Bible*. Cambridge: Cambridge University Press, 2014.

Vessey, Mark. "The Tongue and the Book: Erasmus' *Paraphrases on the New Testament* and the Arts of Scripture." In *Holy Scripture Speaks: The Production and Reception of Erasmus' Paraphrases on the New Testament*, ed. Hilmar Pabel and Mark Vessey, 29–58. Toronto: University of Toronto Press, 2002.

Von Nolcken, Christina. "Lay Literacy, the Democratization of God's Law, and the Lollards." In *The Bible as Book: The Manuscript Tradition*, ed. John Sharpe and Kimberly van Kampen, 177–95. London: British Library, 1998.

Wailes, Stephen. "Why Did Jesus Use Parables? The Medieval Discussion." *Medievalia et Humanistica* ns 13 (1985): 43–64.

Wakelin, Daniel. *Scribal Correction and Literary Craft: English Manuscripts, 1375–1510*. Cambridge: Cambridge University Press, 2014.

Waldron, Ronald. "Trevisa's Original Prefaces on Translation: A Critical Edition." In *Medieval English Studies Presented to George Kane*, ed. Edward Donald Kennedy et al., 285–99. Woodbridge: Boydell and Brewer, 1988.

Walmsley, Conrad. "Two Long Lost Works of William Woodford and Robert of Leicester." *Archivum Franciscanum Historicum* 46 (1953): 458–70.

Warner, J. Christopher. "John Bale: Bibliographer between Trithemius and the Four Horseman of the Apocalypse." *Reformation* 18 (2013): 36–47.

Waters, Claire. *Translating Clergie: Status, Education, and Salvation in Thirteenth-Century Vernacular Texts*. Philadelphia: University of Pennsylvania Press, 2016.

Watson, Nicholas. "Censorship and Cultural Change in Late Medieval England: Vernacular Theology, the Oxford Translation Debate, and Arundel's Constitutions of 1409." *Speculum* 70 (1995): 822–64.

"The Idea of Latinity." In *The Oxford Handbook of Medieval Latin Literature*, ed. Ralph Hexter and David Townsend, 124–48. Oxford: Oxford University Press, 2012.

Richard Rolle and the Invention of Authority. Cambridge: Cambridge University Press, 1991.

Wei, Ian. *Intellectual Culture in Medieval Paris: Theologians and the University, c. 1100–1330*. Cambridge: Cambridge University Press, 2012.

Wenzel, Siegfried. *Latin Sermon Collections from Later Medieval England: Orthodox Preaching in the Age of Wyclif*. Cambridge: Cambridge University Press, 2005.

Preachers, Poets, and the Early English Lyric. Princeton: Princeton University Press, 1986.

The Wycliffite Bible: Origin, History, and Interpretation. Edited by Elizabeth Solopova. Leiden: Brill, 2017.

Zieman, Katherine. "Compiling the Lyric: Richard Rolle, Textual Dynamism, and Devotional Song in London, British Library Additional MS 37049." In *Middle English Lyrics: New Readings of Short Poems*, ed. Julia Boffey and Christiania Whitehead, 158–73. Woodbridge: Boydell, 2018.

"The Perils of *Canor*: Mystical Authority, Alliteration, and Extragrammatical Meaning in Rolle, the *Cloud* Author, and Hilton." *Yearbook of Langland Studies* 22 (2008): 131–63.

Index of Manuscripts

Aberdeen, University Library MS 243: 250, and see Fig. 8
Alençon, Bibliothèque municipale MS 26: 203–4, 259, and see the source notes to the text edited in Appendix C
Cambridge, Christ's College MS 11: 42–43, 45–49, 71, 225, 228, 246, and see Fig. 3
Cambridge, Corpus Christi College
   32: 271–72
   365: 193–200, 245
   387: 250
Cambridge, Fitzwilliam Museum MS McClean 133: 256, 261
Cambridge, Gonville and Caius College MS 803/807: 254
Cambridge, Pembroke College MS 262: 225
Cambridge, Trinity College
   B.1.15: 193–99, 245, 248
   B.1.38: 150–53, 156, 162, 261–62, and see Fig. 16
   B.2.12: 254
   B.15.12: 236, 242–43
   B.16.2: 234
   R.3.21: 220
Cambridge, University Library
   Additional 3470: see Fig. 2
   Additional 3571: 83–85, 241–44
   Dd.5.64: 248
   Ii.2.12: 136, 144–45, 204, 216–17, 221, 256–57, 260
   Ii.6.26: 133, 255
   Kk.2.9: 149–50, 261, and see Fig. 15
Dallas, Bridwell Library MS 7 (Protho B-01): 219
Dresden, Sächsische Landesbibliothek MS Od. 83: 264

Dublin, Trinity College
   76: 264
   242: 234
   244: 229
Durham, Cathedral, Dean and Chapter Library
   A.I.10: 137–39, 143–45, 203–16, 257–60
   A.II.9: 250–51
   A.III.7: 250
Edinburgh, National Library of Scotland
   6124: 261
   Advocates 18.7.21: 242
Edinburgh, University Library MS 331: 248
Glasglow, University Library MS General 223: 264
Hereford, Cathedral Library MS O.viii.1: 193–201, 245
Krakow, University Library MS 1628: 193–99
London, British Library
   Additional 10046: 161
   Additional 18299: 246
   Additional 28026: 149–50, 154, 156–58, 161, 256, 261
   Additional 37049: 91, 95, 129–32, 244, 255, and see Fig. 6
   Additional 41175: 153–54, 161, 166–67, 171, 221, 262–63, 266
   Arundel 158: 250, 271
   Arundel 254: 160, 264
   Cotton Faustina B. VI (part 2), 129–32, 255, and see Fig. 10
   Cotton Tiberius A. XV: 270–71
   Egerton 842: 136–39, 144, 256–58, 260–61, and see Fig. 12 and 13

Index of Manuscripts

Harley 1706: 220
Harley 1806: 250
Harley 3838: 268
Harley 4894: 260
Harley 6333: 264
Harley 7301: 268
Lansdowne 409: 254
Royal 2 D. xxviii: 192–99
Royal 2 E. vi: 225
Royal 3 B. xi: 223–24
Royal 6 E. vi: 255
Stowe 39: 129–32, 255, and see Fig. 11
London, Lambeth Palace Library MS 352: 193–200, 247

Manchester, John Rylands Library
    32826: 225
    English 5: 253
    English 77: 264

Newcastle upon Tyne, Public Library MS Th. 1687: 252

Oklahoma City, Green Collection MS 148: 250
Oxford, Balliol College
    36: 190
    80: 237, 242
Oxford, Bodleian Library
    Auctorium E inf. 6: 247
    Bodley 143: 147, 149, 153, 161, 168, 261–62, and see Fig. 14
    Bodley 243: 153–54, 161, 262
    Bodley 377: 265
    Bodley 716: 67–72, 75–79, 234–42, and see Fig. 5
    Bodley 738: 38–40, 227–28
    Bodley 861: 96–101, 111, 115, 193–202, 218, 245–47, 249–54
    Bodley 877: 271
    Bodley 953: 250, and see Fig. 7
    Digby 18: 220
    Douce 332: 220
    English Poetry a. 1 (Vernon): 129, 255
    Laudian miscellaneous 5: 143, 203–17, 259, 261
    Laudian miscellaneous 235: 158–66, 256, 261, 263–67
    Laudian miscellaneous 286: 103, 250
    Laudian miscellaneous 448: 250
    Lyell 20: 125–27, 254
    Rawlinson A. 389: 253, and see Fig. 9
    Selden supra 64: 183
    Tanner 1: 250

Oxford, Christ Church College MS Allestree L.4.1: 264
Oxford, Corpus Christi College
    193: 193–200, 245, 270–71
    236: 221
Oxford, Lincoln College MS Latin 119: 161
Oxford, Magdalen College
    Latin 52: 250
    Latin 55: 68–72, 78–79, 235–37, 240
    Latin 115: 193
Oxford, Oriel College MS 77: 232
Oxford, Pembroke College MS 39: 225
Oxford, St. John's College
    171: 59–64, 188–91, 230–33, and see Fig. 4
    195: 193–96, 199, 245, 247, 253
Oxford, University College
    64: 222
    96: 161, 264

Paris, Bibliothèque nationale de France
    Latin 431: 193–97, 199, 248
    Latin 11683: 224
    Latin 15588: 242
Peterborough, Cathedral Library MS 8: 264
Prague, Národní knihovna
    III.F.20: 234
    IV.E.1: 193
    V.D.4: 193–96, 199
    X.D.3: 193–96, 199

Rheims, Bibliothèque municipale MS 132: 226

San Marino, Henry E. Huntington Library
    HM 148: 14–15, 104–5, 110–12, 115–18, 222, 248–54, and see Fig. 1
    HM 268: 255
Shrewsbury, Shrewsbury School MS 25: 193–200, 202, 245

Troyes, Médiathèque du Grand Troyes
    227: 204, and see the source notes to the text edited in Appendix C
    488: 65, 254
    815: 190–91, 231–34
    988: 188

Urbana, University of Illinois
    106: 192–96, 199, 248–49
    144: 253

Vatican City, Bibliotheca Apostolica Vaticana MS Reginensis Latinus 320: 250

Vienna, Österreichische Nationalbibliothek
  1342: 68–70, 234–37, 239, 242
  4133: 250, 253

Windsor, Eton College MS 10: 250

Worcester, Cathedral Library
  F.158: 250
  F.172: 255

York, Minster Library MS XVI.D.2: 261

General Index

Abelard, Peter, 173
Albertus Magnus, 180, 182, 246
Alcuin, 180
Alexander of Hales, 25–26, 73
Allen, Hope Emily, 91, 95, 192
Ambrose of Milan, 24, 157–58, 265–66
Anselm of Canterbury, 204
Anselm of Laon, 143, 203–15
Apocalypse, anon. Middle English commentary on, 183, 220
Aquinas, Thomas, 16, 38, 51, 53
   Catena Aurea, 12, 163, 166–70, 263
   Psalter commentary, 31–32, 34, 43
   Quodlibetal Questions, 27
   Summa Theologiae, 27, 200
Aristotle, 34, 75
Augustine of Hippo, 24–25, 33, 44, 58–59, 67, 71, 79, 86–87, 137, 156–59, 164, 169, 173–74, 195–96, 225–27, 236, 246, 251
Augustine of Hippo (Ps.), *De laude Psalmorum*, 102, 104
Auriol, Peter, 60–61, 64, 66, 69, 81, 85, 87–89
Autographs, and authorial working copies, 15–16, 46–49, 70–72, 78–79, 83–84, 102

Baconthorpe, John, 84–86, 236, 242
Bale, John, 19, 176–87
   Anglorum Heliades, 178
   Catalogus and *Summarium*, 182–85
   Image of Bothe Churches, 178–82
Bartholomaeus Anglicus, 250
Basil of Caesarea, 248
Bede, 163, 180, 182–83, 238, 269
Benrath, Gustav, 57
Bernard of Clairvaux, 71, 156, 158, 236–37
Bernard of Trilia, 269
Betteridge, Thomas, 186
Bonaventure, 16, 26, 49–50, 73–74, 86
Bradwardine, Thomas, 129

Bryan, Jennifer, 169
Bühler, Curt, 192
Burgundio of Pisa, 105–6
Burnett, Charles, 106

Capgrave, John, 254
Cassiodorus, 24, 34, 44, 104, 226, 246, 249, 251
Catto, Jeremy, 83, 85, 87, 125
Chastising of God's Children, 12
Chaucer, Geoffrey, and marginal glosses, 240
Cholinus, Maternus, 204
Chrysostom, John (Ps.), *Opus Imperfectum*, 12, 67, 87, 156–58, 164–67, 239
Clark, John P. H., 192, 194, 199
Cole, Andrew, 172
Commentary
   and classicism, 34–37
   and devotional literature, 4, 11–13, 53, 94, 101, 111, 128–29, 136, 160, 175, 245, 249
   in Middle English, 4, 6–9, 103–22, 134–75, *and see* Translation, as commentary
   presentation in manuscript, 8, 13–16, 46–49, 60–62, 70–72, 83, 107–9, 113, 137–39, 144, 147–56, 159, 163, 188–91, 246, 257
   scholastic attitudes toward, 3–6, 9, 21–24, 28–29, 49–52, *and see* Senses of Scripture
   use of *quaestiones* in, 84–88
Constable, Giles, 146
Copeland, Rita, 155, 172
Cossey, Henry, 16, 29, 41–49, 51–53, 71, 90
Courtenay, William, 10, 90
Cummings, Brian, 185

Dahan, Gilbert, 23, 51
Deanesly, Margaret, 104

299

Dickens, A.G., 186
Divisio textus, 59–61, 69–70, 85–87, 96–97, 144, 240
Dobson, R. B., 146
Docking, Thomas, 73, 85
Dove, Mary, 56, 133
Doyle, Ian, 129
Durham, Benedictine monks of, 143–46

Erasmus, Desiderius, 178
Ezra (prophet), 39, 58–60, 64, 102, 227–28

Faber, Johannes, 192, 200

Gameson, Richard, 144
Geoffrey Babion, 143, 203–15
Ghosh, Kantik, 10, 55–57, 65–66, 173
Gilbert of Poitiers, *Media glosatura in Psalmos*, 61–66, 68, 169, 188–91
Gillespie, Vincent, 122, 142, 169
Glossa ordinaria, 11–12, 29, 53, 61, 87, 163, 169, 269
Glossed Gospels, 7, 12, 16, 19, 134–36, 147–75, 185
  and theories of exegetical authority, 158
  gradual development of, 150–54, 156–58, 161–63, 168
  organization of glosses, 164–67
  presentation in manuscript, 147–56, 158–59
  prologues as retrospective descriptions of, 154–56
  prologues as treatises on exegetical theory, 158–61
Gospels
  and parabolic language, 74, 76, 238–39
  and problem of authorial foreknowledge, 140–42
  historicist approaches to, 73–74, 76, 139, 141–42, 170–71, 238
  Monarchian prefaces to, 70, 80, 84, 236
  tropological approaches to, 74–82, 139–40, 142, 171
Gradon, Pamela, 68
Gratian, 261
Gregory the Great, 88, 156–59, 163–65, 167, 169, 227, 243
Grimestone, John, 242
Gross-Diaz, Theresa, 188–89
Grosseteste, Robert, 25, 46, 86, 158, 189
  Superscriptio Lincolniensis, 228
Gullick, Michael, 143

Haimo of Auxerre, 269
Hanna, Ralph, 94, 104, 145, 160, 198

Harvey, Margaret, 146
Hebrew, Latin exegetes' knowledge of, 28, 39, 41, 46–49, 52
Henry of Ghent, 50–51
Henry of Kirkestede, 21, 24–25, 27
Herbert of Bosham, 227
Higden, Ranulf, 270
Hilary of Poitiers, 24, 58, 137, 158, 265–66
Hilton, Walter, 117–18, 121–22
Hoffman, Melchior, 182
Holcot, Robert, 128
Holi Prophete Dauid, 133–34
Horstman, Carl, 91
Hrabanus Maurus, 25, 156–58, 164, 166, 171, 251, 265–66
Hudson, Anne, 14, 71, 122, 133–34, 154, 156, 161, 163
Hugh of St. Victor, 225
Hugh of Strasbourg, 249
Huguccio of Pisa, 106
Hunt, Richard, 23, 189

In þe Bigynnyng of Holi Chirche, 160
Innocent V, 269
Intentio auctoris, 23, 37–38, 42, 45, 52, 54, 66, 69–70, 81, 88–89, 97, 99, 101, 104, 142, 172, 204, 206, 211, 214, 230, 235–36, 241, 246 *and see Sensus auctoris*
Isidore of Seville, 86, 178

James, Thomas, 271
Jerome, 24, 59, 70, 88, 105, 156–58, 164–67, 169, 227–28, 261
John of Damascus, 200
Josephus, 25
Julian of Norwich, 81
Juvencus, 165

Kempe, Margery, 11–13
King, John, 180
Kirkeby, Margaret, 103
Klepper, Deeana Copeland, 53

Lawton, David, 8, 30
Levy, Ian Christopher, 56
Livy, 34–37
Love, Nicholas, 11–13
Lubac, Henri de, 21
Luke, anon. Middle English commentary on, 271–72
Luther, Martin, 178, 182

Maidstone, Richard, 118–22
Mark, anon. Middle English commentary on, 271–72

General Index

Materia libri, 17, 32, 42, 45, 49, 60–62, 64–65, 69–70, 91, 96–97, 104, 188–91, 214–15, 230–33
Matthew, anon. Middle English commentary on, 18–19, 136–47, 171, 174, 203–4, 216–17
Minnis, Alastair, 23, 55, 89
Misyn, Richard, 221
Modus procedendi, 23, 25–27, 39, 42, 73–74, 104, 214

Nicholas of Lyre, 17, 27–28, 41–44, 46, 48, 53, 58–59, 62–75, 79, 82, 84, 86–90, 124–27, 135

Olivi, Peter John, 84–85
Oon of Foure, 160
Openness, as interpretive principle, 171–75
  opposite of darkness, 172
Orcherd of Syon, 170
Otter, Monika, 30
Oxford, University of, and biblical exegesis, 9–10, 90, 134

Parkes, Malcolm, 191
Paues, Anna, 145, 272
Pauline Epistles, anon. Middle English translation of, 271
Peter Comestor, *Historia Scholastica*, 73
Peter Lombard, *Magna glosatura in Psalmos*, 2, 18, 24–25, 29, 31–34, 37, 39, 44, 46, 49, 51–52, 61–62, 94, 96–104, 107, 109–13, 128, 137, 143, 194–96, 198, 238, 247–48
Peter of Herentals, 124–25, 128
Piper, Alan, 145
Pliny the Elder, 250
Psalms
  and *persona*, 31, 33–34, 36, 40–41, 46, 53, 89, 94, 97–100, 110–11, 116, 120
  as lyric poems, 25, 31, 33, 39, 42–43, 94, 101
  as prophecy, 31–33, 35, 38–46, 59, 88–89, 94, 102
  authorship of, 57–59, 101–2, 227–28
  structure of, 39, 59–60, 96, 102, 230

Rashi, 28, 59
Reading, medieval modes of, 13–15, 93–94, 168–70, 245
Reason, use in interpretation, 173–74
Reformation, and biblical commentary, 19–20, 176–87
Remigius of Auxerre, 24, 34, 167
Ridevall, John, 241
Ringstead, Thomas, 129

Rolle, Richard
  catalogued by John Bale, 183–85
  Commandment, 248
  Commentary on Lamentations, 184
  Commentary on the Apocalypse, 184
  De amore Dei contra amatores mundi, 127, 129, 251–53
  De vita activa et contemplativa, 247
  depictions of, 91, 129–32
  Ego Dormio, 95–96, 248
  Emendatio Vitae, 123–24, 127, 245–46, 253, 255
  English Psalter, 8, 14–15, 18, 93, 103–18, 122, 127–29, 134–39, 142, 146, 156, 174, 184–85
  English Psalter, Wycliffite revisions to, 114–17, 121–22
  Expositio super nouem lecciones mortuorum, 247, 251, 253
  Form of Living, 248
  Incendium Amoris, 100, 198, 247, 252–53
  influence of, 114–29, 136–37, 170
  Latin Psalter, 1–3, 5, 17, 93–105, 110–11, 122–23, 125–29, 135, 184
  –, manuscripts of, 192–93, 245, 247, 253
  –, possible revision of, 103, 192–202
  Melos Amoris, 198, 245
  relevance of university exegesis to, 93, 101
  Super Psalmum XX, 252–53
  theory of translation, 105, 137
Rouse, Mary, and Richard Rouse, 62, 189
Rupert of Deutz, 269

Scase, Wendy, 129
Senses of Scripture, 17, 21–23, 27–29, 38, 62–65, 80–81, 89, 135, 140, 166, 170–72, *and see* Commentary, scholastic attitudes toward
Sensus auctoris, 54, 57, 66, *and see Intentio auctoris*
Smalley, Beryl, 4, 10, 21, 34, 56–58, 60, 62, 64–66, 68–70, 73, 83, 86, 90, 140–42
Somerset, Fiona, 115, 135
Sutherland, Annie, 118, 256

Thomas of Jorz, 225
Translation
  as commentary, 106–7, 185
  theories of, 105–7
Trevet, Nicholas, 16, 29, 37–42, 45–49, 51–53, 59, 63
Trevisa, John, 145, 169, 220, 267
Trithemius, Johannes, 178
Twelve Cambridge Tracts, 133–34, 157, 160

Tyconius, Rules of, 159
Tyndale, William, 176–82, 184–86

Ullerston, Richard
De translatione sacrae Scripturae in vulgare, 106–7, 123
Defensorium Dotationis Ecclesiae, 123–24
Expositio canticorum Scripturae, 124–28, 135

Van Dussen, Michael, 192
Virgil, 24, 39

Walafrid Strabo, 180, 250
Waleys, Thomas, 16, 29–30, 32–37, 43, 49, 52–53
Watson, Nicholas, 91
William of Malmesbury, 270
William of Nottingham, 242

Woodford, William, 17, 135, 170
Defensorum Fratrum Mendicancium, 243
Postilla super Matthaeum, 83–90
–, as aid for confessors?, 244
Quattuor determinationes, 89
Wyclif, John, 6–7, 53, 84–85, 135, 169–70
catalogued by John Bale, 182–85
De veritate sacrae Scripturae, 54–55, 82
Opus Evangelicum, 67–68, 71–72, 80
place in Reformation historiography, 185–86
Postilla super totam Bibliam, 17, 55–83, 89–90, 188–91
–, revision of, 68–72, 78–79, 80–82
Trialogus, 55
Wycliffite Bible, 6–7, 11, 147, 156, 162, 183, 185, 260–61, 267, *and see Glossed Gospels*
Prologue to the Later Version, 147, 159–61, 172, 183, 265

CAMBRIDGE STUDIES IN MEDIEVAL LITERATURE

1 ROBIN KIRKPATRICK
  Dante's Inferno: Difficulty and Dead Poetry

2 JEREMY TAMBLING
  Dante and Difference: Writing in the "Commedia"

3 SIMON GAUNT
  Troubadours and Irony

4 WENDY SCASE
  "Piers Plowman" and the New Anticlericalism

5 JOSEPH J. DUGGAN
  The "Cantar de mio Cid": Poetic Creation in its Economic and Social Contexts

6 RODERICK BEATON
  The Medieval Greek Romance

7 KATHRYN KERBY-FULTON
  Reformist Apocalypticism and "Piers Plowman"

8 ALISON MORGAN
  Dante and the Medieval Other World

9 ECKEHARD SIMON (ed.)
  The Theatre of Medieval Europe: New Research in Early Drama

10 MARY CARRUTHERS
   The Book of Memory: A Study of Memory in Medieval Culture

11 RITA COPELAND
   Rhetoric, Hermeneutics, and Translation in the Middle Ages: Academic Traditions and Vernacular Texts

12 DONALD MADDOX
   The Arthurian Romances of Chrétien de Troyes: Once and Future Fictions

13 NICHOLAS WATSON
   Richard Rolle and the Invention of Authority

14 STEVEN F. KRUGER
   Dreaming in the Middle Ages

15 BARBARA NOLAN
   Chaucer and the Tradition of the "Roman Antique"

16 SYLVIA HUOT
The "Romance of the Rose" and Its Medieval Readers: Interpretation, Reception, Manuscript Transmission

17 CAROL M. MEALE (ed.)
Women and Literature in Britain, 1150–1500

18 HENRY ANSGAR KELLY
Ideas and Forms of Tragedy from Aristotle to the Middle Ages

19 MARTIN IRVINE
The Making of Textual Culture: 'Grammatica' and Literary Theory, 350–1100

20 LARRY SCANLON
Narrative, Authority, and Power: The Medieval Exemplum and the Chaucerian Tradition

21 ERIK KOOPER (ed.)
Medieval Dutch Literature in its European Context

22 STEVEN BOTTERILL
Dante and the Mystical Tradition: Bernard of Clairvaux in the "Commedia"

23 PETER BILLER AND ANNE HUDSON (eds.)
Heresy and Literacy, 1000–1530

24 CHRISTOPHER BASWELL
Virgil in Medieval England: Figuring the "Aeneid" from the Twelfth Century to Chaucer

25 JAMES SIMPSON
Sciences and the Self in Medieval Poetry: Alan of Lille's 'Anticlaudianus' and John Gower's 'Confessio Amantis'

26 JOYCE COLEMAN
Public Reading and the Reading Public in Late Medieval England and France

27 SUZANNE REYNOLDS
Medieval Reading: Grammar, Rhetoric and the Classical Text

28 CHARLOTTE BREWER
Editing 'Piers Plowman': The Evolution of the Text

29 WALTER HAUG
Vernacular Literary Theory in the Middle Ages: The German Tradition, 800–1300, in Its European Context

30 SARAH SPENCE
Texts and the Self in the Twelfth Century

31 EDWIN D. CRAUN
 Lies, Slander and Obscenity in Medieval English Literature: Pastoral Rhetoric and the Deviant Speaker

32 PATRICIA E. GRIEVE
 "Floire and Blancheflor" and the European Romance

33 HUW PRYCE (ed.)
 Literacy in Medieval Celtic Societies

34 MARY CARRUTHERS
 The Craft of Thought: Meditation, Rhetoric, and the Making of Images, 400–1200

35 BEATE SCHMOLKE-HASSELMANN
 The Evolution of Arthurian Romance: The Verse Tradition from Chrétien to Froissart

36 SIÂN ECHARD
 Arthurian Narrative in the Latin Tradition

37 FIONA SOMERSET
 Clerical Discourse and Lay Audience in Late Medieval England

38 FLORENCE PERCIVAL
 Chaucer's Legendary Good Women

39 CHRISTOPHER CANNON
 The Making of Chaucer's English: A Study of Words

40 ROSALIND BROWN-GRANT
 Christine de Pizan and the Moral Defence of Women: Reading Beyond Gender

41 RICHARD NEWHAUSER
 The Early History of Greed: The Sin of Avarice in Early Medieval Thought and Literature

42 MARGARET CLUNIES ROSS (ed.)
 Old Icelandic Literature and Society

43 DONALD MADDOX
 Fictions of Identity in Medieval France

44 RITA COPELAND
 Pedagogy, Intellectuals, and Dissent in the Later Middle Ages: Lollardy and Ideas of Learning

45 KANTIK GHOSH
 The Wycliffite Heresy: Authority and the Interpretation of Texts

46 MARY C. ERLER
 Women, Reading, and Piety in Late Medieval England

47 D. H. GREEN
The Beginnings of Medieval Romance: Fact and Fiction, 1150–1220

48 J. A. BURROW
Gestures and Looks in Medieval Narrative

49 ARDIS BUTTERFIELD
Poetry and Music in Medieval France: From Jean Renart to Guillaume de Machaut

50 EMILY STEINER
Documentary Culture and the Making of Medieval English Literature

51 WILLIAM E. BURGWINKLE
Sodomy, Masculinity, and Law in Medieval Literature: France and England, 1050–1230

52 NICK HAVELY
Dante and the Franciscans: Poverty and the Papacy in the "Commedia"

53 SIEGFRIED WENZEL
Latin Sermon Collections from Later Medieval England: Orthodox Preaching in the Age of Wyclif

54 ANANYA JAHANARA KABIR AND DEANNE WILLIAMS (eds.)
Postcolonial Approaches to the European Middle Ages: Translating Cultures

55 MARK MILLER
Philosophical Chaucer: Love, Sex, and Agency in the "Canterbury Tales"

56 SIMON A. GILSON
Dante and Renaissance Florence

57 RALPH HANNA
London Literature, 1300–1380

58 MAURA NOLAN
John Lydgate and the Making of Public Culture

59 NICOLETTE ZEEMAN
'Piers Plowman' and the Medieval Discourse of Desire

60 ANTHONY BALE
The Jew in the Medieval Book: English Antisemitisms, 1350–1500

61 ROBERT J. MEYER-LEE
Poets and Power from Chaucer to Wyatt

62 ISABEL DAVIS
Writing Masculinity in the Later Middle Ages

63 JOHN M. FYLER
   Language and the Declining World in Chaucer, Dante, and Jean de Meun

64 MATTHEW GIANCARLO
   Parliament and Literature in Late Medieval England

65 D. H. GREEN
   Women Readers in the Middle Ages

66 MARY DOVE
   The First English Bible: The Text and Context of the Wycliffite Versions

67 JENNI NUTTALL
   The Creation of Lancastrian Kingship: Literature, Language and Politics in Late Medieval England

68 LAURA ASHE
   Fiction and History in England, 1066–1200

69 J. A. BURROW
   The Poetry of Praise

70 MARY CARRUTHERS
   The Book of Memory: A Study of Memory in Medieval Culture (Second Edition)

71 ANDREW COLE
   Literature and Heresy in the Age of Chaucer

72 SUZANNE M. YEAGER
   Jerusalem in Medieval Narrative

73 NICOLE R. RICE
   Lay Piety and Religious Discipline in Middle English Literature

74 D. H. GREEN
   Women and Marriage in German Medieval Romance

75 PETER GODMAN
   Paradoxes of Conscience in the High Middle Ages: Abelard, Heloise, and the Archpoet

76 EDWIN D. CRAUN
   Ethics and Power in Medieval English Reformist Writing

77 DAVID MATTHEWS
   Writing to the King: Nation, Kingship, and Literature in England, 1250–1350

78 MARY CARRUTHERS (ed.)
   Rhetoric Beyond Words: Delight and Persuasion in the Arts of the Middle Ages

79 KATHARINE BREEN
   Imagining an English Reading Public, 1150–1400

80 ANTONY J. HASLER
Court Poetry in Late Medieval England and Scotland: Allegories of Authority

81 SHANNON GAYK
Image, Text, and Religious Reform in Fifteenth-Century England

82 LISA H. COOPER
Artisans and Narrative Craft in Late Medieval England

83 ALISON CORNISH
Vernacular Translation in Dante's Italy: Illiterate Literature

84 JANE GILBERT
Living Death in Medieval French and English Literature

85 JESSICA ROSENFELD
Ethics and Enjoyment in Late Medieval Poetry: Love after Aristotle

86 MICHAEL VAN DUSSEN
From England to Bohemia: Heresy and Communication in the Later Middle Ages

87 MARTIN EISNER
Boccaccio and the Invention of Italian Literature: Dante, Petrarch, Cavalcanti, and the Authority of the Vernacular

88 EMILY V. THORNBURY
Becoming a Poet in Anglo-Saxon England

89 LAWRENCE WARNER
The Myth of "Piers Plowman": Constructing a Medieval Literary Archive

90 LEE MANION
Narrating the Crusades: Loss and Recovery in Medieval and Early Modern English Literature

91 DANIEL WAKELIN
Scribal Correction and Literary Craft: English Manuscripts 1375–1510

92 JON WHITMAN (ed.)
Romance and History: Imagining Time from the Medieval to the Early Modern Period

93 VIRGINIE GREENE
Logical Fictions in Medieval Literature and Philosophy

94 MICHAEL JOHNSTON AND MICHAEL VAN DUSSEN (eds.)
The Medieval Manuscript Book: Cultural Approaches

95 TIM WILLIAM MACHAN (ed.)
Imagining Medieval English: Language Structures and Theories, 500–1500

96 ERIC WEISKOTT
English Alliterative Verse: Poetic Tradition and Literary History

97 SARAH ELLIOTT NOVACICH
Shaping the Archive in Late Medieval England: History, Poetry, and Performance

98 GEOFFREY RUSSOM
The Evolution of Verse Structure in Old and Middle English Poetry: From the Earliest Alliterative Poems to Iambic Pentameter

99 IAN CORNELIUS
Reconstructing Alliterative Verse: The Pursuit of a Medieval Meter

100 SARA HARRIS
The Linguistic Past in Twelfth-Century Britain

101 ERIC KWAKKEL AND RODNEY THOMSON (eds.)
The European Book in the Twelfth Century

102 IRINA DUMITRESCU
The Experience of Education in Anglo-Saxon Literature

103 JONAS WELLENDORF
Gods and Humans in Medieval Scandinavia: Retying the Bonds

104 THOMAS A. PRENDERGAST AND JESSICA ROSENFELD (eds.)
Chaucer and the Subversion of Form

105 KATIE L. WALTER
Middle English Mouths

106 LAWRENCE WARNER
Chaucer's Scribes

107 GLENN D. BURGER AND HOLLY A. CROCKER (eds.)
Medieval Affect, Feeling, and Emotion

108 ROBERT J. MEYER-LEE
Literary Value and Social Identity in the Canterbury Tales

109 ANDREW KRAEBEL
Biblical Commentary and Translation in Later Medieval England